AN EXPOSITION OF **GALATIANS**

CHRISTIAN CLASSICS
P.O. BOX 2722 GRAND RAPIDS, MICHIGAN 49501

CONTENTS.

PART I.

INSCRIPTION OF THE EPISTLE.

"Paul, an apostle (not from men, nor by man, but through Jesus Christ and God the Father, who raised Him from the dead), and all the brothers with me to the churches of Galatia. Grace and peace to you from God the Father and our Lord Jesus Christ, who gave Himself for our sins so that He might deliver us out of the present evil age, according to the will of our God and Father, to Him be the glory forever and ever. Amen." Galatians 1:1-5.

According to the custom of the age, the apostle begins with a short description of himself and his correspondents, connected with a wish for their happiness.

Paul was above the affectation of singularity. In the form of his epistles, he follows the ordinary custom of his country and age; and he thus teaches us that a Christian ought not to be unnecessarily singular. By readily complying with innocent customs, we are the more likely, when we conscientiously abstain from what we account sinful customs, to impress the minds of those around us that we have some other and better reason for our conduct than whim or humor. Yet the apostle contrives to give, even to the inscription of his letter, a decidedly Christian character; and shows us that, though we should not make an ostentatious display of our Christianity, yet, if we are truly religious, our religion will give a color to the whole of our conduct: even what may seem most remote from direct religious employment will be tinged by it. The manner in which the apostle manages the inscription of this and his other letters, is a fine illustration of his own injunction, "Whatsoever ye do in word or deed, do all in the name of the Lord Jesus, giving thanks to God and the Father by Him" (Col. 3:17). He shows his Christianity even in the mode of addressing his letters.

SECT. I. – THE AUTHOR.

1. HIS NAME.

But let us look a little more closely into the terms of this inscription. "Paul." It is probable that the apostle, from his infancy, had two names: "Saul," a Jewish, and "Paul," a Roman name.

It was common among Roman citizens to give their children what was called a *cognomen*, in addition to the *nomen* answering to our family name, and the *praenomen* answering to our Christian name; and this *cognomen* often referred to something in the appearance, or to some remarkable event in the history, of the individual. It is not unlikely that our apostle received "Paul" as his *cognomen* from his "weak bodily appearance" (2 Cor. 10:10.). Ecclesiastical tradition represents him as a person of diminutive size.[1]

It was no uncommon thing among the Jews to have two names. In ancient times, Solomon and Jedidiah, Azariah and Uzziah. Under the Chaldeans and Persians we find Jews with two names, – one Jewish, the other Chaldean or Persian: Daniel, Belteshazzar; Hananiah, Shadrach; Mishael, Meshach; Azariah, Abednego; Nehemiah, Attirshatha. A similar custom prevailed under the Greek successors of Alexander: Joshua, Jason; Onias, Menelaus.[2] Under the Romans, Latin surnames seem to have been common among the Jews. In the royal family of the Herods, we find Agrippa and Drusilla. The custom seems to have extended to the common people also. John, sister's son to Barnabas, besides his Hebrew name, had the Roman name Marcus. Paul's companion, Silas, is also denominated Silvanus.

Paul seems to have used his Roman name exclusively after his solemn separation to the ministry of the Gentiles (Acts 13:2,9.). His object, probably, was to show, that he had divested himself of all Jewish prejudices, and to secure to himself that respect and attention, which Gentiles were more likely to show to one who bore a name which seemed to imply that he who bore it was a Roman citizen, than to one whose very name told them he belonged to the obnoxious nation, hating, and hated by, all the world. If this is the true account of the matter, we have here a display of Paul's prudence, and knowledge of human nature; his attention to the most minute circumstances which might affect his usefulness; his care not to increase the difficulties in the way of men's conversion by awakening their prejudices; — in one word, to use his own language, his "becoming all things to all men, that by all means he might save some." It was not, however, to his dignity, as a descendant of Abraham, or a citizen of Rome, that the apostle wished to draw the attention of his Galatian correspondents. It was to the office which he held in the Christian church. The style and appellation by which he was anxious to be known, was neither a Hebrew of the Hebrews, nor a Denizen of the Imperial City, but a Christian Apostle.

2. HIS OFFICE.

Paul describes himself as "an apostle." The word "apostle" is precisely of equivalent meaning with the term "messenger."[3] It indicates a person employed by another to execute some commission. Thus, the persons appointed by the churches of Macedonia to carry, along with Paul, their contributions to the poor saints at Jerusalem, are termed "the messengers," or apostles, "of the churches" (2 Cor. 8:23.). And Epaphroditus is termed the "messenger," or apostle, of the Philippians (Phil. 2:25.). It is ordinarily employed in the New Testament as the appropriate appellation of the highest order of the Christian ministry. The twelve disciples chosen by our Lord Himself, as distinguished from evangelists, prophets, and ordinary pastors, — Matthias, who was chosen to occupy the place of Judas, the traitor, — Paul, and Barnabas, — are the only individuals who, in this sense, receive this honorable name. The distinguishing marks of an apostle seem to have been, direct instruction by, and commission from, Jesus Christ; the power of communicating the Holy Ghost by the laying on of their hands; and authority to superintend and guide the catholic Christian church.[4]

As there were false apostles[5] and as Paul's apostleship had been called in question, and represented as if a secondary and inferior kind — as if he had been an apostle of the apostles, or an apostle of the church of Jerusalem, rather than an apostle of Christ, — he is not contented with merely calling himself an apostle, but goes on to describe what kind of an apostle he was. Christians, and especially Christian ministers, ought not to be ambitious of distinctions, nor very forward in claiming, in every case, the respect which properly belongs to them; but when their usefulness is endangered by men endeavoring to rob them of the authority which belongs to their office or character, it is a false modesty which would keep them back from asserting their rights. Paul was a modest man; but he would not silently allow any man to deny or extenuate the official authority with which Jesus Christ had invested him.

He was "an apostle, not of men, neither by[6] men." The full expression is, 'not constituted or commissioned by men.'[7] Some have supposed, that all that the apostle meant by these words, was merely to assert that his commission was not of human but of Divine origin.[8] "This imports something, not only greatly more than a Divine permission, or even what is brought about in the course of ordinary providence, it is the same thing as the express appointment and authoritative order of that God whose apostle he was."[9] The apostolic office was not what Peter says civil government is, an "ordinance of man."[10] I cannot help thinking each of the phrases has its own peculiar meaning. Of those who have been of this opinion, some think that the emphasis is to be laid on the different numbers, plural and singular, *men* and *man*; thus 'I received my commission neither from any body of men, nor from any individual man.' 'I am not an apostle of the church at Jerusalem, nor am I an apostle of Peter, or of James or John, or any of those who are "accounted pillars" in the church.' We rather think that the sense of the apostle is to be brought out by laying the emphasis on the particles *of* and *by*. Paul was not an apostle of[11] men, i.e., he did not derive his commission or authority from men. He was employed on no human errand. No man had told him what he was to say — he had received credentials from no man. Neither was he an apostle by[12] man. A man may have a divine communication made to him, and a divine authority and command to impart this to others, and yet he may have obtained both the one and the other through the instrumentality of man. That is the case with every rightly called gospel minister. That was the case with Timothy. His message and authority were both divine. But he received the one from Paul's instructions, and the other from the laying on of his hands and of those of the presbytery. But the apostle was divinely appointed to his office, and furnished with his commission from Jesus Christ, without human intervention.[13] This is no way inconsistent with the history recorded in the thirteenth chapter of the Acts of the Apostles.

I may be allowed to remark by the way, that though there is a most material difference between the Apostle Paul and ordinary Christian ministers, yet there is a sense in which it may be said even of them, if they are what they ought to be, that they are not *"of* men," neither *"by* man." There are too many who are ministers *of* men, who have no authority but what men gave them, and no message to deliver but what men have taught them. These men may be ministers of the Roman church, or of the Greek church, or of the English church, or of the Scottish church, but they are not ministers of Christ. There are others who though not ministers *of* men are yet ministers *by* men. In one sense, in ordinary cases, all ministers must be *by* men, as it is by the call of the faithful and the laying on of the hands of the presbytery, that they are regularly invested with their office. But many good ministers are ministers *by* men in another sense. Their views of divine truth are scriptural in their substance, and that they are so, is the ground of their belief of them; but still they have gained their views chiefly through the medium of human writings, and it is in this form only that they can bring them forward to others. How much better is it when a minister has drawn directly from the Word of God what he makes known to his people; and, freed from the trammels of human system, can clearly state to others what he has clearly seen for himself in the Holy Scriptures! There is a similar distinction to be observed among private professors of Christianity.[14]

In opposition to his being an apostle of men, or by men, Paul states that he was an apostle "by Jesus Christ," the Messiah — who, in his estimation, was not a mere man[15] but "God manifest in flesh,"[16] — "and God the Father, who raised him from the dead." It is a just remark of the acute Leslie, that "if Christ were not more than man, and considered as such in this passage, the apostle's words cannot be made consonant." I can scarcely help thinking that the apostle meant to contrast the two members of this last clause with the two members of the former clause, — 'An apostle, not of men, but of God the Father; an apostle, not by men, but by Jesus Christ.'[17] He was "an apostle of God the Father." God the Father is uniformly represented in the New Testament as, in the economy of grace, the fountain of authority — "the God and Father of our Lord Jesus Christ." Our Father, because His Father; our God, because His God. It is of Him that "the whole family in heaven and in earth is named." Whatever Jesus Christ does, he does in the Father's name. From Him came the apostle's commission; and it came to him, not through the medium of any man, but through Christ Jesus. He was made an apostle by God, through Christ Jesus. Jesus directly called him; and directly, too, instructed him. What Paul declared, was not what he had learned of men, but what he "received of the Lord" (1 Cor. 11:23; 15:3.). The apostle takes notice by the way, of the important fact — the radical principle of Christianity — that God the Father had raised Christ from the dead. This was a truth ever present to the apostle's mind in its pre-eminent importance; and consequently he was always ready to give it utterance. It is not unlikely that, in mentioning it here, he meant to suggest the idea, — that as an apostle called by the Savior raised from the dead by the power of the Father, he was certainly not inferior to those who had been called by Him when in his suffering state. For it does seem to have been one of the circumstances of which the false teachers in different churches availed themselves, in endeavoring to lessen Paul's authority, that he had not, like the other apostles, been the companion of Jesus Christ while on earth.

3. HIS ASSOCIATES.

In the kind wish which he is about to express for the Galatian churches, he connects with himself (verse 2) "the brethren" who were with him. It is common in the New Testament to call all Christians "the brethren."[18] But it seems probable that here the word is used to designate the evangelists who accompanied Paul, such as Sosthenes, Apollos, Timothy, Titus, Silvanus, (1 Cor. 1:1; 16:12. 2 Cor. 1:1. Tit. 2:12. 1 Pet. 5:12.), Tychicus, (Eph. 6:23.), Epaphroditus, (Phil. 2:25.), Onesimus, (Col. 4:9.), or the pastors of the church of the city where he was when he wrote this epistle. This mode of explaining the term is supported by a parallel passage in Phil. 4:21,22 — *"The brethren which are with me, salute you — all the saints salute you"* — where "brethren," as distinguished from "saints," obviously points out ministers as distinguished from the body of the faithful. It has been supposed that the use of "all," proves the "brethren" here refers not to official brethren, but to Christian brethren generally;[19] but there is no force in the remark. It would be quite a natural thing for a minister in this country, writing to another, when two or three of his brethren were with him at the dispensation of the Lord's Supper, to say, — "all the brethren with me beg to be remembered to you." The phrase seems to mean here, as in the case referred to, not brother Christians, but brother ministers. All true ministers of Christ, though in the present disjointed state of the church they belong to different demoninations, should consider one another as brethren, and act accordingly. Paul does not join the brethren along with him to intimate that they had any hand in the composition of the epistle, or that his declarations as an apostle required any support from them; but he mentions them as a token of his affection for them, and of their affection for the Galatians, and also likely to show the Galatians that his sentiments respecting the points discussed in the epistle were by no means peculiar to himself.

SECT. II. – THE PERSONS ADDRESSED.

The epistle is addressed (verse 2) "to the churches of Galatia."[20] It has often been asserted, but I do not think it has yet been proved, that the word "church," as used in reference to Christians, is never used but in two senses, to denote either a particular congregation of Christians who are accustomed to meet together for Christian worship, or the whole body of Christians. In the New Testament, it does seem sometimes to be used to signify a number of congregations united together by a common government. In Jerusalem, in Antioch, and in many other places, there were far more Christians than could meet in one place; and we ought to remember, that from the iniquity of the times, they had generally to meet in private houses; yet we read not of the *churches* of Jerusalem or of Antioch, but of the *church*. Here the word is used in the plural number; and the reason seems obvious. Galatia was a large district of country containing many cities. The congregations scattered over the country could not have such frequent and intimate intercourse as those residing in the same city, and therefore they are called not the church, but the churches of Galatia; and it is not improbable that the one expression may have been chosen rather than the other, because, though many of the churches of Galatia had embraced the false doctrines of the Judaising teachers, there might still be some who retained the simplicity of the truth.

SECT. III. – THE GREETING.

The salutation of the apostle and his fellow-laborers in the gospel to the churches of Galatia, contained in verse 3, includes a prayer, a statement of doctrine, and a doxology.

1. A PRAYER.

"Grace be unto you and peace from God the Father and from[21] *the Lord Jesus Christ."* "Grace" signifies favor, kindness; and "Grace be to you from God the Father and the Lord Jesus Christ," is equivalent to, — 'May you be the objects of the kind regard of God

the Father and of the Lord Jesus Christ, and may you receive from them abundant tokens of their kindness in all heavenly and spiritual blessings.' "Peace" is a general word for happiness. The ancient Jewish salutation, still common among the Orientals, "Peace be with you," is just equivalent to, 'May you be happy.' "Peace be to you from God the Father, and the Lord Jesus Christ," then, signifies, – 'May you receive from God the Father, and the Lord Jesus Christ, all that is necessary to your happiness both here and hereafter.' These benedictions are indeed prayers, and they show us that the apostle looked for happiness both to himself and others from "God the Father and our Lord Jesus Christ;" that he considered the Father and the Son as equally the object of Divine worship, and that he reckoned prayer to them the appointed way of obtaining saving blessings. One of the best ways in which Christian ministers can manifest their love to their people, is by praying for them. "The ministry of the word" and "prayer" should be conjoined.

2. A STATEMENT.

Having been led to mention our Lord Jesus Christ in the benediction, the apostle does not finish the sentence, but, according to a very common practice with him, introduces, as it were by-the-bye, a statement of one of the most important truths of the gospel (Gal. 1:4), *"who gave Himself for our sins, that he might deliver us from this present evil world."*[22] The meaning of the phrase, "He gave Himself for our sins," is, 'He voluntarily by His sufferings and death made atonement for our sins' – 'He offered Himself a sacrifice for our sins.' This is, if I mistake not, implied in the very words before us;[23] and that this is the apostle's meaning is very plain from parallel passages where he uses similar language, – 1 Tim. 2:6, *"He gave Himself a ransom;"* Tit. 2:14, *"He gave Himself for us that He might redeem us;"* Eph. 5:2, *"He gave Himself for us a sacrifice and an offering."* He here states the doctrine which pervades the whole volume of revelation, and is the very corner-stone of the gospel, 'that Jesus Christ, God's incarnate Son, voluntarily took the place of guilty men, did what they were bound to do, suffered what they deserved to suffer, and thus rendered their pardon and deliverance consistent with, and illustrative of, all the perfections of the Divine character, His holiness and righteousness as well as His mercy, and all the rights and interests of His moral administration. In the language of the Old Testament, *"He was wounded for our transgressions, He was bruised for our iniquities, the chastisement of our peace was on Him;"* and in that of the New, "He became a curse for us" – "He was made sin in our room" – "He died for us" – "died for our sins" – "He bare our sins on His body to the tree" – "He bore away the sins of the world." The phrase "gave Himself" brings out strongly the complete voluntariness of our Lord's expiatory sufferings; and the fact that the procuring cause of salvation, is the entire acting and suffering, the whole course of complete conformity in thought, feeling, and conduct to the Divine law in its precept and sanction, of the God-man Jesus Christ. He *became poor* – He *made Himself* of no reputation – He *emptied Himself* – *'humbled Himself.* "No man took His life from Him – He laid it down of Himself. He made His soul an offering for sin, pouring it out unto death." His sacrifice was the sacrifice of Himself – His whole self.'

The design of our Lord's propitiatory sacrifice is pointed out by the apostle in the following clause: – *"He gave Himself for our sins, that He might deliver us from this present evil world."* Some render it 'from the evil of this present world;'[24] but had this been the apostle's meaning, the phraseology would have been different. The word "world" has, I believe, been most commonly considered as equivalent to 'men of the world' – wicked men, and the word "delivered" as equivalent to 'separated from – taken out from among;' and the whole phrase as equivalent to 'that he might separate us from the great body of mankind, who are sunk in ignorance, vice, and wretchedness, and make us his peculiar people.' In this case the passage would be nearly synonymous with Tit. 2:14, *"who gave Himself for us, that He might redeem to Himself a peculiar people, zealous of good works."* This affords a very good meaning, but I doubt if it exactly conveys the apostle's idea. There can be no doubt that in our English New Testament the word "world" is often equivalent to *worldly* men — men entirely occupied with present and secular things, who have always formed by far the greater part of the inhabitants of the world. Thus, *"therefore the world knoweth not us, even as it knew not Him"* (1 John 3:1.). — *"If ye were of the world, the world would love its own; but because ye are not of the world, the world hateth you.* " (John 15:19.). But in every case where the *world* certainly signifies worldly men, it is the translation of a different word in the original.[25] I have not been able to find any passage in the New Testament where the word here used certainly signifies worldly men. From the undoubted facts that the apostle uses here the word,[26] by which the different states of mankind before and after our Lord's coming in the flesh are denoted, and that "the world to come" is used by the author of the Epistle to the Hebrews (though the word employed by him is a different one)[27] to denote the New Testament order of things, some have concluded that the apostle had here the Jewish state under the Mosaic law in his eye; and that he means to tell those who wished so much to be under that dispensation, that when Christ gave Himself for our sins, there was an end put to that dispensation, and that it was His design to take His people out of that state, "to redeem them from the law," — to take them out of the world which had been, and to bring them into a new world which, in the times of the law, had been called "the world to come." That such was the design and consequence of our Lord's expiatory death there can be no doubt; yet, as Riccaltoun well observes, "the state under the law neither was, nor is ever in Scripture called, evil in itself; and even had it been otherwise, the great body of those to whom the apostle was writing were never in that world, and could not with any propriety be represented as taken out of it." Besides, that economy was abolished, and could not, therefore, with propriety be termed the *"present* world."

By "the world," then, I apprehend is to be understood here 'the present state of things,' including the external frame of nature, and the opinions, dispositions, and habits of mankind. I do not think it is called the *present* age or world to mark the precise state of the world when Paul wrote, but to distinguish it both from the original state of things and the final state of things — from the primitive world and the celestial world.[28] It is termed an "evil,"[29] *i.e.,* according to the primitive meaning of the term, a corrupted, a diseased, a disordered, "world." When the world was made by God, it was pronounced by the unerring Judge very good; every thing was as it ought to be; and when it is remade, if I may use the expression, it shall again be very good; and *"Jehovah shall 'again' rejoice in all His works."* In the "new heaven and in the new earth" there is to be nothing but righteousness; but the present world, as opposed both to the past and the future, is an *"evil* world," full of physical because full of moral evil, full of misery because full of sin.

Now, what is meant by being *"delivered*[30] *from this present evil world"*? It does not mean solely nor principally the being taken out of this evil world by death; it signifies the being delivered from all the evils of whatever kind that men are involved in from their living in, and forming a part of, *"this present evil world."*

The *"present evil world"* is under the malediction of God. The same God who blessed the world at its creation, laid it under a curse after the sin of man. *"Cursed is the ground for thy sake,"* (Gen. 3:17.), said Jehovah. *"The whole creation was made subject to vanity"* (Rom. 8:20.). This province of the universe of God was laid as it were under the ban of the Divine empire. The intelligent portion of it particularly lies under an awful curse. *'Cursed is every one who continueth not in all things written in the book of the law to do them"* (Gal. 3:10.). They are *"cursed in their basket and store, when they go out and when they come in;"* cursed for time and for eternity. Their very blessings are cursed. To sue the sublime language of the prophets, there is a curse *"gone forth over the face of the whole earth"* (Zech. 5:3.), and this curse is *"devouring the earth, and making desolate those that dwell therein."* Now, to be *"delivered from this evil world"* certainly implies the being removed from this state of condemnation — the having our happiness rendered consistent with the purity of the Divine character, the righteousness of the Divine law, and the faithfulness of the Divine declarations.

But this is not all. The present world, so far as it is intelligent, is, in a religious point of view, wholly evil, except so far as it is under the influence of another world. All that is good in it comes from above; and all its influences on the minds of its inhabitants in their natural state, are of an irreligious and demoralising tendency. A man of this world, exposed only to worldly influences – to influences arising from present sensible things – from *"all that is in the world, the lust of the eye, the lust of the flesh, and the pride of life, which are of the world and not of God"* (1 John 2:16.), – may become worse. but he will never become better. In the world, as God made it, all intelligent beings were good, and all the influences of surrounding objects were of a kind calculated to make them better. But it is otherwise now. To be "of the world" is just another way of expressing what is ungodly, what is "not of the Father." He who is "in the world" is "without God."[31] Now, to be *'delivered from the present evil world"* implies in it the being delivered from this demoralising influence of the present world – the being formed to a character entirely different from that which is the result of any combination of mere worldly influences. And this is done by bringing to bear on the mind the influences of the Divine Spirit – by subjecting it to *"the powers of the world which is to come."*

Still further, *"this present evil world"* shall certainly ultimately be visited with that destruction to which it is doomed. *'The world and the lusts thereof must pass away"* (1 John 2:17.), – *"The heavens and the earth which are now are kept in store reserved unto fire"* (2 Pet. 3:7.). These heavens must *"pass away with a great noise, and elements must melt with fervent heat, the earth also and the works which are therein must be burnt up;"* – *"all these things must be dissolved"* (2 Pet. 3:10,11.); and in this destruction those men who are identified with the present system of things, "the men of the world," shall be involved. That day of doom to the present evil disordered world, is "the day" also *"of judgment and perdition of ungodly men,"* when they shall be *"punished with everlasting destruction from the presence of the Lord and from the glory of His power."* (2 Thess. 1:9.). Now, to be delivered from this present evil world is to be secured from this destruction, which is the merited portion of every human being; it is to be secured of a species of happiness not liable to change or dissolution – *"an inheritance incorruptible, and undefiled, and that fadeth not away"* (1 Pet. 1:4.) – an interest in the *"new heavens and the new earth, wherein dwelleth righteousness"* (2 Pet. 3:13.). It is to have for our chief good something which is entirely independent of "the present evil world," and to the full enjoyment of which the dissolution of "the present evil world" is absolutely necessary. This is to be "delivered from the present evil world" – from the curse which lies on it – from the immoral character it forms and cherishes – and from the dreadful destruction to which it is doomed. It thus appears that deliverance or redemption from "this present evil world" is a comprehensive expression, including every part of the Christian salvation – the *"redemption that is in Christ through his blood, even the forgiveness of sins"* – the *"redemption from all iniquity,"* which makes its subjects *"a peculiar people, zealous of good works"* – and the "deliverance" or redemption *"from the wrath that is to come"* – in one word, *"the salvation that is in Christ, with eternal glory."*

Thus to deliver us from "the present evil world" was the grand design of our Lord's voluntary, vicarious sacrifice. He *"gave Himself for our sins, that He might deliver us from this present evil world."* And the sacrifice was well fitted to serve the purpose.

He *"redeemed us from the curse, by becoming a curse for us."* By His sufferings and death in our room, He rendered our salvation consistent with the honor of God, and the stability of His government.

By the same means He removed out of the way the obstacles which prevented the communication of that divine influence, which alone can counteract the depraving influences of *"the present evil world."* He did more: He secured the communication of those influences to those given Him by the Father; and the plain, well-attested record of His giving Himself for us is the grand instrument, in the hand of the Spirit, for transforming the character by the renewing of the mind.

The doctrine of the cross, understood and believed, is the wondrous talisman which breaks all the spells of that most powerful of all enchantresses, "the present evil world" – making what appeared real and important vanish into empty air, and what was unseen and unfelt assume a distinct visibility and a palpable reality; making God and eternity burst on the mind in a resistless but delightful effulgence, which overpowers the false lights of present and sensible things, and opens up a new, and wider, and happier region, in which the mind may exert all its faculties, and the heart find enough to fill all its capacities of hope, and love, and enjoyment, though continually enlarging for ever.

Finally, it was by thus giving Himself for our sins that He secured to us deliverance from *"the wrath that is to come,"* and purchased for Himself those powers, in the exercise of which He shall save His people amid the horrors of the dissolution of "this present evil world," and make them for ever happy in the world which is to come. God hath given Him *"power over all flesh," "because he has laid down His life for the sheep."*

To be 'delivered from the present evil world' is a phrase, in some of its bearings, nearly synonymous with *"having the world crucified to a person by the cross of Christ"* (Gal. 6:14.), and with having *"our old man crucified with Christ"* (Rom. 6:6.), – with our being "dead," while *"our life is hid with Christ in God"* (Col.3:3.). But it is more comprehensive than any of these expressions. It is equivalent to Christ's having expiated our sins by the sacrifice of Himself, that we might be made new creatures, and brought into a new world,[32] or system of things, – a state of things directly opposed to "this present evil world," – an orderly, holy, happy, permanent state, the perfection of which is heaven.

The apostle adds that Christ *"gave Himself for our sins, that He might deliver us from this present evil world, according to the will"* – the benignant good pleasure – *"of God and our Father."*[33] An English reader would readily suppose that *"God and our Father"* are two different persons. The original text suggests no such idea.[34] The meaning is, *'our God and Father.'* God is the God of believers. He treats them as His people; they regard Him as their God – the object of their supreme esteem and love, obedience and submission. He is their Father – the Author of their new and better being. Having begotten them again – having brought them into the relation, and formed them to the character, of children, – He regards them with complacency, and treats them with kindness. This clause is to be viewed as connected with both the preceding. It is equivalent to a declaration that it was the will of God that men should be delivered from "this present evil world," and that this should be done by Jesus Christ giving Himself for our sins. To this gracious determination of God is to be attributed our salvation, and the means of our salvation. The best commentary on this passage is to be found in the following quotations from the Epistles to the Ephesians and Hebrews: – *"Blessed be the God and Father of our Lord Jesus Christ, who hath blessed us with all spiritual blessings in heavenly places in Christ; according as He hath chosen us in Him before the foundation of the world, that we should be holy and without blame before Him in love: having predestinated us unto the adoption of children by Jesus Christ to Himself, according to the good pleasure of his will, to the praise of the glory of His grace, wherein He hath made us accepted in the Beloved: in whom we have redemption through His blood, the forgiveness of sins, according to the riches of His grace; wherein He hath abounded toward us in all wisdom and prudence; having made known unto us the mystery of His will, according to His good pleasure which He hath purposed in Himself: that, in the dispensation of the fulness of times, He might gather together in one all things in Christ, both which are in heaven, and which are on earth, even in Him: in whom also we have obtained an inheritance, being predestinated according to the purpose of Him who worketh all things after the counsel of His own will; that we should be to the praise of His glory, who first trusted in Christ. In whom ye also trusted, after that ye heard the word of truth, the gospel of your salvation: in whom also, after that ye believed, ye were sealed with that Holy Spirit of promise, which is the earnest of our inheritance, until the redemption of the purchased possession, unto the praise of His glory." "Wherefore, when He cometh into the world, He saith, Sacrifice and offering Thou wouldest not, but a body hast Thou prepared Me: in burnt-offerings and sacrifices for sin Thou hast had no pleasure: Then said I, Lo, I come (in the volume of the book it is written of me) to do Thy will, O God. Above, when He said, Sacrifice, and offering, and burnt-offerings, and offering for sin, Thou wouldest not, neither hadst pleasure therein; (which are offered by the law;) then said He, Lo, I come to do thy will, O God. He taketh away the first, that He may establish the second. By the which will we are sanctified, through the offering of the body of Jesus Christ once for all"* (Eph. 1:3-14. Heb. 10:5-10.). We are never to think of God the Father as indisposed to save man till prevailed on to do it by the labors and sufferings, and prayers of His incarnate Son. The whole scheme originated in the will of the one God; and the mediatorial economy is nothing more than the means adopted by infinite wisdom to execute the purpose of infinite mercy, in consistency with the claims of infinite justice.

3. A DOXOLOGY.

This concise but complete account of the Christian salvation, in its procuring cause, its constituent elements, and its primary source, is concluded by an ascription of praise to its gracious Author, – *"To whom be glory for ever and ever. Amen."*[35] It is difficult to say whether the apostle meant this ascription of praise to be understood as addressed to the Father or to the Son. There is no doubt *'God the Father"* is the nearest antecedent; but there is as little doubt that *"Jesus Christ, who gave Himself for us,"* is the principal subject of the preceding proposition. It matters very little how it is understood. We know, from many other passages of Scripture, that Jesus Christ, as well as the Father, is the object of religious worship, and that to the Father and the Son is due the ascription of equal praise for the work of our salvation. Whoever understands, in any good measure, that plan of salvation – which well deserves to be called *"the manifold wisdom of God, according to the eternal purpose which He purposed in Christ Jesus our Lord,"*[36] – will readily agree with the apostle that glory should be ascribed to both for ever, that the power and the wisdom, and the righteousness and kindness, displayed in the formation and execution of this plan, deserve to draw forth the highest sentiments of adoring esteem and affectionate love, and the most fervent expression of these from men and angels for ever and ever.

It is delightful to think that the apostle's wish shall assuredly be gloriously realised. It is pleasing to think that what, owing to the fascinations of "the present evil world," attracts so little attention in time – on earth, – shall be the grand subject of thought – the grand center of feeling – the grand theme of acknowledgment and praise in heaven, throughout eternity. There they sing a song which will be ever new – *"Salvation to our God who sitteth on the throne, and unto the Lamb." "Thou art worthy to take the book, and to open the seals thereof: for thou wast slain, and hast redeemed us to God by Thy blood out of every kindred, and tongue, and people, and nation; and hast made us unto our God kings and priests: and we shall reign on the earth." "I beheld,"* says the rapt John the divine, *"and I heard the voice of many angels round about the throne, and the beasts, and the elders: and the number of them was ten thousand times ten thousand, and thousands of thousands; saying with a loud voice, Worthy is the Lamb that was slain to receive power, and riches, and wisdom, and strength, and honor, and glory, and blessing. And every creature which is in heaven, and on the earth, and under the earth, and such as are in the sea, and all that are in them, heard I saying, Blessing, and honor, and glory, and power, be unto Him that sitteth upon the throne, and unto the Lamb, for ever and ever. And the four beasts said, Amen. And the four-and-twenty elders fell down and worshipped Him that liveth for ever and ever"* (Rev. 7:10; 5:9-14.) Oh, who that has even in the smallest degree experienced the efficacy of the Savior's sacrifice, in a deliverance from "the present evil world," can refrain from wishing, even here, to join the song of angels, and the spirits of just men made perfect, and say, *"To Him that loved us, and washed us from our sins in His own blood, and hath made us kings and priests unto God and His Father; to Him be glory and dominion for ever and ever. Amen"* (Rev.

1:5,6.).

"Amen" is a particle expressive of approbation – it is right that it should be so; of faith – it shall be so; of desire[37] – oh, that it were so! So ought it to be – so let it be – so shall it be.

PART II.

INTRODUCTION TO THE EPISTLE.

"I marvel that you are so quickly moving away from Him who called you into the grace of Christ, to another gospel – which is not another, but there are some who trouble you and desire to twist the gospel of Christ. But even if we or an angel from Heaven should preach any other gospel to you than that which we have preached to you, let him be anathema. As we have said before, I also now say again, If anyone preaches any other gospel to you contrary to what you received, let him be anathema. For now do I persuade men or God? Or do I seek to please men? For if I were yet pleasing men, I would not be the servant of Christ." – Galatians 1:6-10.

SECT. I. – INTRODUCTORY REMARKS.

That man, as a religious and moral being, is radically and totally depraved, – that the bias of his nature is decidedly towards what is false in sentiment, and towards what is wrong in feeling and action, – is a principle which is not only frequently stated, in the plainest terms, in the Holy Scriptures, but the admission of which is forced on us by our experience of what takes place within us, and our observation of what takes place around us. Notwithstanding the completeness of that system of moral means for making men wise and good, for giving a right direction to their religious and moral views and dispositions, contained in the Bible – a plain and well-attested revelation of the Divine will, – how comparatively rare are the instances in which its application is found effectual for the purpose it is obviously intended, and as obviously calculated, to serve – the favorable, and the permanently favorable, transformation of the human character! Though the statements of divine revelation are most perspicuous, though its evidence is most satisfactory, though the arguments it employs are most conclusive, and the motives it urges altogether overwhelming, – yet what a very small proportion of those to whom this revelation is presented, and even of those with regard to whom the most powerful human means are employed to fix their attention on it, ever really understand and believe its doctrines, or experience its renovating, guiding, controlling influence, over the active principles of their nature! Indeed, in no case does this take place but as the result of a peculiar divine energy. No man is "born again" till he is "born of the Spirit." And I know no fact which, well understood, places in a stronger point of light the religious and moral depravity of man than this, that no man ever does really understand, and believe, and live under the influence of the remarkably simple, perfectly rational, most clearly attested principles of the Christian revelation, till he become the subject of the supernatural operation of the Holy Ghost.

And even after a man has thus become the subject of divine influence, how much ignorance, misapprehension, and error, – how much imperfection and impropriety, – still remain, just because he is not completely subject to that influence! And suppose that influence intermitted, the natural bias to error and to sin manifests itself, – truths the most firmly believed become in his view doubtful, – and sinful dispositions, apparently mastered, begin to assume their former energy; and could that influence be entirely withdrawn, the renewed man would soon be entirely divested of his peculiar character, and "the latter end would be worse than his beginning." The partial apostasies of genuine Christians are fearful demonstrations of the power of natural depravity, – clear evidences that, but for the constant operation of the good Spirit, every good man would soon become a bad man; and everything like right religious thinking, and feeling, and acting, would be banished from the earth.

Of the strong tendency of the human mind, even after having been in a good measure enlightened in the knowledge of the truth, to revert to former, or to fall into new, errors, we have a striking exemplification in the history of the Galatian churches. They had been

11

instructed in the principles of Christian truth by the Apostle Paul. No man better understood these principles, and no man could more distinctly and clearly exhibit them. Most distinctly had he taught the Galatians that Christ crucified was the only and the all-sufficient Savior; and that faith in the truth respecting Him, was the only way in which men could be interested in the blessings of His salvation. And most satisfactorily had he proved the truth of all his declarations by working miracles. The Galatians, under the influence of the Holy Spirit, believed the gospel, as preached and confirmed by the apostle; and were so delighted with the message, that they received the messenger "as an angel of God," and, if it had been possible, would have *"plucked out their own eyes, and have given them to Him"* (Gal. 4:14,15.). Yet, in the course of at most a few years, many of those converts were induced, by the artful discourses of false teachers, who gave no satisfactory evidence of the divinity of their mission or the truth of their doctrines, materially to renounce the principles which they had learned of the apostle, and adopt a system utterly irreconcilable with them, and entirely subversive of them. This sad and sudden change excited in the mind of their spiritual father mingled sentiments of astonishment, and sorrow, and indignation, at that inconstancy which the Grecian orator terms "the greatest of all reproaches."[1] These emotions are very powerfully expressed in that introductory paragraph of the epistle which now lies before us for explication.

SECT. II. – THE CHANGE THAT HAD TAKEN PLACE AMONG THE GALATIANS, THE CAUSE OF IT, AND THE APOSTLE'S FEELINGS IN REFERENCE TO IT.

"I marvel that ye are so soon removed from Him that called you into the grace of Christ unto another gospel: which is not another; but there be some that trouble you, and would pervert the gospel of Christ" (Gal. 1:6,7.).

1. THE FACT.

The apostle represents the Galatian churches as "removed from Him that called them."[2] What are we to understand by the "calling" of the Galatians? and whom are we to understand by "Him who called them"? The word "call" is very frequently used in the New Testament in reference to Christians; and it is obvious, that to be called, and to be a Christian, are, if not equivalent terms, two descriptions of the same class of individuals. The phrase seems, like most of the distinctive appellations of Christians in the New Testament, borrowed from the Old Testament, and to have originated in the manner in which Abraham was set apart to be the father of the peculiar people of God. He was called by the voice of God when in his native country, and induced to comply with that call, – to come out from among his idolatrous relations, and go to a distant land, and become the founder of a family which was, through many succeeding ages, to be the repository of the true religion (Gen. 12:1-4. Isa. 48:12.). To be called, in the New Testament sense (Matth. 9:13. Luke 5:32. Rom. 8:30; 9:24,25. 1 Cor. 1:9,26. Gal. 5:13. Eph. 4:1. Col. 3:15. 1 Thess. 4:7. 2 Thess. 2:14. 1 Tim. 6:12. Heb. 9:15.), is, by means of the invitations of the gospel accompanied by the power of the Holy Spirit, to be induced to believe the truth, and make a profession of this faith. The Galatians were *"called,"* when through the preaching of the apostle Paul, they were invited, and induced to accept of the invitation, to participate in the blessings of the Christian salvation.[3]

But whom are we to understand by *"Him that called"*[4] them? Some interpreters have been of opinion, that by "Him that called" them, the apostle means himself. This is, however, entirely inconsistent with the uniform usage of the phrase, 'calling men.' It is always, without an exception so far as I know, referred to God the Father, or to our Lord Jesus Christ; and, indeed, calling, in the sense in which we have explained it, is a word to which human agency is altogether inadequate. Calling is ascribed to God the Father, Rom. 8:30; 9:24; 1 Cor. 1:9; 7:15,17; 1 Thess. 2:12; 5:24; 2Thess 2:14; 2 Tim. 1:9, 1 Pet. 1:15; 2:9; 5:10; 2 Pet. 1:3. It may be understood as ascribed to Christ, Rom. 1:6;

perhaps John 10:16. Nor need we wonder at calling being ascribed to both, when we recollect that *"what things soever the Father doeth, these also doeth the Son likewise"* (John 5:19.); and that *"all power in heaven and in earth is given unto Him"* (Matth. 28:18.). In the whole process of bringing sinners of mankind into His kingdom, the Father does nothing but by the Son (John 5:22.). It is plain our translators understood the appellation of God the Father; but I cannot help thinking, with the Syriac and Arabic translators, that the apostle meant the phrase to be understood of Jesus Christ. This is also Jerome's opinion; and has been adopted in later times by Erasmus, Calvin, Cornelius a Lapide, Junius, Hyperius, Grotius and Vitringa. The words, literally rendered, are, "Him who called you in grace, Christ;"[5] or, more in our idiom, 'Christ, who hath graciously called you.' This gives the natural meaning to 'in grace.'[6] It is harsh to render it as if it were 'through grace;'[7] and still harsher to render it as if it were 'into the grace,'[8] as our translators have done.[9] Christ, by the instrumentality of Paul's preaching, and by the effectual operation of the Holy Ghost, had converted many of the Galatians from idolatry and from Judaism to Christianity, — had led them to "believe with the heart," and to "confess with the mouth," the truth as it is in Jesus. And this he had done "in grace," or graciously. It was a most important favor he bestowed on them; and it was a blessing equally undeserved and unsolicited, entirely the result of sovereign kindness.

The next phrase that comes to be considered is, "Ye are removed from Him that called you." What is meant by the Galatians being removed from Christ? The expression is, literally, "Ye have removed yourselves."[10] To remove themselves from Christ, who had called them, is plainly to abandon the principles which He had taught them, — to give up the peculiarities of His religion, — to leave Him for another teacher, — to deny His Gospel, — and to adopt another creed. This appears plainly to be its meaning from what follows: 'Ye are removed from Christ, who graciously called you, "unto another gospel."

The apostle uses the word "gospel,"[11] here, plainly not in its original appropriate meaning of "good news,' but just as equivalent to a religious system taking the name and laying claim to the character of Christianity. 'Ye have abandoned the religion of Christ for another religion, which has nothing in common with it but the name — a name of which it is utterly unworthy.' And it is to show this distinctly that he immediately adds, — "which is not another."[12]

These words are, by Tyndale and others, connected with what follows. Understanding "which" not as referring to the word "gospel," but to the whole subject of the apostasy of the Galatians, they render the clause, — "which is nothing else but this; there be some that trouble you," etc.; q.d., 'this is the true account of the matter.' In this case, however, the apostle would probably have adopted a phraseology[13] which admitted of but one rendering and reference. It seems far more natural to connect the clause with what goes before, considering it as a parenthesis. It deserves notice that the words employed by the apostle in the 6th and 7th verses are not the same.[14] Perhaps the force of the original expression might be thus given to an English ear, — 'Ye are removed from Christ, who graciously called you, into a *different* gospel, which yet is not another *gospel*.' It is as if he had said,, — 'The doctrine you have embraced is a very different doctrine from the doctrine of Christ. It may be called — it is called — *gospel*, but it is misnamed. There is no *gospel* but one, and that ye have abandoned. What you have embraced is not *gospel* in any proper sense of the word. It is not *Christ's doctrine;* and it is not *good news* for sinful men.' Just contrast the two doctrines, — *"Believe in the Lord Jesus Christ and thou shalt be saved." "All who believe shall be justified from all things from which they could not be justified by the law of Moses."* That is Christ's doctrine — this is 'good news.' Now for the other doctrine, — *"Unless a man be circumcised after the manner of Moses, and keep his law, he cannot be saved."* This is not Christ's doctrine — this is not 'good news.'

The apostle refers to their having very generally, as it would appear, embraced the notion, — that in order to their salvation, submission to the Mosaic law was necessary as well as faith in Christ. It is not at all probable that the Galatians had made a formal renunciation of Christianity. It is all but certain that a proposal of this kind would have been received by them with abhorrence. It is likely that many of them did not see how the doctrines of their new teachers were subversive of those of their old. But they were so; and the apostle very distinctly shows in the sequel that they were so.

And he here, without mincing the matter, states the truth, dreadful as it was, — that the reception of the new doctrines was in reality a renunciation of the old; and that in going over to the Judaisers, they were not only deserting him, but denying his Master.

They had "soon"[15] removed themselves — in the course of a very few years at most. "Soon" may refer to the time that had elapsed, not since their conversion, but since the appearance of the Judaising teachers among them to their change of mind.[16]

2. THE APOSTLE'S FEELINGS IN REFERENCE TO THE FACT.

At this change which had taken place, the apostle expresses a high degree of astonishment. *"I marvel*[17] *that ye should so soon have removed yourself from Christ who graciously called you to another gospel: which is not another."* And well might he marvel. There were many grounds of astonishment; and almost every word in the sentence is big with significance. That any Christian church — any Christian man — should change the pure principles of Christianity for any humanly devised system, is strange. But there were many peculiarities in the case of the Galatians rendering such a change peculiarly wonderful. That they who had been so well instructed, and who had received the instructions given them with so much avidity, should, unmindful of their obligations to Jesus Christ, who, when they were utterly undeserving of His kindness, "called them out of darkness into His glorious light," throw off His easy yoke, and put on the burdensome yoke of Mosaic ceremony, imposed on them by persons who had no right to do it, — that they should exchange liberty for bondage — that they should do this not in consequence of the application of external force, but voluntarily — that they should not have been driven but "removed themselves" from Him who called them — and that they should do this, not after a long course of years, but while the instructions given them by the apostle and the miracles wrought among them could scarcely fail to be fresh in their recollection, — was indeed marvellous.

3. THE CAUSE OF THE FACT

While the apostle expresses his astonishment at the conduct of the Galatian churches, he intimates also that he was not unacquainted with its cause. *"But there be some that trouble you, and would*[18] *pervert the gospel of Christ."*[19] The apostle here plainly refers to the Judaising teachers, who are described in the act of the council of Jerusalem as *"troubling the Gentile churches with words subverting their souls."*[20] They harassed the minds of the disciples individually by filling them with doubts and alarms as to the safety of their state while they remained uncircumcised and unsubjected to the Mosaic law; and they troubled them as a body, laying the foundations of schism and divisions. And they wished to "pervert"[21] the gospel of Christ." It was their wish, their determination, to have the gospel so modified, as to secure themselves and their followers from the persecution of the unbelieving Jews, and in doing so they absolutely changed the very nature of the gospel. As Luther says, — "they made good works, which are the effect of justification, its cause." This was to "pervert;"[22] and by thus perverting the gospel, they "subverted the souls of the disciples."[23] They might suppose that they were not materially altering the gospel, — they were only adding to it the observance of the Mosaic law. But this addition was in reality a most important alteration, — indeed, a complete perversion. The gospel as taught by Paul was a system of pure grace — this was converting it into a variety of the law of works. In Paul's system good works were represented as the necessary fruit of justification; whereas in this system, they, along with faith in the Messiah, were represented as the procuring cause.

It is a most hazardous thing to tamper with the gospel of Christ. It must neither be abridged nor enlarged. It cannot admit of either without injury. An apparently very simple addition may completely "pervert" it. It seems to many no great harm to substitute, in the room of the plain scriptural statement of the gospel, a system which makes our faith and repentance, in connection with Christ's sacrifice, the ground of pardon; but we find the apostle pronouncing a similar system a perversion of the gospel of Christ – a turning of things upside down – a making Christ of none effect. No greater curse can befall a Christian church than to have teachers who, by their confused and erroneous statements, trouble the minds of believers, and attempt to pervert the gospel of Christ.

"But"[24] is an elliptical expression; it intimates, that though the apostle was astonished, his astonishment was not that of ignorance; he well enough knew the cause of the strange change. It implies something like an apology for, or at any rate an extenuation of, the conduct of the Galatians. 'I know the arts which have been practised on you. I blame you; but I blame them still more. Your folly fills me with wonder and pity: their wickedness excites my disapprobation and horror.'

SECT. III. – THE MANNER IN WHICH CORRUPTERS OF THE GOSPEL OUGHT TO BE REGARDED.

What the apostle Paul thought of these men is abundantly plain from what he says of them in the 8th verse. *"But though we, or an angel from heaven, preach any other gospel to you"* – preach as the gospel any thing different from,[25] opposite to – *"that which we have preached unto you, let him be accursed."* The apostle obviously means to state, not only that his gospel was true, but complete – nothing needed to be added to it. The Jewish teachers might have said, – We do not contradict, we only modify, add to, and so improve the gospel as preached by Paul. The grand subject of the gospel of Christ is the way in which a sinner may be restored to the Divine favor, and obtain the pardon of his sin and the salvation of his soul. It is because the gospel of Christ contains the only true account of the only way of justification, and that a way exactly suited to our wretched circumstances, that it receives its name of *gospel* – "glad tidings of great joy." "Another gospel" means, then, a system of doctrine teaching a way of obtaining the Divine favor different from that laid down in Christ's gospel. The leading principles of Christ's gospel are two, – 'that men are restored to the Divine favor *entirely* on account of the doings and sufferings of Jesus Christ,' and 'that men are interested in these doings and sufferings *entirely* by believing.' Now, every plan of restoring men to God's favor, which does not embrace these two principles, or which embraces what is inconsistent with either of them, is another gospel. Every plan, for example, which, like that of the Judaising teachers, leads men to depend on their own obedience to any law to any extent, in any degree, either as the ground of their justification or the means of their justification, is another gospel. It is a most momentous consideration, that "the avowed deist does not more effectually reject the record of God concerning His Son, than the nominal Christian who believes something else than this under the name of a gospel, and trusts in some other Christ than this Christ under the name of a savior."[26]

If such a system should be preached to the Galatians by an angel from heaven, or by the apostle himself, what were they to do? Were they to receive it? No; they could not receive it without renouncing the true gospel – that gospel which they had already received on the best foundation. Instead of receiving it, says the apostle, "let him" who proclaims it "be accursed." It is not probable that the apostle conceived it possible that either he or an angel could preach another gospel. But he puts the thing in the strongest way to impress on the minds of the Galatians the danger of receiving it, and the extreme folly of their conduct in receiving such a gospel, though preached neither by angels nor apostles, but by unauthorised, self-constituted teachers. The original words[27] are obviously to be translated, not 'a messenger from heaven,' but, as in our version, "an angel from heaven;"q.d., 'even if one of the holy angels should dare to corrupt the gospel, let him be accursed.' And good reason why even *his* gospel should be rejected; for, as Richard Baxter says, "the gospel hath fuller evidence than if an angel spake from heaven, and is to be believed before, and against, any such angel." Tertullian strangely supposes that the reference is to a fallen angel – an angel once in heaven,[28] but now out of heaven.[29] This is one of "the African schoolmaster's" many crotchets; and I do not know if he has had any followers in this opinion. Luther's observation is characteristic, – "He casteth out very flames of fire, and his zeal is so fervent that he beginneth almost to curse the angels."

But what are we to understand by those words of the apostle in reference to the preacher of another gospel? "Let him be accursed." Some consider them as a denunciation of vengeance on the corrupters of the gospel of Christ. I have no doubt that corrupters of the gospel of Christ, and especially such corrupters as the apostle speaks of, are in extreme danger of aggravated condemnation – of deepest perdition; and this seems implied in the words; but I apprehend that the apostle's object is to point out the manner in which the Galatian Christians ought to consider and treat such persons. They ought not to receive them. They ought not to listen to their doctrines, nor to follow their advice. They ought to consider them as a devoted thing.[30] They should treat them in the way in which the Israelites were to treat the accursed or devoted thing (Josh. 6:18.). I apprehend it is nearly equivalent to the injunction of the apostle John, – *"If there come any unto you, and bring not this doctrine, receive him not into your house, neither bid him God speed: for he that biddeth him God speed is partaker of his evil deeds"* (2 John 10,11.). "I have never conceived," says a very acute expositor of Scripture, "the words, 'let him be accursed,' as denoting a prayer that the curse of God should ultimately fall upon him (though we must be sure that it shall, if he obtain not repentance to the acknowledgment of the truth), but as a direction that he should be regarded as an accursed thing – as one (however specious and esteemed) upon whom the wrath of God lies. He that will not heartily join with the apostle in the solemn words, must be animated by some spirit very different from that of the truth."[31] At first sight, there may appear a discrepancy between the sentiment expressed here and that contained in 2 Cor. 11:4, but the apparent contradiction is very easily removed.

How those Christians, who receive as ministers men whom they are ready enough to say preach another gospel, satisfy their own consciences, I cannot tell. To acknowledge such men as ministers, and receive Christian ordinances at their hand, is certainly not to treat them as a devoted thing. We should be very cautious how we charge men with preaching another gospel; but whenever we are conscientiously persuaded that they do so, the line of conduct to be followed by us is very plain. We must not acknowledge them as teachers; we must not listen to their instructions. They must be to us "anathema." I wonder what amount of worldly good could have induced the Apostle Paul to have acknowledged such men as ministers, and to have treated them as brethren. Never was there a man more disposed to bear with weak brethren; but never was there a man more determined to oppose, and to expose, false brethren; and I believe it will be always found that, when the love of the truth renders men kind and forbearing to others who really love the truth, it renders them just in the same degree intolerant (so far as church-fellowship is concerned) in reference to those who are the enemies of the truth. It was plainly a feature in Paul's character, as well as in that of the church of Ephesus, that he "could not bear them who were evil." "It is a false charity which represents it as of no essential consequence what we believe under the name of gospel. It is, indeed, but another form of human ungodliness, holding it of little consequence what God we acknowledge."[32] The sentiment was an important one, and the apostle repeats it to show the Galatians that this was no excessive, exaggerated statement, into which passion had hurried him, but his calmly formed and unalterable opinion. *"As we said before,[33] so say I now again, If any man (man is a supplement – being, man or angel) preach"* as gospel any other doctrine *"unto you than that ye have received, let him be accursed."* These words, "as we said before," *may* refer to the words immediately preceding; but we think it more likely that the apostle alludes to what he had again and again said to the Galatians when he was among them. There is a similar expression, 2 Cor. 7:7, where the reference is to what is said in the same epistle, but in another place. Important truth, especially if it happens to be unpalatable truth, needs often to be repeated. For ministers to speak the same things to their people, ought not to be grievous to themselves; and to their people it is not only safe but necessary.

SECT. IV. – THE APOSTLE'S DEFENCE OF HIMSELF AGAINST THE CHARGE OF BEING A MAN-PLEASER.

In the 10th verse, I apprehend the apostle states the reason why he found himself under the necessity of using such strong language. There is an abruptness in the transition here. What follows is either an apology for the preceding language, or an appeal to the Galatians whether the imputation of being a time-server was not in his case a gross calumny. It was a conviction of duty which dictated his words. His great object was to please God; and this object he must prosecute, however much men might be displeased. Perhaps the train of thought which connected the 9th with the 10th verse in the apostle's mind may be thus expressed, – 'I am aware this language will not be very agreeable either to the Judaising teachers or to those who have been deluded by them, but I cannot on this account desist from it. My leading object is to please God, and this can only be done by plainly stating and strongly defending the truth.' And it is not unlikely that it was intended to suggest this idea, – 'A man who thus plainly asserts the most unpalatable truths is not very likely to be such a selfish time-server and man-pleaser as the Judaising teachers had represented the apostle.'

But let us look at the verse a little more closely.

"For do I now persuade men, or God? or do I seek to please men? for if I yet pleased men, I should not be the servant of Christ." In the first clause of this verse we have a proof that a version may be too literal. The translation is so literal as to be unintelligible. It is easy to understand what is meant by "persuading men," though it is not so easy to see what connection such an idea has with what goes before, or what comes after; but what meaning can be attached to the phrase, "persuading God"? The ordinary sense of the original word translated "persuade,"[34] with an accusative, is to prevail on another, by argument or persuasion, to credit a statement or do an action. This is plainly inappropriate to God. Luther, Erasmus, Vatablus, Cramer, and Michaelis, render the clause, – 'Are human or Divine things the subject of my argument? Do I preach man's doctrine or God's?' Calixtus and Piscator, – 'Do I persuade you to believe men or God?' Calvin supposes an ellipsis,[35] – 'Do I respect men or God in my persuasions?' All these expositions are unsatisfactory. If you keep strictly to the primitive meaning of the word, the only sense the clause will bear, is that given by our translators; but then it is obviously inappropriate to the subject. The truth, however, is, that though 'persuade' is by far the most ordinary meaning of the word which occurs here, it is not its only meaning. It means also to 'conciliate,' to 'court favor.'[36] In this sense it occurs in Matth. 28:14; Acts 12:20: *"Having made Blastus the king's chamberlain their friend;"*[37] 2 Mac. 4:45. When Menelaus, the Jewish high priest, found himself convicted of his crimes, he promised Ptolemy a large sum of money to *"pacify"* – to propitiate – *"the king."*[38] The word seems employed with a similar meaning, 1 John 3:19, – We *"shall assure*[39] *our hearts before Him."* Le Clerc seems to think that in all such cases there is an ellipsis. That this is its meaning here there can scarcely be a doubt. 'For do I seek the approbation or favor of men or of God? or do I seek to please men?' These interrogations are plainly equivalent to a strong denial. 'I seek God's approbation, not man's. I am no time-server, no man-pleaser, as I have been represented.'

The apostle appeals to his conduct as a proof that the desire of pleasing men was not his regulating principle, – *"If I yet pleased men, I should not be the servant of Christ."* These words have very commonly been understood as expressing the following sentiment: 'The man whose master-principle is a wish to please men, cannot be a consistent servant of Christ.' It has been considered as a particular application of our Lord's general maxim, *"No man can serve two masters"* (Matth. 6:24.). In this way the words, which viewed by themselves are well fitted to convey this sentiment, express a truth of the last importance, to be seriously weighed by all, especially by those who are ministers of religion. The man, whom fear of human resentment or desire of human favor can induce to keep back any part of the truth, or pervert any part of the truth, is altogether unworthy of the name of a minister of Christ. There are truths which ought to be told, and which cannot be told without displeasing some men; but then they cannot be concealed without displeasing Christ; and certainly he is not a faithful servant of Christ who, in a case of this kind, can be silent. But this does not seem to be the apostle's idea here. It would not serve his purpose. His adversaries would have said, 'We have no objection to that conclusion; that is just what we say — you are not a servant of Christ.' Besides, in this way of explaining the phrase, the word "yet"[40] loses its force. The meaning seems to be this — 'If I were *now* a man-pleaser, as I once was, I would not be a servant of Christ.' Paul was once very ambitious to secure the favor of his countrymen; and, to obtain it, he took his place in the foremost ranks of the persecutors of Christianity. His exertions to obtain human favor were successful, and he stood high in the estimation of his countrymen. 'Now,' says the apostle, 'were worldly ambition now my leading principle, as it once was, I should not be a servant of Jesus Christ. The course I have chosen is not the path to worldly honor. Whatever I may be seeking, it is obvious I am not seeking to please men.'[41] It is a happy circumstance if a Christian minister, when slanderously reported of, can fearlessly appeal to the tenor of his life, and leave the decision with those who know him best.

PART III.

THE APOSTLE'S HISTORICAL DEFENCE OF HIMSELF AND OF HIS OFFICE.

"But I assure you, brothers, the gospel that I preached is not according to men. For I did not receive it from man, nor was I taught it, except by a heavenly revelation of Jesus Christ. For you have heard of my way of life at one time in the Jewish religion, how I was beyond measure in persecution of the church of God and was destroying it. And I was progressing in the Jewish religion beyond many others of my age in my own race, for I was zealous for the traditions of my fathers. But when it pleased God, who separated me from my mother's womb, and called me by His grace, to reveal His Son in me that I might preach the gospel about Him in the nations, I did not immediately talk it over with flesh and blood. Nor did I go up to Jerusalem to those apostles before me, but I went away into Arabia, and I returned again to Damascus. Then after three years I went up to Jerusalem to make friends with Peter. And I remained with him fifteen days. But I did not see any other of the apostles, except James, the Lord's brother. Now what I write to you, behold, before God I do not lie. Then I came into the regions of Syria and Cilicia. But I was not known by face to the churches of Judea which were in Christ. Only they heard that he who persecuted them in times past was now preaching the gospel, the faith that he once destroyed. And they were glorifying God in me. Then after fourteen years I again went up to Jerusalem with Barnabas, taking Titus with me also. But I went up according to revelation and laid before them the gospel which I preach among the Gentiles – but privately to those thought to be important, for fear that somehow I might be running, or had run, in vain. (But not even Titus, who was with me, being a Greek, was forced to be circumcised) But this was on account of the false brothers brought in secretly, who stole in to spy out our freedom which we have in Christ Jesus, so that they might enslave us – to whom we did not give in, not even for an hour, so that the truth of the gospel might continue with you. But from those who were thought to be something (whatever they were makes no difference to me – God does not accept the person of man,) for those who were thought to be important did not add anything to me. But on the contrary, seeing that I had been charged with the gospel to the uncircumcised (even as Peter to the circumcision – for He who worked in Peter towards the apostleship of the circumcision also worked in me towards the Gentiles,) and when they saw the grace which was given to me, James and Peter and John (those esteemed as pillars) gave the right hands of fellowship to Barnabas and me that we should go to the Gentiles and they to the circumcision. Only asking that we should remember the poor, which very thing I was also trying to do. But when Peter came to Antioch, I set my face against him, because he was to be blamed. For before some came from James, he was eating with the Gentiles; But when they came, he was afraid of the circumcision party, drawing back and keeping himself apart. And the rest of the Jews also acted the hypocrite with him, so that even Barnabas was carried away by their dissimulation. But when I saw that they did not walk uprightly, according to the truth of the gospel, I said to Peter in the presence of all, if you, being a Jew, live like the Gentiles and not like the Jews, why do you force the Gentiles to live like the Jews? We Jews by nature and not sinners of the Gentiles know that a man is not justified by works of the Law, but through faith in Jesus Christ. We too have believed on Jesus Christ that we might be justified by faith in Christ and not by works of the Law – for by the works of the Law shall no flesh be justified. But if, while we seek to be justified in Christ, we were found to be sinners, is Christ then the minister of sin? Let it not be said! For if I build again these things which I pulled down, I make myself a sinner. For I through the Law died to the Law, so that I may live to God. I have been crucified with Christ: nevertheless I live, yet not I, but Christ lives in me. And the life which I now live in the flesh I live by the faith of the Son of God, who loved me and gave Himself for me. I do not set aside the grace of God. For if righteousness is through the Law, then Christ died without obtaining anything." — Galatians 1:11-2:21.

SECT. I. — INTRODUCTORY REMARKS.

Egotism, or a disposition to bring forward a person's self, is a characteristic of a weak mind and a contracted heart. It is not an agreeable feature in any man's character; but it is peculiarly disagreeable when it is a leading trait in the character of a man who, from the office he fills, should be distinguished by the wide comprehension of his views, and the generous liberality of his affections. Such a man is a minister of the gospel; and there is something incongruous and disgusting in one whose mind ought to be habitually employed about the glory of the Divine character — the order and stability of the Divine government — the restoration of a ruined world to purity and happiness — the incarnation and sacrifice of the Son of God — the transforming and consoling influence of the Holy Ghost — the joys and the sorrows of eternity — and whose grand business it ought to be to bring these things, in all their reality and importance, before the minds of his fellow-men — it is incongruous and disgusting in such a man to appear primarily anxious to draw men's attention to himself — seizing every opportunity to bring himself into notice — exhibiting the truths of the gospel chiefly for the purpose of displaying his own talents — calling men's attention to them more as his opinions than as God's truth, and less ambitious of honoring the Savior, and saving those who hear him, than of obtaining for himself the reputation of piety, or learning, or acuteness, or eloquence. This is truly pitiable; and if angels could weep, it would be at folly like this.

A minister of the gospel can scarcely, in ordinary circumstances, keep himself too much in the background. He should try to forget himself, and to make his hearers forget him, in his subject. His ambition should be to be a voice proclaiming, 'Behold Him! behold Him!' attracting no notice itself, but fixing the mind directly and entirely on the subject of the message.

But it is obvious that ministers of the gospel may be placed in circumstances in which duty absolutely requires them to speak a great deal more of themselves than they are disposed to do. The success of a minister's labors depends, in a great degree, on the confidence which those to whom he ministers have in the accuracy of his information and the integrity of his character. Aware of this, no art has been more frequently employed by the enemies of Christianity, whether secret or open, to arrest its progress, than an attempt to blast the reputation of its teachers. In such cases, it becomes an imperious duty, not so much to themselves as to their Master and to His cause, to come forward and defend themselves, to expose the falsehood and malignity of their calumniators, and to turn aside the blows which, though directed immediately at them, are ultimately aimed at Christianity and Christ.

This is far from being the most agreeable part of a Christian minister's duty; but it is a necessary and important part of it, from which, when called to it, he ought not to shrink; and it may console him to think, when such engagements withdraw his thoughts from more pleasant employment, that his case is not a singular one — that it has been so from the beginning — and that that apostle who, if left to his own choice, would never have done anything but preach "Christ, and him crucified," — "the power and the wisdom of God for salvation" to a lost world, was not unfrequently obliged to defend himself against charges which avowed enemies, and, what he felt more keenly, false brethren, brought against him, and which, if uncontradicted, would have gone far to frustrate the great object of his evangelical labors.

In this necessary though unpleasant work, we find the apostle engaged in that portion of the Epistle to the Galatians which now comes before us for explication. Soon after the apostle had left the churches which he had planted in Galatia, false teachers came among them, insisting that submission to circumcision and observance of the Mosaic

Law were necessary to salvation, as well as faith in Jesus as the Messiah; and as these sentiments were directly opposed to the doctrines taught by the apostle, they endeavored to pave the way for their reception by shaking the confidence of the Galatian converts in his authority or integrity. They insinuated that the apostle's doctrine was not consistent with the doctrine of the other apostles — that he was not uniform in his doctrine, but taught sometimes one thing, sometimes another, as it suited his convenience; that, at any rate, he was but a secondary teacher, not belonging to the class of original apostles, and that, if he had any authority, it must be derived from them. It is in rebutting the last of these charges that he is engaged in the verses which now lie before us as the subject of exposition. He asserts the fact of his having derived both his information and his authority as a Christian apostle directly from Christ Jesus, and, by appealing to many of the leading events in his history, evinces the falsehood of those statements by means of which the Judaising teachers had endeavored to undermine his influence on the minds of the Galatians, and seduce them from the simplicity of the truth as it is in Jesus.

SECT. II. — THE THESIS TO BE PROVED, "THAT HE WAS A DIVINELY-TAUGHT, DIVINELY-AUTHORISED APOSTLE."

"But I certify you, brethren, that the Gospel which was preached of me is not after man. For I neither received it of man, neither was I taught it, but by the revelation of Jesus Christ" (Gal. 1:11,12.).

The phraseology adopted here by the apostle, "I certify you," does not at all imply that he now, for the first time, stated to the Galatians the fact he was about to assert. It is the same word he uses when he gives a summary of the gospel to the Corinthians, which he at the same time states that he had before preached to them, 1 Cor. 15., "I declare."[1] It intimates his wish that they should remember it, and hold it fast in opposition to the assertions of the false teachers, and also perhaps refers to the confirmation he was about to give of it by a statement of some of the leading circumstances in his history.

The truth which he was so anxious that they should remember and hold fast was, that *"the gospel which was preached of him was not after man."*[2] The gospel preached by Paul signifies the doctrine which he taught respecting the way of salvation through Christ Jesus. The sum and substance of that doctrine was, that what Christ Jesus had done and suffered was the sole ground of human hope, and that belief in the truth respecting what Christ had done and suffered was the sole mode of obtaining a personal interest in his salvation.

This doctrine, the apostle asserts, was not "after[3] man." Although the preposition rendered "after" with the accusative of a person does not properly denote the author of a thing, but that it is done according to his will, law, or example: yet here it is obviously equivalent to 'was not human but divine.'[4] It was something *"which eye had not seen, nor ear heard,"* nor had it entered, nor could it enter, *"into the heart of man to conceive it"* (1 Cor. 2:9.). It was not human either in its substance or in its form. What he taught was not a cunningly devised fable, nor a curiously constructed theory. It was a true account of the Divine method of saving men. It was an accurate statement of a divine revelation. But this was not all. This may be said of every gospel sermon. It may be said of Apollos' preaching as well as of Paul's, nay, it may be said of every man who declares "the truth as it is in Jesus." Paul's gospel was not only divine in its substance, but in its form. It was not divine truth clothed in such language as human wisdom suggested — it was divine truth clothed *"in the words which the Holy Ghost teacheth."* The gospel, as taught by the apostle, was a direct revelation from heaven. He had not framed it himself — he had not borrowed it from those who framed it — he had not even been taught by those who themselves had received it from above. It was in none of these points of view "after man;" for, adds he, *"I neither received it of man, neither was I taught it, but by the revelation of Jesus Christ."*

The pronoun I[5] here is emphatic: — "I, though not one of those who associated with Jesus Christ while on earth[6] — I was not a man-taught apostle." The phrases, "I did not receive it" — "I was not taught it,"[7] may seem at first view synonymous; but, as tautology is not one of Paul's characteristics as a writer, I rather think they are intended to suggest different ideas. When Paul says, 'I did not receive my gospel from men,' he seems to refer to the authority with which he was invested to preach the gospel. Timothy received the gospel in this way from him. He put it into his hands and authorised him to communicate it to others. But Paul received his gospel directly from Jesus Christ. HE made him a minister. HE directly and immediately invested him with apostolic authority. And as he did not in this way receive his gospel "from man," so neither was he taught it "by man." It is easy to conceive that a man might be miraculously pointed out as a person destined to be a preacher of Christianity, and yet left to be instructed in the message he was to deliver by inspired men. But this was not Paul's, case; he was not taught his gospel, "but by the revelation of Jesus Christ."[8] By a direct revelation similar to that by which God made known His will to the prophets of old, Paul was made acquainted with that gospel which he was to preach among the Gentiles. He was not sent to the apostles to be instructed. In the history of his conversion, nothing is said of his receiving instruction from Ananias or the disciples at Antioch (Acts 9:19.). Jesus Christ took him under His own immediate tuition, and made known to him, not only what may be called the abstract part of Christianity, but its leading facts. He received of the Lord an account of the institution of the Lord's Supper (1 Cor. 11:23.). He received of the Lord the gospel he preached to the Corinthians, *"that Christ died for our sins according to the Scriptures; and that He was buried, and that He rose again the third day according to the Scriptures"* (1 Cor. 15:3.). This statement does not by any means necessarily infer that Paul knew nothing about Christ Jesus but what he learned by revelation. This is certainly in the highest degree improbable. It means that his deep, thorough knowledge of "the truth as it is in Jesus" was of supernatural origin. "As regards the purely *spiritual* part of the gospel, there is no difficulty in conceiving how Paul could have made this his own without any instrumentality from man. For the Holy Ghost, who was imparted to him, filled his inner man as an all-pervading light, and made plain to him, through his belief in Jesus as the Messiah, the whole of the Old Testament, in which all the germs of the New were already laid down. In the Spirit, who is absolute truth — 1 John 5:6 — was given the assured conviction of the truth of the gospel, and insight into its meaning in details. With regard, however, to the *historical side* of Christianity, the case appears to be different; and yet there are points connected apparently altogether with this (as, for example, the institution of the Lord's Supper, 1 Cor. 11:23, etc.), of which the apostle insists that he received them immediately from the Lord. Now, we should undoubtedly be running into an erroneous extreme if we were to assume that *all* historical particulars in the life of our Lord were imparted to him by revelation. The general outlines of Christ's outward life, the history of His miracles, of His journeys, and what belongs to them, were no doubt related to him by Ananias or other Christians. But whatever in that life was necessarily connected with the peculiar doctrines of the gospel, as, for instance, the institution of the sacraments, the resurrection, and similar points, came no doubt to the apostle in an extraordinary manner, by immediate revelation of the Lord; so as to accredit him as an independent witness, not only before the world, but also to believers. No one could come forward and say, that what Paul knew of the gospel had been received from him. For it was from no man, but from the highest Teacher Himself, that he had received, as well the commission to preach, as also the essential facts of the gospel, and the Holy Spirit who gives light and life to these facts."[9] This statement the apostle confirms by referring to his past history.

It would be high presumption in any Christian minister to use those words of the apostle, which we have been illustrating, in the sense in which he used them. Yet there is a sense, and an important one, in which every Christian minister should be able to say, "the gospel which I preached unto you is not after man." No man should enter the Christian ministry, for no man is fit for its functions, unless he has been "taught of God."[10]

SECT. III. – HISTORICAL PROOF OT THE THESIS.

1. HIS CHARACTER AS A JEW.

"For ye have heard of my conversation in time past in the Jews' religion, how that beyond measure I persecuted the church of God, and wasted it; and profited in the Jews' religion above many my equals in mine own nation, being more exceedingly zealous of the traditions of my fathers" (Gal. 1:13,14.).

The word *conversation* in modern English is confined in its signification to mutual talk – colloquial intercourse. Here, however, and in many other passages of the New Testament, it is used as equivalent to behavior, general conduct, and is the translation of a word of which this is a common meaning.[11] "Ye have heard of my conversation in the Jewish religion"[12] is just equivalent to 'You have heard of my behavior when I was a Jew, that I had a peculiar hatred at Christianity and Christians, and I had a peculiar zeal for Judaism.'

When he was a Jew, Paul "persecuted the church of God, and wasted it beyond measure."[13] The best illustration of these words is to be found in the sacred history. *"As for Saul, he made havock of the church, entering into every house, and haling men and women, committed them to prison."* – *"Then Ananias answered, Lord, I have heard by many of this man, how much evil he hath done to thy saints at Jerualem."* – *"I verily thought with myself, that I ought to do many things contrary to the name of Jesus of Nazareth. Which thing I also did in Jerusalem: and many of the saints did I shut up in prison, having received authority from the chief priests; and when they were put to death, I gave my voice against them. And I punished them oft in every synagogue, and compelled them to blaspheme; and, being exceedingly mad against them, I persecuted them even unto strange cities"* (Acts 8:3; 9:13; 26:9-11.). And as he was an inveterate opponent of Christianity, so he highly admired, diligently studied, carefully practised Judaism. He "profited in the Jews' religion above many of his *equals,"*[14] *i.e.,*, his contemporaries, men of the same age among his countrymen – "being more exceedingly zealous of the traditions of my father." By these "traditions" we are to understand the doctrine of the Old Testament as understood by the Jewish teachers, and the additional dogmas which had no foundation there, but had been handed down by unwritten tradition.[15] He was not only a Jew, but, after the "most straitest sect of that religion, he lived a Pharisee." There is a very striking similarity between the 13th and 14th verses, and Acts 26:4,5.[16] The apostle seems to notice these things, in order to impress on the minds of the Galatians this truth, that the gospel he taught them was not the natural result of his education. In the succeeding verses he shows how he came to entertain his present views.

2. HIS CONVERSION AND CALL.

"But when it pleased God, who separated me from my mother's womb, and called me by His grace, to reveal[17] His Son in me, that I might preach Him among the heathen; immediately I conferred not with flesh and blood" (Gal. 1:15,16.).

It is obvious that the apostle did not learn his gospel of men before his conversion; and it is as plain that he did not learn it of them afterwards. The apostle's short account of his conversion deserves notice. He describes it as the work of God. God "called him by His grace." God "revealed His Son in him." In the new creation, *"all things are of God"* (2 Cor. 5:13.), and it is as true of every man that is converted, as of Paul, that his conversion is the work of God. He speaks of God as "separating him from his mother's womb, and calling him by His grace." The first of these expressions has been explained by a reference to Psal. 22:9,10; but it seems rather parallel to Jer. 1:5. It is equivalent to – 'Who destined me from my birth, and indeed from all eternity, to the office I now fill.' The second of them, "Who called me by His grace," is equivalent to — 'Who graciously,' *i.e.*, kindly, mercifully, 'at the appointed period, by a voice from heaven, accompanied by the power of His Spirit, made me at once a Christian and a Christian apostle.'

It pleased this God "to reveal His Son" in Paul, "that he might preach Him[18] among the heathen." The expression, "to reveal His Son *in me*," is singular. It is a very literal translation, — so literal as to be obscure.[19] The words may either signify, to 'reveal His Son *to* me,' or, to 'reveal His Son *by* me.' As, in the latter case, the phrase would be nearly synonymous with the succeeding clause, we apprehend the former is its meaning. God "revealed His Son" to Paul. But there is more in the phrase than *to reveal to*, in the ordinary sense of these words.[20] It refers to an *inward* revelation, in contrast to the *outward* revelations made to Paul.[21] The declaration is quite parallel to that in the Second Epistle to the Corinthians: "God, who commanded the light to shine out of darkness, shined [22] *in* his heart" (2 Cor. 4:6.)., for the purpose of its being diffused.[23] He made a miraculous revelation of the truth respecting His Son to Paul's mind, for this purpose, "that he might preach Him among the heathen." This was the result of His good pleasure: It "pleased" Him. It was in the exercise of the sovereign benignity of His nature.

And here I cannot but call the attention of all aspirants to the sacred office to the fact, that when God intended to make Paul a public teacher of Christianity, He "revealed Christ in him." They have no reason to expect *such* an internal revelation as he received; but unless, in a very important sense, God "reveals His Son" in them, they cannot be fitted for the office to which they are looking forward. The words of Perkins are weighty: "Ministers of the gospel must learn Christ as Paul learned Him. They may not content themselves with that learning which they find in schools; but they must ιproceed further to a real learning of Christ. They that must convert others, it is meet that they should be effectually converted. John must eat the book, and then prophesy; and they who would be fit ministers of the gospel, must first themselves eat the book of God. And this book is indeed eaten, when they are not only in their minds enlightened, but in their hearts are mortified, and brought in subjection to the word of Christ. Unless Christ be thus learned spiritually and really, divines shall speak of the word of God as men speak of riddles, and as priests in former times said their matins, when they hardly knew what they said."

3. HIS CONDUCT IN CONSEQUENCE OF HIS CONVERSION.
(1.) HE "CONFERRED NOT WITH FLESH AND BLOOD."

Now when God had thus "revealed His Son" in Paul, "immediately,"[24] says he (verse 16), "I conferred[25] not with flesh and blood." The word translated "conferred," properly signifies 'to impose a new burden.' In the classics, the middle voice is used in the sense, — 'I allow a burden to be imposed on myself — I undertake some difficult affair.' It is sometimes used by the later writers with the dative of a person, to signify 'to take counsel or advice of a person,' as he who asks advice lays a burden on the person consulted. This is its meaning here. "Flesh and blood"[26] are here equivalent to 'human nature' in himself or in others. — 'I neither consulted my own reason or inclination, nor did I seek instruction from others: I committed myself entirely to Divine guidance and teaching. I did not consult with any man. I did not seek instruction from any man. I did not inquire at other Christians if the views of Christiantiy which had been conveyed into my mind were correct or not. I asked at no man what I was to preach, or where I was to preach. I gave myself up to the guidance of the Divine impulse; and immediately commenced speaking the things of the Spirit, not in words which man's wisdom teacheth, but which the Holy Ghost teacheth.'[27]

(2.) HE DID NOT GO UP TO JERUSALEM.

"Neither went I up to Jerusalem to them which were apostles before me;[28] but I went into Arabia, and returned again to Damascus" (Gal. 1:17.). On his conversion, Paul immediately began to teach in Damascus; and when, in consequence of the persecutions of his countrymen, he found it necessary to leave Damascus, he did not go up[29] to

Jerusalem to be better instructed in Christianity, or to have his mission confirmed.

(3.) HE WENT TO ARABIA.

Instead of going to Jerusalem, he went into Arabia,[30] for the purpose, it may be, of yielding himself up in its solitudes to solemn meditation and communion with his divine Master. No proof can be derived from these words that Paul preached in Arabia. There is no trace of that in the Acts of the Apostles.

(4.) HE RETURNED TO DAMASCUS.

After continuing in Arabia for some time, he returned to Damascus, which at that time was under the government of Aretas, the king of Arabia (2 Cor. 11:32.). During all this time he had never met with one of the apostles, nor does it appear that he had intercourse with any individual of note among the Christians. And when, after three years, he did at length go up to Jerusalem, he received neither instruction nor authority from the apostles.

4. *Three years after, he went to Jerusalem to become acquainted with Peter; remained only three days, and saw only two of the apostles.*

"Then, after three years, I went up to Jerusalem to see Peter, and abode with him fifteen[31] days. But other of the apostles saw I none, save James the Lord's brother" (Gal. 1:18,19.). It is impossible to say certainly whether these three years are to be dated from Paul's departure from Jerusalem to Damascus, or from his return from Arabia to that city.[32] This is probably the visit of which we have an account, Acts 9:26,27. His object was to "see Peter."[33] He gained his object, and was Peter's guest for a fortnight.[34] It was natural that Paul whould wish to make the acquaintance of such a man as the apostle Peter: the man who made the noble declaration, Matth. 16:16; the man to whom had been given the keys of the kingdom of heaven; the man who had preached the sermon at Pentecost, which made three thousand converts (Acts 2:14-41.). The only other apostle seen by Paul on this occasion was "James the Lord's brother." This was probably James the son of Alpheus, who was our Lord's cousin – the word rendered "brother,"[35] like the corresponding Hebrew term, being used for a near relative. Some[36] have supposed, but without sufficient reason, that it was another James, a brother-german of our Lord. If such an individual existed, which is not improbable, he was not an apostle. On this visit Paul met with only two of the apostles, and he remained with them only fifteen days; so that it is plain there was no time for him to learn his Christianity from them. Dr. Paley well observes, "The shortness of St. Paul's stay at Jerusalem is what I desire the reader to remark. The direct account of the same journey in the Acts (Acts 9:28-30.), determines nothing concerning the time of his continuance there: 'And he was with them (the apostles) coming in and going out at Jerusalem. And he spake boldly in the name of the Lord Jesus, and disputed against the Grecians: but they went about to slay him. Which when the brethren knew, they brought him down to Caesarea.' Or rather this account, taken by itself, would lead a reader to suppose that St. Paul's abode at Jerusalem had been longer than fifteen days. But turn to the twenty-second chapter of the Acts, and you will find a reference to this visit to Jerusalem, which plainly indicates that Paul's continuance in that city had been of short duration: 'And it came to pass, that, when I was come again to Jerusalem, even while I prayed in the temple, I was in a trance; and saw Him saying unto me, Make haste, and get thee quickly out of Jerusalem: for they will not receive thy testimony concerning me.' Here we have the general terms of one text so explained by a distant text in the same book, as to bring an indeterminate expression into a close conformity with a specification delivered in another book; a species of consistency not, I think, usually found in fabulous relations."[37] It seems likely that it was Paul's intention to remain for some time in Jerusalem; but his Master ordered it otherwise (Acts 9:29; 22:17, etc.) It was not the apostles, but their Master, who determined where Paul was to labor.

In the 20th verse, the apostle makes a strong declaration of the truth of his relation:

"Now the things which I write unto you, behold, before God, I lie not." This is a plain intimation that oaths, on proper occasions, are not unlawful. We have similar declarations equivalent to oaths, Rom. 1:9, 2 Cor. 1:23; Rom. 9:1; 2 Cor. 11:31; 1 Thess. 2:5.

5. He went then into the regions of Syria and Cilicia, being personally unknown to the churches of Judea.

In the following verses the history is continued: "Afterwards I came into the regions of Syria and Cilicia; and was unknown by face unto the churches of Judea which were in Christ: but they had heard only, that he which persecuted us in times past, now preacheth the faith which once he destroyed. And they glorified God in me" (Gal. 1:21-24.). After the apostle's departure from Jerusalem, he went "into the regions[38] of Syria and Cilicia." The parallel passage in Acts is chap. 9:30. How long Paul remained in these regions, we have no means of ascertaining.

"The churches of Judea" is a phrase descriptive of 'the churches out of the capital.' To the members of these churches Saul was personally unknown. All they knew of him was by report. "They had heard"[39] both what he had been – a destroyer of the faith, – and what he had become – a preacher of that faith.[40] "The term by which the apostle expresses the subject of his preaching, " the faith,"[41] has occasioned no small contention among the learned part of the Christian world. He calls it *the faith;* and it seems that was the term then commonly used. As it is allowed by all that it (faith) is the same with *belief,* the meanest day-laborer knows as well as the most learned divine that it is commonly used to express *what* they believe, and the actual believing of it; or, as the schools speak, the *act* of believing, and its *object;* and can easily distinguish when the one or the other is to be understood by that word. And one cannot help saying, that the learned labors of those who have made it their business to explain it, have contributed more to darken a plain subject, and perplex common understandings, than to clear the important subject, which every man knows better than the most learned can define it. No man can believe, or not believe, what and when he pleases. He must perceive the thing to be true, either by his own observation or the testimony of others. Never was there any testimony which deserved half so much regard as that does which God has given us in the record we have in our hands. The facts recorded there are of two kinds: what God has done, and what He has promised to do. By the first, 'His eternal power and Godhead' are set before us in the only way we can come to the knowledge of Him; that is, by such works and ways with His creatures, as we can form some notion of. By the second, we learn what we have to expect from Him; and, from both taken together, we may be enabled to form such apprehensions of the Divine character, as may show us what measures of regard and duty we owe Him. This is the Christian faith, and the belief of these facts is what makes a Christian; and believed they cannot be, without producing such measures of love to Him, and confidence in Him, as answer to the measures of our faith: and 'love is the fulfilling of the whole law;' the whole of our obedience to His law being only the native effect and actings of love."[42]

This intelligence produced its proper effect on the minds of these Christians: "They glorified God," says the apostle, "in me."[43] Well they might; – and so may – so ought – we. Divine grace never had a more glorious trophy, Christianity never made, in one individual, so important an acquisition. "We may still glorify and praise God for the grace manifested in the conversion of Saul of Tarsus. What does not the world owe to him! What do we not owe to him! No man did so much in establishing the Christian religion as he did; no one among the apostles was the means of converting and saving so many souls; no one has left so many and so valuable writings for the edification of the church. To him we owe the invaluable epistles – so full of truth, and eloquence, and promises, and consolations – on one of which we are commenting; and to him the church owes, under God, some of its most elevated and ennobling views of the nature of Christian doctrine and duty. After the lapse, therefore, of eighteen hundred years, we should not cease to glorify God for the conversion of this wonderful man, and should feel that *we* have cause of thankfulness that He changed the infuriated persecutor to a holy and devoted apostle."[44] "Here we see what is the right way of honoring the saints, and that is to glorify God *in* them and *for* them. As for religious worship of adoration and invocation, it is proper to God, and the saints desire it not."[45]

It appears, then, from these statements, that Paul was engaged for three years in preaching the gospel before he had any intercourse with a Christian apostle; that, when he did see them, he saw only two of them; that he went, not to learn from them as a scholar, but to visit them as an equal; that he was only fifteen days in Jerusalem upon that occasion; that he then went into Syria and Cilicia, where there were no apostles, and where he exercised all the powers of an apostle — planting churches; and that the churches of Judea, though he stood in no peculiar relation to them, and was not even personally known to them, glorified God on account of his being converted from one of the most furious persecutors, into one of the most devoted supporters, of the faith of Christ, and of course considered him as having a title to the name and place he occupied in the church: all which particulars were obviously fitted to answer the apostle's object — the assertion of his dignity as an apostle, and of his integrity as a man.[46]

6. He visited Jerusalem again after an interval of fourteen years.

The apostle proceeds with his apologetical narration in the passage which follows. There should obviously have been no new chapter here. "Then, fourteen years after,[47] I went up[48] again to Jerusalem with Barnabas, and took Titus with me also. And I went up by revelation,[49] and communicated unto them that gospel which I preach among the Gentiles, but privately to them which were of reputation, lest by any means I should run, or had run, in vain" (Gal. 2:1, 2.). It is uncertain from what period the apostle dates these fourteen years,[50] whether from the time of his conversion — a period which must have been always present to his mind, — or from the time of his first visit to Jerusalem after his conversion; and it matters very little how this question be determined.[51] Interpreters also differ as to what particular visit to Jerusalem the apostle here refers: some supposing that he refers to the visit he and Barnabas made to Jerusalem as the bearers of the alms of the church of Antioch, mentioned Acts 11:27-30; others, that he refers to the visit occasioned by the dispute respecting the obligation of the Mosaic law, of which we have an account, Acts 15.; and others, that it refers to a visit not mentioned in the Acts of the Apostles. The second of these opinions appears to me the more probable one.

On this journey Paul was accompanied by Barnabas and Titus; and, as appears from the narrative in the Acts of the Apostles, by others of the church of Antioch (Acts 15:2).

(1.) HE "WENT UP BY REVELATION "

On this occasion Paul was not summoned by the apostles to give an account of his conduct. He "went up by revelation."[52] These words are strangely interpreted by the learned Hermann as equivalent to, 'for the sake of explanation,' but their obvious force is, 'in consequence of a direct communication from his only Lord and Master, Christ Jesus.' Of the nature of this revelation we are not particularly informed. It is plain that revelations were common occurrences with the apostle. According to his own account, 2 Cor. 12:7, he was favored with "abundance of revelations;"[53] and these revelations were made to him in various ways: sometimes directly to himself; sometimes to other inspired men respecting him; sometimes in one way, sometimes in another. The following passages contain accounts of revelations made to Paul, or about Paul: — Acts 9:6; 22:17; 13:2; 16:6; 18:9; 21:10; 23:11; 27:23. In some such way was Paul instructed that it was the will of his Master that he should go to Jerusalem. This is no way inconsistent with the history in the Acts of the Apostles, where it is stated that "it was determined" that Paul should go to Jerusalem.[54] That determination was probably the result of the revelation.

(2.) HE COMMUNICATED TO THE APOSTLES HIS MODE OF PREACHING THE GOSPEL AMONG THE GENTILES.

On his going to Jerusalem on this occasion, he communicated[55] not to the church there as a body, but "privately[56] to them who were of reputation"[57] — *i.e.*, to the apostles, or perhaps to the more distinguished of the apostles — "the gospel which he preached[58] among the Gentiles." By "the gospel which he preached among the Gentiles," some understand the doctrine of the freedom of the converted Gentiles from the yoke of the Mosaic law. But this does not seem likely, as certainly, on this occasion, Paul did publicly declare his opinion on this question. Others suppose that the phrase denotes the doctrine that the Mosaic law was not obligatory even on the Jewish converts, though they were not prohibited from observing it. I rather think the phrase denotes generally Paul's mode of stating the grand fundamental doctrines of Christianity. The apostles all preached the same gospel, but each of them had probably his own way of preaching it In Paul's way of preaching it, the non-obligation of the Mosaic law on Christians and the extreme hazard of connecting anything with the merits of Christ as the ground of hope, or with faith in Him as the instrument of justification, were made peculiarly prominent, far more so than in Peter's or James's. or John's mode of preaching it.[59]

Now, Paul stated to his apostolic brethren the way in which he was accustomed to preach the gospel among the Gentiles. He made this statement not publicly, because it is quite possible that many of the weak Christians at Jerusalem, overrun with Jewish prejudices, and accustomed only to James's, or Peter's, or John's way of preaching the gospel, might be disposed to think Paul's gospel, though substantially the same with theirs, another gospel.

And he made this statement to the apostles, "lest by any means he should run, or had run, in vain," *i.e.,* that his past labors might not become, and that his future labors might not be, fruitless. The apostle seems to have been fond of agonistic metaphors drawn from the *stadium* and *arena,* 1 Cor. 9:24-26; Phil. 2:16; 2 Tim. 4:7. We have the same idea in plain words, I Thess. 3:5.[60] It would have been a great obstacle in the way of Paul's success, if the apostles had been ignorant of his peculiar mode of teaching Christianity. In this case, when inquired at respecting Paul's doctrine by those who were stumbled at it, they could only have said, 'We do not know what Paul teaches;' but when Paul had stated his doctrine to them, and when they had approved it as substantially the same gospel which they themselves preached, no danger was to be feared from that quarter.[61]

That the apostles were not dissatisfied with that part of Paul's doctrine which was peculiarly obnoxious to the Judaising teachers, 'that gentile converts were not bound to be circumcised or submit to the Mosaic law" was made very evident by their conduct in reference to Titus. "But neither Titus, who was with me, being a Greek, was compelled to be circumcised: and that because of false brethren unawares brought in, who came in privily to spy out our liberty which we have in Christ Jesus, that they might bring us into bondage: to whom we gave place by subjection, no, not for an hour, that the truth of the gospel might continue with you" (Gal 2:3-5.). The construction of this paragraph is a little involved.[62] Some, following a different reading from our translation, have in rendering it left out *"'no, not,"*[63] in the 5th verse. They suppose that Titus was circumcised, and that the apostle is explaining the circumstance. Titus was not *compelled* to be circumcised, but he (Paul) acted on principles similar to those on which he took and circumcised Timothy. It is a very important remark of Dr. Paley, that "whenever Paul's compliance with the Jewish law is mentioned in the history of the Acts of the Apostles, it is mentioned in connection with circumstances which point out the motives from which it proceeded, and this motive seems always exoteric, namely, a love of order and tranquillity, or an unwillingness to give unnecessary offence." Acts 16:3; 21:26. The apostle's *conduct* in such cases was in no degree inconsistent with his *doctrine*. He yielded for a time to the prejudices of others to gain a good purpose. There are, however, many objections to this way of interpretation. There is no evidence of Titus having been circumcised. The various reading on which this interpretation rests is not so well supported as that adopted in the *textus receptus,* which is, as usual, followed by our translators; besides, the reason given at the conclusion of the 5th verse is a very good reason for Paul's opposing Titus's circumcision, but it is difficult to see how it could be a reason for his consenting to it.

By supposing the language elliptical − not more so than is common in letters, not more so, at any rate, than is common in Paul's letters − the whole passage may be made plain enough.[64] It is as if he had said, 'Nothing can be a more satisfactory proof that the apostles did not object to my doctrine respecting the non-obligation of the Mosaic law on gentile converts than this, that Titus my companion, though known to be a native Gentile, was not required to submit to circumcision. There was, indeed, an attempt to enforce something of this kind by a certain class of men, but I resisted it, and successfully resisted it, from the regard I had to the interests of the Gentile Christians.' The idea of an attempt having been made to enforce the obligation of the Mosaic law, is probably implied in the phrase *"was not compelled."*[65] That such an attempt was made, is plain enough from the history as recorded in the 15 chapter of the Acts of the Apostles, verse 5, which refers, I apprehend, not to what had taken place at Antioch, but to what took place at Jerusalem. At the same time, it is obvious that what took place at Jerusalem was the consequence of what had taken place at Antioch. The question was stirred by these false brethren, and it is to them and their introduction into the church at Antioch that the apostle seems to refer here.

The persons who made the attempt are described by the apostle as "false brethren unawares brought in, who came in privily to spy out our liberty which we have in Christ Jesus, that they might bring us into bondage"(Gal. 2:4.). Here, as in so many other places of the epistles, we want the light of contemporary history to make the meaning of these words perfectly plain. It has been supposed by some, that the apostle alludes to unbelieving Jews, who, on profession of a pretended faith, had sought and found admission into the Christian society, for the purpose of acquiring a more accurate knowledge of the principles and manners of the new sect, that they might the better be able to hold them up to the hatred of their countrymen as violators and despisers of the law of Moses. But the apostle seems to have had a totally different class of persons in his eye − persons who admitted the Messiahship of Jesus Christ, but did not understand His religion − who carried into their new religion all their old prejudices, or rather who merely had added to their old creed this new article, 'that Jesus was the Messiah.' These persons were brethren, *i.e.* Christians in name; but they were "false brethren,"[66] Jews in reality.

They had been "brought in unawares;"[67] for whatever may have been the practice in later times, in the apostolic ages no man was admitted to the communion of the Christian church except under the impression that he really was a Christian. They "came in privily."[68] Had they avowed the opinion, that circumcision was necessary in order to salvation in the same way as faith in Christ, they would never have been acknowledged Christians at all. I think it most likely, however, that the apostle is not here speaking so much of admission into the Christian church as of admission into the church of Antioch; and that he refers to those men mentioned in the fifteenth chapter of the Acts, who, first at Antioch and then at Jerusalem, opposed the doctrine of the apostle respecting the freedom of gentile converts from the yoke of the Mosaic law. These men "privily crept into the church of Antioch" to spy out the Christian liberty which the gentile Christians there enjoyed: and they did this for the purpose of bringing them into bondage, by subjecting them to the requisitions of the ceremonial law. The phrase, "which we have in Christ Jesus,"[69] is equivalent to, 'which we enjoy by Christ,' or rather to, 'which we in Christ Jesus − we Christians − enjoy.'

But to those persons Paul "would not give place, no, not for an hour" (Gal. 2:5.). He opposed them at Antioch − he opposed them at Jerusalem; and the reason why he thus opposed them was, "that the truth of the gospel might continue with the Gentiles." *i.e.*

that "the true gospel" might continue with them – the glad tidings, that "whosoever believeth in Christ Jesus should not perish, but have everlasting life." Had the apostle yielded, the conclusion to be drawn would have been, that something besides Christ's merits was necessary as the ground, and something besides faith in Him necessary as the means, of justification; and the admission of both or of either of these principles was materially a denial of the truth of the gospel. "Let us learn this kind of stubbornness from the apostle," as Luther says. "We will suffer our goods to be taken away, our name, our life, and all that we have; but the gospel, our faith, Jesus Christ, we will never suffer to be wrested from us: and cursed be that humility which here abaseth and submitteth itself; nay, rather let every Christian be proud and spare not, except he will deny Christ. Wherefore, God assisting me, my forehead shall be harder than all men's forheads. Here I take for my motto, 'Cedo nulli.' I will give place to none. I am, and ever will be, stout and stern, and will not one inch give place to any creature. Charity giveth place, 'for it suffereth all things, believeth all things, endureth all things;' but faith giveth no place."

While the apostle thus asserts that his doctrines were sanctioned by the approbation of the other apostles, he as unequivocally declares that he derived neither instruction nor authority from them, but was treated by them as a person who stood in no need of their sanction, but was invested with equal authority with themselves.

(3). HE RECEIVED FROM THE APOSTLES THE MOST UNEQUIVOCAL ACKNOWLEDGMENT OF HIS QUALIFICATIONS, CALL, AND AUTHORITY, AS AN APOSTLE.

"But of those who seemed to be somewhat, whatsoever they were, it maketh no matter to me: God accepteth no man's person: for they who seemed to be somewhat in conference added nothing to me."[70]

"To be somewhat"[71] is an idiomatical expression for dignity of rank or station. "They who seemed to be somewhat"[72] is no disparaging expression. It is equivalent to the expression in a succeeding verse, *"they who seemed"* – were accounted, justly accounted – *"to be pillars,"* and probably refers to the same persons, "the chief apostles."[73]

"Whatsoever they were, it maketh no difference to me."[74] 'Whatever advantages in some points of view they may seem to have had over me, it matters not.' "God regardeth no man's person,"[75] a Hebraistic expression, Deut. 10:17, *i.e.,* 'He is sovereign in the dispensation of His gifts. In the bestowal of His favors, He is not regulated by external appearances or relations.' It does not follow that, because James was Christ's kinsman, or Peter and John His personal friends, that therefore they should have higher authority in His church than one who had, perhaps, never seen Jesus Christ till after His resurrection.[76] These chief apostles "added nothing"[77] to Paul. The word may mean either 'they communicated to him no new information – no additional authority,' or 'they found no fault with his way of preaching the gospel.' They could not in any way improve him who had been taught of their common Master. They never tried it: they were under the influence of a very different spirit. They rejoiced in the grace that had been given to him in common with themselves, and gladly acknowledged him a brother-apostle.

"But contrariwise, when they saw that the gospel of the uncircumcision was committed unto me, as the gospel of the circumcision was unto Peter; (for He that wrought effectually in Peter to the apostleship of the circumcision, the same was mighty in me toward the Gentiles): and when James, Cephas, and John, who seemed to be pillars, perceived the grace that was given unto me, they gave to me and Barnabas the right hands of fellowship; that we should go unto the heathen, and they unto the circumcision. Only *they would* that we should remember the poor; the same which I also was forward to do" (Gal. 2:7-10.).

On hearing Paul state "the gospel which he preached among the Gentiles," the apostles instead of finding fault with it, saw clearly "that the gospel of the uncircumcision was committed[78] to Paul, as the gospel of the circumcision to Peter." "Uncircumcision" here means the Gentiles, and "circumcision" the Jews,[79] Rom. 2:26, etc.; Eph. 2:11; Col.

3:11. "The gospel of the uncircumcision," or of the Gentiles, has generally been understood as meaning the ministry of the gospel among the Gentiles; and "the gospel of the circumcision," or of the Jews, the ministry of the gospel among the Jews; and the meaning of the whole phrase, 'when they saw that it was the will of God that I should labor among the Gentiles, and that Peter should labor among the Jews.' I rather think that "the gospel of the uncircumcision" means that way of preaching the gospel which was peculiarly fitted for the Gentiles; and "the gospel of the circumcision" that way of preaching the gospel which was peculiarly fitted for the Jews. On hearing Paul, they distinctly saw that the Holy Spirit had taught him to preach the gospel in a way peculiarly calculated for the conversion of the Gentiles, just as He had taught Peter to preach the gospel in a way peculiarly fitted for the conversion of the Jews.

"For" (Gal. 2:8.), says the apostle by the way, "He that wrought effectually in Peter to the apostleship of the circumcision, the same was mighty in me toward the Gentiles." These words are ordinarily referred to the *success* of the apostles' preaching, but I apprehend they refer rather to their *qualifications* for preaching. Christ by His Spirit "wrought effectually in Peter to the apostleship of the circumcision," *i.e.*, Christ by His Spirit gave to Peter those qualifications which peculiarly fitted him to do the duties of an apostle among the Jews; and Christ, by the same Spirit, who has a diversity of gifts and operations, gave to Paul those qualifications which peculiarly fitted him to do the duties of an apostle among the Gentiles.

The apostles, James, Peter, and John, who perhaps were all that then were at Jerusalem, were reckoned "pillars,"[80] the ornaments and support – *decora et tutamina* – of the Christian church. It is common for Paul to compare the church to an edifice or temple, 1 Cor. 3:16; Eph. 2:21; 1 Tim. 3:15. The order in which the apostles are mentioned deserves notice, when we recollect the insolent pretensions of the men who assume that they are the successors of Peter. James, not Peter, has the first place. James, too, presided in the council of Jerusalem. Peter, so far from usurping the title of universal bishop, confines his charge to the circumcision, and resigns the rest of the world to Paul. Peter opened the gate to the Gentiles, but Paul gathered them in. A universal bishop could make out a better claim by proving his succession to Paul than to Peter. The apostles James, Peter, and John, "perceived the grace" – 'the tokens of the peculiar favor and love of Christ Jesus' – conferred on Paul and his companion. "The grace" here signifies the favor bestowed on Paul, in authorising and qualifying him to preach the gospel among the Gentiles. The best commentary on this passage is to be found in his own words, "Unto me, who am less than the least of all saints, is this grace given, that I should preach among the Gentiles the unsearchable riches of Christ" (Eph. 3:8.). Perceiving this, they readily acknowledged Paul and Barnabas as brethren: they gave them the right hand of fellowship,[81] as a token of agreement in sentiment, an acknowledgment of their possessing the same authority as themselves, and a pledge that they would mutually assist one another in the great work in which they were engaged; and at the same time it was agreed, that while James, Peter, and John continued to labor chiefly among the Jews, Paul and Barnabas should continue to labor chiefly among the Gentiles. Not that either party was scrupulously to confine their labors within these bounds; but that, generally speaking, they should respectively occupy those fields of labor for which the Holy Spirit had peculiarly qualified them. This was not, however, an appointment laid upon Paul as by superiors. It was a mutual agreement of equals,[82] arising out of their clearly perceiving the will of their common Master. Accordingly they gave Paul and Barnabas no instructions. They knew that he needed none. The only subject on which they gave anything like advice, was one of a practical, not of a doctrinal, kind; and even then it was a friendly hint, not a magisterial command. "Only they would[83] that we should remember the poor." They requested them to keep in mind the distressed condition of many of the believers in Judea, who, for the gospel's sake, had suffered the loss of all things, and recommend their situation to the sympathy of their gentile brethren who might be able to help them. The Jewish poor found a considerable resource in the sacrifices of the temple, on which they greatly depended. Such of them as became Christians were probably deprived of this advantage, and were rendered more necessitous than the poor in other places. "Which thing," says the apostle, "I was forward to do."[84] How the apostle remembered the poor appears from Acts 11:29-30; 24:17; Rom. 15:17; 1 Cor. 16:1; 2 Cor. 8. He was forward to do this for more reasons than one. He was a benevolent man; he was a patriotic man; and he was persuaded that few things had a greater tendency to break down the walls of prejudice between Jewish and Gentile believers, than this fellowship of love – this communion in giving and receiving.

How many jealousies and strifes might be prevented in the church, if the conduct of Paul and his apostolic brethren were generally followed! "If there was, on the one hand, the same readiness for a full and frank explanation, and if, on the other, the same freedom from envy at remarkable success, how many strifes that have disgraced the church might be avoided! The true way to avoid strife, is just that which is here proposed. Let there be on both sides perfect frankness – let there be a willingness to explain and state things just as they are – and let there be a disposition to rejoice in the talents, and zeal, and success of others, though it should far outstrip our own, – and contention in the church would cease; and every devoted and successful minister of the gospel would receive the right hand of fellowship from all, however venerable by age or authority, who love the cause of true religion."[85]

7. HIS REPROOF OF PETER FOR DISSEMBLING AT ANTIOCH, AND HIS ASSERTION OF THE TRUE GOSPEL.

In the succeeding paragraph (verses 11-21) Paul shows from an incident that took place at Antioch, both how consistently he had all along asserted the freedom of gentile believers, and of Christians generally, from the obligation of the Mosaic law; and how far he was from being only a secondary apostle. He had not hesitated to differ from, aye, and to reprove, Peter, one of "the chiefest of the apostles," when his conduct was not according to the truth of the gospel.

"But when Peter was come to Antioch, I withstood him to the face, because he was to be blamed" (Ga. 2:11.). 'Cephas' is considered the preferable reading by Mill and Lachmann; and some interpreters, both ancient and modern, have supposed, in opposition to the plainest evidence, that not Peter the apostle, but some other *Cephas* is intended. Hardouin, the whimsical but learned Jesuit, is as might be expected, a supporter of this opinion. Antioch was a celebrated, wealthy, magnificent, populous city, the capital of Syria, the most illustrious city in Asia, as Alexandria was in Africa, and Rome in Europe, situated on the river Orontes, the seat of one of the most flourishing of the primitive Christian churches, remarkable as the place where the disciples of Jesus received the name by which they have ever since been universally known.[86]

The exact period of this visit of the apostle Peter cannot be fixed. Semler's notion, that it was previous to the visit of Paul to Jerusalem, mentioned in the beginning of the chapter, is in the highest degree improbable. We know that after the apostles and elders at Jerusalem had, by their decree, sanctioned the doctrine of the non-obligation of the Mosaic law on the gentile converts, and enjoined on them abstinence "from fornication, and from things offered in sacrifice to idols, and things strangled, and blood," Paul and Barnabas, along with Judas, Silas, and others, returned to Antioch,[87] and continued there for some time, after which they went to visit the churches which they had formerly planted. It seems highly probable that it was during the interval which elapsed between the return from Jerusalem and Paul's setting out on this itinerant mission, that Peter visited Antioch. He came probably to enjoy the satisfaction of seeing so numerous and flourishing a gentile church, and to give the weight of his personal sanction to the decree of the apostles and elders.

This visit seems for a considerable time to have been agreeable and useful to all parties; but towards the close of it, Paul found it necessary to reprove Peter on account of conduct which appeared to him calculated to injure the Christian cause. "I withstood him"[88] – is equivalent to, 'I opposed him' – "to the face."[89] Some of the fathers, as

Chrysostom and Jerome, have represented this disagreement between the two apostles as merely apparent, and the whole affair got up by mutual agreement to serve a purpose.[90] There is nothing in the narrative which gives the least countenance to such a notion. Such management would have savored too much of the "craftiness,"[91] and "the hidden things of dishonesty,[92] which both the apostles had renounced, and indeed would not have been consistent with integrity. Such a hypothesis would never have been thought of, but to defend the infallibility of Peter. It is, however, an odd way to defend one apostle from a mistake in judgment, by representing two apostles as guilty of something approaching at least to deliberate falsehood.[93] But even in Jerome's and Chrysostom's time, the maxim that the end sanctifies the means, had gained extensive currency among Christians; and they readily attributed to apostles motives and modes of action with which they themselves were but too familiar. It is of great importance, especially in these days, to be impressed with the conviction that primitive Christianity and ancient Christianity, apostolical Christianity and patristic Christianity, are two very different – in many respects two directly opposite – things.

Paul did not keep silent as if he had been afraid of Peter as a superior; he was not awed by the example of so great an apostle into the silent sanction of what he thought wrong; and he did not oppose Peter by secret insinuation – by speaking evil of him when he was absent, – he avowed to himself his dissatisfaction with his conduct.

And he did this "because he was to be blamed."[94] Some interpreters suppose that the apostle's meaning is, 'because he was blamed,' – every person, except the Jews who came down from James, blamed his conduct as inconsistent, unchristian, and unmanly. We apprehend, however, that our translators have given the true meaning.[95] That other people were blaming Peter, would have been no reason with Paul for blaming him. It would have operated rather in the opposite way. The reason that he withstood him was, that he was conscientiously persuaded he was wrong, and that a public statement of this conviction was necessary to serve the purpose of general edification. Of the manner in which Peter received this correction, we have no account. We know it produced no lasting alienation. It was long after this that Peter styled his reprover, "our beloved brother Paul."[96] It has been supposed, but we are very unwilling to entertain the thought, that the occurrences here recorded had their effect in predisposing Barnabas' mind to that irritation which made a comparatively very slight difference of opinion the occasion of breaking up that close companionship with his illustrious friend which had been so full of holy delight to both parties, and so advantageous to the churches.

Let us learn from Paul's conduct, not to allow the authority or example of any man, however great or good, to interfere with the convictions of our own minds respecting truth and duty. Let us be certain that a man is to be blamed before we withstand him; and when we do so, let it be to his face.

The apostle goes on to give a more particular account of this unpleasant affair. "For before that certain came from James, he did eat with the Gentiles: but when they were come, he withdrew, and separated himself, fearing them which were of the circumcision. And the other Jews dissembled likewise with him; insomuch that Barnabas also was carried away with their dissimulation" (Gal. 2:12,13.).

For some time after his arrival, Peter mingled familiarly in social intercourse with the gentile converts who had not been circumsiced, and who did not observe the law of Moses. This is the meaning of his "eating with them." It does not refer to eating the Lord's Supper or religious communion; for we have no reason to think that even after the Jewish brethren came, either he or they refused to have this sort of intercourse with their gentile brethren. The Gentiles were accustomed to eat a variety of articles prohibited by the Mosaic law; and it would appear that Peter, without scruple, sat down with them at table, and, it may be, without scruple partook of what was placed before him, – acting on the principle which he had been miraculously taught, that "what God had cleansed, he ought not to account *common* or unclean" (Acts 10:15.) Such conduct on the part of Peter was certainly well fitted to confirm the Gentiles in their attachment to their new faith, to show that there was no design to proselyte them to Judaism; and that the observance or non-observance of Mosaic ceremonies was no way essentially connected with the grand leading doctrines and duties of Christianity.

But this agreeable state of things was soon interrupted. "Some came from James,"[97] *i.e.* from Jerusalem, over the church of which James seems to have presided, who, like most of their brethren, were "zealous for the law." It does not seem that they directly attempted to impose the law on the Gentiles; but they seem to have insisted that the converted Jews should keep it, and, of course, should avoid unrestrained social intercourse with their Gentile brethren.

Peter "feared"[98] these men."[99] The meaning of these words is not very obvious. I am disposed to think that Peter was afraid of their being so disgusted at seeing the unreserved intercourse of Jews and Gentiles, a thing so abhorrent to their prejudices, as to be tempted to renounce Christianity and revert to Judaism. This is a sentiment much more likely to influence the conduct of a man like Peter than a mean selfish fear of losing his popularity among these prejudiced Jews. Under the influence of this fear he "withdrew, and separated himself;"[100] not at all, as I apprehend, from their religious meetings, but he became more reserved and cautious in his intercourse with them, and carefully abstained from anything that looked like a violation of the law of Moses.

This conduct the apostle calls "dissimulation."[101] For Peter's opinion remained unaltered. On the great question he and Paul were completely at one.[102] But Peter adopted a mode of conduct which had a natural tendency to lead the Jews to think that his opinion and that of Paul were different, and to lead the Gentiles to think that he had altered his opinion. A man dissembles when, either by words, or actions, or silence, or inaction, he gives others reason to think that his sentiments are different from what they really are. The other Jewish converts at Antioch went along with Peter; and even the excellent Barnabas was "carried away,"[103] it is likely, partly by regard to Peter's authority, and partly by the fear of offending the Judaising brethren.

This passage teaches us the importance of consistency of conduct; the danger of worldly wisdom in the management of ecclesiastical affairs; the great caution with which men distinguished for their office, talents, and influence should act; and the extreme danger of making any man's opinion and conduct the rule of ours.

Let us now attend to Paul's account of his own behavior in these difficult circumstances. "But when I saw that they walked not uprightly, according to the truth of the gospel, I said unto Peter before them all, If thou, being a Jew, livest after the manner of Gentiles, and not as do the Jews, why compellest thou the Gentiles to live as do the Jews" (Gal. 2:14.)?

Paul saw that Peter, Barnabas, and the other Jewish converts "did not walk uprightly,[104] according to the truth of the gospel." "To walk uprightly," in the English language, means to act with integrity — to conduct a person's self according to his convictions of truth and duty. It does not necessarily imply that the person's conduct is right: it merely intimates that it is honest. Paul "walked uprightly" when he persecuted the church, as well as when he preached the gospel. It has been very common to understand the phrase here in this way, and to suppose that Paul charges Peter and the others with a want of integrity. I see no ground for such a supposition. I apprehend that Peter and Barnabas acted with perfect integrity, — *i.e.,* they acted according to their views of present duty, though these views were mistaken ones. They did not think that their conduct compromised any truth, and they conceived that it was necessary to prevent "the offence" — in the Scripture sense of the term, the "stumbling" — of their brethren from Jerusalem. And I am quite sure that there never was a man less disposed than the apostle Paul, to ascribe the conduct of his brethren to bad motives. The original term,[105] which occurs only in this place in the New Testament, does not refer to motives at all. It literally signifies *to walk straightly,* and refers to propriety of conduct, viewed in reference to some rule. "When I saw that they walked not straightly" means just 'when I saw that their conduct was not right.' Paul does not question their motives, but he condemns their conduct.

"According to the truth of the gospel."[106] These words are generally understood as nearly synonymous with those which precede them, – 'according to that sincerity which the gospel teaches.' I rather think their meaning is, 'corresponding to the true gospel.' The conduct of Peter and the rest seemed to the apostle calculated to throw obscurity and doubt on the true gospel, – that men are saved entirely "by faith," "through the redemption that is in Christ Jesus;" and accordingly you find, in his address to them, not a reproof of insincerity, but a representation of the tendency which their conduct had to lead to false views of the way of salvation, and a clear statement of those principles which, in his apprehension, their behavior was calculated to obscure. When he saw that their conduct was not right, and did not correspond with the truths of the gospel, he "said to Peter *before them all.*"[107'] The apostle observes the injunction he lays on Timothy, "Them that sin rebuke before all, that others also may fear" (1 Tim. 5:20.). If he had known that Peter really thought differently from him on the general subject and that the apostles had given a judgment consistent with Peter's views, and inconsistent with his own, Paul durst not have thus acted. In the public assembly of the brethren Paul declared his dissatisfaction with the conduct of Peter, and those who had followed his example.

His speech on this occasion is indeed an admirable one, and, in our apprehension, reaches to the end of the chapter. On this subject expositors are not of one opinion. Grotius, Semler, and Koppe, consider the 14th verse as containing the whole of Paul's address to Peter, and the part, from verse 15-21, as addressed to the Galatians. Rosenmüller, Tittmann, Knapp, and Jaspis, consider the whole passage, to the end of the chapter, as Paul's address. In this last view we concur. Everything in the passage has a peculiar propriety, as addressed to Peter. Had verse 15 been addressed to the Galatians, this would have been marked in some way;[108] and, in the commencement of the third chapter, the apostle names the Galatians, as again returning to direct address.[109]

"If thou, being a Jew, livest after the manner of the Gentiles, and not as do the Jews, why compellest thou the Gentiles to live as do the Jews?" Peter, though a Jew, "lived after the manner of the Gentiles,[110] and not as did the Jews,"[111] – *i.e.* he did not strictly conform to the requisitions of the Mosaic law. He did not regulate himself by its prohibitions. This was plain, for before these men from Jerusalem came he ate with the Gentiles. 'Now,' says the apostle, 'how inconsistent is it in you, who, though a Jew, do not think yourself under obligation to observe the Mosaic law, to act in a manner which is calculated to lead the Gentiles to think that they ought to observe it!' When Paul says, "thou compellest,"[112] etc., he refers not to what Peter actually did, nor to his intention, but to the plain tendency of his conduct. It is as if he had said, 'Is not the natural tendency of your conduct to lead the Gentiles to think that surely something more than faith in Christ is necessary to justification, and to induce them to imitate you, and to subject themselves to ceremonial restrictions in order to secure their salvation? Is not your conduct calculated to sanction the false doctrines which the apostles have condemned? and can anything be more inconsistent than such conduct on your part? Even though you had been conscientiously of opinion that the law is obligatory on Jews, you ought to have avoided everything that could lead to the conclusion that it was obligatory on the Gentiles; but as you believe, and have acted on the belief, that its obligation, even on Jews, now no longer subsists, why do that which naturally leads to the conculsion that its observance is a matter of importance, and that its non-observance ought to exclude even Gentiles from free intercourse with those who do observe it?'

The apostle goes on to declare the truth of the gospel, which he was afraid would be obscured by the conduct of Peter and the rest. He declares that Christians among the Jews trusted entirely to Christ for salvation, and that, when they acted in any way which seemed to cast into the shade the necessity and completeness of his salvation, they acted both criminally and inconsistently; and that, for himself, he was, and was determined ever to be, and to appear to be, a Christian, a thorough Christian, and nothing but a

Christian.

"We who are Jews by nature, and not sinners of the Gentiles, knowing that a man is not justified by the works of the law, but by the faith of Jesus Christ, even we have believed in Jesus Christ, that we might be justified by the faith of Christ, and not by the works of the law: for by the works of the law shall no flesh be justified. But if, while we seek to be justified by Christ, we ourselves also are found sinners, is therefore Christ the minister of sin? God forbid. For if I build again the things which I destroyed, I make myself a transgressor. For I through the law am dead to the law, that I might live unto God. I am crucified with Christ: nevertheless I live; yet not I, but Christ liveth in me: and the life which I now live in the flesh I live by the faith of the Son of God, who loved me, and gave Himself for me. I do not frustrate the grace of God: for if righteousness come by the law, then Christ is dead in vain" (Gal. 2:15-21.).

"We who are Jews by nature" — native Jews, not proselytes,[113] — *"and not sinners of the Gentiles."* These words may either mean, 'We who by birth are Jews' — worshippers of the true God, according to the Mosaic law, — 'and not idolatrous Gentiles' — whom the Jews were in the habit of calling 'sinners,' by way of eminence; or, 'We who are Jewish, and not Gentile sinners.'[114] I am partial to this last view of the phrase. I do not think that Paul, in the circumstances in which he was placed, was likely to use language which, even by implication, could be considered as a reflection on the Gentiles, when considered as in contrast with the Jews; and it was much to his purpose to bring forward the fact, that Jews as well as Gentiles were sinners; for it was neither as Jews nor as Gentiles, but as sinners, they had to do with Christ and his salvation. The *usus loquendi* seems in favor of the other view, which also brings out a good sense: 'We Jews have found it necessary to abandon the law, and betake ourselves entirely to Christ for justification. What absurdity, then, to require submission to the law from the Gentiles, as if that were necessary to their salvation, which we have found to be utterly useless in our own case!'

"We Jews," sinners, *"knowing"* — *i.e.* being persuaded — *"that a man is not justified"*[114] — *i.e.* cannot obtain the Divine favor — *"by the works of the law, but by*[115] *the faith of Jesus Christ."* The apostle does not seem here to refer merely to obedience to the Mosaic law, but states the general truth, that it is not by obedience to any law — not by works of righteousness — that men are restored to the Divine favor, but by the faith of Christ. Some would understand "the faith of Christ" as equivalent to 'the gospel;' but, when viewed in contrast with works of law, its plain meaning is, 'the belief of the truth about Christ.' 'Well,' says the apostle, 'we Jews, convinced that we are sinners, and that it is not by obedience to law that sinners are to be restored to the Divine favor, but by faith in the Messiah, by the belief of the truth respecting Him and the way of salvation through Him, — under these convictions "we have believed in Jesus Christ;"*[116] we have credited the testimony of God concerning His Son, "that we might be justified" — *i.e.* in the hope that we shall be restored into God's favor entirely "through the faith of Christ," and not at all by any obedience on our part to any law; "for by the deeds of the law shall no flesh be justified."[117] The reason here stated is plainly a most cogent one. Every Jew has broken the law under which he is placed. Every man has broken the law under which he is placed; and therefore law may — must — condemn men, but it cannot justify them. This is a gloriously clear statement of the way of salvation, which, rightly understood, puts down at once all attempts to join anything with Christ's righteousness as the ground of justification, or with faith as the means of justification. 'This, then,' says the apostle, 'is what we Jewish converts have done — we have given up with everything but Christ as the ground of our justification, and everything but faith as the means of it.'

"But," proceeds the apostle, "if, while we seek to be justified by Christ, we ourselves also are found sinners, is therefore Christ the minister of sin? God forbid." These words, viewed by themselves, might signify, what I believe they are generally thought to signify, 'If, while men are professing to seek justification through Christ, they are found living in the neglect of duty, and commission of sin, is Christ to blame?' *i.e.* 'Christ is not to blame.' They are abusers of the grace of God. "Sinners" is by some considered here, as in Rom. 5:8, as equivalent to 'guilty,' 'unjustified.' They consider the apostle as saying, 'If, while seeking justification by faith in Christ, we are yet found unjustified (which seems to be the fair conclusion from seeking, in obedience to the law, for some additional ground of justification), then Christ is the author, not of justification, but of condemnation.' This, however, would require another inference, — such as, 'Then Christ's expiation has been incomplete;' and it would not connect well with what follows. From its connection, it seems obvious that neither of these can be its meaning. The true sense seems to be this, — 'If, in seeking justification solely by Christ Jesus, without laying any stress on the works of the law, we are to be accounted sinners — offenders — if we are to be viewed as acting improperly, "then Christ is the author of the sin"[118] — he has led us into the error and fault; for this is the sum and substance of his doctrine, and, in embracing it, we are but following him.' "God forbid," says the apostle, starting back from the revolting thought, — i.e. 'It is impossible that Christ can be the author either of error or sin.' In embracing the doctrine of justification by faith, through the redemption that is in Him, and in acting accordingly, we certainly follow Him, and therefore as certainly we cannot be wrong.[119]

'But to embrace this doctrine of Christ, and yet to do what is calculated to obscure it, to overthrow it, that is obviously self-inconsistency and impropriety, — that were to be sinners indeed.' This is the sentiment contained in the 18th verse. "For if I build again the things which I destroyed, I make myself a transgressor." The reference here is plainly to the conduct of Peter; but according to Paul's wisdom, he makes the statement in the way least fitted to hurt or to offend.[120] To pull down with one hand what we build up with the other, that is inconsistency; and this is what Peter was doing, though not aware of it. He preached the doctrine of full and free salvation which he had defended in the council of Jerusalem; but his present conduct was in its tendency quite opposed to these exertions.

In conclusion, Paul declares that whatever others might be or do, he was a thorough, and he was determined to be a consistent, Christian. "For I through the law am dead to the law, that I may live to God."[121] The expressed personal pronoun is emphatic, and its position strengthens the emphasis.[122] 'Whatever may be the case with others, this is MY experience.' "I through the law am dead to law." Some rendering the words, 'I through law am dead to law,' understand the assertion as equivalent to, 'I through one law am dead to another law. I through the law of faith am completely released from obligation to the law of works;' in the same way as we say, 'man serves man,' or 'hand washes hand.' Others understand the word in both cases in the same meaning, and in both cases consider it as referring to the law to which Paul, as a Jew, was originally subject.[123] 'I through means of the law convincing me of sin, and showing me the utter impossibility of justification by itself, have become dead to the law — have ceased to expect justification and salvation by obedience to its requisitions — "that I might live to God;"[124] that, consecrated to God more effectually than I could be by obedience to the law, I might live a divine life — a life of reconciliation with God — conformity to God — fellowship with God.' This second interpretation is preferable to the first; but still it is not satisfactory. It does not naturally introduce the thought that follows. I am persuaded that the apostle expresses here the same sentiment with regard to himself as an individual which he states in reference to Christians in general, when he says, "Ye are become dead to the law by the body of Christ." (Rom.7:4.) And how that is brought about, is described by him (Rom. 6:1-11). 'By the law having had its full course so as to be glorified in the obedience to death of Him *in whom* I am, I am completely delivered from the law. The law has no more to do with me, and I have no more to do with it in the matter of justification. And this freedom from law is at once necessary and effectual to my living a truly holy life — a life devoted to God.' What follows is explanatory of this thought, which was ever present to the mind of the apostle, — 'I consider myself as identified with the Lord Jesus Christ.' "I am crucified with Christ."[125] I view myself as so connected

38

with Christ, as that when He was crucified I was, as it were, crucified; and I am as much interested in the effects of that crucifixion as if I had undergone it myself. He, in being crucified, endured the curse, and I in Him endured it; so that I am redeemed from the law and its curse, He having become a curse for me. "Nevertheless I live."[126] Christ died, and in Him I died; Christ revived, and in Him I revived. I am a dead man with regard to the law, but I am a living man in regard to Christ. The law has killed me, and by doing so, it has set me free from itself. I have no more to do with the law. The life I have now, is not the life of a man under the law, but the life of a man delivered from the law; having died and risen again with Christ Jesus, Christ's righteousness justifies me, Christ's Spirit animates me. *My* relations to God are *His* relations. The influences under which I live are the influences under which He lives. Christ's views are my views; Christ's feelings my feelings. He is the soul of my soul, the life of my life. My state, my sentiments, my feelings, my conduct, are all Christian. "And the life which I now live[127] in the flesh[128] I live by the faith of the Son of God, who loved me, and gave Himself for me." "The life I live in the flesh" is the life I live in this mortal body, this embodied state. The belief of the truth is the regulating principle of my conduct. It is as it were the soul of the new creature. I no longer think, or feel, or act like a Jew — or like a man born merely after the flesh. All my opinions, sentiments, and habits, are subject to the truth about Him "who loved me and gave Himself for me;" and I *live* devoted *to* Him who *died* devoted *for me.'*

The force of these last words plainly is, — 'It is but right that it should be so.[129] It is but right that I should be entirely devoted to Him who devoted Himself entirely for me.' It seems also to intimate, — 'It is the faith of this truth, that Jesus Christ so loved me as to give Himself for me, that makes it impossible for me to build again the things I have destroyed. The faith of the truth keeps me from seeking justification anywhere but in Him, and from doing anything which could lead others to seek for justification anywhere but from Him.'[130]

"I do not frustrate the grace of God" (Gal. 2:21.). "The grace of God" is plainly the grand manifestation of the free sovereign love of God in the way of salvation through the sacrifice of Christ and the faith of the gospel. To frustrate that, is to act in such a way as to lead to the inference, that this display was either unnecessary or insufficient for its avowed purpose. They who give their support in any way to the doctrine of justification by works, do thus frustrate the grace of God. "We despise grace when we observe the law with the expectation to be justified by it. The law is good, holy, and profitable; but it justifieth not. He, then, that keepeth the law in order to be justified thereby, rejecteth grace, denieth Christ, despiseth His sacrifice, and will not be saved by this inestimable price, but will satisfy for his own sins through the righteousness of the law, or deserve grace by his own righteousness. This man blasphemeth and despiseth the grace of God."[131]

The last clause depends on an elliptical clause. "But whosoever wills to be justified by the law, he frustrates the grace of God."[132] Paul did not thus "frustrate the grace of God." To do this is, indeed, to frustrate, or represent as useless, this grace of God, "for if righteousness come by the law, then is Christ dead in vain." "Righteousness"[133] is here obviously equivalent to, 'justification.' If men's works are sufficient for their justification, Christ's death was entirely needless.[134] If men's works are in any respect necessary for this purpose, Christ's death was so far insufficient for the purpose for which it was intended. In either case "Christ died in vain."[135]

"This interesting paragraph is one among many proofs," to use the words of the learned and ingenious Hallett,[136] "that we Gentiles are indebted inconceivably more to the Apostle Paul than we are to any man that ever lived in the world. He was the apostle of the Gentiles, and gloried in that character. While Peter went too far toward betraying our privileges, our Apostle Paul stood up with a courage and zeal becoming himself. For us in particular, as for the Gentiles in general, our invaluable friend labored more abundantly than all the apostles. For us he suffered. He was persecuted for this very reason, because he labored to turn us from darkness to light, and to give to us the knowledge of salvation upon our repentance towards God, and faith in our Lord Jesus Christ. How dear, then, should his memory ever be to us! While it would be intolerably weak," as well as inexcusably wrong, "in us to worship him, we should always think and speak of him with the highest veneration and respect, — remembering the strong reason, the elevated understanding, the accurate discernment, the consummate knowledge, the fine address, the affectionate zeal, the unshaken fidelity, the undaunted courage, the firmest patience, the incomparable writings, the unwearied labors, and the uncommon sufferings of this truly Christian hero; whose character, after he became a Christian, is the most uniform and finished, the most unspotted and amiable, of all the characters of mere man that ever adorned the world." But we shall make it evident that we have very imperfectly imbibed his principles, if we rest in the admiration of him as an individual, and do not clearly perceive and plainly acknowledge that it was not he, but the grace of Christ in him, that made him the great and good man he became; that by the grace of God he was what he was; and imitating the churches of Judea, "glorify God in him." For "all things" in the new creation "are of God; to whom, through Christ Jesus, be glory for ever. Amen."

PART IV.
THE APOSTLE'S DEFENCE OF HIS DOCTRINE.

"O foolish Galatians, who has bewitched you that you should not obey the truth — before whose eyes Jesus Christ crucified was openly set out among you? This only I desire to learn from you: Did you receive the Spirit by works of the Law? or by the hearing of faith? Are you so foolish? Having begun in the Spirit, are you now made perfect by flesh? Did you suffer so many things without cause? If indeed it was also without cause. He then who supplies the Spirit to you and works miracles among you, is it by works of the Law, or by the hearing of faith? It is even as Abraham believed God and it was counted to him for righteousness. Know then that they that are of faith, these are the sons of Abraham. And the Scripture, foreseeing that God justifies the Gentiles by faith, preached before the gospel to Abraham saying, "All the nations shall be blessed in you." So that those who are of faith are being blessed with the believing Abraham. For as many as are of the works of the law are under a curse — for it is written, "Cursed is everyone who does not continue in all things which have been written in the book of the Law to do them." But that no one is being justified by Law in the sight of God is plainly seen, because, "The just shall live by faith." But the Law is not of faith, but, "The man who has done these shall live by them." Christ redeemed us from the Law's curse — being made a curse for us, for it is written, "Cursed is everyone who hangs on a tree" — that Abraham's blessing might come to the Gentiles in Christ Jesus, so that we might gain the promise of the Spirit through faith. Brothers! I speak in the way of man — no one sets aside even a confirmed covenant of man, or adds to it. But to Abraham and to his seed the promises were spoken. He does not say, And to seeds, as of many, but as of one — "And to your Seed," which is Christ. I say this now, the covenant settled first by God to Christ, the Law (which came four hundred and thirty years after) cannot set aside, so as to do away with the promise. For if the inheritance is by Law, it is no longer by promise — but God gave it to Abraham by promise. Why then the Law? It was added because of transgressions, until the Seed should come to the promised ones (having been ordained through angels in a mediator's hand). But a mediator is not a mediator of one, but God is one. Is the Law then against the promises of God? Let it not be! For if a law had been given which was able to give life, indeed righteousness would have been by Law. But the Scripture shut up all things under sin so that the promise by faith of Jesus Christ might be given to those that believe. But before faith came, we were kept under Law, being shut up to the faith which was going to be revealed. So that the Law has been our schoolmaster until Christ, so that we might be justified by faith. But faith coming on, we are no longer under a schoolmaster — for you are all sons of God through faith in Christ Jesus. For as many as were baptized into Christ have put on Christ. There is not Jew or Greek, nor is there slave or freeman, nor is there male or female, for you all are one in Christ Jesus. But if you are Christ's, then you are Abraham's seed and heirs as to the promise. But I say, for as long a time as the heir is an infant, he does not differ any from a slave — though he is lord of all. But he is under guardians and managers until the times set before by the father. So we, too, when in infancy, were held in slavery under the principles of the world. But when the fullness of time came, God sent out His Son, coming from a woman, coming under Law, so that He might redeem the ones under Law, so that we might receive sonship. But because you are sons, God sent the Spirit of His Son into your hearts, crying Abba — Father! So that you are no longer a slave, but a son — and if a son, also an heir of God through Christ." — Galatians 3:1-4:1-7.

SECT. I. – INTRODUCTORY REMARKS.

In an epistolary composition, it is not reasonable to expect the same strictness of method as in a regular treatise. Yet, even in the letters of a man of well-informed and well-disciplined mind, the materials will be disposed in the order best fitted for gaining the object he has in view. There will be much method, though there may be little display of it.

This is precisely the character of the letters of the Apostle Paul; and they equally mistake who represent them as regular logical discussions of certain theological principles, and who view them as a collection of cursory unconnected hints. In all his epistles he has some one leading object in view, of which he never for a moment loses sight. Whatever he brings forward has a tendency more or less direct towards the attainment of this object; but in making his particular statements and reasonings bearing on his grand purpose, he adopts a method more analogous to the course which thought naturally takes in a free, unreserved conversation, than to the artificial form which it assumes in continuous spoken or written discourse.

These general remarks are applicable to that particular epistle, in the interpretation of which we are at present engaged. The leading purpose of the apostle in this epistle is, to point out to the Galatian Christians the falsehood and danger of the principle which some Judaising teachers had been attempting, with but too much success, to impose on them, *"that the observance of the Mosaic law was equally necessary with faith in Jesus as the Messiah to secure for them the Divine favor and everlasting happiness,"* and to recall them to, and establish them in, the great fundamental truths of the gospel which he had taught them, 'that Jesus Christ was the only and all-sufficient Savior; that His vicarious obedience, sufferings, and death, were the *sole* ground of the sinner's justification; and that faith, or believing the gospel, was the sole means of the sinner's justification.' Instead of entering directly into the argument, he first vindicates his own integrity as a man, and his authority as an apostle, both of which had been questioned or denied by the Judaising teachers; and after having most satisfactorily shown, in a narrative of some of the leading incidents of his past life, that he was no time-server − no man-pleaser − that his doctrine on the point in question had always been uniform and consistent − and that his knowledge of the principles of Christianity, and his authority to teach it, had been derived from no human source, through no human medium, but were obtained directly from God the Father and the Lord Jesus Christ − that his character as an independent inspired teacher of Christianity had been acknowledged by the most distinguished of the apostles − and that, in his conduct in reference to one of the chief of them, he had at once shown the strength and consistency of his attachment to those doctrines which the Judaising teachers were endeavoring to overthrow, and asserted his independent authority as an apostle of Christ − he proceeds, in the passage which now lies before us for explication, to expose the falsehood of the dogmas of the Judaising teachers, and to confirm the doctrine which he had originally taught respecting the true ground and means of a sinner's justification before God.

The manner in which the apostle makes this transition is beautifully natural. In the course of his apologetical narration, he has occasion to recite the address which he made to Peter at Antioch, when, by his conduct, that apostle seemed to give countenance to the opinion that the observance of the Mosaic law was, even under the Christian dispensation, a matter of importance, in which he places in a very strong point of view the grand peculiarities of the gospel scheme, the fulness and the freeness of the Christian salvation, the absolute completeness of the Christian scheme, and the abundant provision which it makes at once for the holiness and the happiness of all who sincerely embrace it, while the undivided glory of the whole deliverance is secured to the free sovereign benignity of the Divine Being, manifested in a consistency with His righteousness through the mediation of His Son; and expresses, in very glowing terms, his own thorough satisfaction with, his unbounded admiration of, and exultation in, Christ and Christianity. The contrast between this true gospel, so simple, so complete, so full of glory to God and advantage to mankind, and that system of inconsistency and error, those "beggarly elements," as he phrases it, which the Judaising teachers were endeavoring, and endeavoring with but too much success, to induce the Galatians to receive in its room, strongly struck his mind; and, in the words that follow, he gives utterance to a mingled feeling of astonishment, displeasure, and sorrow.

SECT. II. – THE APOSTLE'S ASTONISHMENT, DISPLEASURE, AND SORROW, AT THE CHANGE IN THE SENTIMENTS OF THE GALATIANS.

"O foolish Galatians, who hath bewitched you, that ye should not obey the truth, before whose eyes Jesus Christ hath been evidently set forth, crucified among you" (Gal. 3:1.)? These words are obviously expressive of deep and powerful emotion, profound sorrow, strong displeasure; but the degree of feeling will not appear excessive when we have attended to the circumstances which called it forth. The Galatians had enjoyed very peculiar advantages in the clear and ample statements made to them, by the apostle, of evangelical truth. "Jesus Christ had been evidently set forth before their eyes crucified among them." The collocation of these words in our version obscures their meaning. It becomes obvious by a very slight change. "Jesus Christ crucified had been evidently set forth before their eyes among them."

"Christ crucified," and "the cross of Christ," are phrases which, in Paul's epistles, are expressive of the whole doctrine of the gospel respecting the way of salvation through the sufferings and death of Christ. This is plainly the meaning in such phrases as "We preach Christ crucified" (1 Cor. 1:23.). – "I am determined to know nothing among you, save Christ and Him crucified" (1 Cor.2:2.). – "God forbid that I should glory, save in the cross of our Lord Jesus" (Gal. 6:14.). When the apostle says, then, that "Christ crucified had been set forth among them" he means, that they had been taught that Jesus Christ, the incarnate Son of God, had submitted to die, and to die on a cross, as the victim of human transgressions; that he had been "delivered for our offences" (Rom. 4:25.); that he had "offered Himself" (Heb. 9:14.) a sacrifice for our sins; that his sufferings and death had completely answered their purpose; that "His blood cleanseth from all sin" (1 John 1:7.); that no human being can be saved but through the efficacy of that sacrifice which He offered; and that every believing sinner, whether Jew of Gentile, shall, through the power of this bloody atonement, assuredly escape everlasting destruction, and obtain everlasting salvation; in one word, that what He did and suffered is at once the sole and the sufficient procuring cause of salvation to every one that believeth.

The apostle states, not merely that "Christ crucified had been set forth among them,"[1] but "set forth evidently before their eyes."[2] These words seem to refer to the remarkable distinctness with which the doctrine of Christ crucified had been set forth among them.[3] It is not impossible that there may be here an allusion to the ordinance of the Lord's Supper, in which the death of Christ is "showed forth" – in which, by the significant emblems of bread and wine – broken bread and poured-out wine – broken bread eaten, and poured-out wine drunk, are presented to the mind through the medium of the senses, these truths, 'that Jesus Christ, God's incarnate Son, suffered and died in our nature, in our room, and for our salvation, and that whosoever believeth in Him shall not perish, but have everlasting life.'[4]

These doctrines, then, had been clearly stated to the Galatians, and accompanied with the most satisfactory evidence. They had professed to receive them, and to rest the interests of their eternity on them – to repose with undivided and undoubting confidence on the crucified Jesus as the only and the all-sufficient Savior. But in embracing the doctrines of the Judaising teachers, they materially relinquished these doctrines, and showed that they did not "obey the truth."[5]

"The *truth*" is here obviously what the apostle elsewhere calls "the truth as it is in Jesus," – 'the truth respecting the way of salvation through His mediation.' "To obey the truth" has often been considered as equivalent to faith. I rather think it refers to that complete transformation of character which results from the truth when it is allowed to exert its full influence over the mind. To obey the truth is just to think, and to feel, and to act, like a person who understands and believes the truth.

Now, the Galatians were not doing this. Had they obeyed the truth they would have looked to Jesus, and to Jesus only, for salvation; they would have seen that there was no necessity, and no possibility, of adding anything to what He had finished on the cross as the ground of acceptance. They would have seen and felt that there is no need of conjoining anything with faith in Him as the means of obtaining an interest in the blessings of His salvation. Trusting in Him, and in Him alone, for salvation, they would have cheerfully devoted themselves to His service in all the spiritual and rational duties of His religion, constrained by His love to live to Him who died for them. Instead of this, they were seeking some other ground of confidence – some other method of salvation. As if His atonement had been either unnecessary or insufficient, they were endeavoring, in their circumcision and legal observances, to find something else on which they might rest their hopes of acceptance with God.

Now, to a person whose views of Christianity accord in any good degree with those of the apostle Paul, it will not appear strange that the apostle should pronounce the persons who acted such a part emphatically "fools."[6]

The Galatians were proverbially stupid, as the Galileans were;[7] but there is no reason to think that the apostle has any allusion to this.[8] The apostle, in astonishment, displeasure, and sorrow, asks them, who had "bewitched" them that they should have acted so unreasonable a part? What could be more foolish than to take up with a human invention instead of a Divine appointment – to exchange the immoveable rock of the Redeemer's all-perfect atonement for the broken reed of imperfect, uncommanded, human services – to part with that peace of God which passeth all understanding, which arises from a belief of the truth, for a false confidence constantly liable to be disturbed with doubts and fears, and certain ultimately to issue in disappointment and ruin? This surely was to leave "the fountain of living waters," and to take up with "cisterns which can hold no water" (Jer. 2:13.). Well might the apostle ask, "Who hath bewitched you?"[9] There is a peculiar beauty and appropriateness in the phrase. 'Jesus Christ has been "plainly set before you crucified." You saw Him, and said you were looking to Him as "the Lamb of God" – the only, the all-sufficient sacrifice – bearing – bearing away the sin of the world. How have ye lost sight of Him? – for ye must have lost sight of Him, else you never could have been expecting to be justified by the law of Moses. How have you been fascinated? How is it that ye have mistaken delusion for truth – truth for delusion – shadows for realities – realities for shadows.' The apostle refers here to the opinion generally entertained in his time of the power of charms or incantations in leading persons into error and folly; but he is not to be considered as sanctioning these opinions.[10] It is as if he had said, 'Your conduct is so foolish that it looks like infatuation. You seem fascinated. Surely it has not been argument, but something like enchantment that has led you to adopt the views of your new teachers.'

There seems to be something emphatic in the question, "Who[11] hath bewitched you?" It seems the apostle's wish to turn their attention to the attainments and character of the men who had seduced them. 'Who are they who have had such an influence over you? Have they the gifts of apostles? Are they distinguished for their wisdom, worth, and piety?'

The conduct of the Galatians is by no means singular. There are multitudes who, like them, enjoy a clear dispensation of the gospel, who "do not obey the truth;" who, though "the righteousness of God" – the Divine way of justification – is plainly pointed out to them, go about to establish "their own righteousness" – a way of justification of their own. Such conduct is extremely foolish, and, if persisted in, will be fatal.

The apostle's mode of expression shows that ministers are warranted, in peculiar circumstances, to use very strong language – to express their amazement, their displeasure, and their sorrow. This is no way inconsistent with the most tender affection. It is the same apostle who says, "O foolish Galatians!" who says to the same individuals,

"My little children, for whom I travail again in birth till Christ be formed in you."

SECT. III. – ARGUMENT FROM THEIR OWN EXPERIENCE.

In illustrating the folly of the Galatians, the apostle brings forward a very strong proof of the falsehood of the new principles they had adopted, and the truth of the doctrines which the apostle had taught them. "This only would I learn of you, Received ye the Spirit by the works of the law, or by the hearing of faith" (Gal. 3:2.)? The force of these introductory words is, – 'An answer to this question will go far to settle the whole controversy.' The argument necessarily involved in the only answer that could be given to it was, in the absence of all other arguments, sufficient to determine the point in question. By "receiving the Spirit" many understand exclusively the receiving the miraculous gifts of the Holy Spirit – such as prophecy, speaking with tongues, the power of working miracles, etc. I have no doubt these are included, for in all the primitive churches which enjoyed the ministry of the apostles, these gifts seem in some measure to have been bestowed. But I do not think that we are so to confine the meaning of the phrase, as to exclude the ordinary saving influences of the Holy Spirit – such as love, peace, and joy. 'Tell me,' as if the apostle had said, 'what was the origin of these miraculous gifts which many of you possess, – what the origin of that inward peace, that love of God, and of one another, – that joyful expectation of immortal glory, by which many of you were once distinguished?'

Did you receive this by, or through, "the works of the law"?[12] i.e. 'Was it by means of obedience to the Mosaic institution that you obtained these blessings?' No, the most of the Galatian believers were strangers to the Mosaic institution till after they had obtained these blessings; and such of them as were Jews previously to their becoming Christians knew very well that, while they continued Jews, they continued unacquainted with them. Or, did ye "receive the Spirit by the *hearing of faith*"? "The hearing of faith" is a phrase which admits of being variously interpreted. The word rendered "hearing"[13] may signify either the act of hearing, or the thing heard; and the word "faith"[14] may signify either the act of believing, or the thing believed. As "hearing" is obviously contracted with "working," and "faith" with the "law," I apprehend that "the hearing of faith" is just equivalent to the reception of the gospel – hearing being often, in the New Testament, equivalent to attending to and believing; – as, "This is My beloved Son, *hear* ye Him" (Matth. 17:5.). "Today, if ye will *hear* His voice" (Psal. 95:7.). The question, then, is – 'Did ye receive the Spirit on your receiving the gospel?' and the answer must be in the affirmative. It was on the profession of faith that the miraculous gifts were given; and all the saving fruits of the Spirit naturally grew out of the belief of the truth. 'If, by the belief of the gospel, and not by obedience to the law, ye obtained such important privileges, is it not extremely foolish in you to give up with the truth of the gospel for Mosaic observances? and is not the Spirit, the seal of God, attached to those doctrines which you are so strangely and causelessly abandoning?'

The apostle presses this consideration home in the next verse: "Are ye so foolish? having begun in the Spirit, are ye now made perfect[15] by the flesh?"[16] The general force of the question is this, – 'Is there not gross incongruity and absurdity in your conduct? To begin with what is imperfect, and to go forward to what is perfect, is the natural and proper order of things; but you are reversing it. You have begun,[17] as Christians, "in the Spirit;" you have adopted the pure, spiritual religion of Jesus Christ – a religion to which the Holy Spirit has given, even in your case, the most distinct evidences of His approbation, – and "are ye now made perfect" – *i.e.* are you seeking to be made perfect, by adopting what, in its very best state, was comparatively a *carnal, material* form of religion, and which, in present circumstances, has no claim of any kind on your adoption? The religion you at first adopted was a religion which, from its perfection, renders any addition utterly useless. You may – you must – debase it, but you cannot possibly improve it, by any supplement. Your progress is not improvement, it is degeneracy. It is not the child becoming the man, but the man becoming the child. To pass from Judaism to Christianity is — having begun in the flesh — to be perfected by the Spirit. For the Jew to become a Christian, was for the child to become a man — a natural, desirable course. For the Christian to become a Jew, is for the man voluntarily to sink into a second childhood — a most unnatural and undesirable course. They, in receiving the gospel, began with what was spiritual — knowledge, faith, holiness, hope, joy; in submitting to the law, they end in "meats, and drinks, and divers washings." '[18]

The apostle still farther illustrates the folly of their conduct in the 4th verse: "Have ye suffered so many things in vain? if it be yet in vain" (Gal. 3:4.). The ordinary mode of interpreting this verse, which it is plain from their version our translators adopted, goes on the supposition that the Galatians, on embracing the gospel as taught them by Paul, had been exposed to severe persecution, and that that persecution had proceeded from the Jews either directly or indirectly. We have no account of such persecutions, though it is by no means improbable they did take place in Galatia, as we know they did in many other places; and in no country or age can a consistent Christian profession be made without sacrifice and suffering. What the apostle says, cahp. 5:11, and 6:12, gives plausibility to this supposition. In this case, the apostle's argument is this, — 'For your attachment to the truth of the gospel you willingly submitted to much persecution; and are you willing that all this suffering should be lost? Are you ready to acknowledge yourselves fools in submitting to it? For be assured it is all lost if you go into the dogmas of these new teachers, which involve in them a virtual renunciation of the gospel.'

He adds, "If it be yet in vain." He is unwilling to think that, after all, they would abandon the truth. They had not yet fairly shifted their ground. He intimates to them that, if they stood firm, their afflictions would be amply compensated. In this case they would find that, "if they suffered with Christ, they would also reign with Him;" but if they renounced the truth, their past suffering would serve no good purpose. "How skilfully, how gently, yet how soundly, does he probe the dangerous wound!"

It deserves, however, and perhaps requires, to be remarked, that the words admit another rendering. The word "suffered," in the original, is used generally of what a man experiences, whether of a pleasant or painful kind.[19] And the idea the apostle meant to convey may be, — 'Have ye experienced so many things in vain? if it yet be in vain' — i.e. 'Have ye seen so many miracles — have you enjoyed, in such variety and abundance, the gifts of the Holy Spirit, all attesting the truth of the gospel, — have you experienced all these in vain? and if you indeed adopt these opinions respecting the necessity of circumcision, and other Mosiac observances, ye have experienced them in vain.' This view of the passage has the recommendation of giving unity to the whole paragraph.

In the 5th verse, the apostle puts what is materially the same argument in a somewhat different form: "He therefore that ministereth to you the Spirit, and worketh miracles among you,[20] doeth He it by the works of the law, or by the hearing of faith?" The language is elliptical. When the ellipsis is filled up it runs, — 'He then that ministereth to you the Spirit, doth He minister it by the works of the law, or by the hearing of faith? He that worketh miracles among you, doth He work miracles by the works of the law, or by the hearing of faith?' The point on which the right interpretation of this verse hinges, is the ascertaining of the person whom the apostle here describes as "He that ministered to them the Spirit, and wrought miracles among them."[21] The appellation has very generally been referred to God. In that case, the phrases, "by the works of the law," and "by the hearing of faith," must be referred to the Galatians, and the force of the interrogation be, 'When God gave you the Spirit, and wrought miracles among you — or in you, or by you — was it in consequence of your yielding obedience to the Mosaic law, or in consequence of your receiving the gospel?' And the meaning is precisely the same as in the 2d verse.

It not only prevents tautology, but seems to give a more natural meaning to the words — to understand "Him that ministereth the Spirit, and worketh miracles" — of the apostle. The Holy Spirit, in His miraculous influences, was given by the "laying on of Paul's hands;" and, in His saving influences, was communicated through the instrumentality of

Paul's preaching. And no doubt, among them as well as among the Corinthians, were "the signs of an apostle"[22] distinctly exhibited — "the seal of apostleship"[23] plainly affixed. The ministry of the gospel is expressly termed "the ministration of the Spirit" (2 Cor. 3:8.), as well as the "ministration of righteousness" — that is, of justification, — the ministry by which both justification and sanctification are conferred on believers. "What a solemn thing is the work of the ministry! The gospel is 'the ministration of the Spirit;' and the business of them who preach it is to minister or convey the Spirit — the Spirit of God and His blessed Son. If this be not done, nothing is done at all; and 'who is sufficient for these things?' "[24]

In this case the force of the apostle's question is, 'Was the person by whose instrumentality ye received the Holy Ghost, and who confirmed His doctrine among you by miracles, an upholder of the Mosaic law? or was he a preacher of the simple gospel?' and it is in some good degree a new argument. 'Not only was the Spirit conferred on you as *believers* not as *workers,* but he who was the instrument in conveying this blessing to you was no teacher of Judaism, but an explicit preacher of "the truth as it is in Jesus." ' Besides, the question naturally enough suggested another, the answer to which was quite decisive on the point. 'Have any of those who are of "the works of the law" and not of "the hearing of faith," have any of *them* "ministered to you the Spirit, or wrought miracles among you?" ' A very strong proof of the reality of the miracles wrought in the primitive ages arises from these fearless appeals to them in the apostolic writings. It is a just and important remark of Mr. Baxter, that "it was a great display of Divine wisdom to suffer such contentions to arise thus early in the church, as should make it necessary for the apostle to appeal to the miracles wrought before and upon those who were afterwards in some degree alienated from them, that future ages might be convinced by the certainty of these miracles as matters of fact beyond all possibility of contradiction."[25]

SECT. IV. — ARGUMENT FROM THE HISTORY OF THE JUSTIFICATION
OF ABRAHAM.

In the passage which follows, the apostle brings forward another argument, borrowed from the history of Abraham, the object of almost religious regard to his descendants. There could be no doubt that Abraham was a justified person, the object of the peculiar Divine regard, "the friend of God" (Isa. 41:8.). He surely was in possession of all that is necessary to justification. Now, if it appeared that Abraham was justified, not by his circumcision, but by his faith; if it was not Abraham the circumcised, but Abraham the believer, that was justified — that single fact would go far to settle the point that circumcision was not necessary, and that faith was sufficient for justification. This is the argument the apostle states in the 6th verse, and is, indeed, the same which he urges with so much effect in the beginning of the fourth chapter of the Epistle to the Romans. The Judaising teachers said, 'Ye cannot be the children of Abraham, the heirs of his blessings, except ye be circumcised.' The apostle says, 'Ye are the children of Abraham, and the heirs of his blessings, if ye be believers.'

"Even as Abraham believed God, and it was accounted to him for righteousness. Know ye therefore that they which are of faith, the same are the children of Abraham."[26] These verses may either be considered as forming one sentence or two separate ones. In the first case, the construction is, 'Since Abraham believed God, and it was accounted to him for righteousness, ye see that they who are of faith are the children of Abraham.' In the second case, the 6th verse must be considered as elliptical, and the ellipsis must be thus filled, up, 'Your receiving tokens of the Divine favor in consequence of your faith, and not of your obedience to the law, is no departure from God's ordinary mode of procedure. It was so from the beginning. The scripture account of Abraham's justification exactly corresponds with your experience. "Abraham believed God, and it was accounted to him for righteousness." '

This is a quotation from Genesis 15:6, — "And he believed in the Lord; and he accounted it to him for righteousness." The phrases, "Abraham believed God,"[27] and "Abraham believed in God,"[28] are precisely synonymous, the latter being merely a

Hebraism.[29] The common doctrine on this subject — that they express different ideas, the former simple belief, the latter belief and such emotions as accompany or rise out of it — seems to have originated with Augustine, who certainly was not overburdened with Hebrew or Greek learning. The declaration, "Abraham believed God," is just equivalent to, 'Abraham counted true what God said to him, because God said it.'[30]

The result of Abraham's faith is stated in the words that follow, "and it was counted to him for righteousness." These words have received two very different interpretations. One class of interpreters, more distinguished for orthodox theology than accurate exegesis, have held that what was imputed to Abraham was not the act of faith — the fact that he believed — but the object of faith, which they say was either Christ Himself or the surety-righteousness of Christ, that was reckoned to his account as *his* righteousness on believing; and thus he was justified. Now, we do not deny that this is substantially a just account of the way in which Abraham was justified, though expressed in a very artificial and non-natural way. Nor do we deny, that what is properly the name of a mental act is often used to designate the object of that act. Faith is often equivalent to 'what is believed,' and hope equivalent to 'what is hoped for.' But we do deny that this is the true exegesis of these words. The object of Abraham's faith was the truth he believed, and *surely* that could not be reckoned to him as his righteousness.

Another class, much worse theologians and somewhat better philologists, have insisted that the words express this sentiment, 'Abraham's faith was reckoned to him instead of righteousness — or a full obedience to the law — and on account of it he was justified.' This is a doctrine altogether subversive of the apostle's doctrine of justification, and the words, rightly interpreted, do not give any support to it. There can be no reasonable doubt that "his faith"[31] is the nominative to "was reckoned."[32] But then, what is the meaning of that phrase? In the Hebrew idiom, for an action, quality, privilege, to be reckoned to a person, is just equivalent to that person being reckoned to have done that action, to possess that quality, or to enjoy that privilege. For faith to be reckoned or imputed to Abraham is, then, just equivalent to, 'Abraham was reckoned (by God) a believer, and he was so reckoned, because he was really a believer — God always reckoning men and things to be what they are. The phrase, "for righteousness,"[33] hangs equally by the two clauses, "Abraham believed God," and "his faith was reckoned to him." God reckoned him a believer. "Righteousness"[34] is used in the sense in which the apostle ordinarily employs it, as equivalent to 'justification.' "For" rather '*unto* righteousness"[35] is equivalent to "unto justification," or, 'so that he was — so that he was *thus* justified.' The phrase is used in the same sense as in Rom. 10:10, "with the heart man believeth unto righteousness;[36] and with the mouth confession is made unto salvation."[37] Abraham does not obey — he does not submit to circumcision, he believes, "unto justification;"[38] and not obedience or circumcision, but faith, is reckoned to him "unto justification."[39] He is not considered in this matter by God as an obedient, or a circumcised man, but as a believing man. Abraham believed God: God reckoned Abraham a believer, and as a believer he was justified by God. The exact place of *faith* in the Divine method of justification, as not in any degree the ground, but the sole means of restoration to the Divine favor, is not fixed by this passage. It merely shows, what the apostle's argument required, that Abraham was justified, not by works, but by faith — not by obeying the law, but believing the promise — not as a worker, but as a believer.

The conclusion the apostle wishes the Galatians to draw from this fact is, that *believers* not *workers* are the imitators of Abraham's conduct and the heirs of Abraham's privileges. "Know ye, therefore, that they who are of faith are the children of Abraham."[40] "They who are of faith"[41] is just equivalent to 'they who belive'[42] in opposition to them who are "of the law," or "of the works of the law." "They who are of faith" are plainly those who are expecting justification by faith and not by works; who are not working that they may obtain the favor of God as a meritorious reward, but who are believing that "God was in Christ, reconciling the world unto Himself, not imputing their trespasses unto them" (2 Cor. 5:19.); and that "the gift of God is eternal life through Jesus Christ our Lord" (Rom. 6:23.); and consequently are looking for it as a gratuitous benefit. These persons, and these persons alone, appear, from this account of Abraham's justification, to be entitled to the honorable appellation of "his children."

To be the children of a person in a figurative sense, is equivalent to, 'to resemble him, and to be involved in his fate, good or bad.' The idea is, similarity both in character and circumstances. To be "the children of God," is to be like God; and also, as the apostle states it to be, "heirs of God." To be "the children of Abraham," is here to resemble Abraham, to imitate his conduct, and to share in his blessedness (John 8:39. 1 John 2:29; 3:1,8,9.). It is as if the apostle had said, 'These Judaising teachers talk much of the glory and advantage of being children of Abraham, and insist that it is by circumcision that men attain to this dignity and happiness. But how far is this from the truth? Abraham's highest distinction was, that he was a justified person, "a friend of God;" and this distinction he attained not by circumcision, but by faith. It follows, then, that they who believe like Abraham, are like Abraham justified through believing, they — they alone — are his true spiritual descendants. Though a man should be "a Hebrew of the Hebrews, circumcised the eighth day, and touching the righteousness that is in the law, blameless" (Phil. 3:5,6.), if he is not a believer, he is not spiritually a child of Abraham. And if a man be but a believer, be he Jew or Gentile, he is spiritually a child of Abraham. And this fact, that all who believe, whether they were descendants of Abraham or not, were to be made partakers of his blessedness, was distinctly enough taught in the ancient oracles given to Abraham.' This is what the apostle states in the 8th verse.

SECT. V. — ARGUMENT FROM THE PROMISE TO ABRAHAM.

"And the Scripture, foreseeing that God would justify the heathen through faith, preached before the gospel unto Abraham, saying, In thee shall all nations be blessed" (Gal. 3:8.).

The language is somewhat peculiar, but the meaning is not obscure. That is ascribed to the Scripture which properly refers to God in that transaction which the passage of Scripture quoted describes. Similar modes of expression are to be found in other parts of the New Testament (Mark 15:28. John 7:38,42. Rom. 4:3; 9:17.). The meaning plainly is, 'God, who foresaw that in a future period many of the Gentiles were to be received into His favor and treated like His children on their believing the revelation of mercy through His Son, gave an intimation of His design to Abraham in the promise which He made to him.' The Syriac version reads, — "And God knowing before hand." The phrase, "preached the gospel beforehand," in consequence of the very definite idea we generally attach to the word *"gospel,"* and the technical sense in which we use the word *"preach,"* does not, I am persuaded, convey distinctly the apostle's idea to most English readers. It is just equivalent to, 'made known these good tidings to Abraham long before the period when they were to be realised.'[43] Tyndale's version here, as in many other passages, is better than the authorised translation, — "showed before hand glad tidings to Abraham." And this intimation was given in these words, — "In thee shall all nations be blessed."[44] The word translated "nations," is the same as that rendered "the heathen" in the beginning of the verse. The same word should have been retained to mark more clearly the point of the apostle's argument.

But it may be said, What intimation is there in these words of God's purpose to "justify Gentiles by faith"? This will appear if we consider that the particle translated *"in,"* signifies, *in connection with, along with, in the same manner as.*[45] The declaration of the oracle, in this way of viewing it, is that, 'all the nations,' *i.e.* that multitudes of all Gentile nations, 'shall be blessed along with Abraham.' "By 'the nations' in this promise we cannot understand all and every one in the nations; nor can we consider them *as such,* political bodies of men in the earth; but according to the New Testament explication, "it is a great multitude of all nations, and kindreds, and people, and tongues" (Rev. 7:9.). This will be evident if we consider that the blessedness spoken of in this promise, is spiritual and eternal, and must be acknowledged so to be by those who take the New Testament account of it (Gal. 3:8,9,14.). It is manifest no nation of this world can, in a national capacity, be the subject of justification by faith, and of the promise of the Spirit, which we receive through faith; and it is as certain that every person in the nations of the world is not to partake of this blessedness. What remains, therefore, but that it should be those who are redeemed by Christ out of every nation? And thus we find out the intent of the writings of the phophets about the nations. For these are enlargements upon this promise to Abraham."[46] The promise is fulfilled in God's "visiting the Gentiles to take out of them a people for His name" (Acts 15:14.). Thus, all nations shall be blessed along with Abraham, in connection with Abraham, members of the same body, possessed of the same privileges, made happy in the same way as he was made happy.

Now, how was he blessed? 'To be blessed' and 'to be justified,' seem to be here used as synonymous, and it is not wonderful they should; for, how can he be blessed who is condemned of God? and how can he be otherwise than blessed who is the object of God's favor (Psal. 32:1-5.)? In the declaration, then, that with him all nations should be blessed, God beforehand gave an intimation to Abraham that it was His design to justify Gentiles by believing; in other words, to make them blessed in the same way in which he had been made blessed.

The conclusion he states in the 9th verse is obviously a well founded one. "So then they which be of faith are blessed with faithful Abraham."[47] 'It is plain, then,' as if the apostle had said, 'that they who are justified by believing are justified in the way Abraham was.'[48] They that believe are blessed along with, in the same way as, believing Abraham. Abraham believed and was justified, and thus became blessed. They also believe and are justified, and thus become blessed. And they who are seeking for justification by circumcision, or in any other way than by faith, by believing, are seeking after it in a way totally different from that in which Abraham obtained it, and that in which God had foretold it was to be extended to the Gentiles.

Having thus showed that justification is by faith, or through believing, the apostle goes on to show that it is not — that it cannot be — by the works of the law; that to expect to secure the divine favor as a merited reward by obedience to the requisitions of the Mosaic law, was to indulge an expectation equally unreasonable and unscriptural. The unreasonableness and absurdity of the expectation are illustrated in the 10th verse; the unscripturalness of it is illustrated in the 11th and 12th verses. Let us examine these illustrations somewhat more minutely.

SECT. VI. – JUSTIFICATION BY THE LAW IN THE NATURE OF THINGS IMPOSSIBLE.

"For as many as are of the works of the law are under the curse;[49] for it is written, Cursed is every one that continueth not in all things which are written in the book of the law to do them" (Gal. 3:10.).

This is a new paragraph containing a new argument. The particle translated *for*[50] here, and in may other places, does not denote that what follows is a reason for what has been just stated, but merely marks transition, and is equivalent to, – 'Further, moreover.' "They who are of the works of the law," is a phrase denoting, they who are seeking for justification, who are expecting to obtain the Divine favor, by their obedience to the law, who are "following after the law of righteousness not by faith, but, as it were, by the works of the law,"[51] just as "they who are of faith," in the preceding verse, denotes them who "through the faith of the truth as it is in Jesus," are expecting to be treated as objects of the Divine favor, "freely by God's grace through the redemption that is in Christ Jesus" – who believe in Christ Jesus that they may be justified by the faith of Christ, and not by the works of the law.[52]

'Now,' says the apostle, 'all persons of this description who are expecting justification, are indulging a most unfounded expectation; for they are already under the curse of that law, by obedience to which they are flattering themselves that they shall obtain the Divine favor. They are already condemned by the law; surely the same law that condemns cannot justify.' That all who were seeking justification by their obedience to the law, were already condemned by that law, or, in other words, were "under its curse," the apostle makes evident by quoting the words in which the curse of the law is couched. It is written, "Cursed is every one that continueth not in all things which are written in the book of the law to do them." The quotation is made from Deut. 27:26,[53] where we have a command, that the Israelites, on their getting possession of the promised land, were to inscribe the law on stone; and that, on this being done, one set of priests should pronounce the blessings which should descend on the obedient, and another the curses which should fall on the disobedient. The words quoted are the conclusion of the curses which were to be pronounced, and contain, as it were, the sum and substance of them all. It is a declaration, that whosoever violated any one of the precepts of the Mosaic law exposed himself to the displeasure of God, and to punishment, as the expression of this displeasure. The apostle's version, though slightly different from that given by our translators, accurately exhibits the meaning of the original words. They literally are, – "Cursed is he who maketh not to stand the words of this law to do them." He who obeys the precepts makes them to stand; he who disobeys them does what lies in his power to overturn them.

This argument, like many others employed by the apostle, is elliptical in its statement; but the ellipsis is easily supplied. In its completed form it would run thus, – 'None of those who are seeking for justification by the law, uniformly and perfectly obey all its precepts; but it denounces a curse on all who do not thus obey its precepts. It follows of course, then, that they are "under its curse;" in other words, they are in a state of condemnation – the objects of the judicial displeasure of God. It is absurdity, it is madness, thus to seek for justification from that which, to persons in their circumstances, is and must be the source of condemnation. To expect to be warmed by the keen northern blast, or to have our thirst quenched by a draught of liquid fire, were not more, were not so, incongruous. This were merely to expect that a positive appointment of God should be altered, which is not in the nature of things impossible – which, in particular cases, has actually taken place. That were to expect a revolution to take place in the moral nature of Him "with whom there is no variableness or shadow of turning." '

The remark made by the apostle has a direct reference to those who were expecting justification by obedience to the Mosaic law; but it is equally applicable to all who, by their own obedience to any law, are expecting to stand approved before God. It is true of that law under which all intelligent creatures are placed, as well as of the Mosaic law, that every violation of it exposes to the Divine displeasure; and that every man, having violated this law, is a proper object of the Divine judicial displeasure, and cannot obtain the Divine favor by obedience to a law which already condemns him to punishment. We find the argument stated in this general form in the Epistle to the Romans, chap. 4:15, – "Because" – or rather, 'moreover' – "the law worketh wrath: for where no law is, there is no transgression." To complete the argument, you must supply the implied cause, – 'But where there is law, with a being like fallen man there is transgression, and therefore "wrath," or punishment.'

So much for the apostle's illustration of the *unreasonableness* of the expectation of justification by the law: it is contrary to the nature of things. Let us now examine his illustration of its *unscripturalness.* This is contained in the two following verses.

SECT. VII. – JUSTIFICATION BY LAW INCONSISTENT WITH SCRIPTURE.

"But that no man is justified by the law in the sight of God, it is evident: for, 'The just shall live by faith.' And the law is not of faith: but, 'The man that doeth them shall live in them' " (Gal. 3:11,12.).

That no man can be justified by the law, has already been made evident from the nature of the thing. The proposition is equally clearly proved by the declaration of God. He has stated distinctly the way in which men become just in His sight, which is by believing. To be justified by the law is, however, quite another thing from being justified through believing; and, of course, it cannot be the way of justification. This is, I apprehend, the force of the argument couched in these words.

The apostle's reasoning appears disjointed and inconclusive in our version, in consequence, I apprehend, of our translators mistaking the meaning of the quotation on which the apostle grounds his argument. The quotation is made from Habakkuk 2:4.[54] It is an important principle, that the verbal adjective is sometimes employed for the participle.[55] It is but right to state, that the Hebrew words in the prophet, and the Greek words in the apostle, taken by themselves, admit of the rendering given them by our translators, and convey an important truth — that it is by the continued belief of the truth that the new life of the Christian is sustained; or, in other words, that he continues good and happy, and grows better and happier. This is the truth stated by the apostle above, in the end of the preceding chapter, — "The life which I now live in the flesh I live by the faith of the Son of God." But we must also state, that the words admit of another rendering, and that the object of the prophet in primarily using them, and of the apostle in quoting them, both here and elsewhere, requires that other rendering, — "The just by faith shall live." 'The man who is the object of God's favorable regard in consequence of his faith, that man shall live, or be happy.'[56]

In the Book of the Prophet Habakkuk, the prophet is required to write a prophetic vision, and to "make it plain upon tables, that he may run that readeth it." Jehovah declares that this oracle would certainly in due time be fulfilled; and then it is added, "Behold, his soul which is lifted up is not upright in him." He is obviously speaking of a promise, and he says, 'Where there is a proud rising of mind, distrusting the fulfilment of the Divine promises, there the mind is not right — not in the state which is well-pleasing to God; but the person who is "just," or righteous, and of course well-pleasing to God "on account of his faith" — his believing the promise, and trusting that, notwithstanding all contrary appearances, it shall be accomplished, — that person shall live.'

The apostle quotes then the passage in the same general meaning that it has in the prophet, and draws from it this conclusion, — that it is not the man righteous by law, but the man righteous by faith, that lives, or is truly happy in the enjoyment of God's favor and its consequent blessings.[57]

But are not justification by the law and justification by believing reconcileable? — may they not be co-incident? How does it appear evident that a man cannot be justified in the sight of God by the law because Habakkuk says, "The just by faith shall live"? May not the just by works live too? To this question we have an answer in the 12th verse. "And the law is not of faith." Here, as in some other cases, it is much easier to perceive the apostle's general meaning than to give a clear satisfactory exposition of the phraseology in which it is couched.[58] "The law" is plainly equivalent to, 'the way of justification by the law;' this is, not "of faith," or, 'by believing.'[59] No; it is entirely different. Its statement is not, 'The just by faith shall live;' but, "the man that doeth them he shall live in them;" — it is, 'the just by works shall live.' This is quoted from Lev. 18:5. It seems to have passed into a proverb among the Hebrews. [60] The opposition between faith and works as the means of justification, is strikingly stated elsewhere by the apostle. "For Moses describeth the righteousness which is of the law, That the man which doeth those things shall live by them. But the righteousness which is of faith, speaketh on this wise, Say not in thine heart, Who shall ascend into heaven? (that is, to bring Christ down from above;) or, Who shall descend into the deep? (that is, to bring up Christ again from the dead). But what saith it? The word is nigh thee, even in thy mouth, and in thy heart: that is, the word of faith which we preach; that if thou shalt confess with thy mouth the Lord Jesus, and shalt believe in thine heart that God hath raised him from the dead, thou shalt be saved. For with the heart man believeth unto righteousness; and with the mouth confession is made unto salvation. For the Scripture saith, Whosoever believeth on Him shall not be ashamed" (Rom. 10:5-11.). The apostle's conclusion then is quite a warranted one. 'If God in His word has stated, that it is the just by faith that shall live, it is evident that no man is justified by the law before Him, for justification by faith and justification by works are utterly incompatible.'

SECT. VIII. – REDEMPTION FROM THE CURSE OF THE LAW NECESSARY FOR JUSTIFICATION BOTH TO JEWS AND GENTILES.

It is customary with the apostle to meet objections likely to rise in the mind of his readers without formally stating them. We apprehend we have an instance of this in the passage to the interpretation of which we are now to proceed. It seems a fair conclusion from the apostle's statement, that not merely all who are of the works of the law, *i.e.* who are seeking for justification by obedience to its requisitions, but that all who are under it, are condemned; and that, of course, the justification of Jews is an impracticable thing. It was then a natural question on the part of the Galatians, 'If this be the true statement of the case, how are Jews condemned by the law to obtain the Divine favor? Is the thing possible? and if it be so, how is it brought about?' To these questions the 13th and 14th verses contain a satisfactory answer.

"Christ hath redeemed us from the curse of the law, being made a curse for us: for it is written, Cursed is every one that hangeth on a tree: that the blessing of Abraham might come on the Gentiles through Jesus Christ; that we might receive the promise of the Spirit through faith."[61] The first question to be resolved here is, 'Of whom is the apostle speaking when he says, "Christ hath redeemed *us* from the curse of the law, that we might receive the promise of the Spirit through faith" '? The pronoun 'we" is used by the apostle with very considerable variety of reference. It is sometimes, we *men;* sometimes, we *sinners;* sometimes, we *Jews;* sometimes, we *believers,* whether Jew or Gentile; sometimes, we *believing Jews;* sometimes, we *apostles;* and it is obvious that to the right understanding of any particular passage in which it occurs, it is absolutely necessary that we should understand the reference in which it is employed; and, in most cases, there is little difficulty of ascertaining this from the context.

I believe the more ordinary method among orthodox interpreters has been to understand the statement in the text as referring directly to all the saved – as a general statement of the way of salvation, and equivalent to, 'Christ had delivered *us elect sinners,'* or, *'us believers,* from the punishment which the Divine law denounces on us as sinners, by having sustained that punishment in our room.' This, no doubt, is a truth, a most important truth; and a truth which the words contained in the first clause of the verse, taken by themselves, not unnaturally convey.

But to a person who is familiar with the modes of thinking and speaking of the primitive age, and who carefully attends to the context, it will appear plain that this is not the apostle's meaning. It is obvious, that they who are "redeemed from the curse of the law," are distinguished from "the Gentiles," to whom the blessing of Abraham comes through means of their redemption.[62] The direct subject of discussion is the impossibility of being justified by obedience to the Mosaic law; and it is the curse of the Mosiac law which is spoken of in the 10th verse. The Gentile believers were, previously to their conversion, under sin[63] and condemnation,[64] as well as the Jewish believers; but not being subject to the Mosaic law, they could not be considered as exposed to *its* curse, and, of course, they could not be represented as redeemed from a curse to which they were never subject.

Every principle of rational interpretation, therefore, requires us to consider the statement made in this verse as referring to those Jews who had become Christians. They had been under that law which the Judaising teachers were so anxious to impose on the Gentile believers; but so far from being justified by that law, they had incurred its curse, in consequence of their "not continuing in all things written in its book to do them," and must have taken the tremendous consequences had not "Christ redeemed them from the curse of the law, by becoming a curse for them."

"The curse of the law" is expressive both of the denunciation of punishment, and of the punishment denounced. The law of God, as made known to the Jews, denounced a variety of punishments of a temporal nature for different violations of it, specially, an untimely violent death, and generally the displeasure of God against all violations of it, to be manifested in the way most illustrative of the Divine wisdom, holiness, and justice, during the continuance of the offender's existence, or at least till his guilt is expiated. What the curse of the law is may be learned by reading the latter part of the twenty-sixth chapter of Leviticus and the twenty-seventh and twenty-eighth chapters of Deuteronomy. They are fitted to make the ears to tingle of every one who reads them, and to induce the exclamation, "It is a fearful thing to fall into the hands of the living God."

To this curse every Jew was exposed, and such of them as were delivered from it, were delivered by Christ. "Christ has redeemed[65] us from the curse of the law." The meaning of that is not, 'in consequence of what Christ has done, the condemnatory sanction of the law is repealed or mitigated.' "The law" in its sanction as in its precepts, "is holy, just, and good" (Rom. 7:12.), and will for ever continue to condemn every offender and every offence. The meaning is, 'Christ hath delivered us from the punishment which the law denounces against us on account of our sins;' or, 'He hath delivered us from the consequences of the natural operation of the condemnatory sentence to which our sins have exposed us.' If we are delivered from condemnation and misery, it is entirely owing to Jesus Christ, and not at all to the law, which could do nothing but condemn and curse us.

The phrase, "Christ hath *redeemed* us," has often been considered as just equivalent to, 'He hath *delivered* us.' There can be no doubt that the word "redeem" is often used in this general sense; but there is little doubt that its primary and proper signification is to deliver in consequence of paying a ransom or equivalent; and that it has this peculiar meaning in the passage, is plain from the account of the way in which this redemption was accomplished. It was not by a mere exertion of power, nor by a mere display of mercy, that deliverance was obtained, – it was by Christ's yielding to the law in its condemnatory sanction that satisfaction which sinners owed.

"Christ hath redeemed us from the curse of the law, being made a curse for us."[66] "To be made a curse"[67] is a strong expression for becoming accursed;[68] or, in other words, being subjected, by the Divine appointment, to that suffering, the infliction of which sin had rendered necessary for the honor of the Divine character and government, – that suffering which is the manifestation of the Divine displeasure at sin.[69] Christ was thus "made a curse" *for* or *in the room of* those whom He redeemed from the curse; and this substituted endurance of the curse was the ransom-price[70] by which He redeemed them. It was that, in consideration of which they obtained deliverance – pardon and salvation.

The language of the text, and of the many other texts in which Christ's sufferings and death are represented as undergone in the room of His people, by no means necessarily implies that Christ experienced precisely the same kind and degree of suffering that they must have done had He not interfered – a reflecting mind will soon perceive that this is a statement which involves in it many difficulties; – but it does teach us, that the sufferings which Christ endured were sufferings on account of the sins of His people; and sufferings which satisfied the law, or, in other words, rendered it right, safe, and honorable in God to pardon sin, and save those in whose room they were sustained – those who, in the appointed way, were united to Him who sustained them.[71]

The penal, expiatory nature of the sufferings of Christ was intimated by the peculiar manner of His death, when taken in connection with one of the usages prescribed by the Mosaic law. This fact is noticed by the apostle in the close of the verse, – "Christ was made a curse for us: for it is written, 'Cursed is every one that hangeth on a tree.' " This passage is quoted from Deut. 21:23. The quotation seems made from memory, as it does not exactly correspond either with the Hebrew text or with the version of the LXX, but clearly expresses the meaning.[72] There are considerable difficulties in explaining the passage as it stands in Deuteronomy, but there are none of importance in its application to the subject before us. From this passage it is plain that, in all cases in which a person was put to death as a punishment for violation of the law of God, the dead body was to be exposed on a gibbet; and that the being thus exposed on a gibbet was a public demonstration that this person had been put to death on account of sin, as a condemned, an accursed person. From the Talmudical writers, it appears that the dead body was not hung by the neck, but by the hands; and that it was hung, not on a tree, properly so called, but on a piece of timber − a stake.[73] Hanging by the neck was not one of the modes of capital punishment sanctioned by the Jewish law. These modes were four in number: stoning, burning, beheading, and strangling the criminal as he stood on the ground. He was not suspended till after he was dead.

What the apostle says, then, is just this, − 'Christ Jesus, in redeeming us from the curse, was treated as accursed in our room; and of this we have an indication in the very manner of His death − in His being suspended on a cross, or hung on a tree, − which, under the law, was the appointed way of intimating that a person had died a victim to the claims of public justice.'[74]

The design or consequence of Christ's thus redeeming Jewish believers from the curse of the law, by becoming a curse in their room, is stated in the 14th verse, and it is twofold: (1) "That the blessing of Abraham might come on the Gentiles through Jesus Christ;" and (2) That "WE" − i.e. the Jewish believers − "might receive the promise of the Spirit through faith."

The particle "that,"[75] in the commencement of the 14th verse, may either signify that the two events mentioned were the design or object, or that they were the consequence or result, of Christ's redeeming the Jewish believers from the curse of the law by becoming a curse in their room. In fact, they were both; and it does not matter much in which way the particle is here understood.

The first object or result of the redemption of the elect and believing Jews from the curse of the law by Christ becoming a curse is, "that the blessing of Abraham might come on the Gentiles through Christ Jesus." From the preceding context, I think that there can be no doubt that the "blessing[76] of Abraham" is the blessing wherewith Abraham was blessed, i.e. justification through believing. It was then the design, and it has been the result, of Christ's redeeming believing Jews from the curse of the law by becoming a curse in their room, that the blessing of justification through faith has been extended to the Gentiles through Jesus Christ. But it may be asked, What connection is there here? What has Christ's enduring the curse of the Mosiac law in the room of His people who were subject to it to do with another class of persons altogether obtaining justification from the offences they had committed against God in doing what they knew to be wrong and neglecting to do what they knew to be right? There is a most intimate twofold connection.

1st, Those sufferings and that death which, viewed as the execution of the curse of the Mosaic law, were the price of the redemption of all believers who were subject to that law − a law that included the moral law to which all men are subject − and who had incurred its curse, were also the effectual expiation of the sins of such Gentiles as should believe. For, as the apostle John says, when Christ died, He was "the propitiation for our sins; and not for ours only, but also for the sins of the whole world" (John 2:2.). So that what laid a foundation for the deliverance of believing Jews from the consequence of the Divine displeasure as threatened in the law to which they were subject, laid also a foundation for the deliverance of believing Gentiles from that "wrath of God which was revealed from heaven against their ungodliness and unrighteousness." The same satisfaction which redeemed the believing Jews, laid a foundation for the justification of the believing Gentiles. But this is not all.

2d, Christ's endurance of the curse of the Mosaic law in the room of such of His people as were subjected to it, was the honorable and appropriate termination of that economy which, while it continued, presented insurmountable obstacles to "the blessing of Abraham," or justification by believing, being generally extended to the Gentiles. Fully to illustrate this principle, which is of the utmost importance to the right understanding of the apostolic epistles, would require more time than we can here devote to it. A few general hints must suffice. The Mosaic institution may be considered in three points of view, – (1) As an exhibition of the claims of God, as the righteous moral governor, on His intelligent creatures; (2) As an obscure intimation both of the fact, that God was disposed to pardon the human violators of His law, and of the way in which this pardon was to be dispensed; and (3) As a means of preserving the Israelitish people distinct from other nations, that this exhibition of the character, and claims, and intentions of God might not be lost in the prevailing moral darkness which covered the earth. Under this order of things, it is plain that it was inconsistent with one of its principal ends that the blessing of Abraham should generally come on the Gentiles during its continuance. The peculiar relation in which God stood to one nation as His own people[77] must be dissolved in order to the formation of a covenant relation with a peculiar people, which was to consist of persons of all nations. The two constitutions on which these relations rested, were incompatible; and "He taketh away the first, that He may establish the second" (Heb 10:9.). It is equally plain, that, under this order of things, God claimed no more than His right; that right had been withheld from Him; and it would have been inconsistent with the honor of the Divinity that this order of things should pass away without *His* rights being fully vindicated. In reference to all believers, whether they lived before or at the coming of the Messiah, His endurance of the curse in their room fully compensated all the wrongs which their transgressions had done the Majesty of heaven; and in reference to all the unbelieving and disobedient, the law would vindicate its honor by inflicting on them personally the punishment they deserved. *The law,* as an economy, thus not destroyed but fulfilled, ceased to exist; the Mediator of the new covenant having, by means of death, expiated the transgressions under the first covenant (Heb. 9:15.). That which was "a middle wall of partition,"[78] was removed, and justification through believing extended generally to men of every kindred, and people, and nation. The close connection between the death of Christ as making expiation for the violations of the Mosaic law, and its terminating that peculiar order of things, and throwing open the door of salvation to the Gentiles, is often adverted to by the apostle, and illustrated at some length in the concluding paragraph of the second chapter of the Epistle to the Ephesians: "Wherefore remember, that ye being in time past Gentiles in the flesh, who are called Uncircumcision by that which is called the Circumcision in the flesh made by hands; that at that time ye were without Christ, being aliens from the commonwealth of Israel, and strangers from the covenants of promise, having no hope, and without God in the world: but now, in Christ Jesus, ye who sometimes were far off are made nigh by the blood of Christ. For He is our peace, who hath made both one, and hath broken down the middle wall of partition between us; having abolished in His flesh the enmity, even the law of commandments contained in ordinances; for to make in Himself of twain one new man, so making peace; and that He might reconcile both unto God in one body by the cross, having slain the enmity thereby: and came and preached peace to you which were afar off, and to them that were nigh. For through Him we both have access by one Spirit unto the Father. Now therefore ye are no more strangers and foreigners, but fellow-citizens with the saints, and of the household of God; and are built upon the foundation of the apostles and prophets, Jesus Christ Himself being the chief corner-stone; in whom all the building, fitly framed together, groweth unto an holy temple in the Lord: in whom ye also are builded together for an habitation of God through the Spirit" (Eph. 2:11-22.).

The second object of the redemption from the curse of the law by Christ's becoming a curse, is, that the believing Jews "might receive the promise of the Spirit through faith."[79] "The promise of the Spirit" is a Hebraism for 'the promised Spirit.'[80] To "receive the promise,"[81] is plainly 'to receive the blessing promised.' And "the promise of the Holy Ghost"[82] is obviously 'the Holy Ghost promised.' By *"the promised Spirit,"* we understand the enlightening and enlivening, the sanctifying and consoling, influence of the Holy Spirit vouchsafed to believers, not excluding the extraordinary influences which distinguished the primitive ages. The Spirit is termed *"the promised Spirit,"* for the communication of His influences was promised by the ancient prophets as one of the grand characteristics of the Messiah's reign. – "For I will pour water upon Him that is thirsty, and floods upon the dry ground: I will pour My Spirit upon thy seed, and My blessing upon thine offspring.'"And I will put My Spirit within you, and cause you to walk in My statutes, and ye shall keep My judgments, and do them." "And it shall come to pass afterward, that I will pour out My Spirit upon all flesh; and your sons and your daughters shall prophesy, your old men shall dream dreams, your young men shall see visions: and also upon the servants and upon the handmaids in those days will I pour out My Spirit."[83] The Spirit had also been promised by our Lord. — "And I will pray the Father, and He shall give you another Comforter, that He may abide with you for ever; even the Spirit of truth; whom the world cannot receive, because it seeth Him not, neither knoweth Him: but ye know Him; for He dwelleth with you, and shall be in you." "These things have I spoken unto you, being yet present with you. But the Comforter, which is the Holy Ghost, whom the Father will send in My name, He shall teach you all things, and bring all things to your remembrance, whatsoever I have said unto you." "But when the Comforter is come, whom I will send unto you from the Father, even the Spirit of truth, which proceedeth from the Father, He shall testify of Me." "Nevertheless I tell you the truth; it is expedient for you that I go away: for if I go not away, the Comforter will not come unto you; but if I depart, I will send Him unto you" (John 14:16,17,25,26; 15:26; 16:7.).

Now the communication of this Spirit to Jews, through their believing, was one of the objects and results of this redemption from the curse of the law by Christ's being made a curse in their room. Divine influence is one of the most precious blessings God can bestow; and He never bestows it on sinners but on account of the expiatory sufferings of Jesus Christ. Pious men under the law enjoyed the Spirit, though not in the same degree as it is enjoyed under the gospel. But if they did so, it was bestowed on them with a reference to the atonement to be offered, and received by them through faith in the obscure revelation of that atonement. And Jews who lived after this atonement was offered, could receive the Spirit in no way but through this atonement, and faith in this atonement. Christ did not redeem them from the curse of the law that they might obtain the promised Spirit through obedience to its precepts, but through believing the gospel.[84]

The sum, then, of what the apostle says in these two most important verses is this: 'We believing Jews owe our salvation not to the law, but entirely to Christ, and obtain it entirely through believing. We, by violating the law, to which we were subject, had incurred its curse; but Christ has delivered us from this curse by enduring it in our room. As His sufferings and death are sufficient and intended to avail, not only as the propitiation for our sins, but also for those of the whole world; and as, by completely satisfying all the demands of the Mosaic law, they have put an honorable termination to that order of things, which, during its continuance, necessarily excluded the great body of the Gentiles from the blessing of Abraham — an order of things which, now that the Messiah is come, has completely served its purpose, — the consequence is, that justification by believing is extended to men of every nation; and we Jews obtain the promised Spirit through believing the gospel, and not by obedience to the law.'[85]

Behold, then, the plan of salvation in its grand characteristic features! An all-perfect atoning sacrifice, — an all-powerful quickening, sanctifying Spirit, — and a plain well-accredited revelation, laying a foundation for *faith,* which interests whosoever believes, at once and for ever, in thy justifying righteousness and in this transforming Spirit, which secure, and prepare for, perfect, unending, holy happiness, in heaven.

> "Oh, how unlike the complex works of man
> Heaven's easy, artless, unincumbered plan!
> No meretricious graces to beguile;
> No clustering ornaments to clog the pile.
> From ostentation as from weakness free,
> It stands, like the cerulean arch we see,
> Majestic in its own simplicity.
> Inscrib'd above the portal, from afar

Conspicuous as the brightness of a star,
Legible only by the light they give,
Stand the soul-quickening words—BELIEVE AND LIVE."
This is the "gate of God," the entrance into true peace, holy joy, permanent happiness.
Let us all enter in by it. It stands wide open, and all are invited to enter. And having
entered, let us, in the enjoyment of these blessings, praise the name of the Lord. Blessed
be He who came in the name of the Lord to save us; and blessed be He who sent Him.
Blessed be He who spared not His Son; and blessed be He who loved not His own life to
the death for our salvation; and blessed, too, with equal honors, be that good Spirit who,
by His all-powerful, all-persuasive influence, puts us in possession of all the blissful results
of the love of the Father and the mediation of the Son.

SECT. IX. – FREE JUSTIFICATION BY BELIEVING SECURED IN A RATIFIED DIVINE ARRANGEMENT WHICH CANNOT BE DISANNULLED BY THE LAW – A SUBSEQUENT DIVINE ARRANGEMENT.

In the paragraph that follows, the apostle shows that the Mosaic law was not, and could
not be, the means of justification, from the fact, that the giving of the Mosaic law was
long posterior to the period when Abraham was justified, and when it was declared that
the Gentiles were to be justified in the same way that he was justified; and that the plan
of justification by the law was not only different from, but altogether inconsistent with,
that plan of justification which was exemplified in the case of Abraham, and which, in a
Divine oracle, was declared to be intended at some future period to be extended to the
Gentiles.

1. THE THESIS STATED AND PROVED.

"Brethren, I speak after the manner of men; though it be but[87] a man's covenant, yet if
it be confirmed, no man disannulleth, or addeth thereto. Now to Abraham and his seed
were the promises made. He saith not, And to seeds, as of many; but as of one, And to
thy seed, which is Christ. And this I say, that the covenant, that was confirmed before of
God in Christ, the law, which was four hundred and thirty years after, cannot disannul,
that it should make the promise of none effect. For if the inheritance be of the law, it is
no more of promise: but God gave it to Abraham by promise" (Gal. 3:15-18.).
The apostle often uses the phrase, "I speak as a man," or, "I speak after the manner of
men." He uses this phrase with some variety of meaning; but it seems uniformly to imply
this idea, – 'I use language frequently adopted;' or, 'I reason on principles which are
generally admitted among mankind.' In the present case, it is obviously equivalent to, 'I
will illustrate this subject by an example borrowed from the ordinary business of human
life.' The phrase is used in the same way, I Cor. 9:8; Rom. 6:19.
The word here translated "covenant,"[88] as well as the corresponding word in the Old
Testament, of which it is a version,[89] is of considerably more comprehensive signification
than the term by which it is rendered in our version. The English word *covenant*, means 'a
bargain,' an agreement between certain parties on certain terms. To this there is a
corresponding term in Greek,[90] but that word never occurs in the New Testament, and
rarely in the LXX, or in the other Greek versions of the Old Testament. The Hebrew and
Greek words rendered "covenant,"[91] signify, 'a disposition,' 'arrangement,' and are
applicable not only to *covenants* or bargains, properly so called, but to *laws* and *promises.*
It is plain that it is necessary to the apostle's argument that "the promise"[92] spoken of
(verse 16), should be considered as a διαθήκη, or rather the statement or record of a
διαθήκη.[93] "A man's covenant," is just equivalent, then, to 'a human arrangement or
transaction involving the interests of others.'
Now the apostle says, when such a transaction is "confirmed, no man disannulleth or
addeth to it."[94] To "confirm" is to sanction, ratify, make or declare valid. Such a
transaction is confirmed when it is fully settled, and the appropriate evidence given that it
is settled. The royal assent confirms or ratifies a law in this country, after it has received

the approbation of the other two branches of the legislature. The signature or seal of the individual appended to particular legal deeds ratifies or confirms them. When any disposition is thus finally settled and ratified, it is understood to be valid. After this, without the consent of all parties concerned, the arrangement[95] cannot be disturbed or altered. It cannot be annulled; no addition can be made to it.[96]

And if, while this deed remains unrevoked, some other arrangement or disposition should take place which might seem inconsistent with it, if we have a perfect confidence in the wisdom and integrity of the author of the two arrangements, the conclusion to be come to is, the second arrangement does not really interfere with the first, and their apparent discordance must arise from our misconception of them. The application of this principle to the apostle's object is natural and easy. God had, in the case of Abraham, showed that justification is by believing; He had, in the revelation made to Abraham, declared materially that justification by faith was to come upon the Gentiles. This arrangement was confirmed or ratified, both by circumcision, which the apostle tells us was "the seal of justification by faith,"[97] and by the solemn promise made to Abraham that, "in him," along with him, in the same way as he was, "all nations should be blessed."[98] It follows, of course, that no succeeding arrangement of God could contradict this arrangement; and that if any succeeding Divine arrangement seemed to do so, the cause of this was to be sought in our misapprehension of its true nature and design, which, when clearly perceived, would distinctly show the perfect harmony of the two apparently inconsistent arrangements. This is the line of argument which the apostle pursues in the following verses.

"Now to Abraham and his seed were the promises[99] made. He saith not, And to seeds,[100] as of many; but as of one, And to thy seed, which is Christ" (Gal. 3:16.).

These words admit of two renderings: either 'Now to Abraham and his seed,' or 'now in, through, or in reference to Abraham and his seed.' In either case they are expressive of a fact. "To Abraham and his seed promises were made;" or, in other words, blessings were promised. The following are examples of such promises, — Gen. 12:3; 17:4-8; 22:16,17. This has been generally understood to be the meaning of the apostle; and it has been supposed that his argument is, — 'Certain blessings were by God freely promised to Abraham and his spiritual seed long before the law was given, and therefore their communication cannot be suspended on obedience to the requisitions of that law.' The great objection to this mode of interpretation is, that it obliges us to understand the word "Christ," not of the Messiah personally, but of the collective body of those who are saved by Him.

We are rather disposed to consider the apostle as stating, 'Now the promises were made through or in reference to Abraham and his Seed.' Not only were blessings promised to Abraham and his seed; but blessings were promised through Abraham and his Seed to the nations (Gen. 12:3; 22:18.). It is to one of these promises that the apostle refers in the proceding context, verse 8. The blessing promised through Abraham and his Seed was, he informs us, the justification of the Gentiles by faith. We consider the apostle then as saying in the first clause of the verse, 'Now the promises of justification by faith were made to the Gentiles through Abraham and through his Seed.'

The word "seed"[101] is a word of ambiguous meaning. It may either signify descendants generally, or one class of descendants, or a single descendant.[102] The apostle in the concluding part of the verse tells us how it is to be understood in the passage he alludes to. "He saith not, And to seeds, as of many; but as of one, And to thy Seed, which is Christ."

These words have very generally been understood as if they embodied an argument, — as if the apostle reasoned from the word "seed" being in the singular, inferring from that circumstance either that the word referred to one class of descendants, and not to descendants of all classes, or to one individual descendant, and not to descendants generally. That this is not the apostle's reasoning we apprehend is certain; for it is obviously inconclusive reasoning. The use of the plural term might have laid a foundation for the inference that he spake of more than one; but *seed* being a *collective* word, its use in the singular lays no foundation for an opposite inference. Even supposing that his Jewish readers might have been imposed on by such a sophism, which is not at all probable, it would not only have been unworthy of his dignity as an apostle, but of his integrity as an honest man, to have used it.

The truth is, there is no ground to suppose that it is the statement of an argument at all. It is just as Riccaltoun observes, "a critical, explicatory remark." It is just as if he had said, 'In the passage I refer to, the word *seed* is used of an individual, just as when it is employed of Seth, Gen. 4:25, where he is called "another seed,"[103] and said to be given in the room of Abel, whom Cain slew. In looking carefully at the promise recorded, Gen. 22:16-18, the phrase "seed" seems used with a different reference in the two parts of the promise — the first part of the 17th verse plainly referring to a class of descendants; the last clause and the 18th verse to an individual, and that individual is Christ.' There is no doubt that this is the fact — that in the promise, "In thy Seed shall all the families of the earth be blessed," the reference is not to the descendants of Abraham generally, nor to his descendants by Isaac, nor to his spiritual descendants, but to his great descendant, the Messiah.

The words will, indeed, admit of another meaning, *q.d.* — 'The sacred oracle does not refer to all the descendants of Abraham, but to one particular class of them; not to his descendants by Ishmael, or to his descendants by the sons of Keturah, nor even to all his descendants by Isaac, nor to his natural descendants, but to his spiritual descendants.' But this obliges us to understand the word "Christ" in a very unusual, if not altogether unwarranted, sense. Besides, if the apostle alludes, as is natural, to the promise he had already quoted, there is no doubt that the reference there is to the Messiah personally considered.[104] We therefore prefer the former mode of interpretation. The promise of justification by faith to the Gentiles was made through Abraham and his seed, meaning by his seed, the Messiah. The reason why this is so particularly noticed will appear in the course of the discussion.

The apostle proceeds with his argument. "And this I say,[105] that the covenant,[106] *that* was confirmed before of God in Christ, the law, which was four hundred and thirty years after, cannot disannul, that it should make the promise of none effect" (Gal. 3:17.).

The only phrase which is obscure in this verse is the clause rendered "in Christ."[107] Some would render it *to* Christ; others *till* Christ, *i.e.* till Christ came, which is undoubtedly its meaning at chapter 5:24.[108] I apprehend the true rendering of the particle is *concerning*, or *in reference to* — a meaning which the term by no means uncommonly bears in the New Testament. I shall give a few examples, — Eph. 5:32; Acts 2:25; Heb. 7:14; Luke 12:21; Rom. 4:20; 16:19; 2 Cor. 2:9. The covenant in reference to Christ is just the arrangement or settlement as to justification by faith to be extended to the Gentiles through the Messiah, which was made known in the Divine declaration to Abraham. This Divine arrangement was "confirmed of God," ratified by God in the ordinance of circumcision which was given to Abraham as a person justified in uncircumcision (Rom. 4:9-13.), and made known as a fixed appointment in the Divine declaration so often referred to. It was "confirmed *before*,"[109] That is, it was a finished, ratified deed, long previously to the law.

'Now,' says the apostle, 'this completed and ratified covenant or arrangement about Christ, as to the justification of the Gentiles by believing, could not be disannulled by the giving of the law, which was four hundred and thirty years after, so that the promise should be of none effect.' There is some uncertainty as to the period of four hundred and thirty years mentioned, some chronologers insisting that it is the exact period from the time the promise was given till the law was given,[110] others that it refers only to a part of that period, namely, to the time of the Israelites sojourning in Egypt.[111] In either case it is true that the law was at least four hundred and thirty years after the promise in which the covenant about Christ was exhibited as confirmed. The law being a subsequent covenant or arrangement, could not make of none effect the promise, which was a previously ratified and unrepealed covenant. The person who thinks the promise thus made void, must labor under some misapprehension with regard to the nature and design of the law.

But it might be said, How does the making the observance of the law the condition of justification disannul the covenant or make the promise of none effect? The answer to that question is to be found in the next verse. "For if the inheritance be of the law, it is no more of promise: but God gave it to Abraham by promise" (Gal. 3:18.).

"The inheritance"[112] here is, I apprehend, the same thing as the blessing of Abraham, which, we have seen, is justification – the being treated by God as righteous; or, what is necessarily connected with, indeed implied in, it – the heavenly and spiritual blessings of which the possession of Canaan is the type. The "covenant,"[113] "the promise,"[114] and "the inheritance,"[115] all refer to substantially the same thing; but it would be absurd to say these three words have the same meaning. The "covenant" refers to the Divine arrangement as to conferring on men the blessings of the Divine favor, "the promise" is the revelation of this in the form of a promise, and "the inheritance," is this as enjoyed by men. It is termed "the inheritance," because it is as the spiritual descendants of Abraham, "the father of the faithful," that we come to enjoy it. Now, if the enjoyment of this inheritance be suspended on our obedience to the law of Moses, "it is no more of promise," *i.e.* it is no more a free donation in fulfilment of a free promise. But this is the character which belongs to the blessing as originally promised to Abraham. "God gave it to Abraham by promise," *i.e.* 'God freely promised it to Abraham;' or, 'God in promising it, acted from free favor.' He meant to give a favor, a free favor; not to make a bargain, however favorable. Abraham's justification was not suspended on his circumcision; and the justification of the Gentiles was to be like Abraham's.[116]

This, then, is the sum of the apostle's argument, 'A ratified, unrepealed constitution cannot be set aside by a subsequent constitution. The plan of justification by believing was a ratified and unrepealed constitution. The law was a constitution posterior to this by a long term of years. If the observance of the law were constituted the procuring cause or necessary means of justification, such a constitution would necessarily annul the covenant before ratified, and render the promise of none effect. It follows, of course, that the law was appointed for no such purpose. Whatever end it might serve, it could not serve this end; it could never be appointed to serve this end.

2. DESIGN, AND MODE OF GIVING THE LAW.

This naturally introduces the inquiry, What then was its design? This is the question which, in the next paragraph, the apostle considers; and in its discussion he makes it evident, that the Mosaic law, so far from being opposed to the covenant or arrangement revealed to Abraham, was a necessary means of securing the accomplishment of its provisions. Let us look at the passage with that closeness of attention which it at once requires and deserves.

"Wherefore then serveth the law?[117] It was added because of transgressions, till the seed should come to whom the promise was made; and it was ordained by angels in the hand of a mediator" (Gal. 3:19.).

There can be no reasonable doubt as to the meaning of the term *"the law"*[118] here. It is obviously the Mosaic institution viewed as a whole. It is neither what has been termed the moral law, nor the ceremonial law, nor the judicial law, which theologians have been accustomed to treat of as three distinct codes; but it is the whole arrangement or covenant under which the people of Israel were placed at Sinai.

The apostle has showed that that law could not be the means of justification, and that it was never intended for this purpose. Now, if it cannot serve this purpose, what purpose does it serve?[119] I do not think we are to consider the question as an inquiry into the designs and uses of the Mosaic law generally, but as to its design and use in reference to the arrangement that justification was to be by faith through the Messiah; and especially, that justification by faith through the Messiah was to be extended to the Gentiles. If this is not kept in view, the apostle's account may appear defective, while in reality it is complete, so far as his object required.

The answer is, "It was added because of transgressions." The law was added or appended.[120] It was a separate subordinate institution, not an alteration of or addition to the original arrangement. Now, in what way was it added? The question is easily answered. The revelation of justification by believing,[121] which was substantially the same revelation that was made to our first parents after the fall, was given to Abraham, and was to be preserved by his descendants. This was a sacred deposit which they were to preserve pure and entire, till the great Deliverer, to whom it referred, should make his appearance. To this revelation, termed "the promise," committed to the Israelites, "the law" was added or appended. God, who gave the promise to Abraham, thought fit, at least four hundred and thirty years after, to impose the law on his posterity.

For what reason was it imposed? It was, "because of transgressions."[122] This passage has very generally been considered as parallel with the declaration of the apostle, – "Moreover, the law entered that the offence might abound" (Rom. 5:20.), and has been very variously interpreted. The ordinary interpretation is very well given by Barnes. "The meaning is, that the law was given to show the true nature of transgressions, or to show what was sin. It was not to reveal a way of justification, but it was to disclose the true nature of sin; to deter men from committing it; to declare its penalty; to convince men of it, and thus to be 'ancillary' to, and preparatory to, the work of redemption through the Redeemer. This is the true account of the law of God as given to apostate man, and this use of the law still exists."[123] It is strange that so acute an interpreter did not see that the clause, "till the seed should come," is quite inconsistent with this exegsis. If "the law," referred to could do all this, "why," as Riccaltoun shrewdly remarks, "why was it limited to the time that the Seed should come who had the promised blessing to bestow, as the apostle plainly says it was?" Without noticing any more of the different ways in which these words have been explained, I shall state as clearly and briefly as I can what appears to me to be the apostle's meaning.

"The transgressions," on account of which the law was added refer, I apprehend, to the criminal conduct of the Israelites, which rendered the introduction of such a system as the law necessary in order to the attainment of the great object of the covenant about Christ. and justification by faith through him. This arrangement was first made known in the first promise, but from the prevalence of human depravity, it seems to have been in the course of ages almost entirely forgotten. "All flesh corrupted its way on the earth" (Gen. 6:12). The deluge swept away the whole inhabitants of the ancient world, exception of one family, among whom the true religion was preserved. In the course of no very long period, the great body of their descendants, the inhabitants of the new world, became idolaters. To prevent the utter extinction from among mankind of the knowledge of God and the way of obtaining His favor, Abraham was called, and a plainer revelation made to him of the Divine purposes of mercy, and his descendants by Isaac and Jacob chosen as the depositaries of this revelation, till *He* should come to whom the revelation chiefly referred. In consequence of the descendants of Jacob coming down into Egypt, they gradually contracted a fondness for Egyptian superstitions, and were fast relapsing into a state of idolatry, which must soon have terminated in their being lost among the nations, and the revelation with which they were entrusted being first corrupted and then forgotten, when God raised up Moses as their deliverer, brought them out of Egypt, and placed them under that very peculiar order of things, which we commonly term the Mosaic law — an order of things admirably adapted to preserve them a distinct and peculiar people — and by doing so, to preserve the revelation of mercy through the Messiah, of which they were the depositaries, and to prepare abundant and satisfactory stores of evidence and illustration when the great Deliverer appeared — evidence that He was indeed the person to whom the hopes of mankind had from the beginning been directed, and illustration rendering in some measure level to human apprehension what otherwise would have been unintelligible.[124]

Every person acquainted with the principles of depraved human nature, and with the history of the Jews at and subsequent to their deliverance from Egypt, will see that their "transgressions" rendered some such arrangement as the Mosaic law absolutely necessary, on the supposition that the Messiah was not to appear for a course of ages, and that the revelation of salvation through Him was to be preserved in the world by means of the Jewish people. We are not so much, if at all, to consider the Mosaic law as a punishment for the transgressions of the descendants of Abraham. We are rather to consider it as the means which their transgressions rendered necessary in order to secure the object of their being chosen to be God's peculiar people. To be preserved from being involved in the ignorance, and idolatry, and vice in which the surrounding nations were sunk, was a blessing, at whatever expense it might be gained. At the same time, had it not been for the transgressions of the Isrealites, the more spiritual and less burdensome order of things under which Abraham, and Isaac, and Jacob were placed, might have been continued, and the law as a distinct order of things never have existed because never needed.

The law was for this reason added, "till the seed should come to whom the promise was made."[125] I have already stated my reasons for understanding "the seed" here of the Messiah, and of course rendering the words "till the seed should come, in reference to whom the promise was made." The promise referred to is, "in thy seed shall all the families of the earth be blessed" — a promise made not *to* the Messiah, but *in reference to* the Messiah.[126] This view of the law being rendered, by the transgressions of the Israelites, necessary to preserve them a separate people, and to gain the ends connected with this till the coming of the Messiah, when the necessity of this order of things should cease, exactly corresponds with what the apostle afterwards says of the Israelitish people, as "kept" imprisoned, confined, "shut up[127] by the law" (Gal. 3:23.).

The apostle adds that this law was "ordained[128] by angels." The word translated "ordain," means to arrange, to appoint, to establish. The law was ordained or established by Jehovah Himself as its author. All its particular injunctions are introduced with, "And the Lord spoke to Moses." But while it was ordained by God as its author, it was ordained through the instrumentality of angels. Michaelis[129] supposes the reference to be to winds and flashes of lightning, which he, following a mistaken exegesis, considers as termed "angels" in Psalm 104:4. There can be no reasonable doubt that the reference there and here is to angels in the ordinary sense of the term. Some have been disposed to understand the words as meaning, 'it was established in the presence of angels.' The particle here translated *by*[130] has certainly this meaning in 2 Tim. 2:2, *"before* many witnesses."[131] We are rather disposed to understand it in its ordinary meaning of instrumentality — "through means of." That angels were somehow or other employed in the giving of the law, there seems no reason to doubt.[132] There is, indeed, nothing said about them in the nineteenth chapter of Exodus; but in the thirty-third chapter of Deuteronomy, verse 2, Jehovah is said to have come with "ten thousand of his holy ones." In the sixty-eighty Psalm, verse 17, we have these words, "The chariots of God are twenty thousand, even thousands of angels: the Lord is among them, as in Sinai, in the holy place." Stephen in his speech before the Sanhedrim says that the Israelites received the law by "the disposition of angels;"[133] and the apostle in the Epistle to the Hebrews, calls the law "the word spoken by angels."[134] It seems doubtful for what purpose the apostle brings forward this fact. It appears to me probable that he introduces it as characteristic of the law, which was not a method of reconciliation, but a transaction showing that God was displeased with Israel for their transgression.[135] The supplement *and it was* is an unhappy one. It is not needed to bring out the sense; it rather obscures it, breaking tne close connection with the statement in the first clause. Perhaps there is a tacit contrast as to the manner in which the promise was given, "not by the ministry of angels," not "by the hands of a mediator," in the same sense as the law was. God conversed with Abraham as with a friend; and if an angel spoke the promise after the intended sacrifice of Isaac, it was the angel of Jehovah's presence — the angel in whom Jehovah's name was, *the angel of Jehovah*. It is obviously the apostle's design to exalt the *promise* viewed alongside of the law. The promise is first, the law second in order. The promise is the principal transaction, the law is secondary and subservient. The promise speaks of nothing but blessing. The law is "added because of transgressions," and curses transgressors. The promise is for ever; the law only "till the seed should come." The promise was made directly by God; the law "given by angels." The promise was given directly to Abraham — God speaks to him as a man with his friend; the law to Israel by the hand of a mediator, the people not being able to bear the things which were spoken. He comes to them not as to Abraham, as a man comes to converse with his friend, but in awful majesty as an offended, though still merciful and placable sovereign. If it be admitted, as has been supposed with considerable appearance of probability, that angels were the agents of the Divinity in the production of those terrific phenomena with which the giving of the law was attended, this view of the matter acquires increased plausibility. The law was not only ordained by angels, but also "in the hand of a mediator."[136] "In the hand" is just a Hebraism[137] for through, or by means of.[138] Though some learned men have been of opinion that the mediator here mentioned is the Son of God, yet I think no reasonable doubt can be entertained as to its denoting Moses. Strictly speaking, Aaron, or rather the priesthood, was the mediator of the old covenant. *It* answers to the Great High Priest,[139] Mediator,[140] and Surety[141] of the new covenant. But the reference seems here to the *giving* of the law; that was, by Moses. "The law was given by Moses."[142] We know that the law, with the exception of one proclamation of the decalogue, was given through the medium of Moses.[143] God speaks to Moses, and Moses to the people; and this arrangement was entered into by the express request of the people themselves. The following is the inspired account of this circumstance, "And all the people saw the thunderings, and the lightnings, and the noise of the trumpet, and the mountain smoking: and, when the people saw it, they removed, and stood afar off. And they said unto Moses, Speak thou with us, and we will hear: but let not God speak with us, lest we die. And Moses said unto the people, Fear not: for God is come to prove you, and that His fear may be before your faces, that ye sin not. And the people stood afar off: and Moses drew near unto the thick darkness where God was."[144] Moses Himself says, "I stood between the Lord and you at that time."[145] This statement seems plainly introduced as characteristic of the economy. The existence of a mediator is certainly no proof that a dispensation is not a dispensation of mercy, for the new covenant has a mediator. But the facts connected with the law being given by the hand of Moses as a mediator, plainly show that the law was not, in its literal meaning and direct object, a revelation of the way of obtaining the Divine favor.

Hitherto all is comparatively plain and easy. The law was never intended as a means of justification. It was a means, rendered necessary by the sins of the Israelitish people, of gaining the accomplishment of the promise; and the circumstances of its revelation, so different from all the revelations of the scheme of mercy, mark its character.

But while there is little difficulty in apprehending either the meaning of the terms or their bearing on the apostle's object in the verse we have considered, there is extreme difficulty of both kinds in reference to the short verse which immediately follows, one of the most perplexing passages in the whole "Book of God."

"Now a mediator is not *a mediator* of one; but God is one" (Gal. 3:20.). Perhaps no passage in Scripture has received so many interpretations as this. Winer says they were about 250 when he wrote some twenty years ago, and the number has since been considerably increased. Who does not see in this an illustration of the honor done to the Word of God? On what other book would the same amount of time, and mental labor, and literary attainment, have been expended for the illustration of an occasional remark?[146]

The causes of the diversity of sentiment are various. Some suppose the apostle to speak in his own person; others consider either the whole verse, or at any rate the first part of it, as the words of an objector. Some by the mediator understand any mediator; others Moses; others Christ. Some understand "one"[147] as a substantive; others as an adjective which requires a substantive to be supplied to bring out the sense, and that substantive they have supplied very variously; some of one party;[148] others of one seed;[149] others of one law;[150] others of one race;[151] others of one thing,[152] etc. Some understand the assertion "is not of one"[153] of the person; others of the condition; others of the design and business of the mediator.[154] Some consider the last member of the sentence, "God is one,"[155] as philosophical or dogmatic; others as historical, looking to the times of Abraham, or of the giving of the law at Sinai. Luther's notion is quite singular, – "God offendeth no man, and therefore needeth no mediator; but we offend God, and therefore we need a mediator." The mode of connecting the passage has also given origin to diversity of view respecting its meaning.

Before inquiring particularly into the meaning of these words, there are two remarks which we must make and carry along with us, and which may probably be of some use in the subsequent discussions, if not in enabling us to discover the truth, at least in preserving us from falling into error. The first refers to the words themselves, and the second to the principle on which they must be interpreted. The repetition of the word "a mediator" is not in the original. It is marked as a supplement by our translators. The original text literally runs – "Now a" – or the – "mediator is not of one."[156]

The second observation to which I solicit attention is that the words must contain in them some statement which lays a foundation for the conclusion which the apostle deduces from them in the next verse, to wit, 'that the law is not against the promises of God.' However plausible in other respects an interpretation may be, it cannot be the just one if it does not bring out a sense which justifies the apostle's inference.

The almost innumerable opinions of interpreters as to the meaning of these words may be all reduced to two classes, – those in which the words "Now a mediator is not of one," are understood as a general proposition, true of all mediators, and applied by the apostle in the course of his reasoning to the subject before him; and those in which they are considered as a particular statement, referring exclusively and directly to the mediator spoken of in the close of the 19th verse, by whose hands the law was given.

Those who are agreed in opinion that the words are a general proposition, differ widely in the way in which they understand it, and in which they make it bear on the apostle's argument. One class consider the words as equivalent to – 'Now a mediator does not belong to a state of unity or agreement. The use of a mediator seems to intimate that the parties between whom he mediates are not at one.' This mode of interpretation labors under great difficulties. For, first, it is not true that the use of a mediator necessarily supposes disagreement. There are causes of the use of a mediator besides this. God continues to deal with those with whom He is reconciled through a mediator. And secondly, it breaks the connection between the two clauses of the verse, which obviously is very intimate.

Another class consider the words as equivalent to – 'a mediator does not belong exclusively to one party; a mediator belongs to both parties;' and they consider the apostle as arguing thus: 'No man can be a *mediator* who is not appointed by both parties. There were two parties in the original agreement – God and the spiritual seed of Abraham. Moses was indeed appointed by God; but God was but *one* of the parties, so that whatever such a mediator could do could not affect the interests of the other party.' This, though supported by such names as Pareus, Capillus, Locke, Whitby, Chandler, is anything but satisfactory, because in the appointment of the Great Mediator of the better covenant, God alone was concerned.[157]

A third class consider the words as equivalent to – 'a mediator is not peculiar to this one dispensation. There have been various mediators, but there is but one God. The mediator may be changed, but God continues the same.'

If obliged to choose a meaning from this class of interpretations, I should prefer this, which is that adopted by Cameron and Koppe. It is not peculiar to the law to have a mediator; other Divine dispensations have mediators also; but while there may be different mediators, God is one, and therefore His dispensations must be all like Himself

— consistent. Judaism had its mediator; Christianity has its mediator; God is *one*. The same God appointed both economies and their mediators; therefore they cannot be opposed to each other. But even this is not satisfactory. The objection to this meaning is a strong one — that the words do not naturally convey it. But I apprehend that an insuperable objection lies against all the views of the passage which regard it as the announcement of a general proposition. The words of the original seem to me to oblige us to understand the mediator in the 20th verse as the mediator mentioned in the 19th. They literally are now *the* mediator, *i.e.* the mediator just mentioned, *this* mediator is not of one.[158] We have thus narrowed the field of discussion to that class of interpretations in which the words are considered as a statement in reference to the mediator mentioned. But the field is still very extensive.

Some consider the mediator by whose hands the law was given as Jesus Christ. Of those who take this view of the subject, some regard the verse before us, not as consisting of two distinct yet connected propositions referring to different subjects, the one to the mediator, and the other to God, but as a continued description of the mediator. They consider the apostle as saying, 'the *law* was given by a mediator — Jesus Christ — and *this* mediator is no inferior being, is not the subject or property of Him who is one, but He is the one God Himself.' To state this exegesis, though it has been held by learned men,[159] is to refute it.

It is a much more plausible view of the subject which those give who consider the apostle as saying, 'The law was given by the hand of the mediator — of Jesus Christ, the great mediator. Now He is not the mediator of this *one* dispensation only; He is the mediator also of the better covenant, and God is one. It is the same God who gave the promise and who established the law; and it is the same mediator whom He employed in both cases. Can the law then be against the promise?' This is an argument which hangs very well together; but unhappily it is one which cannot be brought out of the words of the apostle. Christ is nowhere in Scripture called the *mediator* of the *law.* "The word" may be considered rather as the giver of the law than the mediator through whom it was given; and if the reference had been to Christ, the language in the 19th verse would not have been *a* mediator, but *the* mediator, if not the apostle's expression elsewhere, "the *one* mediator between God and men" (1 Tim. 2:5.). This renders it unnecessary to examine more particularly the following view, which otherwise might appear plausible — 'Now the mediator, Jesus Christ, does not belong exclusively to one part of the human race — He is the mediator of men, of both the great divisions of mankind; even as God is the one God, the God equally of Gentiles and Jews.'

We have thus still further narrowed the field of discussion. We have now only — taking for granted that the mediator is Moses — to seek for a meaning which the words of the apostle will bear, and which will support his conclusion, that "the law is not" — cannot be — "against the promises of God." One of the most judicious of the ancient interpreters[160] thus comments on the text, — "But Moses was not the mediator of one, for he mediated between God and the people; but God is one. He gave the promise to Abraham; He appointed the law; and He has shown to us the fulfilment of the promise. It is not one God who did one of these things, and another another. It is the same God who is the author of all these dispensations." This is, upon the whole, excellent sense; it gives substantially the meaning of the second clause; but it throws no light on the bearing of the two clauses on each other, or on the words, "Now the mediator is not of one," or on the apostle's object.

Some learned and judicious men have considered the apostle as saying, 'Now this Moses was not the mediator of the *one* seed mentioned in the preceding context.' But this is to interpret the expression the *"one* seed" in a way which we have showed the apostle's argument will not warrant; for the one seed is Christ personally,[161] and besides breaks the connection between the two clauses of the verse. It is impossible to make sense of the words 'that mediator did not belong to the one seed, Jesus Christ.'

The following view of the passage, though by no means clear of objections, seems to me, upon the whole, the most probable that has been given. If the first part of the verse be read interrogatively, and if the word *one* be understood, not numerically, but morally, as signifying, uniform and unchangeable, always self-consistent, a plain meaning may be deduced from the words – the two clauses will be found naturally to follow each other – and a broad and solid foundation to be laid for the conclusion which the apostle draws in the first clause of the 21st verse, 'The law was given by the hands of Moses as a mediator. But was *he* not the mediator of Him who is one and the same for ever? Now God, who appointed Moses mediator, is one and the same – unchanged, unchangeable. Can, then, the law be against the promises of God?'[162] Moses was not the author of the law, he was but the mediator. The law was God's law, and Moses was God's mediator: the one was enjoined, the other appointed, by Him. The promise is *His* promise. *He* cannot by His law contradict His promise. He is one and the same; always like Himself. The two divine institutions, the law and the promise, cannot be inconsistent, coming, as they do, from the immutable God.[163] The apostle had already shown in another way that the promise was not made void by the law; now he proves the same thing by the immutability of God, their common author.

This mode of interpretation has the advantage, that the sense it attaches to the words is true in itself, and exactly suits the purpose of the apostle's argument. The interrogative form given to the words is not foreign from the apostle's usage. The word *one* is explained in the same sense in both clauses of the verse, and the connection of the clauses is kept up. The principal difficulties arise from the present tense being used where we would have looked for the imperfect,[164] and from the meaning, certainly unusual, given to the word *one*. That the meaning, though unusual, is not unexampled, will appear from the following passages, – Gen. 41:25; Lev. 24:22; 1 Cor. 12:11.[165]

I cannot say with confidence that this is the meaning of the inspired writer;[166] but it appears to me the most probable sense which has yet been given to his words.[167] To suppose with Michaelis, in direct opposition to all critical evidence, that the passage is spurious, is a very unjustifiable mode of cutting the knot.[168] What is so difficult to us might be, probably was, perfectly plain to the Galatians, calling up a train of thought which the apostle, by his discourses when with them, had made familiar to their minds.[169]

3. THE LAW NOT CONTRARY, BUT SUBSERVIENT, TO THE PROMISE.

The conclusion the apostle draws from these statements, with regard to the design and circumstances of the giving of the Mosaic law, is contained in the first clause of the next verse, and is couched in the form of an interrogation, – "Is the law then against the promises of God?[170] God forbid;"[171] or rather, "Let it not be, by no means."

To those at all acquainted with the apostle's mode of writing, it is needless to remark that these words are just equivalent to a very strong negation. 'The law is not opposed to the promise.'[172] On the contrary, he has showed that the law is subservient to the promise: that it was added to secure the fulfilment of the promise; and that it proceeds from the same author as the promise, who is one and the same – "Jehovah, who changes not:" "the same yesterday, today, and for ever."

What a sad aptitude is there in our depraved nature to misapprehend the design of the gifts and works of God, and to pervert that to our destruction which was meant for our salvation, rendering such an exuberance of illustration necessary to prevent fatal mistake as to the purpose of "the law!"

The apostle proceeds to show that as the law was not, could not be, *against* the promise, so it was altogether unfit to serve the purpose of the promise. If the law had been so constituted as that through it guilty men might have obtained life or happiness, there might have been some plausibility in supposing that it should have taken the place of the promise. But since the very reverse of this is the case, its great use is not to take the place of the promise, but to evince the necessity of the promise.

"For if there had been a law given which could have given life, verily righteousness should have been by the law. But the Scripture hath concluded all under sin, that the promise by faith of Jesus Christ might be given to them that believe" (Gal. 3:21,22.).

It is plain that the apostle's object is to show from the design of the law, that it is not inconsistent with the promise; and his argument in the passage just read seems to me to be this, — 'If a law had been given which furnished all the means necessary for making men really and permanently happy, then in that case, justification by law — legal justification — restoration to the Divine favor, on the ground of something done by the sinner, would have been a possible thing. In this case there would have been a practicable legal way of justification by working — different from, and opposed to, the gratuitous method of justification by believing, made known in the promise. But no such law has been given. Neither the law of nature nor the law of Moses is such a law; for the Scriptures represent all men as violators of the law under which they are placed — of course not justified but condemned; and thus it appears that the promised blessing can be obtained in no other way than as a free gift to be received by believing.' Let us endeavor to make it evident that this important and conclusive argument is indeed expressed by the apostle in the words under consideration.

The connective particle "for"[173] may either be understood, as it often must, as a mere connective equivalent to, *indeed, farther, moreover;* or, as intimating that the words which follow contain in them a corroboration of the sentiment just stated, that the law is not against the promises of God.

A law that could give life[174] is, in scripture language, a law which could secure happiness — true permanent happiness.[175] To understand the apostle, we must recollect that he is speaking of mankind in their present guilty and depraved state. To secure the happiness of innocent creatures, a law distinctly pointing out to them what to do and what to avoid, is quite sufficient. Such a law was imposed on the angels; such a law was imposed on man at his creation. It has been found sufficient for its purpose in the case of the angels; and but for man's fault, it would have been found sufficient in his case too. But a law which is capable of giving life to mankind in their fallen state, of making them truly and eternally happy, must, while it is quite practicable on his part to yield obedience to it, make provision for rendering his happiness consistent with the perfections of the Divine character and the principles of the Divine government, and for effecting such a change in his character as shall make him susceptible of happiness in the only form, that of holiness, in which it becomes God to bestow it on His intelligent creatures.

"If such a law was given, verily," says the apostle, "righteousness would have been by the law," or rather, "by law."[176] "Righteousness"[177] here, as in most other parts of the epistle, is justification. If such a law had been given, then justification by law, a legal justification in opposition to gratuitous justification, would have been a possible thing. A law, by obedience to which the sinner could have made atonement for his past offences and secured those Divine influences which are necessary to make him holy, and thus obtained for himself true and permanent happiness, — a law of this kind would certainly have furnished the means of justification; and they who were justified in this way would have had no need of that gratuitous justification by believing made known in the promise. Such a law would have been against the promises of God. It would have frustrated the grace of God.[178]

But no such law has been given.[179] No such law could have been given. This sentiment, though not expressed in so many words, is obviously implied in the apostle's statement. "If there had been," etc. Neither the law of nature nor the law of Moses was such a law. They make no provision for efficacious atonement for past offences, or for that change of character which is necessary to prevent new offences. They show us what is right and what is wrong; and tell us that obedience, if it is perfect in every point of view, will secure reward, and that disobedience will incur punishment. But they do not, they cannot, give life; they do not, they cannot, justify.

So far from that, "the Scripture hath concluded[180] all under sin." "Sin"[181] is here, as in many other parts of the apostle's writings, equivalent to 'guilt,' exposure to punishment on account of sin. To be "under sin,"[182] is just, in other words, to be guilty, or, condemned. The apostle says, "the Scripture," *i.e.* the old Testament Scriptures, "hath concluded," or shut up,[183] "all," both Jews and Gentiles, "under sin." Guilt is here considered as a mighty tyrant, under whose power "all"[184] men are confined, shut up. 'To shut up,' is equivalent here to, 'to show, to prove, to be shut up.'[185] The Scriptures distinctly state, that all men, both Jews and Gentiles, are imprisoned, as it were, under guilt – are condemned criminals.[186] The law under which either Jews or Gentiles have been placed, so far from giving them life, delivers them over to death; so far from justifying, condemns them. The best illustration of the apostle's declaration, that all men are shut up under sin, and that the Scripture says so, is to be found in the concluding part of the first chapter of the Epistle to the Romans, the whole of the second chapter, and the first part of the third chapter; the substance of which is, 'It is obviously the uniform doctrine of Scripture, that the whole world is become guilty before God.' It is plain that the law of Moses cannot – that no law that had been given, that can be given to a being like fallen man can – come in competition with the way of justification indicated in the promise made known in the gospel. Law in every form, so far from being fitted to take the place of the promise or the gospel, only proves the necessity of some such plan of salvation as they reveal, if man is to be saved at all.

This is what the apostle states in the close of the 22d verse, "that the promise by faith of Jesus Christ may be given to them that believe." "The promise," is plainly the blessing promised; the same thing as the blessing of Abraham, justification – restoration to the Divine favor.[187] This promised blessing is by believing. It is obtained not by working, but by believing on Him who justifies the ungodly. It was bestowed on *believing* Abraham, and it is promised to all believers who are His spriitual children.

The particle "that"[188] either states the design of the Scriptures concluding all men under sin, or the consequence of its doing so. The Scriptures declare all men condemned on account of sin, *that it might be,,* or *so that it is,* evident that if men are justified at all, that blessing originally promised to believers must be bestowed as a free gift on men, not purchasing it for themselves by their service, but in the belief of the truth, humbly and gratefully receiving it. This is the true design of the law, whether that under which all men are placed, or that under which the Jewish nation was placed, to demonstrate the absolute necessity, if man is to be saved at all, of such a method of salvation as was dimly made known in the promise to Abraham, and which is now made manifest, being "witnessed by the law and the prophets."

The statement contained in these words has lost none of its truth or of its importance in the lapse of ages, and is just as closely connected with our duties and interests as with those of the Galatians to whom it was originally made. We are indeed in no danger of reposing our hope of an interest in the Divine favor on our enjoyment of the privileges, or our performing the ritual observances, of the Mosaic economy. But we all are in imminent danger of building our expectations of final happiness on a foundation equally insecure. Are there not thousands and tens of thousands among us who are flattering themselves that they are Christians, merely because they were born in a Christian land and baptised in the name of Jesus? Are there not countless multitudes who, without any reference whatever to the Savior's atonement, on the ground of their comparative innocence or excellence, or of their repentance and reformation, or of their alms and their prayers, are expecting to obtain a share in the felicities of heaven? And are there not countless multitudes more who, while they profess to depend on what the Savior has done and suffered, look on his merits merely as an ample store out of which is to be supplied the deficiency in their own deserts – relying a little on the Savior, but principally on themselves? Indeed, are not by far the greater part of those who name the name of Jesus obviously ignorant and unbelieving respecting the very elementary principle of his religion, that "eternal life is the gift of God," and that men are justified freely by God's grace through the redemption that is in Christ Jesus"? Are not the great majority even of those who appear to be religious, going about to establish their own method of justification, and obstinately refusing to submit to this Divine method of justification. They will do anything and everything rather than credit God's testimony concerning his Son, rely entirely on His finished work, and humbly and heartily accept of a full and free salvation.

To such persons we proclaim with the apostle, "If there had been a law given which could have given life, verily righteousness should have been by the law." But no such law has been given. No such law could be given. You may indeed imagine remedial and reduced laws, and you may depend on your obedience to these laws, and cherish lively hopes of thus obtaining the Divine favor and everlasting happiness. But remember, God will acknowledge no law as His but that which He Himself has promulgated, and He will gratify no hopes but those which He Himself has awakened.

May I be allowed to speak a PARABLE on this subject? A ship's crew mutinied against their commander, who was the king's son; and not only refused to obey him, but threw him overboard with the intention of depriving him of life. Feeling their situation desperate, they commenced pirates, and while disorder and every evil work prevailed among themselves, they carried terror and misery over the ocean and into all the surrounding coasts. The prince, contrary to all probability, reached the shore in safety, and on arriving at his father's palace, instead of urging the punishment of those who meant to murder him, employed all his influence, and with success, to induce his justly offended parent to lay aside all thoughts of vengeance, and even to despatch immediately heralds of mercy offering a free pardon to them if they would but acknowledge the prince as their savior and ruler, and submit to be guided by him in all their future proceedings; but reminding them that if they did not accede to this overture of mercy, sooner or later they must fall into the hands of some of his war-vessels, and must count on being dealt with according to the rigor of the law. On the messengers of mercy approaching the vessel, some of the most determined villains were for treating them as they had done their commander, but this proposal being overruled, they were taken aboard, and their sovereign's proclamation was made in the hearing of the piratical rebels. Some mocked at it; others said it was a stratagem to get them into the king's power; and even the most sober thinking among them, though they were tired of this scene of discord and ravage, both in the vessel and when they were on the shore, said that really they could not give the king credit for such extraordinary kindness, nor bring their mind to acknowledge the authority of the prince, but that they would endeavor to behave better as individuals, to establish better order in the ship, and to restrain their companions from those excesses of cruelty and rapine in which they had formerly indulged, to that if the king's cruisers should lay hold of them, as they feared might be the case, the king might be induced to pardon them, perhaps reward them for their good conduct.

The time dreaded by them all at last arrived. Their vessel is boarded by the king's servants in irresistible force, and the whole crew are safely lodged in prison, and in due time brought before the king for judgment. With a calmness of inflexible determination, more appalling than the most furious passion, the sovereign pronounces their sentence. 'You most causelessly violated your allegiance; you transgressed the law; you, in intention, murdered my son; yet, on his intercession, I proffered you forgiveness – free, full forgiveness. You refused to give me credit for the generosity I manifested, and dishonored me by supposing me false and malignant like yourselves. You persisted in contemning my authority and opposing my will. And even such of you as have not run to the same enormity of licentiousness and cruelty, have formed laws to yourselves which ye have observed; but my laws ye have not regarded. And you have trampled on my grace as well as my authority. You have spurned mercy on the only terms consistent with my honor to offer it; and you have had the insufferable arrogance of attempting to dictate to me in what way I should bestow my favor. You have had your choice, and you must abide by it. As for those men who would not that I should reign over them, bring them forth and slay them before me.'[189]

Let the self-righteous sinner see, in a figure, the doom which awaits him if mercy prevent not. The law by which he must be judged is none of the laws of human device, but the law of God. By that law, "no flesh living can be justified." Let him be thankful that the promised blessing is still held forth as the gift of God to the believer in Jesus. The Scripture has shut us all up under sin, but it is that the promise may be given to us believing. This is the way − this is the certain, the only way − to justification and peace, to holiness and heaven. The oath which has secured that the believer shall enter, and that the unbeliever shall not enter, into God's rest, is unrepealed and unrepealable. God grant that we all may seek and find this good old way, and walk in it, and find rest to our souls.

The greater part of the apostle's answer to the question, "wherefore serveth the law," has hitherto been negative, except the statement, "it was added because of transgressions, till the Seed should come." The sum of what he has said is this, 'The law cannot, it never could, justify. It was never intended to serve this purpose.' In the words which follow, and which we consider to be just an expansion of the statement contained in the clause, "the law was added because of transgressions, until the Seed should come" in reference "to whom the promise was made," etc. the apostle states the purpose which the law was intended to serve, and which, in fact, it did serve; and in making that statement he makes it evident, that to be under the law, though a great blessing to those who lived before the coming of the Messiah, was by no means a state to be envied by those who lived under his reign; and that indeed the two states were quite incongruous.

4. STATE OF THE CHURCH UNDER THE LAW.

"But before faith[190] came, we were kept under the law, shut up unto the faith which should afterwards be revealed. Wherefore the law was our schoolmaster to bring us unto Christ, that we might be justified by faith" (Gal. 3:23,24.).

The first thing to be inquired into here is the meaning of the phrase, "the coming of faith."[191] Some interpreters understand by "faith" Jesus Christ, whom they represent as the object of faith, and consider the phrase, "before faith came," as synonymous with, "till the Seed should come." In strict propriety of language, it is not Jesus Christ personally considered, but the truth about Jesus Christ, which is the object of faith; and though we have no doubt that the coming of the Seed, in reference to whom the promise was made, and the coming of faith, refer to the same period, yet it does not follow that the expressions are synonymous. The Son of God and the Messiah are descriptive denominations of the same individual, but they are by no means synonymous terms; just as the prince of Wales, and the eldest son of the monarch of Great Britain, and the heir-apparent to the British throne, may all be descriptive appellations of the same individual, though each appellation has its own distinct signification. The departure of the sceptre from Judah and the coming of the Messiah, are descriptions of the same period; but it would be absurd to say the two phrases mean the same thing. In the same manner, the coming of the Seed and the coming of faith refer to the same period, but it does not follow that the phrases are synonymous.

By "faith" others understand the system or order of things in which faith is the grand means of justification. But this mode of interpretation is obviously inadmissible. For in this sense "faith" came immediately after the fall, or in the revelation of the first promise. There has been but one way of justifying sinners all along. Adam, if he was justified, as we have reason to hope he was, was justified by believing. Abraham was justified by believing. It was true under the Old, as well as under the New Testament dispensation, that it was the person justified by faith that *lived* − enjoyed true happiness in the possession of the Divine favor, which is life.

By faith, I apprehend we are to understand, not the *act of believing,* but *the revelation believed,* just as our language we call the article which a man believes his creed, his belief, his faith. The expression literally rendered is,[192] *the faith,* and looks back to the phrase, *faith of Christ,* in the preceding verse. "Before the faith of Chrsit came," is just equivalent to, 'before the Christian revelation was given.'

Now, what was the state of the Jewish church previously to this period? "We," says the apostle, "were kept under the law shut up." The apostle in using the pronoun "we," plainly speaks of himself as belonging to the Jewish church previously to the coming of the Messiah. 'We Jews were kept under the law shut up,' or, 'shut up under the law.'

It has been common to connect the words "shut up"[193] with the concluding clause "to the faith," and to consider the words as conveying the idea, that the design and effect of the commands and threatenings of God's law on the mind of an awakened sinner, is to close every avenue of relief but one, and shut him up to accept of the free and full salvation of Christ by believing the gospel. But though this is a truth, and an important one, it is not the truth taught here.

The apostle is speaking of the design of the law in reference to the Jewish church or people as a body, and their situation under it. They were kept shut up under it. They were kept as under the case of a sentinel; they were shut up as in a fortress, or confined within certain limits. The general idea is, they were in a state of restriction. They were kept from mingling with the rest of mankind, preserved a distinct people; and to gain this object, were subjected to many peculiar usages. The law was "the middle wall of partition" which kept them distinct from the other nations of the world. The making one city the seat of religion, the laws with regard to food and ceremonial pollution, the institutions directly opposed to the prevailing customs of the surrounding nations, and the express prohibition to form alliances with heathen nations, all these formed a more powerful barrier to commixture with the surrounding nations than any physical separation of mountains, or seas, or distance could have done.

The apostle seems obviously to have intended to convey the assessory idea of *uneasy confinement*. Their state was necessary, and it was happy when compared with that of the heathen nations; but still it was a state of restriction and confinement, and in this point of view not desirable. This state was, however, never designed to be permanent. It was intended to serve a purpose, and when that purpose was served, it was intended to terminate.

"We were," says the apostle, "kept under the law, shut up unto the faith which should afterwards be revealed." "Unto,"[194] is here equivalent to 'until.' A parallel mode of expression, though the subject is different, is to be found, 1 Pet. 1:5. The phrase is parallel, though not quite sysnonymous, with that used in the 19th verse, *"till the Seed should come in reference to whom the promise was made."* "The faith" here, is plainly the same thing as the faith in the first clause of the verse. The Jewish church was not without a revelation as to the way of justification, for in that case they could not have been justified by faith. We know that the Divine method of justification is "witnessed[195] by the law and the prophets." But it was not *manifested*[196] – fully, clearly, made known – till the fulness of the time, when "the mystery which had been kept secret" was disclosed. The phraseology adopted by the apostle, the revelation of *faith*, makes it evident that faith here refers to doctrine. He speaks of it as *"afterwards to be revealed."*[197] The gospel revelation formed a principal subject of Old Testament prophecy;[198] and the believing Jews under the law were encouraged to look forward to a period when "the glory of the Lord should be revealed, and all flesh should see it together." When His "salvation should be brought near, and His righteousness should be revealed" (Isa. 40:5; 56:1.). The apostle's assertion then in this verse is, 'previously to the Christian revelation, we Jews were kept in a state of separation from other nations by the restrictive ordinances of the Mosaic law, till that revelation was made to which we had been taught to look forward.' He expresses nearly the same idea under a different figure in the following verse.

"Wherefore the law was our schoolmaster to bring us to Christ, that we might be justified by faith" (Gal. 3:24.). "Wherefore"[199] does not here intimate that what is contained in this verse is a logical inference from what has preceded. It is not properly an inference, but a superadded illustration. It is just as if he had said, 'Thus the law was our schoolmaster,' etc. "Schoolmaster," in the modern use of the term, scarcely answers the

apostle's idea. A pedagogue, a tutor,[200] was anciently among the Greeks and Romans —
and let it be remembered Paul is writing to a Gentile church — a servant or slave to whom
the charge of the children was given while they were under age, and whose business was
not sole, or chiefly perhaps, to instruct them, but to keep them from mischief and
danger. The pedagogue and the preceptor were two different persons, and had entirely
different duties to perform.[201] Now, says the apostle, the law acted to us the part of a
tutor or pedagogue, restraining, chastising, and protecting us, and preparing us by its
discipline for a higher and better order of things. The apostle's object is plainly to lower
the idea of the Galatians respecting the state of the Jews, and the economy under which
they were placed. He intimates that they were in an infantine state, and that the economy
they were put under suited it. They were wayward children, put under the care of a
faithful, but somewhat severe and strict, tutor — a servant or slave only temporarily
employed till the children should arrive at maturity.

"The law was our schoolmaster to bring us to Christ." These words have often been
applied to express this idea, — that it is by the commands and threatenings of God's law
brought home to the conscience of the sinner by the effectual working of the Holy
Ghost, that he is induced to believe the revelation of mercy, and gladly to receive Christ
Jesus as the only and all-sufficient Savior. But this, though a very important truth, is
obviously not what the apostle means. He is speaking of the church as a body, and the
law it was subject to. Nor is the somewhat more plausible exegesis, that the apostle means
to say, that the law by its typical ordinances introduced the Jews into an acquaintance
with the Messiah whom they prefigured, satisfactory, for the leading idea in the word
tutor or pedagogue is not teaching, but custody — restriction — correction. You will
notice that *"to bring us"* is a supplement, and is one of the supplements which might as
well have been omitted. "Unto Christ," is equivalent to, 'until Christ,' The three
following expressions are obviously parallel, and throw light on each other. "The law was
added because of transgressions till the Seed should come to whom the promise was
made." "We were kept shut up under the law till the faith was revealed." "The law was
our tutor till Christ, *that we might be justified by faith.*" These last words may either
signify, 'The law was our tutor till Christ, that we might be justified by believing,' *i.e.* that
when the way of salvation through faith in Christ Jesus alone was made known, Jews
might be prepared for gladly accepting it — gratefully hailing a better and more benignant
order of things, which would put an end to all the unpleasant restraints of this severe
tutor.' Or, 'Thus the law was our tutor till Christ; this was its character; so that if we Jews
are justified at all, we are justified by faith. The law restrained, commanded, and
punished, but it did not justify. If we Jews are justified, it is not by the law, but by faith.'
It matters not much which of these two modes of interpretation be adopted, though I
confess I lean to the latter. The substance of the apostle's assertion is, that "the law was
added because of transgressions till the Seed should come, in reference to whom the
promise" of justification to the Gentiles by faith "was made;" that "before faith came,"
before the gospel revelation was given, the Jewish church "were shut up under the law,"
till the good news promised afore was announced; and that "the law was the tutor or
pedagogue" of the infant church "till Christ." The apostle now proceeds to show that the
law, though an institution necessary in and suited to that imperfect and preparatory state,
was utterly unnecessary and unsuited to that new and better state into which the church
had been brought by the coming of the Savior, and to the full and clear revelation of the
way of salvation, and therefore to endeavor to perpetuate it was the height of criminal
folly. This is the principle which the apostle lays down in the verse which follows, and
which he illustrates down to the close of the 11th verse of the next chapter.

5. STATE OF THE CHURCH AFTER "FAITH HAS COME."

"But after that faith has come, we are no longer under a schoolmaster: for ye are all the
children of God by faith in Christ Jesus" (Gal. 3:25,26.).

The meaning of the phrase, "the coming of faith," has already been illustrated. By "faith" we understand the gospel revelation, not only as given, but received. "After that faith is come," is, we apprehend, equivalent to, 'After the truth about the come Savior, and the completed revelation, has been made known to us, and believed by us.'

"We are no longer under a schoolmaster."[202] These words seem a statement not only of the fact, but of the reason of it. It is as if the apostle had said, 'We are no longer, and we no longer need to be, under such a restrictive system as that of the law.[203] The necessary imperfection of the revelation of the method of salvation, till the Savior appeared and finished His work, and the corresponding limitation of the dispensation of divine influence, rendered such a restrictive system absolutely requisite; but the cause having been removed, the effect must cease. Till faith came, it was necessary that we should be under the tutelage of the law; but now that faith is come, we need our tutor no longer. When the child, in consequence of the development of his faculties, and the completion of his education, becomes a man, and capable of regulating his conduct by internal principles, the tutor is dismissed, and his pupil is freed from external restraints now understood to be superseded by the expanded, instructed, disciplined, rational and moral powers of his nature.'

It is plainly on this principle that the apostle reasons; for he immediately adds, "For ye are all the children of God by faith in Christ Jesus."[204] 'Faith being come, you no longer need a tutor; for by faith in Christ Jesus ye are all the children of God.' The change of the person from the first to the second, from *we* to *ye*, is easily accounted for. The language in the 25th verse is strictly applicable to believing Jews only, who once were under the tutelage of the law; the statement made in the 26th verse is equally applicable to believers, whether Jews or Gentiles, to all the Galatian converts, and is plainly intended to lay a foundation for this conclusion − 'if the coming of the faith emancipates those believers who were under the tutelage of the law, it surely must prevent those believers who were never subject to it from being brought under its bondage.'

To perceive the force of the apostle's reasoning it is necessary to observe that the figurative appellation *"children of God"*[205] is here used with a certain peculiarity of reference and meaning. When Christians are represented in Scripture as the children of God, we have a view given us sometimes of their state, and sometimes of their character, and sometimes of both conjoined. We are taught either that God regards them as His children, or that they regard Him as their father, or both. To speak in technical language, it sometimes represents them as justified, and sometimes as sanctified, and sometimes as both justified and sanctified.[206] In most of the passages where this figurative expression occurs, it describes the state and character of saints, in opposition to the state and character of unconverted, unforgiven, unsanctified sinners. But in the passage before us, it obviously describes the state and character of saints under the Christian dispensation, in contrast with the state and character of saints under the Jewish dispensation. The persons spoken of as having been under the law, previously to the coming of faith, are not represented as aliens from the family of God. They belonged to it; but being under age, they were "under tutors and governors till the time appointed of the father," when they were to receive,[207] what our translators call, "the adoption of sons" − the privileges of grown-up children. There can be no reasonable doubt then that the phrase "children of God" is here equivalent to *grown-up children.*[208]

The meaning of this language is not obscure. It is as if the apostle had said, 'There is as great a difference between the privileges you possess, and the character of love to God, and confidence in Him, and submission to Him, to which you have been formed, and the privileges and character of those who lived under the law, as there is between the state and feelings of a son arrived at maturity, and having finished his education, and those of the same child while an infant or still under the care of the nurse and the tutor; and it were not more incongruous for such a person to insist on still remaining in the nursery or the school − to have all his movements watched and regulated by servants − than it is in you believers in Christ to seek to remain under the bondage of the law, not to speak of your subjecting yourselves to that bondage.'

It is "through faith in Christ Jesus" that they were introduced into the privileges and formed to the character of *mature children.* "Faith in Christ Jesus," here as in the whole of the context, is equivalent to the revelation of the truth about Christ Jesus viewed as believed. It is by this revelation believed that Christians obtain that knowledge of the Divine Being as "the God and Father of our Lord Jesus Christ," and our God and Father in Him, which at once fills them with joy and peace, and forms them to that love and confidence in Him which leads them to "serve Him without fear," and to "walk at liberty, keeping His commandments." To such persons the restrictions of the Mosaic law are unnecessary, and its carnal ordinances altogether unsuited; and such is the state into which every believer of the gospel is brought, and such is the character to which every believer of the gospel is formed.[209]

We are now prepared to feel the force of the apostle's reasoning. 'Now that the gospel revelation has been made, and believed by us, we stand no more in need of such an elementary, restrictive, external dispensation as the law; for through this gospel believed we are introduced into a state, and formed to a character, to which such an introductory institution, however well fitted to serve its own purposes, is utterly unsuited.'

That this high honor of being "the children of God" is not peculiar to any class of believers, but common to them all, is the principle which the apostle states and illustrates in the succeeding verses. "For as many of you as have been baptized into Christ have put on Christ" (Gal. 3:27.).

To be *"baptized into*[210] *Christ Jesus"* obviously means something more than to be baptized in the name of Jesus Christ. The phrase occurs here only and in the sixth chapter of the Romans, verse 3d, and in both places, something is predicated of those who are "baptized *into* Christ," which cannot by any means be said of all who are baptized, whether in infancy or mature age, in the primary sense of the term.[211] All who are baptized into Christ, are there said to be "baptized into His death," and "buried with Him by baptism unto death, and risen with Him," etc. And here all who are "baptized into Christ Jesus" are said to "put on Christ." Union with Christ as dying and buried, and raised again, is obviously the idea in the sixth chapter of the Epistle to the Romans. To be baptized into Christ is, I apprehend, just equivalent to be united or intimately related to Christ by that faith of which a profession is made in baptism.

We cannot understand the apostle's words as applying to all who, either in infancy or mature age, have undergone the rite of Christian baptism, for they are not true of them all. They plainly refer to those who have received the doctrine of Christ, who "by one Spirit have been baptized into one body, and have been made to drink into one Spirit" (1 Cor. 12:13.); who are saved "by the washing of regeneration," which is not baptism, "and" – even "the renewing of the Holy Ghost" (Tit. 3:5.). The baptism here spoken of is the "one baptism" which belongs to those who have one God and one Lord – one spirit, one faith, one hope. It is that of which external baptism is the emblem – a blessing not at all necessarily connected with, the administration of the external rite. In the case of an adult, the possession of this spiritual baptism is pre-supposed. It is not external baptism that unites to Christ.

All who are thus related to Christ Jesus by faith "put on Christ." The language is figurative. Properly speaking, we put on garments. But the phrase is often used figuratively in reference to the acquisition or exercise of intellectual and moral habits, whether good or bad. We read of being "clothed with cursing" (Psal. 109:18.), of being "clothed with humility" (1 Pet. 5:5.), of putting off "anger, wrath, malice," etc., and putting on "kindness, humbleness of mind" (Col. 3:8-12.), etc. In this use of the figurative expression there is no difficulty. It is sometimes, though less-frequently, used in reference to persons. Thus, "the Spirit of the Lord" is said to have "come on," literally "to have clothed" "Zechariah the son of Jehoiada" (1 Chron. 24:20.). We are exhorted to put off the old man, and to put on the new man (Eph. 4:22-24.). And in the thirteenth chapter, verse 14, of the Epistle to the Romans, Christians are exhorted to "put on Christ." "To put on Christ" in that passage plainly means to imitate Christ, to be distinguished by the graces and virtues which distinguished Him. To clothe ourselves with His habits.

We apprehend the context here requires us to explain the phrase somewhat differently. To put on Christ is plainly something parallel, if not equivalent, to being "a child of God," as being "baptized into Christ" is parallel to having the faith of Christ. "To put on Christ" is to become, as it were, one person with Christ. They are invested, as it were, with His merits and rights. They are treated as if they had done what He did, and had deserved what He deserved. They are clothed with His righteousness, and in consequence of this they are animated by His spirit – the mind that was in Him is in them. To use the apostle's own language, they do not so properly "live," as "Christ lives in them." The apostle's statement, in plain words, is – 'All who believe in Christ Jesus are so closely related to Him as to be treated by God as if they were one with Him.' When He looks at them, He sees nothing, as it were, but Christ.

This is the privilege of all believers. For the apostle adds, – "There is neither Jew nor Greek, there is neither bond nor free, there is neither male nor female: for ye are all one[212] in Christ Jesus" (Gal. 3:28.).

The general idea obviously is, that under the Christian dispensation our religious privileges depend on nothing but our connection with Christ Jesus, which is formed entirely by faith. External distinctions are here of no avail. It is neither as a Jew nor as a Greek[213] equivalent to a Gentile, as a bondman nor as a freeman, as a man nor a woman, but purely and solely as a person "in Christ" that the believer enjoys any spiritual blessings. And all who are in Christ Jesus are blessed with the same privileges. Believers when they have put on Christ, put off these external distinctions, and appear, as it were, all one in Christ Jesus.

The apostle marks here the decided difference of Christianity, both from Judaism and Paganism. There was a great difference in Judaism[214] between Jews and Greeks – a great difference between male and female – the seal of the covenant being confined to the first. Among the pagans, slaves were excluded from the temples where free men worshipped.[215]

The conclusion which the apostle draws from all believers being thus united, and equally united to Christ Jesus, is that they are all equally secured of those blessings which flow entirely from their connection with Him. "And if ye be Christ's, then are ye Abraham's seed, and heirs according to the promise" (Gal. 3:29.).

To be "Christ's," or to be "of Christ," the property of Christ, as it were, a part of Christ – a member of His body – His flesh and bones – one spirit with Him, is the same thing as to be in Him, and to be clothed with Him. "If ye be Christ's," if you be united to Him, "then are ye Abraham's seed."

To perceive the force of the apostle's argument, you must look back to the 16th verse, where we are told that Abraham's seed was Christ. Now, says he, if ye are one with Christ, the seed of Abraham, then are ye also Abraham's spiritual seed. You may be Abraham's natural descendants; but if ye have not put on Christ, if ye are not in Him, if ye are not His, you are not Abraham's seed. And if ye have put on Christ, if ye are in Him, if ye are His, though you may be an utter alien from the Hebrew family, you are one of Abraham's seed. Jews have no claim to the appellation, in its spiritual sense, if they are not Christ's; and Gentiles, if they are Christ's, have just as good a claim as their believing Jewish brethren – they, too, are "heirs according to the promise."

To be "an heir" of Abraham, is to possess the same blessings which Abraham possessed, and to hold them by the same tenure. All who are Christ's, in other words, all who believe, are "blessed with faithful," i.e. believing, "Abraham." Like him, they are justified, and like him justified through believing.

"According to the promise" may either signify 'agreeably to,' in virtue of, 'the Divine promise,' which says, "in Abraham's seed all the families of the earth shall be blessed;" or 'in reference to the promised blessing,' which we have seen above was justification by faith. The same sentiment is to be found strongly expressed, Rom. 8:17, – "And if children, then heirs; heirs of God, and joint-heirs with Christ: if so be that we suffer with Him, that we may be also glorified together." Eph. 2:19, – "Ye" Gentiles "are no more strangers and foreigners, but fellow-citizens with the saints, and of the household of God." Rom. 9:7,8, – "Neither, because they are the seed of Abraham, are they all children: but, In Isaac shall thy seed be called." "The children of the promise are counted for the seed."

6. FIGURATIVE ILLUSTRATION OF THESE TWO STATES.

There is an unhappy disposition in mankind to overlook and underrate the advantages which they enjoy, while at the same time they often attach an utterly disproportioned value to supposed advantages of which they are destitute. It is in consequence of this that they so eagerly, in many cases, exchange real for fancied good; and find, too late, that they have made "a senseless bargain." It is in consequence of this, too, that in circumstances furnishing everything requisite to substantial comfort we find so many completely miserable, just because they are without something or other which, whether right or wrong, they have imagined to be necessary in order to make them happy. It is quite possible that the attainment of this very something might be productive of pain instead of pleasure, – it is absolutely certain it would not produce the effect of perfect satisfaction which is anticipated; but in the meanwhile the want of it embitters every source of enjoyment, and keeps the mind restless and unsatisfied.

It is distance which lends enchantment to supposed advantages and pleasures; and the best way to secure ourselves from this fascination, is to endeavor to bring them near the eye of the mind, and thoroughly scrutinise them alongside of those possessed advantages for which we may be tempted to exchange them. In that case, we shall often find that what was a seeming advantage would be a real and important disadvantage to us; and we shall uniformly find that the most promising of these advantages has its accompanying disadvantages, and is far indeed from that unmingled good which fancy told us of.

The Galatian Christians, chiefly of gentile origin, were in great hazard of being led dangerously astray by that principle in human nature, to the operations of which I have been adverting, at the period the apostle Paul wrote this epistle to them. By the tender mercies of God they had been delivered from a state of heathen ignorance, immorality, and wickedness, and made partakers of that peace and purity which flow from the knowledge and faith of the truth as it is in Jesus. "In Him they had redemption through His blood, the forgiveness of sins;" they were "sanctified in His name, and by His Spirit;" and, in the enjoyment of His consolations, and the hope of His glory, they were "walking in all His commandments and ordinances blameless." How happy must they have been, had they been but aware of their happiness! But, yielding a too ready ear to the statements of some Judaising teachers, they began to think that, to complete their spiritual dignity and happiness, they must submit to the initiatory rite of the Jewish economy, and yield obedience to all its ritual requisitions. Nothing seemed so venerable as this kind of connection with the holy family; and, instead of moving onwards in that holy happy course on which, by the belief of Christian truth, they had entered, they were in extreme hazard of being drawn aside to the by-paths of ceremonial services, in which, whatever exercise for the body they might find, they would experience no improvement to the mind, no rest to the conscience, no peace to the heart.

The apostle, who watched over them with the tender anxiety of a spiritual parent, uses the appropriate remedy. He strips the legal economy, now become obsolete, of the false splendor with which the Judaising teachers had contrived to surround it. He brings it near to them – fully unfolds its nature and design – distinctly shows that it was an introductory, imperfect, and temporary dispensation – that what they strangely had been led to account dignity was indeed in their case degradation – what they called going forward was indeed going backward – what they gloried in as progress was in reality all but apostasy. He sets the state of Judaism alongside the state of Christianity, and distinctly shows the Galatians that in their case the two were utterly incompatible, and certainly not to be for one moment compared with each other: in plain words, he assures them that if they were determined to be Jews, they must cease to be Christians; and that, if they did make such an exchange, they would have to regret it now and for ever.

To make the thing, as it were, palpable to them, he brings it before their minds in a variety of aspects, and illustrates it by various analogies. One of the most striking of these lies now before us. He illustrates the principles he has laid down by a domestic analogy, showing that it would not be more unnatural or absurd for a family of children arrived at majority to insist on being again subjected to all the restraints of the nursery, than it would be for them, after being introduced into the glorious freedom of the children of God, voluntarily to subject themselves to the servitude of the Mosaic institution.

There should have been no division of chapters here. The careful reader of the epistles must often find occasion to notice that the division of chapters and verses is far from being uniformly judicious.[216]

(1.) THE FIGURE.

"Now I say, that the heir as long as he is a child, differeth nothing from a servant, though he be lord of all; but is under tutors and governors, until the time appointed of the father."[217] The expression, "Now I say," is just a phrase of transition.[218] It introduces an explanation or modification of what has been said, as chap. 3:26.

The reference here does not seem to be, as we have remarked, to the case of the proprietor of an estate leaving the management of the education and property of an only son in infancy or childhood, the heir of his property, — the one to the charge of tutors, the other to the care of governors and stewards, — till the period which the father in his will had fixed for his son entering on the uncontrolled possession of his rights. This would not well correspond with what it is intended to express, — that state of the children of the ever-living God. The reference seems plainly to be to what ordinarily took place both in Jewish and Greek families, even during the life of the father. In these families, the son, though destined ultimately to be the possessor of the father's property, and called among the Romans, during his minority, "*herus minor,*" as with us, the "young master," was, in so far as independent management was concerned, in a state not superior to that of a servant. He was obliged to rise and go to bed, to work or rest, to study or amuse himself, according to the will of others. Like the servant, he was altogether a person "under authority." The management of his time and occupation was committed to slaves, who were themselves entirely subject to the command of the father of the family; and this state was continued till the time fixed by the father for his son being freed from this system of restrictions, and entering on the exercise of his independent right.

"Son,"[219] and "servant"[220] are tacitly opposed to one another. 'Ye are now children;' what were they before? what could they be but slaves? Is not the family[221] made up of these two classes? and it is more than hinted that the situation of those whom he was addressing previously to their becoming Christians was comparatively a servile one. This suggestion could not be very agreeable to the Jewish part of the Galatian church; and they might appeal to the Old Testament Scripture for proof that even under the former economy they were "children of God."[222] The apostle does not deny that even under the law they had a sonship;[223] but he clearly implies that that state was by its restrictions very similar to a state of servitude.

The word rendered "children,"[224] signifies persons of immature age, whether in infancy or under training. The word rendered "tutor,"[225] denotes one to whom is entrusted the power of management of property or persons. In a civil sense, it is applied to provincial magistrates; in a domestic sense, to the managers of farms and estates. The word rendered "governor,"[226] signifies a house-steward to whom the management of the domestic concerns was entrusted. Such was Eliezer of Damascus in Abraham, the rich Emir's, establishment. The tutor or governor is not the same as the official styled "the schoolmaster,"[227] whose sole business was to take care of the children; but while under age, the children, as to pecuniary matters, were under the tutor and governor. The expression "until the time appointed of the Father,"[228] is of itself sufficient to prove that the reference is not to the children of a dead proprietor under the care of what we call trustees or tutors; for the period of tutelage was fixed among the Greeks and Romans, not by the testament of the father, but by the civil law. The *minor* son, though "lord of all,"[229] destined to be the proprietor of the estate, "differs," so far as restriction is concerned, "nothing from a servant" – a slave.

The condition of the *minor* son was thus to be borne patiently – it was vastly preferable to abandonment; viewed in contrast to such a state, and in reference to the object in view, the preparing the son for a higher position, it was a condition to be thankful for – but certainly in no point of view was it to be fondly cleaved to when its ends had been answered, or preferred to the liberty for which this state of restriction was intended as a preparation.

Let us now see how dexterously the apostle turns this familiar fact to account, as an illustration of the subject more immediately before him.

(2.) THE APPLICATION OF THE FIGURE.

"Even so we, when we were children, were in bondage under the elements of the world: but when the fulness of the time was come, God sent forth His Son, made of a woman, made under the law, to redeem them that were under the law, that we might receive the adoption of sons. And because ye are sons, God hath sent forth the Spirit of His Son into your hearts, crying, Abba, Father. Wherefore thou art no more a servant, but a son; and if a son, then an heir of God through Christ" (Gal. 4:3-7.).

(a.) THE CHURCH'S MINOR STATE.

"Even so."[230] It is just as if the apostle had said, 'Analogous to the manner in which human fathers manage the education of their offspring, has the Father of the great "family in heaven and earth" conducted the discipline of His children.' "When we were children, we were in bondage under the elements of this world." ' To the question, Whom are we to understand by the persons[231] in whose name the apostle speaks? the answer plainly is, *The family of God, the true church, genuine believers.* And to the question, What are we to understand by their being "children,"[232] that is, children under age? the proper reply as obviously is, It refers to the state of the church under the law, as one of imperfection, comparative feebleness, and preparation. It does not, however, so properly refer to its condition of subjection to the law – intimated in the phrase "were in bondage under the elements of the world" – as to its imperfection which rendered subjection to such an economy as the law necessary.

"When we were children" is just equivalent to, 'When our knowledge of divine things was limited and indistinct, and all our spiritual faculties in an unripe and imperfect state.' We have but to look into the Old Testament and New Testament revelation to see that the one as far more confined and far less distinct than the other. From the very circumstances of the case, it behoved to be so. The salvation was yet a future salvation, and it was to be accomplished by means of the instrumentality of human agency acting according to its ordinary laws. On this supposition, which is the truth, a clearer revelation would have been incompatible with the object in view; so that under that order of things the children of God would, in ordinary circumstances, be in a state of infancy, or at best, childhood.

Now, when this was the state of their spiritual knowledge and faculties, they were obviously utterly unfit to be left to their own management. Something analogous to "the tutors and governors appointed of the Father" was absolutely necessary, and this was found in what the apostle terms "the elements of the world" under "the bondage" of which they were placed.

There are here two questions to which our attention must be turned, What are "the elements of the world"? and, How were the children of God under the law "in bondage under these elements"? The word rendered "element"[233] properly signifies an order or series, and thence is transferred in a variety of ways to things which stand in an order or series, or to things which keep other things in a series or order. In the classics, it is used of alphabetical characters or letters, as their order is fixed; and by joining them, syllables and words are formed, and regular orderly languages are produced. In a more extended sense, it is employed of things which in any view are "elements" – things out of which other things are constituted or compounded. Peter uses the word of the component elementary parts of the universe (2 Pet. 3:10.). Some have thought that "the elements of the world"[234] here refer to the sun, moon, stars, and other bodies; but the apostle is plainly speaking of the Judaeo–Christian Galatians (we), and even as to the Ethnico-Christian Galatians it is doubtful how far they had been in bondage to these as objects of worship.

To be "in bondage under the elements of the world" is obviously opposed to the being "redeemed from the law," so that the reference of the phrase is undoubted. It refers to the commandments and ordinances of the Mosaic law, and they seem to be termed "elements,"[235] as elementary modes of instruction corresponding to the alphabet, and suited to children;[236] and "elements of this world,"[237] as the elementary modes of discipline belonging to, and characteristic of, the preparative Jewish dispensation.[238] Now, by the elements here referred to, I understand the whole system of external observances under the law, which, if I may use the expression, may be considered as elements, rudiments, suited to the comparatively childish state of the church at the period referred to. And they are termed "worldly elements"[239] to mark their sensible and external character. In training children, we are obliged constantly to appeal to their senses; we cannot fix their attention in any other way. It is by sensible representations we convey abstract truth into their minds. In like manner, in the childish state of the church, arising out of the imperfect revelation of the economy of grace, and that, again, proceeding from the nature of the case, the church was taught and disciplined by symbolical representations and external services. This worship, though not destitute of spirituality   for everything had a meaning, and that meaning was by no means all concealed – had a great deal of corporeality. It was very much a thing of time, and place, and circumstance. The constant round of such observances was intended, in some measure, to serve as a substitute for that enlightened spiritual, habitual, service of God, which nothing but a clear revelation, accompanied with a full effusion of divine influence, could have produced.

Under these worldly external elementary institutions, the church, in its childish state, was "kept" as in a state of bondage; that is, its members were kept in a restricted, confined state – they were "kept" "shut up under the law." Chandler remarks, "The Jews were in bondage under these elements. Their very religion made them a kind of slaves; the expense necessary to support their temple worship was very great, and a constant burden on their estates. Their frequent washings and purifications must have been attended with many great inconveniences: their annual journeys to Jerusalem, which all the male Jews were thrice every year obliged to perform, were both costly and troublesome: so that they might well cry out, 'What a weariness is it?' upon which account the apostle Peter calls the Mosaic law, even in Jerusalem itself 'a yoke which neither we nor our fathers were able to bear' (Acts 15:10.). The being under such a law was really a state of slavery and bondage; and therefore the Jews who were heirs of the promises differed nothing whilst they were under it from servants."

This was no doubt a far preferable state to that of the Gentiles; for better be the Lord's bondmen than our own masters, or, in other words, the devil's slaves. But though a state preferable to that of the Gentiles, and necessary in the peculiar circumstances in which the church was placed, it was not, as we have already showed, in itself a desirable state. It was only intended to be introductory to something better. It was God's purpose to bring them, his bondmen-children, into "the glorious liberty of His grown-up children;" and accordingly the apostle states, that when God by the accomplishment of His promise disclosed the mystery, when Christ being come, there could with propriety be given a full and plain account of the way of salvation through Him — such a view of the Divine character as accompanied with divine influence, was quite sufficient without these artificial and worldly elements to lead the believer to the habitual service of God — then the family of God were delivered from that system of restriction to which they had been so long necessarily subjected, and were introduced into the enjoyment of the privilege of grown-up children. This is what is stated in the next verse, one of the most important in the Book of God.[a]

"But when the fulness of the time[240] was come, God sent forth His Son, made of a woman, made under the law, to redeem them that were under the law, that we might receive the adoption of sons" (Gal. 4:4,5.).

Fully to unfold and illustrate the ideas contained in this verse, it will be necessary for us to follow an order somewhat different from that adopted in the verse itself. In such a passage as that before us, the first point is to endeavor to ascertain what is the leading idea, and what are the accessory ones — what is the trunk, and what are the branches. That is easily done in the present instance. "When we were children, we were under bondage; now when the fulness of time is come, we have obtained the adoption of children." To the obtaining of this it was necessary that they who were under the law should be redeemed from it; and in order to gain this, "God sent forth His Son, made of a woman, made under the law."[241]

(b.) THE STATE OF TTTTT, OR, "MATURE SONSHIP," INTO WHICH THE CHURCH HAS BEEN INTRODUCED.

"The fulness of the time"[b] is a Hebraism for 'the full time,' in the same way as "the perfection of beauty" (Psal. 1:2.) is 'perfect beauty, and "the promise of the Spirit" (Gal. 3:14.), 'the promised Spirit.' When the full time was come — when the time appointed of the Father[242] was fully arrived — then we, that is, the church, the family of God, obtained the adoption of sons.

The word "adoption,"[243] here, is not used in the sense in which it is employed in theological writings generally. It does not denote the state of a person newly introduced into the family in opposition to that of a person who is not of the family at all — it describes the state of a member of the family raised to a higher station in the family. "Adoption of sons" is equivalent to, 'the state of mature sons as opposed to the state of infants and children.'[244] It describes not the state of saints as opposed to that of sinners, but the state of saints under the Christian dispensation in contrast with that of saints under the Mosaic dispensation.

Now, in what does that state consist? In the possession of a larger portion of knowledge of the character of God as a father, in a higher measure of filial love and confidence towards Him, and in a system of religious observances in their simplicity and spirituality suited to this extended knowledge and improved character. Under the Christian dispensation there is a much clearer revelation of the character of God as "rich in mercy and ready to forgive;" "just, yet the justifier of him that believeth in Jesus," than under the Mosaic. The glory of God is most illustriously displayed "in the face of His Son Jesus Christ." The natural effect of this revelation believed is to destroy "the fear that has torment," and to fill the mind with filial confidence and love. These sentiments as naturally draw out the thoughts and affections towards God, and thus render unnecessary, and indeed unsuitable, that complicated system of external religious observances which characterised the former economy. Under the Christian dispensation, the ordinances of religion consist chiefly of the simplest possible expression of the sentiments and feelings due to God, and of the direct and obvious means of religious and moral improvement. There is just so much of positive institute, and no more, as to keep us in mind of our duty *implicitly* to submit to Divine authority, while even these positive institutions are so simple and significant as to have far more in them of spiritual, than of bodily, service. To use the powerful language of the first of English authors, "The doctrine of the gospel planted by the teachers divinely inspired, was by them winnowed and sifted from the chaff of over-dated ceremonies, and refined to such a spiritual height and temper of purity, and knowledge of the Creator, that the body, with all the circumstances of time and place, were purified by the affections of the regenerate soul, and nothing left impure but sin; faith needing not the weak and fallible offices of the senses to be either the ushers or interpreters of heavenly mysteries save where our Lord Himself in His sacraments hath ordained."[245]

(c) THE MEANS BY WHICH THIS FAVORABLE CHANGE WAS EFFECTED.

In order to the church obtaining this "adoption of sons" – this state of mature sonship – it was absolutely necessary that the believers under the law should be *"redeemed"* from it. We have already seen that the system of religious observances under that economy was rendered necessary by, and was suited to, that imperfection of revelation, limited exertion of divine influence, and corresponding imperfection of spiritual character, which prevailed under it. That service, as the apostle informs us, "stood only in meats and drinks, and divers washings, and carnal ordinances," which could not make them that performed them perfect as pertaining to the conscience, and was imposed only "until the time of reformation" (Heb. 9:10.).

The removal of that state of things was necessary both in reference to believing Jews who were already in the family of God, and in reference to those Gentiles who by believing were to be brought into it. It was not meet that those in the family, when admitted to the privilege of mature sonship, should continue subject to the restraints necessary in infancy and childhood; and it was not meet that those admitted into the family in this advanced state, should be made subject to these restraints. Thus it was necessary for them who were under the law to be redeemed or delivered from the law "that we" – that is, both Jews and Gentiles – "might obtain the adoption of sons."

The manner in which this great and happy change in the state of the church was brought about, is thus stated, – "God sent forth His Son, made of a woman, made under the law," that He might "redeem them that were under the law, that we might receive the adoption of sons." This change in the Christian state was highly important, and its importance is marked by the manner in which it was accomplished. It was not accomplished by a mere revelation of the Divine will by an ordinary messenger either angelic or human. It was accomplished by the only-begotten Son of God becoming incarnate, and subjecting Himself to the law that He might deliver His church from under it. To bring His ancient church out of the slavery of Egypt and put them in possession of liberty and peace in Canaan, God raised up Moses and Joshua; but to deliver them from the thraldom of the law, and to introduce them into the glorious liberty of God's children, "He sent forth *His Son.*"

"The Son of God" is an appellation given to Him who is our Redeemer, to indicate the identity of His nature with, His personal distinction from, and the intimacy of His relation to, His divine Father, as well as the complacential affection with which they regard each other. When Jesus called God His own Father, and called Himself God's *own,* only-begotten, Son, the Jews understood Him to say He was equal with God; and that they did not misunderstand Him, is plain from our Lord never correcting them. This glorious Personage, in nature and perfection equal to the Father, but in the economy of human salvation subject to Him, was "sent forth" or commissioned by Him to bring His church into the enjoyment of "'the adoption of sons."

The phrase "sent forth"[246] is used of one who sends a person from Him in another direction to execute a commission.[247] Plainly referring here to something preceding our Savior's birth, it contains in it an intimation of the pre-existence of the Savior – a doctrine very distinctly taught in many passages of Scripture.[248]

The Son of God was sent forth "made or born of a woman."[249] This expression obviously describes our Lord's incarnation. He was sent forth in human nature. "The Word was made flesh, and dwelt among us" (John 1:14.). "Forasmuch as the children" whom He came to bring to glory "were partakers of flesh and blood, He also Himself likewise took part of the same" (Heb. 2:14.). It has been thought that there is a reference in the phrase to the peculiar mode of our Lord's becoming incarnate — in being born of a virgin, being the offspring of the woman. The words do not necessarily express this; but I am not prepared to assert that the fact was not present to the apostle's mind when he chose this particular expression which naturally enough suggests this idea in preference to other expressions, which would have merely conveyed the idea of incarnation, without any reference at all to the mode.

He came, not only made or born of a woman, but "made" or born "under the law;"[250] not only a man, but a Jew. Many interpreters consider "the law" here as what they term the moral law in its covenant form. The doctrine which they state in these words, "Christ was made under the moral law in its covenant form" — that is, "Christ Jesus came commissioned by the Father to yield a perfect obedience and satisfaction to the law, which His people, whether Jews or Gentiles, had broken, and thus to deliver them from condemnation, and secure for them eternal life" — is a most important truth; but it seems very plain that it is not the truth here taught.[251]

The law under which Christ is here represented as made is the law under which the church was placed before His coming, and from which it was necessary to deliver her in order to the obtaining the adoption of sons. He was made under that law, inasmuch as He was the substitute of all His believing people who had ever been under it, bound to obey its precepts, and to sustain its curse, which they had incurred. It is not at all unlikely that one of the arguments of the Judaising teachers was, 'Jesus Christ was Himself a Jew; he was under the law, and yielded obedience to all its requisitions; He was circumcised and scrupulously conformed to all its injunctions;' and that the apostle had a reference to this in bringing forward the fact. It is as if He had said, 'It is very true that Jesus Christ was "made under the law," but it was "to redeem them who were under the law." So far was the imposition of the law on the Gentiles from being the object of His coming, one of its designs was to deliver the Jews from under it.'

It only remains, to a full elucidation of this important verse, that we inquire what connection there is between God's sending forth His Son in human nature and subject to the Mosaic law and the redemption of them who were under that law, and the churches obtaining the adoption of sons. We have already seen that the state called *"the adoption of sons"* — the state of New Testament privileges and liberty — could not exist along with the state of legal bondage; and we have seen, too, that the only honorable termination to the legal economy was to be found in its precepts being perfectly obeyed, and its curse fully endured, by the Substitute of those belonging to the spiritual Israel who had lived under it. For this purpose it was obviously necessary that that Divine Substitute should become both a man and a Jew, and in human nature, and subject to the Mosaic law, and as all His people under that law were bound to do, and suffer all they had deserved to suffer, and thus lay a foundation for the honorable termination of a system which had served its purpose, and the continuation of which was inconsistent with the higher and better order of things which was not to take place.

Besides, it was the imperfection of the revelation of the way of salvation, attended with a corresponding limited communication of divine influence, which was the cause of that imperfection of spiritual character which made the law necessary as a restrictive system; and it was the fact that the Savior was yet to come, that the salvation was yet to be accomplished, which rendered the imperfection of the revelation necessary. Now, when the Savior was come, and had "finished transgression, and made an end of sin, and brought in an everlasting righteousness," a foundation was laid for a full and plain revelation, and this revelation, attended by the influence of the Holy Spirit, produced that state of thinking and feeling in reference to divine things to which such a system of carnal ordinances as the law contained was at once unnecessary and unsuitable, and which fitted the people of God for that simple spiritual order of things which distinguishes the gospel economy. Such is the apostle's analogical *illustration* drawn from domestic life.

A question most deeply connected with our highest interests claims our attention ere we proceed farther. This Son of God, sent forth by the Father, has come into our world — made of a woman — made under the law — a man, a Jew, and He has done and suffered all that was necessary to redeem them that were under the law — and in doing so He has laid a broad and sure foundation for all men, whether under the law or without law, whether Jews or Gentiles, on believing, obtaining the high privilege of mature divine sonship. An infinite atonement has been made and accepted — a plain and well-accredited revelation has been given, and a channel wide and deep opened for the communication of divine influence all powerful to purify and to save. We live under the dispensation in which all these things are matters, not of prediction and expectation, but of history and of experience.

But we may live under that dispensation and yet continue personally uninterested in its blessings. The question — the all-important question — is, 'Am I so united to Christ as to be interested in the blessings of His salvation?' Such an union can only be formed by the faith of the truth; and wherever that faith really exists there is that union, and there are all its blessed results. If we are the children of God, it is through the faith of Christ; and if we believe in Christ, we are the children of God. "To as many as receive Him He gives the privilege of being the sons of God — even to as many as believe in His name."

Let us see then that we be not unchanged men, while an economy is in operation around us, in which "old things have passed away, and all things are become new" — that we be not in darkness amid light, and when many once in darkness are now light in the Lord — under condemnation while a free pardon is proclaimed in our ears, and many as guilty as we are actually pardoned — dead while quickening influence is in active operation around us, and many once as lifeless as we are quickened together with Christ. Let us see that we be so united to Christ as to be "made the righteousness of God in Him." Let us see that we be "created anew in Christ Jesus;" for "if any man be in Christ Jesus he is a new creature." Let us see that this double change has taken place on us. Without the first change, heaven is shut against us; without the second, we are unfit for heaven; without them both, it had been better for us that we never had been born. It will be a fearful thing if, with an infinite atonement — an omnipotent Spirit — a plain and well-accredited Bible — a full and a free salvation — we yet perish. No common perdition must be our perdition — deeper than that of Jews or heathens in proportion to the greater number and higher value of our privileges. But why should there be perdition at all? Salvation in Christ with eternal glory is brought very near us, and must be ours if we do not obstinately refuse to receive it. It can be received only in the faith of the truth of the gospel; and why should we not believe? all things are ready — the completed sacrifice — the free Spirit — the plain well-accredited record — nothing in the way but "the evil heart of unbelief" — a state of mind as monstrous as it is wicked, as irrational as it is ruinous.

For a proof that the Galatian believers were indeed introduced into a state analogous to that of grown-up children, the apostle appeals to their state of mind in reference to God produced by the operation of the Holy Spirit.[c]

(d) CONSEQUENCE AND PROOF OF THIS FAVORABLE CHANGE OF CONDITION.

The consequence and proof of this happy change in the church's condition are described in the two following verses, — "And because[252] ye are sons, God hath sent forth the Spirit of His Son into your hearts, crying, Abba, Father. Wherefore thou art no more a servant, but a son; and if a son, then an heir of God through Christ" (Gal. 4:6,7.).

The word "sons"[253] is obviously to be understood as equivalent to grown-up sons, as opposed to sons in a state of infancy and childhood; and the whole phrase "because ye are sons" is equivalent to — 'as a proof of your being introduced into a state of mature sonship, as an evidence that you have indeed obtained the adoption of sons[254] — "God has sent forth the Spirit of His Son into your hearts, crying, Abba, Father." '

It is not very easy to determine whether by "the Spirit of God's Son" we are here to understand the Holy Spirit, that divine person who, along with the Father and the Son, exists in the unity of the Godhead, and is the great agent in the communication of spiritual blessing; or – like the phrase "The spirit of Elijah" – the temper, the disposition, of Christ – the way of thinking and feeling in reference to God, by which He was characterised. Both modes of interpretation are sufficiently agreeable to the use of the language and the object of the apostle. Indeed, it matters very little which is adopted; for the characteristic sentiments and disposition of Jesus Christ, His spirit, was the result of the operation of the Holy Spirit, who, in His enlightening and sanctifying influence, was given Him without measure. At the same time, the phrase "sent forth," which is the same as that used in reference to our Lord in the 4th verse, seems more applicable to a person than to a temper or disposition. And on this account we are disposed to consider the phrase "Spirit of His Son" as an appellation of the Holy Spirit, intimating either His essential or economical relation to the Divine Son – either His proceeding from Him, or His being sent by Him, or His dwelling in Him.

By God's sending forth the Holy Spirit into the hearts of the believing Galatians, we are to understand His making them the subjects of His influence. In the whole of the Christian economy "All things are of God." *He* sends forth His Son; *He* sends forth the Spirit of His Son. "Of Him, and through Him, and to Him, are all things."

The particular nature of the influence of the Spirit of His Son whom He sends forth is described in the conclusion of the verse, – "Crying, Abba, Father." The word "crying" is by a Hebraism used instead of making to cry. The phrase is explained by a similar one in the parallel passage in Romans, – "Whereby we cry, Abba, Father" (Rom. 8:15.). The Spirit of God's Son sent into the hearts of the believing Galatians led them to cry, "Abba, Father." The Holy Spirit, through the faith of the gospel, had formed them to the sentiments and feelings of children, had given them such views of the Divine character as led them to venerate Him, to love Him, to trust in Him, and to express these sentiments and feelings in spontaneous, reverential, affectionate, confidential prayer. "Abba" is a Syrian word, signifying father, and a word which none but children were allowed to use. The Syro-Chaldaic was the apostle's vernacular language as a Jew. The idea he means to express, was that the Galatian believers felt towards God as children, and showed that they felt in this way by the manner in which they approached Him in their devotions. Now, what could be more natural for him than to use the word with which his ear was most familiar as the expression of filial regard, which he had likely a thousand and a thousand times addressed, both to his earthly and heavenly father, as an expression of confidence and tenderness? and then, recollecting that many of those to whom he wrote did not understand the Syriac language, he adds a translation in a language with which they were acquainted.[255] The distinction between slaves and children is strongly marked. Slaves seldom spoke to their master; and when they did, it was in a subdued voice, and then they called Him *Lord,* Baali. Children habitually speak to their parents – they speak boldly. In distress they cry to them, and they call them, *Father,* Abba. Selden quotes the Babylonian Gemara to prove that it was not allowed to slaves to use the title of Abba in addressing the head of the family, or the correspondent title Imma, when speaking to the mistress of it. The possession of such views and feelings in reference to God, and the habitual expression of these in humble, believing, affectionate prayer, are the result of the Spirit of God's Son being sent into the heart, and the most satisfactory of all evidence that we indeed have received the adoption – are the children of God through Jesus Christ.

This is the conclusion which the apostle draws from it in reference to the Galatians in the next verse, – "Wherefore thou art no more a servant, but a son; and if a son, then an heir of God through Christ" (Gal. 4:7.).

The apostle here changes the number in his address from the plural to the singular, *"thou"* art no more," etc. instead of, *"ye"* are no more," etc. Such changes are common in the apostle's writings; and it is not always possible to assign the reason. In the case before us, it is not improbable that the apostle's object was to impress on the minds of the Galatians that the privilege he was speaking of was a personal privilege, not enjoyed in consequence of their connection with any visible society merely, but in consequence of every individual, by his own faith of the gospel, obtaining an interest in the blessings it reveals and conveys.

The verse is obviously a deduction from what goes before. The import of the connective particle[256] "wherefore," or, *so that,* or, *thus,* is — 'since God has by sending His Son,' etc. has redeemed those who are under the law, and introduced His church into the state of mature sonship, and since He has by the operation of His Holy Spirit formed you to a character suited to that state, it is evident that ye are indeed sons of God, grown-up sons of God, and enjoying all the privileges of that exalted state.

"Thou art a son"[257] at once placed in the filial relation and formed to the filial character. God regards and treats thee as His son; and thou art taught by the Spirit to think and feel in reference to Him as thy Father; "and if a Son, then an heir of God through Christ."

To be the "heir" of any person, in strict propriety of language, is to be destined to be the legal possessor of his property after his death. It is plain that in this point of view the word is inapplicable to God. To be "an heir of God" is just to be possessed, and secured, of all the blessings which may be expected from God in the character of a father. The force of the apostle's argument is, 'If thou art indeed a son of God, thou mayest safely count on all the privileges of sonship. if thou art a son, the inheritance assuredly is, or will be, thine.' We have the same argument, nearly in the same words, Romans 8:17, — "And if children, then heirs; heirs of God, and joint heirs with Christ: if so be that we suffer with Him, that we may be also glorified together."

And all this is "through Christ Jesus." It was entirely on account of what Christ had done and suffered in the room of the believing Galatian — it was entirely in consequence of the belief of the truth on this subject — that He was a son and an heir of God; and the conclusion to which the apostle obviously wishes him to come, and to which his statements plainly lead, is this, — 'What object can in your case be secured by subjecting yourself to the law? Ye are already in possession of, or at any rate secured of, all you can possibly wish in the way of dignity and happiness; ye are already the sons and heirs of God through Christ Jesus. Ye are already complete in Christ, — why go to the law then? What can it do for you which He has not done? What can it give you of which you are not already possessed?'

But you will notice the apostle introduces another idea; he not only exhibits the dignity and happiness of their state as believers simply, but he exhibits it as contrasted with the degradation and misery of a situation in which they had been previously placed. "Thou art no longer a servant, but a son," etc. Some interpreters suppose that the apostle is here contrasting the state of believers under the gospel with that of believers under the law. But this is obviously not the case. The apostle in this passage represents the state of believers under the law not as a condition of servitude (though in some respects resembling such a state), but of tutelage; he compares it not with the condition of slaves, but with that of children during their state of minority.[258] Had he been addressing Christian Jews, he would have said rather, — 'Ye are no longer in a state of infancy and childhood, but in a state of mature sonship.' Indeed, from the following verse it is quite plain that he is addressing himself to converted idolaters, persons who never had been subject to the law. The word "servant" properly signifies 'slave,' and strikingly describes that degraded spiritual condition in which the Galatians were previously to their conversion. 'Thou art no longer a slave as thou once wast — the devoted, degraded servant of false divinities — but thou art introduced into the glorious freedom of the children of the true God, and into all the immunities and privileges connected with such a situation.'

PART V.

THE APOSTLE'S EXPOSTULATIONS WITH AND WARNING OF THE GALATIANS.

"But then indeed not knowing God, you were a slave to those who by nature are not gods. But now *that you* have known God (or rather, that you have been known by God,) how can you turn again to the weak and poor principles to which you again desire to be in slavery? You carefully keep days and months and times and years. I am afraid of you for fear that somehow I have labored to no avail regarding you. Brothers! I beg of you, be as *I am*, for I also *am* as you are. You did not wrong me in anything. But you know that through weakness of the flesh I preached the gospel to you at first — and you despised not my temptation in the flesh, nor spit on *me*. But you received me as an angel of God, even as Jesus Christ. What then was your happiness? For I tell you that if possible you would have plucked out your eyes and have given them to me. Have I then become your enemy by telling you the truth? They are eagerly after you, *but* not with honor. But they desire to keep you so that you may *run* eagerly after them. But it is right to be zealous in a right thing at all times, and not only when I am present with you. *You* are my little children, for whom I labor in pain again until Christ shall have been formed in you — and I desire to be there with you now and to change my voice, for I am doubtful about you. Tell me, you who desire to be under Law — do you not hear the Law? For it has been written that Abraham had two sons, one out of the slave-woman and one out of the free woman. But he that was out of the slave-woman had been born after the flesh, and he that was out of the free woman through the promise. Which things are an allegory, for these are the two covenants — one from Mount Sinai, bringing into slavery, which is Hagar. For Hagar is Mount Sinai in Arabia and answers to the present Jerusalem. And she is in slavery with her children. But the Jerusalem which is above is free, which is the mother of us all. For it has been written, "Rejoice, O unfruitful one that does not bear. Break forth and cry, you who have no birth-pains. Because more are the children of the deserted one than of her who has the husband." But, brothers, we like Isaac are children of the promise. But as then he who was born according to the flesh persecuted him *who was born* according to the Spirit, so it is now. But what does the Scripture say? — "Throw out the slave-woman and her son, for the son of the slave-woman shall not in any way inherit with the son of the free woman." So, then, brothers, we are not children of the slave-woman, but of the free woman. Then stand firm in the freedom with which Christ has made us free. And do not be held again in the yoke of slavery. Behold! I, Paul, say to you that if you are circumcised, Christ will be no profit to you. And I again testify to every man being circumcised that he is a debtor to do the whole Law. You are set aside from Christ, you who are being justified in Law. You fell from grace. For we through the spirit wait for the hope of righteousness by faith. For in Christ Jesus neither circumcision or the lack of circumcision is worthy anything, but faith working by love. You were running well. Who kept you back that you did not obey the truth? This false belief is not of Him who calls. A little leaven leavens the whole lump. I am persuaded as to you that you will have no other mind in the Lord. But he who is troubling you shall bear the judgment, whoever he may be. But I, brothers, if I still preach circumcision, why am I yet persecuted? Then the stumbling-block of the cross has ceased. I wish that they who are causing you to doubt would even cut themselves off." — Galatians 4:8-5:12.

SECT. I. — INTRODUCTORY REMARKS.

Man is a being endowed with affections as well as intellect, and these different parts of his mental constitution mutually influence each other. While, on the one hand, you cannot obtain a secure hold of the affections without first bringing the understanding over to your side; on the other, the having the affections on your side makes it a comparatively easy work to obtain the suffrage of the intellect. The same sentiments and arguments wear a very different appearance to the mind when they come from a friend and from an enemy. If I am prejudiced in favor of an individual, I naturally see everything he says in the best light. I am prejudiced in favor of his sentiments and arguments; and if the former are true and the latter conclusive, their truth and force are more readily acknowledged and more strongly felt just because they are his. On the other hand, if I am prejudiced against an individual, I view everything he says and does with suspicion. I am prejudiced against his sentiments and arguments, just because they are his; and though the former should be true and the latter conclusive − so evidently true and completely conclusive that there is no denying the one or resisting the other − yet still there is a struggle against, and a reluctance in, surrendering our understandings into the hands of one who has no hold on the heart.

Hence the importance of a teacher of Christian truth standing well in the affections of those whom he instructs. If a teacher of Christianity be generally viewed as a man altogether destitute of, or greatly deficient in, integrity and piety, anxious to promote his own interest and reputation, but careless of the spiritual interest of those to whom he ministers − however able and eloquent may be his discourses, however clear his statements of truth and powerful his enforcements of duty − it is not at all likely that his labors will either be very acceptable or very useful. On the other hand, if a teacher of Christianity be regarded by his people with reverence and love, as really "honest in the sacred cause," firmly believing every statement he makes, exemplifying in his own character and conduct every virtue and duty he recommends, truly desirous of promoting their spiritual improvement and ultimate salvation, truth from his lips is likely to prevail with double sway, attention will be readily yielded, and conviction, instead of being resisted, will be welcomed, and obedience cheerfully rendered.

Both Paul and his Judaising opposers in the church of Galatia seem to have been aware of the peculiarity in the human constitution we have just adverted to, and to have regulated their conduct accordingly. Perceiving that it was a hopeless undertaking to shake the faith of the Galatians in Paul's doctrine so long as he continued the object of their veneration, esteem, and love, these false teachers appear to have left no means untried to destroy their confidence in his divine mission as an apostle, and his integrity as a man. They seem to have used the most unworthy acts to seduce their affections from their spiritual father and to appropriate them to themselves; and it appears that their nefarious attempts were attended in too many cases with success.

The apostle easily could, and actually did, oppose clear statements to their misrepresentations, and powerful arguments to their sophistical reasonings; but he knew human nature too well to think that statements of truth however clear, and reasonings in its support however powerful, could of themselves regain alienated affection, or, while that affection continued alienated, were likely to produce their own appropriate effect on the mind. To counteract the mischievous design of his enemies and to pave the way for the unprejudiced consideration of his statements and arguments, we have seen him in the two previous chapters of his epistle vindicating his authority as an apostle, and his integrity as a man; and in the paragraph which begins the next division of his epistle, we find him with the skill of a master in the science of human nature making an appeal to the all but extinguished kind affections of those who had once so dearly loved him, bringing before their minds in a manner peculiarly calculated to make an impression on their hearts, that mutual interchange of kind affections and friendly offices by which their original intercourse had been characterised, and assuring them that however they might have changed he remained unaltered, that his heart beat as warm as ever to their best interests, and that all he had endured for them he was willing to endure again, though the more he loved them the less he should be loved.

The object of the apostle in thus adverting to their former situation soon becomes apparent.

It lays a foundation for a new argument against their seeking to be subjugated to the

Mosaic law. The substance of it is this: 'Ye were once slaves; now you are free. Would you wish to be slaves again? for, indeed, there is much in common between the rites of the religion you have abandoned and these over-dated ceremonies for which you are discovering so preposterous a fondness.'

SECT. II. – THE APOSTLE SHOWS THE GALATIANS THAT THEY WERE IN DANGER OF SUBJECTING THEMSELVES TO A BONDAGE SIMILAR TO THAT FROM WHICH THEY HAD BEEN DELIVERED.

"Howbeit then, when ye knew not God, ye did service unto them which by nature are no gods. But now, after that ye have known God, or rather are known of God, how turn ye again to the weak and beggarly elements, whereunto ye desire again to be in bondage? Ye observe days, and months, and times, and years. I am afraid of you, lest I have bestowed upon you labor in vain" (Gal. 4:8-11.).

It is as if the apostle had said, 'Ye are no more slaves; but there was a time when ye were slaves.' "When ye knew not God," – that is, 'when you were ignorant of the true God and Father of our Lord Jesus Christ, when you were in a state of heathenism,'[1] – "ye did service unto them which are no gods." The English phrase *do service,* which suggests no other notion than worship, does not by any means come up to the apostle's idea: "Ye were enslaved[2] to them who are by nature no gods," – ideal beings, dead men, evil spirits, heavenly luminaries. 'You served your false divinities, and you served them like slaves: you had the feelings of slaves in reference to them, and your conduct was like that of slaves engaged in a toilsome, profitless round of external services.' In false religion in all its forms, nothing is more remarkable than its enslaving, degrading influence on the minds of its votaries.

Such was once the situation of the Galatians; but an important change had taken place: "They knew God, or rather were known of God."[3] These words admit of two different modes of interpretation. According to one of these, the words mean, 'They had obtained the knowledge of the existence and character of the true God; or rather, to speak more accurately, they had been made to know by God.[4] Their knowledge of God was not the result of their own research: it was entirely of God. He gave the revelation; He sent it to them; He "opened their understanding" to understand and believe it.' In this case we must suppose the apostle to use a Hebraism. According to the other mode of interpretation, which, upon the whole, I think the preferable one, the word *"know"* is to be considered as equivalent to 'acknowledge,' – a sense which it certainly has in some passages of Scripture; for example, Amos 3:2; Matth. 7:23; John 10:14; 1 Cor. 8:3. 'But now, after ye have acknowledged God, or rather have been acknowledged by God,[5] – now that you have, in consequence of having believed the gospel, taken the true God for your God, and have been acknowledged by Him as His people, by His bestowing on you numerous and important privileges, – how is it that in these circumstances "ye turn again[6] to the weak and beggarly elements whereunto ye desire," or do ye desire, "again to be in bondage?" '

These words may seem at first view inexplicable, as they may appear to involve in them one or other of the two following equally false suppositions: that the Galatian Gentiles had been subject to the law previously to their believing the gospel; or, that they were disposed to return to heathenism. There is a principle that removes all difficulty. – The rites of the heathen worship and the now obsolete ritual observances of the Mosaic economy having much in common, they both deserved the name of "weak and beggarly elements." The leading character of both was externality; they were both "worldly elements;" they consisted "in meats, and drinks, and divers washings." Those rites were "weak and beggarly."[7] These epithets seem synonymous; and intimate that they were incapable of propitiating God, of pacifying the conscience, of improving the character. The apostle (Heb. 7:18.) represents the "weak"[8] and the "unprofitable"[9] as the characteristic features of the law, viewed as a method of salvation.

The apostle's expostulation is obviously very forcible: 'That ye should have been slaves, even the slaves of false deities, when you knew no better, was not wonderful; but now that you have acknowledged God as your God, and that He has acknowledged you, not merely as His servants, but his sons, it is very extraordinary that, after experiencing "the liberty of the children of God" — the walking at liberty, keeping His commandments, ye should discover a disposition again to be subjected to a state of things which, as to externality and restriction, bears a striking analogy to the state from which you have been delivered.'

That the apostle's suspicions were not unfounded, he makes evident from the facts he refers to in the next verse. "Ye observe days, and months, and times, and years" (Gal. 4:10.).

This verse may be rendered interrogatively; but that does not materially affect its meaning. From this passage, it is plain that some of the Galatian converts had yielded to the Judaising teachers, and commenced in good earnest to keep the law. While they were Gentiles, they performed a set of useless ceremonies in honor of their false deities; and now they do the same thing though unintentionally, in honor of the true God. Under the Christian dispensation, with the exception of the Lord's day,[10] all days are alike. God may be worshipped at all times, and in all places. The phrase "days"[11] probably refers to the Jewish Sabbath, and the great day of expiation; "months,"[12] to the festivals at the new moons; "times,"[13] to annual feasts, such as the Passover, Pentecost, the Feast of Tabernacles; "years,"[14] to the Sabbatical year and the year of Jubilee.

It seems plain, from the fourteenth and fifteenth chapters of the Epistle to the Romans, that though the apostle considered the observing of these institutions on the part even of believing Jews as unnecessary, he did not consider it as unlawful, so long as they viewed them not as a means of justification, but merely as institutions originally of Divine appointment, and in their estimation unrepealed. But for believing Gentiles, who never had been subject to the law, to engage in these services, had a very suspicious aspect indeed, and certainly seemed to say that they wanted something more than was to be found in Christ and in Christianity. Accordingly, the apostle adds, "I am afraid of you, lest I have bestowed upon you labor in vain."[15] 'I am afraid that you have rendered of no effect all the labor I have bestowed on you.' The great object of a Christian teacher is to bring men to the enjoyment of the blessings of Christianity, by leading them to understand and believe "the truth as it is in Jesus." And whenever men who profess to believe the gospel act in a manner which gives reason to think that they really do not understand and believe the gospel, then the Christian teacher has reason to fear that he has bestowed labor on them in vain. Such was the conduct of the Galatian Christians. The man who clearly understood and firmly believed the gospel, which Paul had preached among them, found all in Christ of which he stood in need. "Christ" was to him "all in all." He wanted no wisdom but the wisdom of Christ — no propitiation but this propitiation. "Of God Christ was made unto him wisdom;" and in Him he found "justification, and sanctification, and redemption."[16] But when, by submitting to circumcision, offering sacrifices, and performing other ceremonial services, the Galatians seemed to find something wanting in Christ, there was much reason to fear that, notwithstanding their profession, they did not understand and believe the truth; and that, of course, the apostle's labor had been bestowed on them in vain.

There is something peculiarly affecting in these simple words of the apostle. He had labored, labored too with apparent success; but now, through the exertion of false teachers, the fruits of his labor seem in extreme hazard of being completely blasted. How happy would it be for Christ's church if ministers in general were of the apostle's spirit — "jealous over their people with a godly jealousy" (2 Cor. 11:2.)!

SECT. III. — THE APOSTLE REMINDS THEM OF THE CIRCUMSTANCES OF THEIR CONVERSION AND SHOWS THEM THAT NOTHING HAD OCCURRED THAT SHOULD HAVE CHANGED THEIR SENTIMENTS TOWARDS EITHER HIM OR HIS TEACHING.

"Brethren, I beseech you, be as I am; for I am as ye are: ye have not injured me at all. Ye know how, through infirmity of the flesh, I preached the gospel unto you at the first. And my temptation which was in my flesh ye despised not, nor rejected; but received me as an angel of God, even as Christ Jesus. Where is then the blessedness ye spake of? for I bear you record, that, if it had been possible, ye would have plucked out your own eyes, and have given them to me. Am I therefore become your enemy, because I tell you the truth" (Gal. 4:12-16.)?

The meaning and reference of the words in the 12th verse are by no means very evident.[17] The words admit, and they have received, various interpretations. They are obviously an exhortation to imitate the apostle. The question is, In what?

They have very generally been considered as an exhortation to the Galatians by the apostle, enforced by a motive, to cherish the same views which he entertained in reference to a full and free justification by faith in Christ, without the works of the law. The interpreters who take this view of the passage would read the words thus, "Brethren, I beseech you, be as I am: for I *was* as ye are:" as if he had said, 'I once though as ye do; I once considered circumcision and the other observances of the Mosaic institution absolutely necessary to salvation; I once expected to obtain the Divine favor by my own exertions. But I have seen reason to change my opinion; and I am quite sure, that if you saw things in their true light, you would adopt, not those views which, from a full conviction of their falsehood, I have abandoned, but those which I now hold fast as the truth of Christ, and the only foundation of my own hope as a sinner.'

Other interpreters suppose that the apostle does not refer so much to sentiment as to conduct. "Be ye as I am;" — that is, 'Exercise your Christian liberty; imitate me in my disregard of the obsolete requisitions of the Mosaic economy;' — "for I am as ye are." 'I, to use the language of the address to Peter in the second chapter, "I live as the Gentiles do."[18] I, though a native Jew once under the law, disregard these legal restrictions. Why should you Gentiles, who were never under the law, submit to them, now that they are destitute of all obligation even on those who were once bound to observe them?'

I confess that neither of these modes of interpretation seems to me satisfactory. I apprehend that the apostle is in these words neither calling on them to think as he thought nor to act as he acted, but is urging them to regard him with the kind affection which they once cherished towards him and which he still continued to cherish towards them. It is one of the comparatively *few* good *exegetical* remarks (for there are very *many* good *doctrinal* and *experimental* remarks) in Luther's large commentary. "The meaning is not, Think of doctrine as I do; but, Bear such an affection towards me as I do towards you." The apostle's phraseology seems proverbial, and may be illustrated by a passage in the Old Testament Scripture, 1 Kings 22:4. "I am as thou art," is there obviously equivalent to, 'I am united to you in the most cordial friendship, so that you may use my resources as if they were your own.' In like manner, the apostle beseeches the Galatians to lay aside any unkindly feelings they might through the arts of the Judaising teachers be induced to indulge towards him, and to regard him with that perfect affection which they once entertained for him, and which he still continued to entertain for them. It is equivalent to the expostulation, 'Why should you dislike me who so cordially love *you?*'

Alienation of affection is often greatly increased by a consciousness that we have acted unkindly to one whom we once loved, and a suspicion that in consequence of this he cannot but regard us with unfriendly feelings. It is in consequence of this, that when friends quarrel the offender frequently finds it more difficult than the offended to resume that cordiality of affectionate feeling which previously existed between them. It was, I apprehend, for the purpose of removing this obstacle out of the way of a complete restoration of a right state of feeling in the Galatians towards himself that he adds, "Ye have not injured me at all."[19]

These words may either intimate that the Galatians had never done him any personal injury, but on the contrary, as he goes on to state, had heaped on him every mark of affectionate regard; or, that the injury had been done principally not to *him* but to themselves; or rather, that their having deserted his doctrine, and cherished unkind and unfounded suspicions of him, had made no such impression on his mind as to produce in his heart alienation or resentment. 'I do not feel as an injured man in reference to you. I have no resentment. I indulge no feelings but those of affectionate regard.' The apostle acts in reference to the Galatians on the same principle on which the supreme Being acts in reference to sinful men. He seeks to cure their disaffection to *him* by displaying his affection to *them*. His language is, 'O, how can ye hate one who loves you so well that he will do everything but deny himself to make you happy?'

In prosecuting his object of blowing into a flame the almost extinguished embers of affection in the hearts of the Galatian converts, the apostle discovers equal delicacy of feeling and knowledge of the human heart. An ordinary man in the apostle's circumstances would have expatiated on the labor and privation he had exposed himself to, to promote their interests; and if he had touched on the expression they had once given of their attachment to him, it would have been for the purpose of giving greater keenness to his upbraidings for their subsequent unkind, causeless, abandonment of him whom they had once acknowledged as the greatest of their human benefactors. But the apostle takes a different course — a course more corresponding to the dignity and tenderness of his own character, and a course far better fitted to gain his object. He dwells, not on his labors and sufferings, but on their affectionate reception of him and his services; and if he speaks of those at all, it is for the purpose rather of enhancing the display the Galatians gave of their attachment to him. There is nothing like upbraiding. He speaks as if he had been the obliged party, puts them in mind of the marks of regard they had heaped on him, and the happiness they then had felt in the indulgence and expression of their kind affections.

"Ye know how, through infirmity of the flesh, I preached the gospel unto you at the first. And my temptation which was in my flesh ye despised not, nor rejected; but received me as an angel of God, even as Christ Jesus" (Gal. 4:13,14.).

The expression "to preach the gospel *through* the infirmity of the flesh," is idiomatic, but its meaning is obvious.[20] The apostle's statement is plainly equivalent to, 'when I first preached the gospel to you — when I first laid before you the principles of Christianity — I labored under severe bodily indisposition.' The apostle had been *twice* in Galatia previously to his writing this epistle. It is to what happened on his first visit that he here alludes.

It is needless to indulge conjecture as to the particular disease under which the apostle labored at the time he introduced Christianity into Galatia, though it seems to have been one which in some way or other had a tendency to make his ministry less acceptable to strangers. Chandler says, "It was probably some tremor or convulsive motion of his nerves, arising from the extraordinary revelations made to him, or the glory which struck him blind at his first conversion, or the impressions which were made on him when he was snatched up into the third heavens" (2 Cor. 12:1-10.). Some interpreters consider "infirmity of the flesh" as referring to a state of extreme calamity generally — a state of poverty and persecution; but I apprehend the more definite sense is the more natural one.

The apostle does not say, 'I gave a strong proof of my affection to you in preaching to you the gospel when in a state of extreme indisposition,' or leave them to draw that inference; but he does say, 'notwithstanding all the comparative imperfection of my labors among you, arising from this indisposition, you appreciated them at a very high rate.'

"My temptation which was in my flesh ye despised not nor rejected."[21] "Temptation" is often in Scripture equivalent to affliction viewed as a trial of character (Luke 10:2,28. Acts 20:19. 1 Pet. 1:6.). The strongly idiomatical language in the text, translated into plain English, is equivalent to, 'You did not treat me or my labor with contempt or rejection when I was tried by the severe bodily indisposition under which I then labored. On the contrary, you "received me as an angel of God – as Christ Jesus." ' The same Greek word signifies angel and messenger; so that the first clause may mean, 'ye received me as a messenger of God.' At the same time, as the apostle's object is obviously to place in a very strong point of view the high esteem, the warm affection, the Galatians showed to him, I am disposed to acquiesce in the version of our translators, especially as this seems to have been a proverbial expression (2 Sam. 19:27.). 'An angel of God, nay, Christ Jesus Himself, could not have been more respectfully, more affectionately, received by you than I was with all my infirmities.'[22]

The apostle goes on with his description, – "Where is then the blessedness ye spake of? for I bear you record, that, if it had been possible, ye would have plucked out your own eyes, and have given them to me" (Gal. 4:15.). I do not think the rendering of the first clause of this verse is by any means happy. It does not seem to give the natural meaning of the words, and the sense it brings out does not well suit the context. The reading in the margin, 'what was,' is better than that in the text, where.[23] The words literally rendered are, 'What or how great was your mutual congratulation?[24] How did you then felicitate one another! Oh, how happy did you think yourselves in having me, though a poor diseased man, for your teacher. So highly did you value me, so much did you prize my labors, that there was nothing you would not have parted with to make me happy.' This is obviously the meaning of the proverbial phrase, "plucking out the eyes." It has been conjectured, and though ingeniously, it is still a conjecture, that Paul's indisposition was a severe affection of the eyes, and that this suggested the peculiar mode of expression.

These words contain a most beautiful picture of the native effect of the gospel, when believed, to attach the believer to him who has been the instrument of his conversion. It is possible for a minister to be very *popular,* as it is called, among a people to whom, in a spiritual sense, he is utterly useless; but it is not possible for a minister to be really useful to individuals without exciting in the minds and hearts of these individuals a very warm personal affection; and when the gospel is remarkably successful, the danger is not of converts not being sufficiently attached, but of their being inordinately attached, to the minister who has been the instrument of conveying to them so great a benefit. The being greatly applauded, is scarcely any proof that a minister has been successful; the being highly esteemed and cordially loved, is a considerably strong presumption that he has; the being regarded with indifference and dislike, is a clear proof that he has not.

The apostle concludes this affecting expostulation by proposing to them a very touching question. 'Am I therefore become your enemy, because I tell you the truth?"[25]

It is as if the apostle had said, 'Whence has originated the alienation of your sentiments in reference to me? How is it you regard him as an enemy whom you once regarded as your friend? Have I done any thing which warrants such a change? I remain unaltered; I tell you the truth – the same truth I originally told you – that truth on account of which you loved and honored me.'

The word translated, "to tell the truth,"[26] has a more extensive meaning. It refers to conduct generally. It is equivalent to, 'I have acted an honest, upright part. I have "walked uprightly according to the truth of the gospel."[27] I maintain and declare the same truth which, when you understood and believed it, filled you with joy and peace, and made you highly esteem and warmly love him who made it known to you; and my conduct towards you has been constantly influenced by that truth. It is strange that you should cease to love me for the very reason why you began to love me.'

Perhaps there may be some reference in these words to the faithful and somewhat severe language he had used in a preceding part of the epistle. In this case the words imply the following sentiment: – 'If I had used "all plainness of speech" in pointing out to you error and danger, this is no proof that I am your enemy; on the contrary, it is the truest proof of my friendship. "Faithful are the wounds of a friend, but the kisses of an enemy are deceitful." ' We are rather disposed to think the former mode of interpretation the true one.[28]

In the following verse the apostle traces the alienation of the affection of the Galatians to its true source in the unworthy acts of the Judaising teachers.

The change which took place in the estimate formed by the Galatians of the apostle at different times suggests important instruction to the ministers of religion in every age. It teaches them not to be unduly elated by popular applause; and not to be unduly depressed when it is withheld or withdrawn. It is a minister's duty to use every proper means to stand well in the estimation of those to whom he ministers, and it argues not magnanimity, but stupidity and ingratitude, to be insensible to the pleasure which the successful use of these means is calculated to excite. But he is a fool who makes the attainment of what is usually called popularity a leading object — he is worse than a fool who, in order to secure or retain it, conceals or modifies, in the slightest degree, his conscientious convictions, either as to faith or duty. The present approbation of conscience, and the anticipated approbation of his Lord, these are the objects the Christian minister should continually keep in view. When popularity is gained along with these, it is really valuable, for it insures the probability of usefulness; but the hosannas of the crowd are dearly purchased at the expense of one pang of conscience — one frown of the Savior. It is obviously, however, equally the interest of ministers and people that a cordial attachment should subsist between them, and that on both sides everything should be avoided that has a tendency to diminish and alienate mutual affection. It is very difficult for a minister to do his duty in a right spirit to a people when he has reason to think they have little or no attachment to him, and it is all but impossible for a people to derive spiritual advantage from a minister whom they do not respect and love. Happy is that Christian society when the minister loves his people, and the people love their minister "for the truth's sake," and when they manifest their mutual affection, not by warm protestations, but by his honestly and affectionately performing every pastoral duty, and by their "walking in all Christian commandments and ordinances blameless."

SECT. IV. THE APOSTLE EXPOSES THE UNWORTHY ACTS OF THE JUDAISING TEACHERS.

The Christian ministry, if entered on with appropriate sentiments, and prosecuted with conscienctious fidelity, will be found replete with difficulties. Its toils are arduous and unceasing — its trials numerous and severe. He who would "war this good warfare" must "endure hardness as a good soldier of Jesus Christ." The man who assumes the sacred character of a minister of Christ, with the honest intention of performing its duties (and he who resumes it without such an intention will find in the ultimate result of things that he had better have chosen any other profession) must lay his account with submitting to labors often ill-appreciated, sometimes unkindly requited, and with meeting with trials and afflictions which are the more severe as coming from a quarter from which nothing but support and encouragement had been expected.

It is one of the highest and purest pleasures man is susceptible of in the present state, which the faithful minister of Jesus Christ enjoys, when he clearly sees that his labors are answering their great purpose — that under his ministrations the thoughtless are becoming considerate — the ignorant intelligent — the spiritually foolish "wise unto salvation" — the bad becoming good — the good becoming better — those who are far from God brought near to Him, and those who are near Him brought still nearer, multitudes "striving to enter into the kingdom of God," and those who have entered "walking worthy of their high calling," and rapidly "growing up in all things to Him who is the head." Wherever this is in any good measure the case, there is a peculiarly strong and tender attachment between the Christian minister and his spiritual children, and the indulgence and display of it on both sides is a source of heartfelt satisfaction. He loves them for the sake of the truth which dwells in them, and which he trusts will abide in them for ever. He "lives," *i.e.* he enjoys life, if they but "stand fast in the Lord." They are his "joy and his hope" even now, and he trusts they will be his "glory and his crown of rejoicing in the presence of His Lord Jesus at His coming." On the other hand, they "esteem him very highly in love for his work's sake," and, among higher incentives, they feel the pain which their inconsistent behavior would give their best earthly friend, and the satisfaction which their consistent conduct would afford to him – a motive of no slight influence to their "walking in all the commandments and ordinances of the Lord blameless."

This is a delightful state of things, and every faithful minister may reasonably expect to know something of these joys; but at the same time, it is an uncertain state of things, and every faithful minister must be prepared to meet with some of his severest trials from a quarter from which he has already derived some of his highest satisfactions, and from which he was perhaps anticipating with confidence a long continuance of them. It is not an impossible, nor even an uncommon, thing for persons who seemed to be – who were – most tenderly attached to their minister, and attached to him in consequence of having received from him spiritual advantage, to have their affections entirely alienated from him whom they so greatly esteemed and loved; and what is worse still, it is not impossible, nor very uncommon, to find this alienation of affection to their minister rising out of, or at any rate connected with, indifference about, or rejection of, those grand peculiarities of Christian truths, of which, the faith and the love that grows out of it, form "the perfect bond"[29] which unites Christians in the love of their common Lord and of each other.

This is one of the severest trials which a Christian minister can meet with; and perhaps there are few situations in which he is so strongly tempted to indulge something like a resentful, almost a malignant feeling, as when thus situated, in reference to those designing men, whose selfish intrigues have been the means of injuring the best interests of his people, and robbing him of the dearest jewel of his heart. It is comparatively an easy thing for a minister to be reproached, and ridiculed, and persecuted by an ungodly world; but he only knows who has felt it how bitter it is to see those of whose conversion and spiritual improvement he flattered himself he had been the instrument, to guide whom to heaven he felt to be his most delightful work on earth, and to meet with whom in heaven was not one of the least delightful anticipations of eternity – to see them regard him with "hard unkindness, altered eye," especially if, when they are turning their backs on him, they also seem in extreme hazard of making shipwreck of faith and of a good conscience.

It is one of the high excellences of the epistles of Paul that they embody a perfect directory for the Christian minister. He can scarcely be placed in a situation of difficulty and trial which, in all its most prominent circumstances, Paul has not occupied before him, and all that he has ordinarily to do is just to copy his example, to be a follower of him, as he was a follower of his Master. The passage that lies before us exhibits him exposed to that perhaps severest ministerial trial to which I have been adverting, and it is worth our while to inquire somewhat particularly how he conducted himself under it.

In the verses preceding, he had endeavored to revive the almost extinguished embers of the Galatians' affections towards him, by showing how fondly he cherished the recollection of their kind regards and offices, by which their original intercourse had been characterised, assuring them that however they might be changed he remained unaltered, and if he ever deserved their esteem he had not become unworthy of it. He now proceeds to unfold the base acts by which the Judaising teachers had endeavored at once to seduce them from their attachment to their spiritual father, and from the simplicity and integrity of Christian truth, as he had taught it to them. "They zealously affect you, but not well; yea, they would exclude you, that ye might affect them. But it is good to be zealously affected always in a good thing, and not only when I am present with you" (Gal. 4:17,18.).

There can be no doubt as to the persons to whom the apostle here refers, though he does not name them. He plainly speaks of the Judaising teachers. We have here an instance of what I may call the *naturalness* of the apostle's style. When speaking on subjects peculiarly painful, or of persons peculiarly disagreeable to us, we mention their names as seldom as possible. There was no danger of the Galatians misunderstanding him or misapplying what he said, and he saves himself the pain of being more particular.

These verses admit of different interpretation according to the sense you give to the principal word in them rendered 'zealously affect.'[30] If we understand the word in the meaning given to it by our translators – a meaning, by the way, in which it never occurs anywhere else in the New Testament – the apostle states that these Judaising teachers pretended the warmest attachment to the Galatian converts,[31] and endeavored, though neither in the most honorable way, nor for the most honorable purposes, to ingratiate themselves with them – and that it was a leading object with them to exclude the Galatians from all intercourse with the apostle, to cut off all connection between them and him, that they might the more certainly succeed in their plan of retaining the Galatians' affections to themselves.

This is very good sense, and sufficiently well corresponds with the connection. It also presents us with a lesson which is not unneeded in our times, "to be on our guard," to use Riccaltoun's words, "against those who lie in wait to deceive, and to set a mark on those who make no scruple to attack the characters of men as good, if not better, than *themselves*, when they stand in their way – a practice generally disclaimed, but, alas! as generally practised." But we apprehend it labors under insuperable objections. It gives a meaning to the principal word in the sentence which it certainly never has anywhere else in the New Testament, and which it is doubtful if it has in any book, and it obliges us to understand the word with different shades of meaning in each case in which it occurs in these two verses.

The word properly signifies 'to be ardent,' and seems used only in this sense, either literally or figuratively, in the New Testament. It is used to signify 'to desire earnestly,' 1 Cor. 12:31; 14:1,39; 'to be zealous,' Rev. 3:19; and 'to envy,' Acts 7:9; 17:5; 1 Cor. 13:4; James 4:2.[32] It is the last of these senses in which we apprehend the apostle uses it in the passage before us – 'They envy you,' says the apostle, 'but not well or honorably.' Their endeavors to bring you over to Judaism originate, not in a benevolent, but in a very opposite principle. They grudge that Gentiles should be allowed to indulge the hope of sharing in the blessings of Messiah's reign, without submitting, like them, to the yoke of the Mosaic law. They were actuated by the same principle as the unbelieving Jews mentioned by Luke, Acts 17:5, who, "when some of their brethren believed along with a great multitude of the devout Greeks, moved with envy,[33] raised a tumult" in Thessalonica. The same principle operates in different ways, according to the different circumstances in which the person actuated by it is placed. What in an unbelieving Jew produced persecution, in a nominally converted Jew led to artful measures to entrammel the believing Gentiles with the burdensome requisitions of the Mosaic law.

"They envy you," says the apostle; "but not well" – honorably.[34] There is a praiseworthy emulation which, by a tolerable license, may be termed an honorable envy. If the Judaising teachers, on seeing the peace and comfort which the Galatian converts enjoyed in walking at liberty, keeping Christ's commandments, had been so struck with the happiness of their situation as to have set about acquiring those extensive liberal views of the gospel of Christ which Paul had exhibited to the Galatians, and which would have relieved their consciences from the observance of the Mosaic law, and enabled them, too, to "serve" God, "not in the oldness of the letter, but the newness of the spirit," that had been a praiseworthy ambition, an honorable envy. But the object of their earnest desire was not to obtain for themselves the fellowship of that liberty wherewith Christ had made the Galatian converts free, but to bind round their neck the yoke which they refused to have unloosed from their own. Their envy or emulation did not stir them up to rise to the level of the Galatian liberty, but to bring down the Galatians to the level of Jewish bondage.

'To gain their object,' says the apostle, 'they would exclude you,[35] that you may envy them.'[36] The meaning seems to be, They wished to exclude them; that is, they wished to shut out the converted Gentiles from associating with them on equal terms. They refused to "eat along with them" (Gal. 2:12.). They wished to go farther: they wished to exclude them from the privilege of the kingdom of the Messiah, unless they became Jews; for their doctrine was, "Except ye be circumcised after the manner of Moses, ye cannot be saved" (Acts 15:1.). They thus wished to shut out the converted Galatians, that they might envy them, − that they might form so high an estimate of the privilege of the circumcised as to solicit to be introduced into their society as the only true church, or at any rate, the highest form in the true church.

Alas, how much of this spirit has been discovered in the Christian church in every age! Alas, how much of it is to be met in our own age, notwithstanding its boasted illumination and liberality! How do individuals and denominations pride themselves on those distinctive dogmas or usages which separate them from the great body of Christians, − distinctions which must be of minor importance, which often rest entirely on human authority, − and obstinately refuse to admit to their communion men of the purest faith and manners, if they will not assume their badge, practically saying to all around them, "Stand by, I am holier than thou;" and, instead of endeavoring to select everything that is excellent in the various forms of Christianity, are chiefly bent on imposing their peculiarity, which after all may be a defect or a deformity, on the whole Christian world as a term of communion. This attempt to form a sort of privileged order in Christ's kingdom, where all are kings and priests, which originated among the Judaising Christians of the first age, is still made in a variety of ways; but wherever or by whomsoever it is made, every enlightened Christian will regard it with disapprobation; and do what lies in his power to expose its folly and wickedness, and prevent its success. "In reading the history of the church, it is hard to say whether what has gone, and still goes, under the name of *zeal,* has done more good or hurt to religion. When regularly conducted according to the apostle's rule, it is the fervor of love to God and man, the very best thing in the world. But how readily does it degenerate into what the apostle blames in the Judaisers, − zeal for a party; and that, again, into the bitterest enmity, which naturally leads to what we find the apostle cautioning against, 'biting and devouring one another!'"[37]

But to return to the apostle. "But it is good to be zealously affected always in a good thing, and not only when I am present with you" (Gal. 4:18.).

Those who are satisfied with our version explain these words in one or other of the following ways. Some refer them to the Galatians, thus: 'These men have used dishonorable means to attach you to them, and it is not very much to your honor that they have succeeded; but it is truly honorable to remain steadily attached to that which is good. You would act an honorable part, if the same zeal for the truths which you discovered when I was with you were still displayed by you, now that I am absent.' And others refer them to the apostle, thus: 'These men have dishonorably abused the facilities my absence offered them, by alienating your affections from me and fixing them on themselves; but my attachment to you is of that honorable kind in which absence makes no change. I loved you then; I love you now.'

We have already stated the reasons why we cannot accede to this mode of interpretation. Giving the verb its common meaning, and understanding it to be not in the middle but in the passive voice, we read, "But it is good," or honorable, "to be envied in a good thing always, and not only when I am present with you." It is better, and more honorable, to be the object of the envy of these Judaisers, than to be the subject of their triumph. It is as if the apostle said, 'Ye were once the subject of their envy; and I would God ye were the subject of their envy still. I wish your place in their estimation had been the same in my absence that it was when I was present with you.' The good opinion of some men may be bought at too high price.

The words, "in a good[38] thing," − or, literally, 'in that which is good,' − obviously refer to the faith and practice of Christianity; as when the apostle says, "Let not your good"[39] — that good thing of yours — "be evil spoken of." It is an honorable thing so to assert the privileges, profess the principles, perform the duties, and exhibit the influence of Christianity, as to command the respect, and even envy, of the men of the world. And the doing this ought not to depend on accidental circumstances, such as the presence or the absence of influential individuals, as a teacher or a parent. Wherever we are, and in whatever company, let us remember that it is an honorable thing to be envied for Christian attainments.[40]

SECT. V. — THE APOSTLE EXPRESSES HIS DEEP ANXIETY FOR THEM, AND HIS WISH TO BE PRESENT WITH THEM.

In the two succeeding verses, the apostle expresses his affectionate anxiety in reference to the Galatians in terms peculiarly touching. "My little children, of whom[41] I travail in birth again until Christ be formed in you, I desire to be present with you now, and to change my voice; for I stand in doubt of you" (Gal. 4:19,20.). A more beautiful picture of pastoral affection is perhaps not to be found in the sacred volume. He addresses them in terms the most expressive of tender regard, — "My children — my little children."[42] They had been converted to Christianity through his instrumentality; and they had given but too satisfactory evidence that they were to be addressed as "babes in Christ," not as "spiritual" — "men of full age" (Cor. 3:1. Heb. 5:13,14.).

The great object of his anxiety was, "that Christ might be formed in them;"[43] that is, that they might be true, thorough Christians. The phrase is peculiarly expressive. When a man becomes a true Christian, "Christ is formed in him;" that is, Christ's mode of thinking and feeling becomes his. The mind that was in Christ is in him. He has the spirit of Christ; so that he thinks as Christ thought, feels as Christ felt, speaks as Christ spoke, acts as Christ acted, suffers as Christ suffered. He is just an animated image of Jesus Christ. This, and nothing short of this, is to be a Christian; and to have his people thus made Christians, is the great object of every faithful minister. Nothing short of this will satisfy him.

The gaining of this object excited the apostle's most earnest, anxious desires in reference to the Galatians. There was nothing he would not willingly do and suffer to secure it. "I travail in birth again until Christ be formed in you." No figure could more strongly express the apostle's agony of anxiety and desire. "I travail again in birth." He had suffered much painful anxiety in reference to them formerly; and now he is, as it were, constrained by their inconstancy to endure for them a second time the sorrows of a mother.[44] Who that sincerely considers the weight of the interests which hang on Christ's being formed in the soul can wonder at the apostle's anxiety? The true cause of wonder and of regret is that such anxiety is so rare in those to whom is committed the care of souls — the management of the highest interests of the immortal mind.

"I desire to be present with you, that I may change my voice; for I stand in doubt of you." "I stand in doubt of you;"[45] that is, 'I do not know well what to think of you. I do not know well how to address you. I cannot think of treating you as apostates, and yet I cannot speak to you as consistent Christians.' "I desire to be present with you." 'I wish I were with you, and then I should be able to ascertain exactly how the matter stands.' "And to change my voice;" that is, "to vary my mode of address according to circumstances,"[46] as Luther has it. "I could reprove sharply them who are obstinate, and comfort the weak with sweet and loving words, as occasion should require." An epistle can but give what it has — the loving voice of a man can add and diminish, and change itself into all manners of affection, suited to times, places, and persons. The apostle well knew the importance of suiting the applications to the state of the spiritual patient — the importance, to use the apostle Jude's expression, of "making a difference,"[47] "having compassion" on some, and "saving others by fear, pulling them out of the fire." The presence of a minister with his people, and, so far as it is practicable, his intimate acquaintance with them, are of the utmost importance to the proper and successful discharge of the duties of the pastoral office. "Confidence about the profession of others cannot be scripturally regulated — if it vary not in degree according to the scriptural evidences they afford of believing the truth, and it is hard to say whether it be more dangerous when it is on the favorable or unfavorable side."[48]

What an admirable model for a Christian minister is the apostle Paul! May the Great Shepherd of the sheep deeply imbue all His servants with the spirit of Paul, which is, indeed, His own spirit, that they may be enabled to "feed the flock of the Lord, which He purchased with His blood" — to "gather the lambs in their arms, and to carry them in their bosom, and gently lead those which are with young" — to "seek that which is lost, and to bring that again which was driven away, and to bind up that which was broken, and to strengthen that which was sick;" or to adopt another set of figures, that they may be "gentle among the people of Christ, as a nurse cherisheth her children — so affectionately desirous of them as to be willing to impart to them, not only the gospel of God, but also their own souls" — "laboring night and day, exhorting, and comforting, and charging every one of them, as a father doth his children" (Thess. 2:7,11.). When such pastors abound, the church must flourish. From such labors divine influence will not be withheld. Then, as in the beginning, "The word of the Lord would have free course, and be glorified" — then would "the churches have rest, and be edified; walking in the fear of the Lord, and in the comfort of the Holy Ghost, they would be edified" (Acts 9:31.), and "the exalted Savior seeing of the travail of His soul would be satisfied."

SECT. VI. — ALLEGORICAL ILLUSTRATION.

In the paragraph which follows, the apostle endeavors to wean the Judaising Galatians from their strange attachment to an obsolete and servile economy by unfolding to them its true nature. This he does by referring them to an emblematical representation of the two economies taken from the domestic history of Abraham by the prophet Isaiah (ch. 54:1), and amplified by himself.[49]

"Tell me, ye that desire to be under the law, do ye not hear the law? For it is written, that Abraham had two sons; the one by a bond maid, the other by a free woman. But he who was of the bond woman was born after the flesh; but he of the free woman was by promise. Which things are an allegory: for these are the two covenants; the one from the Mount Sinai, which gendereth to bondage, which is Agar. For this Agar is Mount Sinai in Arabia, and answereth to Jerusalem which now is, and is in bondage with her children. But Jerusalem which now is above is free, which is the mother of us all. For it is written, Rejoice, thou barren that bearest not; break forth and cry, thou that travailest not: for the desolate hath many more children than she which hath an husband. Now we, brethren, as Isaac was, are the children of promise. But as then he that was born after the flesh persecuted him that was born after the Spirit, even so it is now. Nevertheless, what saith the Scripture? Cast out the bond woman and her son: for the son of the bond woman shall not be heir with the son of the free woman. So then, brethren, we are not children of the bond woman, but of the free" (Gal. 4:21-31.).

1. INTRODUCTION.

The word "hear"[50] in this place, as in many other places of Scripture, is equivalent to, 'to attend to,' or 'to understand.'[51] The "law" may be interpreted, either of the Pentateuch, the five books of Moses,[52] or of the Mosaic institution of which it gives an account. The latter is its meaning when it occurs the first time, and the former seems to be its meaning when it occurs a second time. It matters little in which way you understand it. The force of the apostle's question is plainly this, 'If you Galatians, who aspire to circumcision, and subjection to the Mosaic law as a privilege, understood the true nature of the law, as described in the inspired account of it, you would not be so anxious to bring yourselves under its yoke — you would find that to you it is fraught, not with safety and honor, but with danger and disgrace.'[53]

The notions about the law which the Judaising teachers had instilled into the minds of the Galatian converts were false. Their attachment to the law was formed on these false notions; and therefore the shortest and surest way of weaning them from their attachment to the law was the exposure of the falsehood of these notions, and the statement of the opposite truth. This statement the apostle does not make in direct terms; but by a reference to a piece of Jewish history which afforded a striking emblematical representation of the truth on this subject, and which had already been employed by the prophet Isaiah.

2. THE ALLEGORY.

"For it is written, that Abraham had two sons; the one by a bond maid, the other by a free woman. But he who was of the bond woman was born after the flesh; but he of the free woman was by promise" (Gal. 4:22,23.).

"For"[54] is, we apprehend, a mere connective particle here. "It is written,"[55] is an ordinary formula of quotation. Here it does not mean that what follows is written in so many words in any of the Old Testament books; but that the facts here stated are related there. Abraham had a number of sons besides Isaac and Ishmael; but it is to these, and to the circumstances of their birth, subsequent conduct, history, and fate, that the apostle's discussion exclusively relates. Ishmael was the son of Hagar, a female slave. Isaac was the son of Sarah, a free woman, of the same rank with her husband. Ishmael was born in the ordinary course of nature. Isaac was born in consequence of a peculiar interference of Heaven, made known "by promise." Such are the facts of the history.

3. THE ALLEGORY EXPLAINED.

"Which things are an allegory: for these are the two covenants; the one from the Mount Sinai, which gendereth to bondage, which is Agar. For this Agar is Mount Sinai in Arabia, and answereth to Jerusalem which now is, and is in bondage with her children. But Jerusalem which is above is free, which is the mother of us all. For it is written, Rejoice, thou barren that bearest not; break forth and cry, thou that travailest not: for the desolate hath many more children than she which hath an husband" (Gal. 4:24-27.).

The introductory words, "which things are an allegory," have occasioned much difficulty to interpreters.[56] Some have considered them as equivalent to, 'these events were intended to typify corresponding events under the Christian 'economy, and their history is to be viewed as an obscure prophecy.' The words certainly do not necessarily imply this; and the admission of the principle on which the interpretation goes, 'that everything, or almost everything, in Old Testament history is typical,' would lay a foundation for the indulgence of the wildest dreams of the imagination,[57] and would withdraw the mind from the rational interpretation of the Old Testament history, and the important religious and moral instruction which thus interpreted it is calculated to convey.[58]

Others consider the words as equivalent to, 'These historical facts may be turned to account as affording an emblematical illustration of the true nature of the two divine economies of which I am discoursing;' but it seems plain that the apostle speaks of these facts as if they had already been used as emblems. He does not make the allegory; but he takes up an allegory formed to his hand, and applies it to his purpose.

I apprehend the phrase, "which things are an allegory," is just equivalent to, "which things are allegorized;"[59] to wit, in the book of the prophet Isaiah, in the passage which the apostle immediately quotes from the fifty-fourth chapter.[60] On no other supposition can you account for his quoting this passage; and this principle of interpretation, as we shall soon see, carries light through the whole paragraph.[61]

Let us first of all examine the passage in Isaiah, quoted by the apostle, in which the allegory is to be found. The passage is quoted from the Greek translation commonly in use when the apostle wrote, and it exactly enough corresponds with the sense of the Hebrew original. The meaning of the closing phrase is better given here than in our translation of the Old Testament — "her that hath *a*," or rather *the*, "husband," conveys the idea of the original phrase better than "the married wife."

The prophet's address obviously goes on the following hypothesis: a man who, as it appears from the apostle's interpretation, is Abraham, has two wives, – the one of whom, Sarah, on account of her barrenness, lives as it were in temporary widowhood; while the other, Hagar, "has the husband," and brings him a son. The mystical Sarah is congratulated by the prophet because the period of her reproach and desertion is hastening to an end, and because her offspring shall ultimately be more numerous than that of the mystical Hagar who long seemed to occupy her place.

In plain terms, the passage is a prediction that a period was coming when the spiritual descendants of Abraham should be far more numerous than his merely natural descendants ever were – when the true children of God should be more numerous than the nominal children of God, the Israelitish people, had been. We have a similar use made of a fact in ancient history by the prophet Jeremiah respecting the Babylonian captivity, and by the evangelist Matthew in reference to the slaughter of the infants of Bethlehem (Gen. 30:1,2. Jer. 31:15. Matth. 2:17.).

But let us look at the apostle's explanation of the allegory. These women spoken of by the prophet allegorically, Sarah and Hagar, "are the two covenants." This is a mode of speech of the same kind as when our Lord says of the bread, "This is My body," that is, it represents it, signifies it; and when the apostle says of the smitten rock, "That rock was Christ." In this allegory, these two women represent or signify the two covenants. Similar modes of expression are to be found, – Genesis 41:26; Matthew 13:20,22,38,39; John 6:41; Apoc. 17:15. I have already stated to you that the English word "covenant" does not exactly answer to the original term,[62] which is much more comprehensive in its meaning. 'Constitution' or "arrangement' comes nearer to it. But what are the two constitutions or covenants here spoken of? Some interpreters explain them of what are ordinarily termed the covenant of works and the covenant of grace. Others, of the two dispensations, the Mosaic and the Christian. An examination of what the apostle says will probably convince us, that while there is an approximation to truth in both of these opinions, neither of them is exactly accurate. "The one," says the apostle, "from the Mount Sinai gendereth unto bondage, which is Agar. For this Agar is Mount Sinai in Arabia, and answereth to Jerusalem, which now is, and is in bondage with her children." The one covenant or constitution is that from Mount Sinai; it is that order of things under which the Jews were placed at Mount Sinai to keep them a separate people, commonly termed "the law." That constitution "gendereth to bondage"[63] – bringeth forth children who are slaves.[64] The children of a constitution or covenant are the persons who are under it, and whose characters are formed by that constitution. The children of "the law" were the Israelites generally, and the Gentiles who submitted to it. It was formed on a servile principle, "do, and live;" and so far as men were influenced by it only, they must have had a servile and not a filial character.

We are never to forget, however, that the promise was before the law, and that the law did not disannul the promise. Believers under the law were not destitute of the filial character; but the law under which they were, infused even into their feelings and services something servile; while, on the other hand, unbelievers under the law, who formed the great majority, were entirely slaves, obeying merely from the fear of external evil and the hope of external good. This is the constitution which Hagar in the allegory represents.

The words which follow, "For this Agar is Mount Sinai in Arabia," have greatly perplexed interpreters[65] Their perplexity seems principally to have originated in supposing that the apostle was speaking of the woman Hagar, while in reality he is speaking of the word only – her name. The truth is, that the words seem not to contain an explanation of any part of the allegory, but merely to embody a passing remark as to the meaning of the word "Agar" in the Arabian language. "For this word Agar in Arabia is," or signifies, "Mount Sinai."[66] The word "Agar" in Arabia signifies a rock, a rocky part of the country, a rocky mountain such as we know Sinai is; and we are told by oriental travellers, that this name is given by the Arabs to that mountain. 'The rock,' by way of eminence.[67] It is just as if the apostle had said, 'By the way, it is a remarkable circumstance, that in Arabia the name of Mount Sinai is Agar.' The words then (whether proceeding originally from the pen of the apostle, or, what is not impossible, being originally a marginal remark afterwards introduced into the text) are to be considered as parenthetical, and the sense goes on just as if they had not been introduced.[68] "Agar," then, in the allegory, "answereth,"[69] or corresponds, "to Jerusalem that now is, and is in bondage with her children." Jerusalem, the metropolis of the Holy Land, the seat of religion, is naturally enough used for Judaism. "Jerusalem that now is,"[70] is just Judaism in its present state. Now Judaism in the apostle's times, was just as it were the embodied representation of the constitution given at Mount Sinai, unmodified by the promise. The unbelieving Jews were under the unmitigated slavish influence of that economy. "Jerusalem which now is, is in bondage with her children." Agar is the emblem of the law, and Ishmael of those who are under it.

The other part of the allegory is more briefly explained, — "But Jerusalem which is above is free, which is the mother of us all."[71] It is quite plain, though it is not expressed, that Sarah the barren woman in the allegory is significant of another covenant or constitution which answereth to what is here termed "Jerusalem from above."[72] What that constitution is, it is not very difficult to perceive. It is not what systematic theologians call the covenant of grace; far less is it what is ordinarily called the Christian dispensation. Let us look at the allegory, and it will guide us in our explanation of it.

Sarah, the barren woman, was Abraham's wife previously to his taking Hagar for his concubine. The constitution of which Sarah was the type in the allegory, must surely then be a constitution which existed prior to that of which Hagar was the type. What is it then but the other constitution which the apostle in the context contrasts with the law, even "the covenant which was confirmed before of God" in reference to the Messiah, and which the law could not disannul? It is just the method of salvation made known to Adam immediately after the fall, more fully made known to Abraham, and still more fully unfolded by the prophet, and "manifested" in the gospel revelation.

This constitution, of which Sarah is the emblem, corresponds to, is embodied in, "the Jerusalem above." These words are often interpreted of the celestial church; but in this way of considering the phrase, it is difficult to see what is meant by its being the "mother of all believers." The word "above"[73] is used in reference to time as well as place. The phrase before us may mean either the Jerusalem that is above in place — that is, the heavenly Jerusalem, or it may mean the Jerusalem above in time, or the ancient Jerusalem.[74] That the last is its meaning here, seems probable from its being contrasted, not with Jerusalem below or Jerusalem on the earth, but with Jerusalem that now is. Jerusalem seems to have been a seat of religion before the Israelitish economy. Melchizedec, the priest of the most high God, was king of Salem, which we know was an ancient name for Jerusalem, and which was embodied in its later appellation.[75] Zedec seems also to have been an ancient name of Jerusalem. This is asserted by the pseudo Josephus.[76] Adonizedec is the king of Jerusalem as Adoni-bezek is the king of Bezek; Joshua 10:1; Judges 1:5; and there seems a reference to this in Isaiah 1:26; Jer. 31:33. In this case, "Jerusalem above," or the ancient Jerusalem, is a very appropriate emblem of the religion of fallen man in its primitive form before "the law was added," which is substantially the religion of the New Testament, the latter being the complete development of the former. It is, I apprehend, in reference to the state of things in which Melchizedec was a priest, that our Lord is termed a priest, not after the order of Aaron, who was the priest of a peculiar people, but after the order of Melchizedec, who was the priest of mankind. The expression means more than this.

If, however, we should understand the word "above" as referring to place, the idea is this, — 'All believers of every age have gone to heaven; and when a man becomes a believer, he joins the great society they belong to.' Thus the conversion of the Gentiles is described as their coming and sitting down "with Abraham, Isaac, and Jacob in the kingdom of their Father;" and the apostle, speaking of believers on the earth, says, That they are "come to the spirits of the just made perfect" (Matth. 8:11. Heb. 12:22.). In either view of it, Jerusalem is the true spiritual church consisting of genuine believers from the beginning down to the present time. That church is free. Its principles are free and generous. They lead men to obey from love. Its first principle is, 'believe and live; and love, and do, and enjoy.' In the original state of the spiritual church, its members were untrammelled by such carnal ordinances as were afterwards enjoined "because of transgressions." With the exception of a very few simple rites, its service was spiritual and rational. It preserved a filial spirit in all who belonged to it. Even under the servitude of the law, and now in the most perfect state as to revelation in which it is to be exhibited on earth, its members are "made free by the Son, and are free indeed."[77]

This primitive catholic church, which is founded on the promise of mercy, is "the mother of us all," says the apostle; that is, of all believers whether they be Jews or Gentiles. They are all Abraham's spiritual seed — all children of the mystical Sarah; and they are a numerous family — "a multitude, which no man can number, of all nations, and kindreds, and people, and tongues" (Rev. 7:9.).

4. THE ALLEGORY EXTENDED AND EXPLAINED.

Such is the apostle's exposition of the prophet's allegory. But he not only explains the prophet's allegory, he also extends it. He has already done so in introducing the idea of the free and servile condition of the emblematical females and their offspring; but he further employs it by showing how strikingly the conduct and the fate of the servile and the free-born offspring of Abraham emblematically represent the conduct and fate of those "who are of the law," and those "who are of the faith of Christ."

Let us consider a little more particularly this application.

"Now we, brethren, as Isaac was, are the children of promise.[78] But as then he that was born after the flesh persecuted him that was born after the Spirit, even so it is now. Nevertheless, what saith the Scripture? Cast out the bond woman and her son: for the son of the bond woman shall not be heir with the son of the free woman" (Gal. 4:28-30.). The word "we" plainly refers to all who, with the apostle, whether Jews or Gentiles, expected salvation by faith in Christ without the works of the law. 'We believers are, as Isaac was, "the children of promise." ' The general meaning of the word is plain enough. 'In this allegory, we believers are represented by Isaac, and those who are of the works of the law are represented by Ishmael. We and they stand in a relation to God, and to one another, similar to that in which Isaac and Ishmael stood to their father, and to one another.'

There can be no doubt that this is the leading idea; but it is not so easy distinctly to perceive in what the similarity consists. At first view, the words may seem merely to state the fact that, as Sarah, in the allegory, represents the promise, — so Isaac represents believers, the children of the promise. Had this, however, been the apostle's meaning, he would not have said "the children of promise," or rather, "children of promise," but 'the children of the promise.'

Some have sought the resemblance in Isaac being "by promise," in opposition to Ishmael "being born of the flesh." The relation between the Israelites and God, originating in the law, was a relation into which they were brought by natural descent: the relation into which believers are brought with God originates in a supernatural divine influence, which is the subject of promise. Others seek it in the fact that Isaac was a genuine believer, and in this sense "a child of the promise." 'As Isaac was by faith an heir of the promise, so are we.' Neither of these views is satisfactory. I am disposed to think the phrase, "children of promise," is a Hebraism, and is equivalent to promised children. Isaac was Abraham's promised son. It was to him that the promise of a son made to his father referred, — not Ishmael, who, though Abraham's son, was not his promised son. Now, in like manner, believers are the promised children — the spiritual seed promised to Abraham, as the father of all who believe. This idea is strikingly expressed by the apostle in his Epistle to the Romans, when he states that 'Abraham was justified while uncircumcised, that it might be plain that uncircumcised believers were his spiritual children, and that no circumcised person was his spiritual child unless he was also a believer' (Rom. 4:10-12.); and when he states that 'all Abraham's children are not reckoned his seed;[79] and that they who are merely the children of the flesh, these are not the sons of God, but the children of the promise are counted for the seed' (Rom. 9:7,8.).

In this statement is plainly implied its counterpart, that they who are of the works of the law — who expect justification and eternal life by observing its requisitions — are, like Ishmael, not promised children. It is not to them that the promises made to Abraham's spiritual seed refer at all: it is to us believers, and to us alone, that all the glorious privileges ascribed to Abraham's seed, mentioned in the promise, belong. Ishmael may possess the wilderness; but Canaan is Isaac's promised portion. Ishmael may obtain a number of gifts, not without their value; but the birthright and inheritance are Isaac's.

The apostle proceeds to show that the analogy holds as to the character and conduct of the two classes, of which Ishmael and Isaac are emblems. "But as then he that was born after the flesh persecuted him that was born after the Spirit, even so it is now" (Gal. 4:29.). The fact on which the analogy proceeds is this, that "he that was born after the flesh" — that is, Ishmael — "persecuted," or maltreated, "him that was born after the Spirit," that is, Isaac. How Ishmael came to be said to be "born after the flesh," we have already explained. He was Abraham's son; and that is all that can be said of him. But how is Isaac said to be "born after the Spirit"? We have no reason to doubt that Isaac was a true saint — a man "born of the Spirit;" but whether he was so at the time Ishmael persecuted him we cannot tell. And, at any rate, there does not seem any reference to what is ordinarily called regeneration here; for it is of Ishmael and Isaac as children of Abraham that the phrases "after the flesh" and "after the Spirit" are employed. The phrase "after the Spirit," as opposed to that "after the flesh," seems equivalent to 'in an extraordinary manner, by Divine agency,' much in the same way as it is used in the following expression: — "Not by might, nor by power, but by my Spirit, saith the Lord of hosts" (Zech. 4:6.).

The fact to which the apostle refers is recorded, Gen. 21:9-12: "And Sarah saw the son of Hagar the Egyptian, which she had born unto Abraham, mocking. Wherefore she said unto Abraham, Cast out this bond woman and her son: for the son of the bond woman shall not be heir with my son, even with Isaac. And the thing was very grievous in Abraham's sight because of his son. And God said unto Abraham, Let it not be grievous in thy sight because of the lad, and because of thy bond woman; in all that Sarah hath said unto thee, hearken unto her voice; for in Isaac shall thy seed be called." What the precise nature of this persecuting or mocking was it is needless to inquire. It is plain from Sarah's opinion, which was sanctioned by the express approbation of God, that it was no trifle — something which made it necessary to banish Ishmael from the family. The cause of Ishmael's dislike, and ill-usage of Isaac, though not recorded, was very probably envy of his brother's peculiar privileges.

In this point, then, says the apostle, the analogy holds. Those whom Ishmael represents in the allegory still persecute those whom Isaac represents. The descriptive appellations given to Ishmael and Isaac are given also to those whom they represent. "They of the law" are represented as, like Ishmael, "born after the flesh." They are mere outward Jews. They become the nominal people of God, either by natural descent, or by submitting to the carnal ordinances of the Mosaic institution. There is nothing spiritual in their relation or character — nothing supernatural in the way in which they are formed. On the other hand, "they of the promise" — they who believe are represented as, like Isaac, born of the Spirit. They are "Israelites indeed," "inward Jews."[80] They become the true children and people of God by the belief of the truth, which belief is of the operation of God. Their relation to God is spiritual, and that relation is supernaturally formed.

'Now,' says the apostle, 'as Ishmael persecuted Isaac, so do those born of the flesh persecute still those who are born of the Spirit.' The Jews, who obstinately rejected Christ and his religion, persecuted those who embraced them. They were the fiercest enemies of the primitive church. It is of them the apostle speaks when he says, "They both killed the Lord Jesus and their own prophets, and have persecuted us; and they please not God, and are contrary to all men; forbidding us to speak to the Gentiles, that they might be saved, to fill up their sins alway: for the wrath is come upon them to the uttermost" (Thess. 2:15,16.). The best commentary on these words is to be found in the book of the Acts of the Apostles (Acts 4:1-6,18; 5:17,40; 6:9, etc; 9:1,2; 13:45; 14:19; 17:5,13; 21:20; 22:22,etc; 23:2,12; etc, etc.). In the words of an accomplished writer,[81] "As Ishmael persecuted Isaac with taunt, and sarcasm, and keen-edged mockery, nay, possibly with heavier weapons, and more substantial tokens of boyish antipathy, and rivalry, and passion, the buffet and the blow, and all the tortures and petty tyranny which Ishmael's superior age and strength enabled him to exercise over his envied brother, most probably a delicate and gentle child, — as he turned out a meek, and tranquil, and meditative man, — even so the children of the servile persecuted those of the free Jerusalem. Stung with jealous rage at the claims of the infant church — which had arisen, as it were, to push them from their stools, to rob them of their birth-right, to supplant them in the prerogatives which they thought and gloried in as rightfully their own — they poured upon the head of the detested sect the last extremes of scorn and cruelty. They smote now the heart of the Christian with the scourge of tongues, and now his person with the lictors' rods; now they sought to overwhelm his character with barbed and venomous reproaches, 'sharp sleet of arrowy shower,' and now hurled at his head missiles of more ponderous and crushing sway. Wherever their influence reached, they labored in stirring up against the church a perpetual and unrelenting persecution, and exhausted all the resources of subtlety and violence in testing to the uttermost the meekness, and patience, and power of endurance which that young church, mighty in weakness, had inherited from its founders."

Those unbelieving Jews were not, however, the only class of the children of the bond woman who persecuted the children of the free woman. A considerable number of Jews professed to believe Jesus to be the Messiah, while at the same time they retained their carnal views as to the character of the Messiah, the design of His mission, and the nature of His kingdom; and these nominal, false Christians harassed those who had juster, more spiritual, and more liberal views of the Christian economy. These men called themselves Christians; but they were in reality "the enemies of the cross of Christ," and the enemies of all those who gloried in it.

But the apostle traces an analogy, not only between the conduct of Ishmael and Isaac, and that of the two classes he is speaking of, but also between their destinies. "Nevertheless, what saith the Scripture? Cast out the bond woman and her son: for the son of the bond woman shall not be heir with the son of the free woman" (Gal. 4:30.). The words here quoted are, as we have seen, the words of Sarah (Gen. 21:10.) to Abraham when she was displeased at Ishmael's mocking and abusing her son. The counsel of Sarah, we are told, "was very grievous in Abraham's sight because of his son;" but it was sanctioned by divine approbation, and was of course followed by Abraham. (Gen. 21:12.). The design of the apostle is plainly to bring before the mind of his readers these ideas. Ishmael was expelled the family of Abraham, and excluded from the inheritance. "They who are of the law" shall be expelled from the family of God, and excluded from the inheritance of his children. Isaac obtained the inheritance; and so also shall all "they of the promise," or in other and equivalent words, "of the faith of Christ."

It is not at all improbable that the apostle here has a reference to the plain and public proof which Jehovah was soon about to give in the complete destruction of the Jewish polity — of His rejection of the unbelieving Jews as His people — "the cutting off of the natural branches," as he phrases it in the eleventh chapter of the Epistle to the Romans. "Ere long the decree went forth from God which stript them of the power they loved so well, and had wielded so unsparingly, of persecuting the chosen seed. As of Hagar and Ishmael it had been said, so of the Mosaic institute, and those who clung to it as their justifying plea, their title to God's favor, their glory, and their hope — of the law and of her children it was said, 'Cast out the bond maid and her sons.' The authority of the Mosaic law was abolished — the system of its institutions was subverted. From the tents wherein they had dwelt so long around the tabernacle and pavilion of their God, from the mountain of Jehovah's heritage, from the pale of his acknowledged people, his chosen family, they were driven forth, and long, like Ishmael, they have had their abiding place in the wilderness, and long have wandered to and fro, 'tribes of the wandering foot and weary eye,' seeking rest, and finding none, fainting often for thirst, like Hagar and her son, in Beersheba's wilderness, yet still by a special Providence sustained and miraculously delivered, earning from the wilderness over which they are scattered a random and scanty sustenance, like that old huntsman of the desert, 'their hand against every man,' or at least every man's hand against them. Meanwhile 'the free Jerusalem, who is the mother of us all,' hath been brought back again in nuptial pomp into the palace of the king, with gladness and with mirth on every side, and now shines forth in matron dignity, rejoicing in the name received from God, of "Sarah" — lady that is, a princess — the acknowledged spouse of her Savior-God, — the consort-queen of the King of kings. The Lord hath looked on her reproach, and she hath become 'the joyful mother of children.' She has broke forth on the right hand and the left, and her seed has inherited the nations. How amply this prediction has been fulfilled since 'the promise' took the name of the gospel, we need not tell.

> 'The world hath seen a nation born—
> A nation in a day.'

And the time is coming when the Lord shall yet more illustriously fulfil His promise to Sarah, that He will make her seed as 'the dust of the earth, innumerable,' — when all of the race of man shall become the children of the church, and even far scattered Israel shall return from their long and weary exile, and with 'the innumerable multitude out of every kindred, and people, and tongue, and nation,' shall be adopted into her glorious and happy household.

> 'Rise crown'd with light, imperial Salem, rise!
> Exalt thy towering head, and lift thine eye,
> See a long race thy spacious courts adorn,
> See future sons and daughters yet unborn,
> In crowding ranks on every side arise,
> Demanding life, impatient for the skies.'[82]

But it would be wrong to confine the apostle's meaning to this particular proof of God's casting the children of the bond woman out of His family. He seems plainly to have meant to bring forward the general truth, 'That no man who sought for salvation by obedience to the Mosaic law could possibly obtain an interest in the blessings of the Christian salvation.' Whether he rejected Christianity altogether, or whether he endeavored to connect an acknowledgment of the Messiahship of Jesus Christ along with obedience to the Mosaic law, as the ground of his hopes of acceptance with God, he equally shut himself out from participating in the blessings of Christ's salvation, by refusing to receive it in the only form in which it is offered — "The gift of God through Jesus Christ our Lord." The leading law of the spiritual church in all ages is, "the man who is just by faith shall live." That law, as more fully and plainly stated under the New Testament dispensation, runs thus, "Whosoever believeth shall be saved" — "God so loved the world that he gave His only begotten Son, that whosoever believeth in Him should not perish, but have everlasting life." He who refuses to accept of salvation in this way must want it: For "there is no name given under heaven, or among men, whereby men must be saved" but the name of Jesus, and no way of abtaining a personal interest in His salvation but by believing. "He that believeth not shall be damned." "He is condemned already, and the wrath of God abideth on him."

While there can be no doubt, then, that the apostle had directly in view the Jewish opposers of true spiritual Christianity, his principles are much more widely applicable. In every age, not only have there been two parties — the church and the world, like Abraham's family and the surrounding nations — but there have been two parties in what is called the church — those who submit to God's method of justification, and those who go about to establish a method of justification of their own — like Isaac and Ishmael, both in the family of Abraham externally. There always have been men who professed to believe Christianity, while they did not understand its true nature; and who, while they called Christ their only Lord and Savior, were in reality the servants of men, and trusting in something else than His righteousness for their salvation. Sometimes this has been the character of the great body of a religious society, as in the case of the Roman church, falsely styled catholic. In all ages it has been the character of some in every religious body. These children of the bond woman have always been persecutors of the children of the free — Rome Papal has been a more cruel enemy of vital spiritual Christianity than ever Rome Pagan was. The worst enemies of the truly evangelical party in every established church are their nominal brethren who think of justification "as if it were by the works of the law;" and, generally speaking, enlightened, consistent Christians, with whom Christ is all in all, are the objects of the peculiar dislike of those who, while they cling to the name Christian, have dismissed from their religion almost all direct reference to Christ as the Lord of their faith, and the ground of their hope.

These two classes of men have always existed, and are likely in some measure to continue to exist to the end. The tares and the wheat will not be completely separated till the harvest. But they shall then be seaprated. "The children of the bond woman shall not be heirs with the children of the free woman." Mere nominal Christians — those who have never been "justified by the faith of Christ," nor regenerated by His Spirit, though they may have had a place in His church here, of which they were unworthy, shall have no place in the church above. They seemed here "children of the kingdom;" but instead of being admitted to "sit down with Abraham, Isaac, and Jacob, in the kingdom of their Father," they shall be "cast out into outer darkness, where there is weeping, and wailing, and gnashing of teeth." This is a consideration which may well alarm us all. Nothing but scriptural, spiritual, Christian, religion will save. Nothing short of an implicit belief of Christ's gospel, an unreserved dependance on His atonement, a universal transformation by His Spirit, a constant reliance on His assistance, a habitual submission to His will, can prove us "children of the promise" — heirs of the inheritance.

The paragraph, the illustration of which I have finished, is perhaps above all others fitted to give distinct and accurate ideas respecting the great economies, or covenants, or arrangements by which God has developed and executed his purpose of mercy to man. I take leave of it, in the words of the author already repeatedly quoted, in his elegant dissertation on this important passage. "Such is the allegory drawn, first by the prophet and then by the apostle, from the history of Abraham's household. We do not need the practical inference, at least in the same shape which Paul intended the Galatian church to draw from its consideration — that they should steadfastly resist the acts and efforts of the Judaising teachers, by whom they were at this time assailed, and against whom he wrote the epistle before us, laboring as they did, and straining every nerve to bring back the Galatian converts unto the yoke of an over-dated bondage, by persuading them of the necessity of submission to the Mosaic institute for ultimate salvation. Be then our first practical lession a lesson of gratitude that we need not this instruction; that to us it has been given distinctly to behold 'the wall of partition' utterly thrown down, and 'the handwriting of ordinances' finally abolished, to exult in the unclouded light and unfettered liberty of the gospel, and to acknowledge as the common 'mother of us all' the mystic Sarah, the free Jerusalem. And be it further ours, to take especial heed that we not merely call ourselves, but are, her children; that our character is befitting those who profess to be the children not of the bond woman, but of the free; that we love our heavenly Father with a filial and ingenuous love, and our Christian brethren with fraternal regard and sympathy; that we imbibe our spiritual mother's spirit, and by her maternal instructions are daily becoming educated and ripe for heaven. So shall we share the present privileges of her holy household; so shall we sympathise and exult in the glorious prospects which are before her, even in our fallen world; so especially shall we share her joy in the anticipation now, in the inheritance hereafter, of 'the glory that is to be revealed,' when she shall be presented to her immortal spouse in sublime, unsullied loveliness, 'a glorious church without spot or wrinkle;' when she shall be acknowledged and welcomed by all the inhabitants of heaven as 'the bride,' 'the Lamb's wife;' when He shall encircle her fair brows with the spouse's diadem, and she shall stand on His right hand as queen 'in the gold of Ophir;' when all her blessed seed shall share her glory and her joy; when she shall take and make them princes in the land of immortality – 'kings and priests unto God, even their Father.' "[83]

5. THE ALLEGORY PRACTICALLY IMPROVED.

That partial obscurity which occasionally perplexes the interpreters of the apostolical epistles is easily accounted for, and is not altogether to be regretted. It is easily accounted for, arising as it does in a good measure out of their very nature as epistolary compositions, written in a remote age to persons whose modes of thought were very different from ours, and of whose particular circumstances we are in a great measure ignorant, except so far as these can be gathered from the epistles themselves;[84] and it is not altogether to be regretted, for not only does it stimulate attention, but it is one of the many marks of authenticity which belong to these writings.

Without that particularity of allusion by which they are so remarkably distinguished, and from which occasionally obscurity must necessarily arise, the internal evidence that the epistles are no forgeries, would not have been by any means so strong as it is. On the supposition of the epistles being what they profess to be, they could not have been without their obscurities to us, unless accompanied by a collection of historical notices and documents more voluminous than the letters they were meant to illustrate.

A careful study of the epistles and of the history of the age in which they were written will frequently suggest important hints for the elucidation of passages which otherwise would be extremely obscure. This is a source of satisfactory interpretation which is by no means yet exhausted. And in the absence of all direct information, it not unfrequently happens that a reference to opinions and customs, modes of thought, and modes of expression, known to have existed at the period when, and among the people to whom, these epistles were written, enables us more distinctly to apprehend the meaning of a statement, the appropriateness of an illustration, and the force of an argument.

This remark applies, we apprehend, to the somewhat difficult paragraph in the exposition of which we are engaged. We know certainly that the Jews were accustomed to plume themselves on their descent from Abraham, Isaac, and Jacob. From connection with these patriarchs, they conceived that the most valuable blessings necessarily flowed. They looked upon all the other nations of the world as belonging to an inferior class, and considered submission to the rite of circumcision and to the other ordinances of that law which had been given to Israel, as the only way in which these nations could find admission into the privileged order of the people of God. Jewish contempt and hatred of gentilism and Gentiles, were proverbial; and this mode of thinking and feeling was not confined in the primitive age to the unbelieving Jews; it prevailed to a considerable degree among the great majority of converts to Christianity, and formed a leading trait in the characters of those Judaising teachers, from whose artful attempts the Galatian gentile converts were exposed to considerable hazard of being induced to sacrifice that entire reliance on Jesus Christ for salvation, which the apostle had taught them, and place at least a portion of their dependance on their being admitted by circumcision among the carnal descendants of Abraham.

In prosecuting their object, there is little doubt that they dwelt much on circumcision being the seal of God's covenant; and that while uncircumcised, men were still aliens from the commonwealth of Israel, and strangers to the covenant of promise; and they not improbably, in illustration of their doctrine, that faith in Christ as the Messiah without circumcision was not sufficient, might in allusion to the history of Abraham state, that they who acknowledged the Messiah yet did not submit to circumcision, were but imperfectly connected with Abraham. If they were of the family at all, it was but as Ishmael was, not as Isaac. Nothing could better comport with the sentiments and feelings of these false teachers. Nothing could be better fitted to gain their object of making their gentile converts envy them than such a statement. 'Ye are but Ishmaelites. We are the ture Israel.'

All this is highly probable; and on the hypothesis of its having been fact, we see an obvious propriety in the peculiar illustration which the apostle uses; and we admire his dexterity in wresting his adversaries' weapons out of their hands, and turning them against themselves, by showing that they were the Ishmaelites and the unbelievers; and that the true Israelites were those who rested entirely and solely in the faith of Jesus Christ.

The apostle shuts up his allegorical illustration of the two economies, and paves the way for the practical inference to which the truth thus illustrated naturally led, in these words: "So then, brethren, we are not children of the bond woman, but of the free" (Gal. 4:31.). This, as is common with the apostle, seems the first half of an antithetic sentence – the second member readily supplied by the intelligent reader, – and for obvious reasons left thus to be supplied, being – 'And the Judaisers are children, not of the free woman, but of the bond.'

These words stand in need of little illustration. We are not to consider them as, strictly speaking, a conclusion from what goes before; for what goes before is an analogical illustration, not an argument. They are merely a brief statement of the sum and substance of that illustration; the justness of which depends not on its intrinsic evidence, but on its having been employed by inspired men – a prophet and an apostle. 'We believers are the true seed of Abraham, the spiritual children of God. We are not children of the bond woman, born to slavery, but we are the children of the free woman born to liberty.'

The idea of the abolition of the legal economy, though not directly brought forward here, is plainly implied. The mystical Isaac is born and weaned; the power of the mystical Hagar is come to an end. She and her children must be banished from the family; and it is not meet that the children of the promise should be longer subject to her control or their persecution.

This view is very closely connected with the verse which follows; and we have here one among very many proofs, that the division of the New Testament into chapters is far from being uniformly judicious. If, indeed, believers are the subjects of the economy of promise, and if the economy of law is come to an end, nothing could be more incongruous than for them to endeavor to attach themselves to it; and a plain and broad foundation is laid for the exhortation which the apostle proceeds to address to them. "Stand[85] fast therefore in the liberty wherewith Christ hath made us free, and be not entangled again with the yoke of bondage" (Gal. 5:1.). The first words of this verse are connected by Lachmann and Schott with the preceding one, – "We are children of the free woman by that liberty whereby Christ has made us free." We prefer the ordinary mode of connection.

This exhortation is obviously addressed to the gentile converts among the Galatians, and this is intimated by the change of person, "we are the children not of the bond woman, but of the free," that is, we believers, whether Jews or Gentiles; "stand," ye gentile believers, "fast in the liberty wherewith Christ has made you free;" and it is further made evident from the persons addressed being persons who had not submitted to circumcision. This remark is of importance to the right understanding of the passage.

By the liberty wherewith Christ had made these gentile converts free has very generally been understood – freedom from the Mosaic law. But they surely could not with propriety be said to be made free from that to which they were never subjected. The liberty with which Christ had made them free is something much more general and extensive than this – something that is common both to believing Jews and Gentiles. It is a deliverance from subjection to the doctrines and commandments of men, and it is a deliverance too from a servile spirit in yielding obedience to the commandments of God. When a man embraces the gospel with an enlightened faith he acknowledges Christ as the alone Lord of his understanding and conscience, of his faith and conduct; he knows and feel that no man, no body of men, have any right to dictate to him what he is to believe, and what he is to do in religion. "One is his master, even Christ." To observe all His ordinances and commandments is the whole of his duty; and in doing so "he walks at liberty."

In embracing the gospel, the man not only obtains this kind of freedom, but he is also delivered from a servile spirit in obeying the commandments of God — knowing and believing that "God is in Christ, reconciling the world to Himself, not imputing to men their trespasses" — persuaded that "in Christ he has redemption through His blood, the forgiveness of his sins according to the riches of Divine grace," he loves God who has so loved him, and constrained by love he "serves Him without fear in righteousness and holiness." This is the liberty wherewith Christ makes all who believe His gospel free.

Luther's description of the liberty wherewith Christ makes His people free, though not perhaps exegetically correct, is doctrinally true, and very beautiful and delightful. "Christ has made us free, not civilly nor carnally, but divinely; we are made free in such a sort that our conscience is free and quiet, not fearing the wrath of God to come. This is the true and inestimable liberty to the excellency and majesty of which, if we compare the others, they are but as one drop of water in respect of the whole sea. For who is able to express what a thing it is when a man is assured in his heart that God neither is, nor will be, angry with him, but will be for ever a merciful and a loving Father unto him for Christ's sake? This, indeed, is a marvellous and incomprehensible liberty, to have the most high and sovereign Majesty so favorable to us that He doth not only defend, maintain, and succour us in this life, but also as touching our bodies will so deliver us as that, though sown in corruption, dishonor, and infirmity, they shall rise again in incorruption, and glory, and power. This is an inestimable liberty that we are made free from the wrath of God for ever, and is greater than heaven and earth and all other creatures. Of this liberty there followeth another freedom from the law, sin, death, and the power of the devil. 'Blessed is he that understandeth and believeth.' "[86]

Now, the apostle's exhortation to the Galatian converts is, "stand fast in this liberty." To stand fast is just equivalent to, 'to persevere in, to maintain.'[87] 'Act like Christ's freemen.' To receive the doctrines of the Judaising teachers, to submit to the ritual observances which they wished to impose, was utterly incongruous with this liberty. They said, "unless you are circumcised, and keep the law of Moses, ye cannot be saved." But Christ had said no such thing; on the contrary, he said, "Whosoever believeth shall not perish, but have everlasting life." To receive their principle, and to act on it, was plainly to renounce Christ's authority, and to submit to the authority of men; and the whole of their system of seeking justification by their own doings was utterly subversive of the filial confidence, that generous spirit, which the faith of the gospel of Christ generates, and was necessarily productive of a servile temper. "Stand fast in the liberty wherewith Christ hath made you free," is thus equivalent to, 'maintain your Christian freedom.' When the Judaising teachers press their principles on you, ask for their authority; request them to show you the sanction of Christ; and let them know that He is your master, and that ye are not, and will not be, "the servants of men." When they call on you to submit to circumcision and other ritual observances, in order to obtain the favor of God, tell them that, "being justified by faith, ye have already peace with God through our Lord Jesus Christ, and have access into the grace wherein ye stand, and rejoice in the hope of the glory of God."

The apostle adds, "be not entangled again with the yoke of bondage," or rather, a yoke of bondage.[88] The apostle plainly refers to the subjection to the law — this was the particular yoke of bondage that the Galatians were in danger of being subjected to — but he speaks generally, and calls it not the yoke, but a yoke, for a plain reason. The Galatian gentile converts had never been subject to this yoke of bondage before, and therefore they could not with propriety be warned against being again entangled in it; but they had been subject to a yoke of bondage, and might with propriety be warned against being again subject to any such yoke.

The state of gentilism, as we have already seen, bore in many respects an analogy to the state of those who were under the law. The heathen were the slaves of human authority even more, if possible, than the Jews were; like them, they were subject to an endless, wearisome series of external services; and like them, their sentiments and institutions naturally produced a servile spirit. It is as if the apostle had said, 'You were once slaves: Christ has made you free: beware of becoming slaves again. If you follow the advice of these Judaising teachers ye will become so. They have no better claim on your belief than the priests and sages of paganism; and the system of observances they would force on you has now no more authority than that burdensome ritual from which you have been so happily delivered.'

The general principle of this exhortation is applicable to Christians in all ages, both in regard to religious doctrine and duty. Let them assert their freedom, and guard against the admission of any principle, or the submission to any imposition, that may entangle their consciences and strip their obedience, even to Christ's law, of that child-like character which the faith of Christ in its purity, and the ordinances of Christ in their simplicity, are so well calculated to produce and cherish.

What an admirable system is pure Christianity! How grateful should we be for the clear and full statement of it we have in the New Testament Scripture! How deeply should we study it! How jealously should we guard it against corruption! How anxiously should we seek to experience more and more of its generous and holy influence — its efficacy to purify and to bless! How grateful especially should all be who have reason to hope that they are in possession of this liberty! He whom the Son makes free is free indeed. Every man is naturally a slave; and he only is truly free whom grace has made a freeman.[89]

Let those who have this freedom act a part worthy of it, and let those who want it gratefully receive what is "freely given them of God. Still does "the anointed of the Lord" proclaim "liberty to the captives, and the opening of the prison doors to those that are bound" (Isa. 61:1.). Let them receive the truth in the love of it, and that truth will make them free; and as it is this truth believed which gives this spiritual freedom, so it is the continued belief of this truth which alone can enable them, in opposition to all the attempts of their spiritual enemies to entangle them again in bondage, to "stand fast in the liberty wherewith Christ has made us free."

SECT. VII. – THE COURSE THE GALATIANS WERE FOLLOWING AN IMPLICIT RENUNCIATION OF CHRISTIANITY AND ITS BLESSINGS.

The paths of error and vice are downward paths; but the descent is sometimes so very gradual, especially at first, that it is often no easy matter to convince those who have entered them that they have left the level ground of truth and duty. To use another figure, the divergence from the straight road is often so very small that he who has abandoned it may easily for a time persuade himself that he is still prosecuting it. The lines of direction seem to be almost parallel; yet at every step he takes they are diverging, and by and by it will become abundantly apparent, even to the individual himself, that the path he now treads and the path he formerly trode are different paths. It is quite possible he may still think that the path he has chosen is the preferable one; but he can no longer indulge the delusive notion that he has not altered his course.

In many cases, I am persuaded, the fatal catastrophe of "making shipwreck of faith, and of a good conscience," might

> No nook so narrow but he spreads them there
> With ease, and is at large. The oppressor
> His body bound; but knows not what a range
> His spirit takes, unconscious of a chain,

And that to bind him is a vain attempt,
Whom God delights in, and in whom He dwells."

         —Cowper, *Task, v.*

be prevented, were the true nature and probable results of commencing apostacy, either in principle or in conduct, brought before the mind. Many a man has begun with doubting or denying some particular doctrine of revelation which seems beset with peculiar difficulties, such as the doctrine of original sin, and has ended with denying the Divine authority of the Bible altogether. Many a man has begun with venturing on what he was afraid was wrong, or at any rate was by no means quite sure was right, who has ended with disregarding all religious and moral obligations. Had these men understood the tendency of the first step, they might perhaps not have taken the second. Had they contemplated the termination of their career they might probably never have commenced it.

Nothing is more unfair than to charge a man with holding principles which he disavows, however justly deducible from his professed opinions. Such a mode of reasoning, however common, is obviously uncandid, and has a much greater tendency to irritate than to convince. To charge a man with crimes of which he knows he is not guilty, though the faults he has committed may naturally lead to the perpetration of these crimes, is certainly not the most likely way of reforming him. But it is a matter of the last importance that the tendency of a false principle, and of a criminal action, should be distinctly and fully laid before the mind of him who has adopted the one, or committed the other; and that he should be faithfully and affectionately warned against holding an opinion or indulging a practice the moral characters of which are very different from what he apprehends them to be, and which will in the ordinary course of things sink him in depths of error and guilt, from which at present he would perhaps recoil with terror.

It is most unfortunate when a person just about to commence the downward road of apostasy falls in with a well meaning, it may be, but most mistaken friend, who flatters him in the opinion he has formed that there is nothing very dangerous or wrong in the course he is taking, who says "peace, peace," to him while there is no peace. A true friend will in these circumstances not thus help forward the delusion; but, at the hazard of displeasing him whom he wishes to save, he will honestly, but at the same time kindly, tell him the truth, and, leading him to the brink of the precipice, bid him ponder ere he goes farther in the path which terminates so fearfully.

This is the kind office the Apostle Paul is doing to the Galatians, who, through means of the arts of Judaising teachers, were in extreme hazard of apostatising from pure Christianity. They in general seemded to have entertained the idea, that they might follow the course recommended by their teachers, and yet continue believers and followers of the Lord Jesus — possessors of the character and heirs of the inheritance of true Christians. The apostle endeavors to dissipate all such delusive hopes, and distinctly informs them, that if they were determined to follow their new teachers they must make up their mind not only to abandon their old teachers, but to give up their Savior; for that to depend on Him for salvation, and at the same time to depend on circumcision or any thing else for salvation, were, whatever their new teachers might tell them, utterly incompatible; that to yield to these Judaising teachers was to sacrifice their Christian freedom, and in effect to renounce Christianity altogether.

"Behold, I Paul say unto you, that if ye be circumcised, Christ shall profit you nothing" (Gal. 5:2.). There are two things which here require our attention — the apostle's statement and the manner in which this statement is made. The statement is, that if the Galatian gentile converts submitted to circumcision in compliance with the wish of the Judaising teachers, "Jesus Christ would profit them nothing." The phrase, "Jesus Christ shall profit you nothing," is equivalent to, 'you will derive no advantage from Jesus Christ — you cannot share in the blessings of His salvation.' The statement is not, that no circumcised person can obtain salvation through Christ. Abraham, the father of circumcision, and all his believing childlren of the circumcision, were saved through the Messiah, and through faith in the Messiah. From the case of Timothy, who was of Jewish descent by his mother, and who, after his conversion to Christianity, was by the apostle taken and circumcised, it seems plain that the mere act of submitting to that rite did not imply in it a renunciation of the blessings of Christ's salvation. The words are to be understood with a reference to the Galatian converts in the particular circumstances in which they stood. For them who were Gentiles never subject to the law of Moses, to submit to it in order to obtain for themselves the favor of God and eternal life, was an implied renunciation of Christianity, and to such persons Christ could be of no advantage.

Actions derive their moral character from the circumstances in which, and the principles from which, they are performed. To eat bread and drink wine in commemoration of Christ's death, had not our Lord commanded us to do so, would have been a superstitious usage — a piece of will-worship. To do so now that He has commanded it, is an important part of Christian worship. To observe this ordinance for the purpose for which it has often been observed, to make atonement for sins, or to qualify for civil office, is gross profanation. To observe this ordinance from a regard to the Divine authority — a wish to honor the Savior, a desire to obtain spiritual improvement — is highly dutiful. In like manner, for a Jew, previously to the coming of the Messiah, to attend to the initiatory rite of his religion, was an imperative duty. For a Jew, even after the coming of the Messiah, to submit to it, if he did not regard it as the ground of his hope, as securing his salvation, was not forbidden, nay, in certain circumstances, as those of Timothy, it might become a duty. But for any person, especially for a Gentile professing to believe the gospel, and to expect pardon and salvation entirely "through the redemption that is in Christ Jesus," to submit to circumcision for the purpose of securing for himself the favor of God and eternal happiness, was obviously most incongruous and criminal conduct.

The doctrine of Judaising teachers, as we have often had occasion to observe, was, "except ye be circumcised and keep the law of Moses, ye cannot be saved." In submitting to the rite in compliance with the wishes of such teachers, gentile converts in effect said, 'The atonement of Jesus Christ as apprehended by faith, is not a sufficient ground of hope; it stands in need of addition.' This is to renounce Christianity. For its leading doctrine is, "Christ is all." In Him we are justified, sanctified, and redeemed. And the apostle's objection to circumcision, now an obsolete rite, would have been equally strong to their substituting anything else in the room of the Savior's obedience to the death, which is the sole foundation of the sinner's hope, or of that faith of the truth by which the sinner lays hold of "the hope set before him in the gospel." Such then is the apostle's statement — that if any gentile convert submitted to circumcision as, either wholly or in part, the means of obtaining the Divine favor, he cut himself off from the blessings of Christ's salvation. Not that there was no room for his repentance — not that if he did repent and believe the gospel his having submitted to circumcision would bar his way to the Savior — but the act when performed in these circumstances, and from these principles, was an implied renunciation of Christ and Christianity.

The manner in which the statement is made deserves notice. "Behold, I Paul say unto you." This form of introducing the statement, marks his sense of its importance, and his wish that it should be well pondered by them. It is equivalent to, 'I Paul, a divinely authorised teacher, "an apostle not of man, neither by man," who "wrought miracles among you and ministered the Spirit," who ardently loved you, and whom you once ardently loved, and who have been artfully and calumniously represented as contradicting the doctrine I taught while among you, I Paul solemnly assure you, in the name of my Master, that if you submit to circumcision that you may be saved by it and the works of the law to which it is introductory, you in effect renounce Jesus Christ, and will cut yourselves off from a participation in the blessings of His salvation.' There is no reason to doubt that the Judaising teachers had told the Galatian converts, that submission to circumcision, even on their principles, was perfectly consistent with the faith of Christ, and that it was under this mistaken notion that some had discovered a willingness to comply with their wishes. Such a declaration was therefore called for on the part of the apostle, and was certainly well fitted to make them pause and consider before they went further.

In the next verse the apostle takes notice of another circumstance which the Judaising teachers had kept out of sight, and which was well fitted to show the Galatian converts how hazardous a step they were taking in submitting to the initiatory rite of Judaism: "For I testify again to every man that is circumcised, that he is a debtor to do the whole law."[90]

As the statement in this verse is a different one from that made in the former one, and indeed different from any made in the previous part of the epistle, we apprehend the word "again"[91] signifies here 'besides,' or, 'moreover.' This is its signification, Matth. 5:33; 13:45. Some consider it as equivalent to, "on the other hand;" and quote in support of this signification, Matth. 4:7; 1 Cor. 12:21; 2 Cor. 10:7; 1 John 2:8.

The phrase, "every man that is circumcised," is obviously to be limited to every one of the persons to whom he is referring. 'Every one of you gentile converts who submit to circumcision, in compliance with the will of your new teachers, I testify to you that by doing so he becomes bound to keep the whole law;[92] that is, on the very same principle that you submit to circumcision as necessary for your salvation, you must observe all things "written in the book of the law to do them." ' Chrysostom remarks that "there is an internal connection of precepts in the law, circumcision was connected with sacrifice, sacrifice implied sacredness of times and places, and sacred places required lustratory rites." The apostle does not say that by doing so they would obtain what they were in quest of. On the contrary, he distinctly tells them that, "by the deeds of the law no man can be justified." But he tells them also what consistency required of them if they submitted to circumcision.

It seems obvious that these Judaising teachers were not very attentive to some of the Mosaic rites (Gal. 6:13.); and it is probable that the gentile converts in submitting to the initiatory rite of Judaism did not contemplate subjecting themselves to all its requisitions. 'But,' says the apostle, 'where can you stop? If obedience in any point be necessary, it is necessary in all. Circumcision is not more obligatory than the other ordinances of the Mosiac economy.' They were thus allowing a heavier yoke to be imposed on them than they were aware of. And all for no purpose — for worse than no purpose.

The principle is of universal application. Whenever a man shifts the ground of his hope in any degree from the finished work of Jesus Christ — whenever he depends on anything he has done, or is to do — he lays himself open to a claim for complete perfect obedience and satisfaction to that law, by obedience to which he is seeking justification. To depend on works at all is absurd, unless we have perfect works. We must choose between the two principles, justification by faith and justification by works — justification as a free gift, and justification as a merited reward. There is no combining the two principles; and if we prefer the law, let us recollect we must stand by its terms. "The soul that sinneth shall die."

This is substantially the apostle's assertion in the next verse. "Christ is become of no effect unto you,[93] whosoever of you are justified by the law; ye are fallen from grace" (Gal. 5:4.). The expression "whosoever of you are justified by the law," is plainly equivalent to, 'such of you as are seeking justification by the law;"[94] for, as the apostle has himself remarked above (Gal. 3:11.), "that no man is justified by the law in the sight of God, is evident." To such of the Galatians as were seeking justification by the law, "Christ had become of no effect." The word here used is the same as that employed in Romans 7:2-6, — "She is loosed"[95] — "We are delivered from the law."[96] The idea, is, 'Christ and you are completely separated.'[97] They had professed faith in Christ, but their conduct in seeking justification by the law was a proof that they never understood the gospel they had professed to believe. Christ for justification and the law for justification, are not only two different, but two incompatible, things. You who are seeking for justification by the law can have nothing to do with Christ, for "Christ for righteousness," or justification, "is the end of the law." The man who is seeking pardon and salvation as the reward of his own doings, either in whole or in part, necessarily, from the very constitution of the gospel, cuts himself off from the benefit of Christ's mediation., God will give freely or He will not give at all. Christ must be the sole Savior, He will not divide His honor with the sinner.[98]

> "No; He as soon will abdicate his own
> As stoop from heaven to sell the proud a throne." — Cowper.

"Ye are fallen from grace." To "fall from grace," is not to cease to be objects of the peculiar favor of God. We have no reason to think the persons spoken of were ever interested in the Divine special favor; and it appears to us very distinctly the doctrine of the Bible, that a man cannot, in this sense of the word, fall from grace. "There is no condemnation to them who are in Christ Jesus." Nothing "can separate them from the love of God," — i.e. His grace "in Christ Jesus" (Rom. 8:1,35-39.). Grace is here used as opposed to works; and what the apostle says is, 'By seeking to be justified by works, you have renounced the way of justification by grace.' There is no combining the two things; for, as the apostle says, "if it be by grace, then is it no more of works; otherwise grace is no more grace: but if it be of works, then is it no more grace; otherwise work is no more work" (Rom. 11:6.). 'You give up all claims on the Divine favor, or kindness, when you go about to establish a method of justification of your own.'

In the general principles laid down here we are just as much interested as the Galatian converts, to whom the Epistle was written. The principle in human nature which led them to seek for justification by the Mosaic law still exists, and is in active operation; leading men, under a prefession of Christianity, to "make void the grace of God," and involve themselves in endless destruction, by "going about to establish their own methods of justification," and refusing to submit to the Divine method of justification. These human methods are various; but their common principle is to substitute something in the room of Christ's obedience to the death as the ground of hope, and something in the room of faith as the means of justification. An error here must be dangerous — may be fatal. Let us all carefully examine the foundation of our hopes. The only secure ground is the finished work of Christ; the only way of making that the ground of our hope is the faith of the truth respecting it. But let us never forget that the only permanently satisfactory evidence of our interest in Christ's atonement, and of our having really believed the true gospel, is our personal experience of its sanctifying and comforting efficacy, — the only sure evidence of our having the faith of the gospel, is our feeling its purifying, and our exemplifying its transforming, influence. Luther's pithy words are worth quoting: — "Some would bind us at this day to certain of Moses' laws which like them best, as the false apostles would have done at that time; but this is in no wise to be suffered. For if we give Moses leave to rule over us in anything, we are bound to obey him in all things; wherefore we will not be burdened with any law of Moses. We grant that he is to be read among us, and to be heard as a prophet and a witness-bearer to Christ, and moreover, that out of him we may take good examples of good laws and a holy life; but we will not suffer him in any wise to have dominion over our consciences. In this case, let him be dead and buried, and let no man know where his grave is. — Deut. 34:6."[99]

To a reflecting mind, few things seem more worthy of considerate remark than that identity of essence which, amid almost endless variety of form, has characterised false religions and corruptions of the true. True religion, in all its forms, has been spiritual in its nature, and humbling in its tendency; and false religions, in all their varieties, have been possessed of directly the opposite qualities. The leading principles of true religion are, "God is all in all;" — man, as a creature, "is as nothing; and less than nothing, and vanity;" — God, as the Governor of the world, has done all things well; — His law is, like Himself, perfect, — its precept is not too strict, its sanctions are not too severe; and man, as a sinner, a violator of the law, is most criminal, and altogether inexcusable; — if man is saved at all, it must be in the exercise of sovereign kindness on the part of Him whom he has offended. "All things are of God." "Of Him, and through Him, and to Him, are all things." The leading duties of true religion are spiritual duties — exercises of the mind and heart; the understanding and affections towards God corresponding to the views given of his character and moral administration, and our relations to Him.

In almost all false religions and corruptions of the true, the pride of man's nature is done homage to. He is not represented as he really is, an inexcusably criminal, an utterly lost, being, and he is flattered by what is a radical principle in every religion but the pure religion of the Bible, that he can either by repentance or sacrifice propitiate the Divinity for any offence he may have given Him, and that he is to be author of his own moral improvement, the builder of his own immortal fortunes. The Divine favor is to be merited, not freely received.

And as in their principles false religions flatter the pride of man, so in their practical requisitions they suit themselves to that part of the depraved human constitution, its supreme attention and attachment to sensible things — things seen and temporal. Externality, if we may use the owrd, is the leading character of the duties enjoined by false religions. A round of ritual observances, a series of outward performances is prescribed, viewed not as the expression of religious thought and feeling, but as constituting the substance of religious duty. These are the great characters of Paganism in its leading forms, both in ancient and modern times. They are the leading characters of false Judaism and of false Christianity. They are the leading characters of Mohammedanism. They are the leading characters of Popery. And one or other of them, will be found in all the numerous essential corruptions of protestant Christianity. In truth, all the forms of false religion are just so many varieties of one religion, the religion of corrupt depraved men; the elements of which rising out of the pride and secularity of that corrupted nature which equally belongs to them all, are essentially the same, though liable to endless modification from the circumstances in which individuals or bodies of men are placed.

We find from the passage which we have been considering, that these characters belonged to the earliest corruptions of the Christian faith. The Judaising teachers, instead of the humbling doctrine of redemption through the blood of Christ and justification by faith, taught, that by submitting to circumcision and obeying the law, men could do something in the way of meriting the Divine favor; and their object was to substitute in the room of the simple and spiritual institutions and duties of pure Christianity the numberless carnal ordinances of the Mosaic institution. In doing so they pretended to be improving on the Christianity taught by the apostle; but he plainly informs the Galatian converts that this was not to improve Christianity but to destroy it; and that if they were determined to receive what in reality was another religion, they must make up their minds to give up that which they had professed to embrace. He states to them, that whosoever submitted to circumcision for the purpose of obtaining justification by doing so, cut himself off from all interest in the blessings of Christ's salvation. That on the same principle, that circumcision was necessary to justification, perfect obedience to every requisition of the law was necessary; that to seek justification by law was an implied apostasy from Christ, and that all who did so of course relinquished all claim on the free favor of God, and came forward as expectants of Divine favor and eternal life, not as humble suppliants, but as persons entitled to a stipulated reward for the performance of stipulated labors. To impress more deeply on the minds of the Galatians the conviction that the gospel of these Judaising teachers was indeed "another gospel:" that the religion to which they were attempting to convert the Galatians was not the religion of Christ, and of course that he had not gone too far in declaring those who embraced such views apostates from the faith they had once professed, the apostle in the following verses shortly, but plainly, states what were the principles held by himself and all true Christians on the subject under consideration. "For we through the Spirit wait for the hope of righteousness by faith. For in Christ Jesus neither circumcision availeth any thing, nor uncircumcision; but faith which worketh by love"(Gal. 5:5,6.).

"Righteousness" is in this verse, as in the epistles of Paul generally, equivalent to, 'justification.' "Hope" is here plainly employed as descriptive not of the affection of hope, but of the object of hope; as, Col. 1:5; Tit. 2:13; Heb. 6:18; 7:19, the thing hoped for. "The hope of justification," is just equivalent either to, 'the justification hoped for — that state of favor with God which is the object of our hope;' or to, 'that final happiness which is the object of the hope of those who are justified by faith.[100]

'Now,' says the apostle, 'we wait for or expect this hoped for justification.' The word "we" is descriptive of the apostle and those who thought along with him in opposition to the false teachers. "We," that is genuine Christians, expect that justification which we hope for, or that salvation which is the object of our hope as justified persons "through the Spirit by faith."

The phrase "through the Spirit," or, "in the Spirit," may either be connected with the word "we," or with the phrase, "expect the justification we hope for." In the first case it describes the character of the persons spoken of; in the other it describes the manner in which they expect justification. In the first way of explaining it is equivalent to, 'We who are "in the Spirit" and "not in the flesh;" we who are spiritual and not carnal; we who by the Spirit of God have been formed to a spiritual character; whatever others may do, WE expect the justification we hope for solely by faith.' This makes very good sense; but the peculiar turn of expression adopted by the apostle, and the connection in which the words are introduced, lead us to prefer the second mode of interpretation, which considers the phrase as describing the manner in which they expect[101] justification. 'We expect the justification we hope for "in the Spirit," or, "through the Spirit;" that is spiritually, in a spiritual manner, not in a carnal manner. We expect justification not by the performance of external ceremonies as the Judaising teachers teach you to expect it. We have "begun in the Spirit," and we are determined to carry on in the Spirit. We expect spiritual blessings in a way corresponding to their nature.'

And as they expected the hoped for justification, or the blessing they hoped for as justified persons, through the Spirit, not through the carnal ordinances of the law, so they expected it not by working but by believing — "we expect the hoped for justification by believing." It was by believing they had obtained a place in God's favor, and it was by believing they hoped to retain it. Justification was a blessing of which they were already in possession; but it is a permanent state into which they enter by faith, and in which "they stand by faith." The sentiment is the same as that more fully expressed by the apostle in the beginning of the fifth chapter of the Romans, "being justified by faith, we have peace with God, through our Lord Jesus Christ: by whom also we have access by faith into this grace wherein we stand, and rejoice in hope of the glory of God," that is, of the Divine approbation at last. It is not by obedience to the law of Moses, but by exercising faith in the gospel of Christ that we hope to continue in the state of favor into which we have been brought, and to receive the Divine approbation at last.

The reason why Paul and all genuine enlightened Christians expected the hoped for justification "through the Spirit," not through the flesh, "by faith," not by works, is stated in the 6th verse, — "For in Christ Jesus neither circumcision availeth any thing, nor uncircumcision; but faith which worketh by love" (Gal. 5:6.).

The phrase "in Christ Jesus," has been variously interpreted, some considering it as equivalent to, 'in the estimation of Jesus Christ;'[102] others, as equivalent to, 'in the kingdom of Christ — under Christ's dispensation.' We see no necessity of receding from the ordinary sense of the phrase, according to which it describes that intimate relation to Christ Jesus in which all true believers stand. The expression by an ordinary ellipsis is equivalent to, 'to the being in Christ Jesus;'[103] to thy being a true Christian — one so related to Jesus Christ as to be as it were in Him, one with Him, interested in all the blessings of His salvation.'

Now, to the being a true Christian, "neither circumcision availeth anything, nor uncircumcision." It is not either as Jews or as Gentiles that men are connected with Christ Jesus. The general idea is, connection with Christ depends on nothing external. It is the same idea that is more fully expressed, 1 Cor. 7:19; Col. 3:11; and Gal. 3:28. The apostle's statement then is, 'We do not look for justification from any external distinction; for we know that to the being a true Christian external distinctions, of whatsoever kind they be, avail nothing; but we do look for justification by faith, for we know that "faith working by love" does avail a man being in Christ Jesus to his being a true Christian.

By "faith" I understand just the belief of the gospel − the counting true the testimony which God has given us concerning His Son − that He "died for our sins according to the scriptures;" that "He was raised again from the dead according to the scriptures;" that "He came to save sinners, even the chief;" that "His blood cleanseth from all sin;" that "He is able to save to the uttermost;" and that "whosoever believeth on Him shall not perish, but have everlasting life." This faith availeth to a man being in Christ Jesus. It is this faith which connects a man with the Savior. He who has it not, whatever else he may have, is not in Christ Jesus; he who has it is in Christ Jesus. "He that believeth not is condemned already. He that believeth is not condemned − he cannot come into condemnation." "We look for justification by believing," says the apostle, for faith avails to a man being in Christ Jesus. And "there is not" − there cannot be − "condemnation to them who are in Christ Jesus." It takes no more to make any man a subject of Christ's kingdom than to be of "the truth" − this truth; and it requires no less. The Jews, notwithstanding all their privileges, are not in Christ if they be not of this truth; the Gentiles are free in this kingdom if they be of this truth. The circumcision of the Jew does not raise him above the Gentile; the uncircumcision of the Gentile does not sink him below the Jew. The Greek has no advantage from his politeness; the barbarian has no loss from his rudeness. The slavery of the bondman cannot hinder his liberty if he be of the truth; and the freeman, if he is not of the turth, has no part in "the liberty wherewith Christ makes free."[104]

This faith, which connects the sinner with the Savior, which avails to the being in Christ Jesus, is described as faith "which worketh," which exerts itself "by love" (1 Thess. 1:3. 1 Tim. 1:5.). Wherever the word of the truth of the gospel is believed it produces an effect on the temper and conduct. "It worketh effectually in all who believe." The apostle James speaks of a "dead faith," that is, either a mere pretended faith − a faith which a man says he has but has not − or it is a faith of something else than the gospel. A man may have a considerably distinct and extensive theoretical view of the gospel without believing it; and such a view may − must − be in a great measure inoperative − will exert itself in any way rather than in love and good works. But wherever the faith of the gospel − of the whole gospel − exists, it will "work,"[105] and "by love."

It is impossible, from the constitution of human nature, that the gospel should be really believed without the man who believes it, just in the degree in which he believes it, loving God, loving Christ, loving his brethren in Christ Jesus, loving his brethren of mankind. It is so easy to impose on a person's self − by mistaking mere speculation about the gospel for the faith of the gospel, or by mistaking the faith of something else for the faith of the gospel − that it is of the last importance to him who would not be deceived in a matter which involves his everlasting interests to take care not to conclude himself a believer if he is a stranger to that love by which the faith of the gospel uniformly exerts itself.

In the verses which follow, the apostle recals to the minds of the Galatians the suspicious commencement of their career − expresses his regret and astonishment at their subsequent conduct, halting and stumbling in the Christian course − states his conviction that the means which had been unhappily effectual for this purpose were not sanctioned by Divine authority, and warns them of the hazard of admitting any, even the slightest, admixture of human error into the system of Divine truth, of which their creed, as received from Him, was originally composed.

SECT. VIII. − ADDITIONAL CONSIDERATIONS FITTED TO ROUSE THE GALATIANS TO SERIOUS CONSIDERATION.

1. They had been arrested in the course they had well begun. Why?

"Ye did run well; who did hinder you that ye should not obey the truth" (Gal. 5:7.)?

The language is figurative, but by no means obscure. The life of a Christian, which is a life of faith in, and obedience to, Jesus Christ, is here represented as a race course on which a man enters when he believes the gospel, and along which he runs while holding fast the faith of Christ — he walks in his ordinances and commandments blameless. "Now," says the apostle, "ye did run well." On embracing the gospel, ye for a while had your conversation in every way becoming the gospel of Christ. Ye "walked at liberty, keeping Christ's commandments" — "having received Christ Jesus, the Lord, ye walked in Him" — finding yourselves "complete in Him." In the words "ye did run well," is obviously implied, that they ran well no longer[106] — a sentiment more plainly brought out in the interrogation which follows, "who did hinder you that ye should not obey[107] the truth?"

The figure is contained in the first clause, 'Who has obstructed you — repelled you — in your onward career;' and in the second clause it is explained, 'Who have induced you "not to obey the truth." '[108] To "obey the truth," is to yield the mind up to the native influence of the truth. The man who yields his mind to the influence of the truth, as it is in Jesus, finds all he needs in Christ — he does not go about to establish a way of justification of his own, but submits to God's method of justification, through the faith of Christ. All halting in the Christian course originates here. While the mind yields itself up to the influence of the truth, the Christian runs well; but whenever this influence is resisted, he is hindered. The question is not answered; nor was it needful. The apostle and the Galatians were perfectly aware how the change had been brought about, and who had been the great agents in effecting it — the Judaising teacher. 'Now,' says the apostle, 'the change has not come from the right quarter.'

2. THE "PERSUASION" WHICH HAD INDUCED THEM TO CHANGE HAD NOT COME FROM CHRIST.

"This persuasion cometh not of Him that calleth you" (Gal. 5:8.). The word "persuasion"[109] may be understood as referring either to the Galatian Christians or to the Judaising teachers who had misled them. In the first case it must refer to the opinion they had been brought to entertain in reference to the necessity and efficacy of submission to the Mosaic law for justification, or rather to their credulous confidence in their false teachers; and according as you understand the phrase, "Him that calleth you" of God, or Christ, or of the apostle, the meaning will be either, 'This opinion you have imbibed, or this submission of mind you have showed, is not of divine origin, or is not of divine requisition;' or it is not an opinion or habit of mind which you have learned from me.[110]

I am rather disposed to view the word as referring to the persuasion — the persuasive arts used by the Judaising teachers, by means of which they hindered the Galatian Christians in their Christian course, and led them to disobey the truth. This persuasion, of which you have been the subjects, "is not of Him who calleth you." In illustrating the sixth verse of the first chapter, I explained the phrase Him who calleth you, and endeavored to show that it refers, not to the apostle, but to Jesus Christ. The apostle's statement seems then to be, 'This persuasion to which you have yielded is not from Christ. It comes from a very different quarter. The men who have employed it are not moved by HIS Spirit. They have no divine authority, and you ought not to yield to them, "no, not for an hour."

3. THE EVIL WAS LIKELY TO INCREASE.

The proverbial adage which the apostle goes on to quote, seems to have been intended to meet a thought which might very naturally rise in the minds of such of the Galatians as had listened to the seductive persuasions of the Judaising teachers — 'Why so much ado about nothing? May we not, in matters of so slight importance as these Jewish rites, accommodate ourselves to our new teachers?' "No," says the apostle. "A little leaven leaveneth the whole lump" (Gal. 5:9.). This is a proverb borrowed probably from some old Greek writer. The principle necessarily involved in submitting to any Jewish rite in order to justification, is one which, once admitted into the mind, will completely change the whole belief in reference to the peculiarities of the Christian faith. It leads directly to the denial of the two grand principles of the Christian system: The necessity and sufficiency of Christ's obedience to death as the only ground, and of faith in the gospel as the only means, of the sinner's justification. "Leaven" is frequently used to denote false doctrine, as Matt. 16:6; 1 Cor. 5:7; and is alluded to, though the word does not occur, 2 Tim. 2:17. By some interpreters the proverb has been applied to the Judaising teachers, as if the apostle had siad, 'Beware of these teachers; they may be few at present; but error is infectious. By and by the whole body of you may be led away from the truth.' This harmonises with the way in which the same apophthegm is applied by the apostle in reference to the Corinthian Church (1 Cor. 5:6.). He exhorts them to cast out the incestuous person, as his continuance in the society was hazardous to the purity of the other members. But there is nothing to hinder the apostle from applying the same proverb to different subjects which it equally answers. Our Lord, for instance, employs this proverb — "The disciple is not above his teacher, nor the servant above his master" — in illustration of two totally distinct statements, — Matt. 10:24; Luke 6:40.[111]

4. THE APOSTLE STILL HOPED WELL OF THEM.

In dealing with those who have apostatised, or are in danger of apostatising, there is a peculiar need of the union of tenderness with fidelity. In warning men of the crime and misery of apostasy the minister cannot be too honest. There is scarcely a possibility of exaggerating here. But he must not take too readily for granted either that apostasy is begun, or that it has become obstinate. To address a man who is but doubting as if he were a confirmed infidel is a very likely method of making him one. The Christian teacher ought always to act under the influence of the charity which "hopeth all things;" and when he stands in doubt of any of those whose souls are committed to his care, he must not conceal his hopes while he makes known his fears.

Here, as in every other department of the duty of a Christian teacher, the apostle Paul presents us with an example which every minister of Christ should endeavor to copy. After having, in the Epistle to the Hebrews, placed before the mind the fearful consequence of apostasy in one of the most alarming passages in the whole book of God (Heb. 6:4-8.), he adds, "But, beloved, we are persuaded better things of you, and things that accompany salvation, though we thus speak." And in the section of the Epistle to the Galatians now before us, after he has stated the very hazardous and criminal conduct of those who should yield to the ensnaring acts of the Judaising teachers, he expresses his hope that the great body of the Galatian converts would adopt a wiser, more dutiful, and safer course. "I have confidence[112] in you through the Lord, that ye will be none otherwise minded: but he that troubleth you shall bear his judgment, whosoever he be" (Gal. 5:10.).

The literal rendering of this first clause is, 'I have confidence in the Lord in reference to you,' or 'I hope in the Lord concerning you.' The confidence of a true Christian, either in reference to his own perseverance, or to that of his Christian brother, rests on the Savior. He trusts in reference to both that the arm of Divine kindness which has laid hold of them will never let them go — that He who has begun the good work will carry it on "until the day of the Lord," and will keep those whom He has brought to the knowledge and belief of the truth by His power "through faith unto salvation." The apostle had reason to hope that many of the Galatian church were genuine converts of Christ; and, with regard to them, he had a confident hope in Christ that, notwithstanding the temptations they might be exposed to, they would continue "rooted and grounded" in Him, and "established in the faith as they had been taught."

That this was the subject of the apostle's confidence is plain from what follows — "I have confidence in the Lord concerning you, that ye will be no otherwise minded."[113] Some interpreters would confine the reference of these words to the apophthegm which immediately precedes them, and the application of it, q.d. 'I trust you will be of my mind, that the beginnings of error are hazardous, and will act accordingly.'

It seems to me much more probable from the solemnity of the preface, that the apostle refers to the great subject of controversy between him and the Judaising teachers. His confidence was that the Galatian converts would reject that "other gospel" which it was the object of their new teachers to obtrude on them, and think on that subject as he thought – as they had thought in the beginning of their Christian profession; and that, in opposition to all attempts to seduce them, they would continue to hold Christ's obedience to the death as the only ground of their justification, and faith in Him as the only means of their justification.

5. THEIR TROUBLERS WOULD BE PUNISHED.

In the concluding clause of the verse he states his conviction that while through the help of Christ they would be preserved "steadfast and immoveable" in the true grace of God wherein they stood, those who had disturbed their peace by harassing their minds with perverse disputings about the law should not pass unpunished. "He that troubleth you,[114] whosoever he be, shall bear his judgment." We cannot conclude certainly from these words that the apostle had in view some individual of considerable note on some ground or other among the Galatians who was the ringleader in these attempts to seduce the church from the apostle's doctrines, and the simplicity of apostolic usages; though this is not at all improbable. The force of the phrase is obviously, – 'Those men who have done so much to disturb the peace of your minds by leading you away from the all-perfect sacrifice of the Savior as the ground of your hopes, and to break the peace of your church by introducing debate and strife among you, however distinguished they may be for rank or wealth, for learning or apparent piety, shall assuredly not pass unpunished, they shall "bear their judgment." "Judgment" (Luke 20:47; 23:40. Rom. 13:2.) is here, as in some other passages of the New Testament, punishment. It is, however, punishment which is the consequence of judgment. Some have supposed that the apostle refers to excommunication, as if he had said, 'I hope you will be of my mind as to the danger of allowing such persons to continue in your body, and punish them by excluding them, as they deserve, from your assemblies.' I rather think the train of thought is, 'I trust that you will not suffer from these attempts; and I know that their authors shall not escape with impunity. They must be judged, and they shall be punished.'

It is a dangerous thing to disturb the Christian Church, especially by the introduction of false doctrine. He who does so incurs a tremendous responsibility. He must stand his trial; he must bear his punishment. Good men, under the influence of mistaken views and wrong feelings, have often troubled the Church, and though they have had "their soul for a prey," they did not escape unpunished. And dreadful indeed is the doom which awaits wicked men and deceivers who, to gratify unhallowed ambition, or for any similar purpose, have introduced error, disorder, and tyranny into the church of Christ. "Offences" of this kind "must come; but woe to the man by whom they come."

6. THE OBVIOUS FALSEHOOD OF THE SUGGESTION, THAT THE APOSTLE HAD BECOME A PREACHER OF CIRCUMCISION.

Among the unworthy arts used by the Judaising teachers to gain over the Galatians to their views, this was one, the representing the apostle as now teaching the same doctrines as themselves. In the following verse the apostle strongly denies and clearly refutes this charge. "And I, brethren, if I yet preach circumcision, why do I yet suffer presecution? then is the offence of the cross ceased" (Gal. 5:11.).

It is probable that the false teachers availed themselves of the fact of Paul's having taken Timothy and circumcised him, and of his having, in certain circumstances, observed Jewish ceremonies – becoming "a Jew to the Jews" to save them, – to give plausibility to their representation that Paul had changed his mind since he was in Galatia, and was now of their opinion. Nothing can be more satisfactory than the apostle's refutation of the charge. It consists in an appeal to facts. The first "yet,"[115] if it be genuine, which is doubtful, must refer to the period previous to Paul's conversion. Certainly at no period posterior to it did he "preach circumcision." Prior to it, nobody could cry up circumcision more than he. 'How is it,' says he, 'that I am still the object of the persecution of the Jews wherever I go? Were I teaching that the Gentiles must be circumcised, and observe the law of Moses, in order to salvation, the principal cause of their extreme dislike to me would be removed.' Had Paul been contented, with the Judaising teachers, to make Christianity a modification of Judaism, and Christians a Jewish sect, distinguished from other Jews merely by a belief that Jesus was the Messiah, in their sense of the Messiah, he would have met with comparatively little opposition. In that case "the offence of the cross would have ceased."

"The cross," when not used in its strictly literal sense, sometimes, perhaps, signifies, in the New Testament, sufferings on account of Christ and Christianity, – e.g. "If any man will come after me, let him take up his cross" (Matth. 16:24.). It more frequently, however, signifies the crucifixion of Jesus Christ as the victim for sin – the fact that He was crucified – the doctrine that His crucifixion was the expiation of sin. "God forbid that I should glory, save in the cross of our Lord Jesus Christ" (Gal. 6:14.). In the first sense, the meaning of the phrase, "the offence," or stumbling-block, "of the cross," is the obstacles which persecution for Christianity throws in the way of the progress of that religion; in the second, it is the obstacles which the doctrine of the crucifixion of Christ, as the victim for sin, throws in the way of its success. Either mode of interpretation will bring out a good sense. If you adopt the first, the meaning is, 'If I had become a preacher of circumcision, the Jews would have ceased to persecute me, and this obstacle in the way of men becoming Christians would no longer exist.' If you adopt the second, it is, 'If I were a preacher of the necessity of circumcision, and the observance of the law of Moses, to salvation, the Jews would cease to persecute, me for the great stumbling-block to them – the representing the obedience of Jesus Christ to the death, the death of the cross, as the sole ground of hope – would no longer exist.' We prefer the latter mode of interpretation. It was not so much the fact of the Messiah being crucified – though even that was not very palatable – which exasperated the Jews, as the holding forth His death on the cross as the only ground of hope for sinners, excluding everything else, particularly all those things in which they had been accustomed to place their confidence, and thus reducing them, as Jews, to a level with the despised, accursed Gentiles; and it is this which has been substantially the great stumbling-block all along. It is this which makes genuine Christianity so much disliked by natural men in all countries and in all ages, – the insisting on relinquishing every ground of hope but one, and that one the death of Jesus Christ on a cross. Whenever Christianity has been so modified as to get quit of this most repulsive principle, it has ceased to excite very strongly the antipathies of natural men. But it is this doctrine which gives Christianity all its peculiar efficacy; and when "the offence of the cross" ceases in any other way than by the eyes of the mind being opened to behold its glory, the triumph of Christianity ceases also. The Jews had no great objection that Jesus should be allowed to be the Messiah, if, at the same time, the law of Moses was admitted to be the only way of salvation; and there are multitudes who are ready enough to admit that Jesus was a divine messenger, if they may be but permitted to depend for salvation on anything but His obedience to death.

It is not a pleasant thing in itself to be an object of censure; but an honest minister of the gospel would rather be censured than praised by persons of a particular mode of thinking. When he hears a discourse praised by those who are "going about to establish their own righteousness," – who are expecting salvation in some other way than "through the redemption which is in Christ Jesus," – he feels alarmed that "the cross" has not had its own pre-eminent place assigned it; for to such persons, wheresoever "the cross" is, there is "a stumbling-block." To the unrenewed mind, Christ crucified – the sole foundation of the sinner's hope – is the grand hindrance to the embracing of

Christianity. Give up this, and what is necessarily connected with this, and the bitterest opponents of Christianity may be softened into complaisance; but you cannot give up this without in effect giving up Christianity itself – with all that gives it peculiarity – with all that gives it efficacy.

7. THE APOSTLE'S WISH THAT THEY WHO TROUBLED THE GALATIAN CONVERT MIGHT BE CUT OFF.

In the next verse the apostle expresses a strong wish that the Galatian church were well rid of those Judaisers who had troubled their peace, and had well-nigh subverted their souls. "I would[116] they were even cut off which trouble you" (Gal. 5:12.). The word translated "trouble" here is not the same as that word in the 10th verse, though it is nearly of equivalent import.[117] The Judaising teachers derived the name of "troublers" on two accounts, both as they troubled the minds of the Galatian converts individually with doubts and alarms, and collectively as a society, producing strifes and schisms among them. To use the language of the apostolic decree respecting the same class of persons at Antioch, "They troubled the disciples with words, subverting their souls" (Acts 15:24.); and they also, to use the apostle's language in reference to the same class in the Church of Rome, "caused divisions and offences, contrary to the doctrine which they had learned" (Rom. 16:17.).

With regard to those persons, the apostle wishes they were "cut off." It is not very easy to say what is the true meaning of the phrase, rendered "I would that they were cut off."[118] Some will have it a wish that, by a sudden stroke of Divine judgment, they were deprived of life, and hurried into the destruction which their conduct merited. This is the view taken of it by the judicious Calvin. He remarks that, though at first sight such a wish may not seem very consistent with the Christian meekness of the apostle, yet, in a certain state of mind, when the glory of God and the welfare of His church occupy the whole attention, and when the criminal conduct of some individuals is seen to be obscuring the one and endangering the other, and there seems no way of the mischief's being stopped but by their death, such a wish as that of the apostle is the natural result of a high degree of spiritual feeling, and is not to be condemned. "When the wolf entereth the fold of Christ," says he, "is the shepherd to be condemned who wishes his destruction, as absolutely necessary to the safety of the sheep"?[119] This is anything but satisfactory, and can be accounted for only on the principle that the reformer had still in him a remnant of the spirit of the church he had abandoned. Surely, when he wrote these words, he knew not what spirit he was of.

It is a more probable interpretation which explains the phrase of excommunication. 'I wish they were cut off from the Christian church; I wish they were distinctly declared to be what they are, not Christians.' At the same time, I think it likely that, if this had been the apostle's meaning, he would, as in the case of the incestuous person in the church of Corinth, have exhorted the Galatian church to excommunicate them (1 Cor. 5:3-5.). The words may be rendered, 'I wish they would cut themselves off; I wish they would renounce all pretensions to Christianity.' This is a wish similar to that of Jesus Christ in reference to the church of Laodicea, – "I would that thou wert either cold or hot" (Rev. 3:15.). Paul would rather that those men had become true Christians; but if not, he would rather they would cut themselves off from the Christian church altogether. It is a very just observation of Mr. Fuller, that "corrupt Christianity is more offensive to God" – and, we may add, more hurtful to the interests of genuine Christianity, "than open infidelity." Every man who has just and extended views will be ready to say, 'We wish there were more real Christians; but we wish there were fewer merely nominal Christians, even although the diminution should be made by these nominal Christians throwing off a profession altogether.' The doctrinal errors and the practical abuses which prevail among nominal Christians are the principal case, of a secondary kind, why Christianity has not long ago gained her promised triumphs.[120]

The general conclusion of a practical kind, to which all this is calculated to lead, is, that, both as individuals and as churches, if we wish to be what we ought to be, we must cling alone to the cross — to Jesus Christ, and to Him crucified — as the sole ground of hope, and the grand channel of Divine influence; and that our worst enemies, whatever guise they may assume, are those who would conceal or obscure the cross, or place anything in its room. "God forbid that we should glory, save in the cross of our Lord Jesus."

PART VI.

PRACTICAL INJUNCTIONS.

"For you were called to freedom, brothers. Only do not use the freedom for an opportunity to the flesh, but serve one another by love. For all the Law is fulfilled in one word, "You shall love your neighbor as yourself." But if you bite and devour one another, be careful that you are not destroyed by one another. But I say, Walk in the Spirit and you will not fulfill the lust of the flesh. For the flesh lusts against the Spirit, and the Spirit against the flesh. And these are contrary to one another: so that you cannot do the things that you want to do. But if you are led by the Spirit, you are not under Law. Now the works of the flesh are clearly revealed — adultery, fornication, uncleanness and lustfulness, idolatry, practicing of evil magic, hatreds — fightings, jealousies, outbursts of anger, party arguments, differences, false teachings, envyings, murders, drunkenness, wild parties and things like these. As to *these* I tell you now, as I also said before, that they who do such things shall not inherit the kingdom of God. But the fruit of the Spirit is love, joy, peace, long-suffering, kindness, goodness, faith, meekness, self-control — against such things there is no law. But they that are Christ's crucified the flesh with its passions and lusts. If we live by the Spirit, we should also walk by the Spirit. We should not seek after self-glory, provoking one another, envying one another. Brothers, if a man is taken in some fault, you, who are spiritual restore him in a spirit of meekness, considering youself for fear that you also may be tempted.

Bear one another's burdens, and so fulfill the law of Christ. For if anyone thinks himself to be something, being nothing, he is fooling himself. But let each prove his own work and then he alone will have rejoicing, not in another. For each shall carry his own load. Let him who is taught in the word share with him who teaches in all good things. Be not deceived, God is not mocked — for whatever a man sows, that he shall also reap. For he that sows to his own flesh shall reap from the flesh everlasting misery. But he that sows to the Spirit shall reap everlasting life from the Spirit. But let us not lose heart in doing well, for in due time we shall reap, if we do not faint. So then as we are able, we should do good to all, and especially towards those of the household of faith." — Galatians 5:13-6:10.

In the verses which follow, down to the 10th verse of the sixth chapter, the apostle gives the Galatians various practical advices, rising out of the previous discussions.

SECT. I. — CAUTION AGAINST THE ABUSE OF LIBERTY.

He first of all cautions the Galatians against the abuse of their Christian liberty. "For brethren, ye have been called unto liberty; only use not liberty for an occasion to the flesh, but by love serve one another" (Gal. 5:13.).

There is a strange disposition in mankind to misapprehend the meaning and tendency of religious truth however plainly stated, and to turn it to purposes which it was never intended to answer, and which, when rightly understood, it obviously appears that it was never intended to answer. The Apostle Paul was well aware of this tendency, and accordingly he often connects with a statement of a Christian doctrine a caution against its abuse. This is what we find him doing here in reference to the doctrine of Christian liberty which he had been stating and defending. The whole of the paragraph which commences with this verse and ends with the 10th verse of the next chapter, is occupied with showing that the liberty wherewith Christ had made them free, by no means relaxed their obligation to religious and moral duty, but, on the contrary, furnished them at once with the most cogent motives and the most powerful encouragements to avoid sin in all its forms, and to cultivate universal holiness both in temper and conduct.

"For"[1] seems here to be merely a particle of transition. The whole clause is equivalent to, 'Brethren, ye have indeed been called to liberty.' To be "called," is, as we have had repeated occasion to remark to you, equivalent to becoming a Christian; so that the apostle's statement is, — 'In being made Christians ye were made freemen.[2] "Called unto liberty,"[3] does not mean merely to be called into a state of freedom from the Mosaic law, but to be called into such a state of spiritual liberty generally as is quite incompatible with subjection to that institution. When men become Christians by the belief of the truth, they are introduced into the state, and formed to the character, of spiritual freemen. Their conscience is delivered from the yoke of human authority, and their obedience, even to the Divine law, flows not from the mercenary spirit of a slave, but from the generous spirit of a son. It is the offspring not of unenlightened fear, but of well-informed love.

In the beginning of the chapter the apostle had exhorted the Galatians to "stand fast" in this liberty, and to resist every attempt to bring them into bondage. In the passage before us, he warns them against the imprudent display and the criminal abuse of this liberty. Ye are indeed called unto liberty, and you ought to assert the liberty into which you have been called; but you ought also to beware of using it as an occasion to the flesh.[4]

"The flesh" here obviously signifies the depraved inclinations which are natural to man in his present state, and which, though subdued, are by no means extinguished even in the regenerate. These inclinations are personified under the name of "the flesh," and are represented as ready to seize every opportunity that is afforded for obtaining their gratification. In the seventh chapter of the Romans we find "sin dwelling in" Paul — which is just a synonyme for "the flesh," — represented as "taking occasion" from the tenth commandment to "work in him all manner of concupiscence" (Rom. 7:8.); and here we find "the flesh" in the Galatians represented as being ready to turn to its own purposes the doctrine of Christian liberty.[5]

Of the manner in which "the flesh" has availed itself of the doctrines of Christian liberty for its gratification, the history of the Christian church is replete with the most melancholy illustrations. At a very early period indeed "the grace of God was turned into lasciviousness," and freedom from sin strangely identified with freedom in sin — freedom to sin. There were men bearing the Christian name who said, "let us continue in sin because grace abounds," and who used the liberty to which they falsely laid claim as a cloak of wickedness. The character and doom of such persons are graphically described by the apostles Peter and Jude: — "They shall receive the reward of unrighteousness, as they that count it pleasure to riot in the daytime: sports they are the blemishes, sporting themselves with their own deceivings while they feast with you: having eyes full of adultery, and that cannot cease from sin; beguiling unstable souls: an heart they have exercised with covetous practices; cursed children: which have forsaken the right way, and are gone astray, following the way of Balaam the son of Bosor, who loved the wages of unrighteousness; but was rebuked for his iniquity: the dumb ass, speaking with man's voice, forbade the madness of the prophet. These are wells without water, clouds that are carried with a tempest; to whom the mist of darkness is reserved for ever. For when they speak great swelling words of vanity, they allure through the lusts of the flesh, through much wantonness, those that were clean escaped from them who live in error. While they promise them liberty, they themselves are the servants of corruption: for of whom a man is overcome, of the same is he brought in bondage. For if after they have escaped the pollutions of the world, through the knowledge of the Lord and Savior Jesus Christ, they are again entangled therein, and overcome, the latter end is worse with them than the beginning. For it had been better for them not to have known the way of righteousness, than, after they have known it, to turn from the holy commandment delivered unto them. But it is happened unto them according to the true proverb, The dog is turned to his own vomit again; and the sow that was washed to her wallowing in the mire." "For there are certain men crept in unawares, who were before of old ordained to this condemnation, ungodly men, turning the grace of our God into lasciviousness." "Wo unto them." "To them is reserved the blackness of darkness for ever" (2 Pet. 2:13-22. Jude 4,11,13.).

It is deeply to be regretted that abuses of the doctrine of Christian liberty are not mere matters of history, but that there are still so many who "use it as an occasion to the flesh." There are not wanting men who avow the principle that Christians have nothing to do with the law of God; and there are many who would not avow such a general statement who are yet acting as if it were true. This is fearful delusion. The madman who has mistaken his tattered garments for the flowing robes of majesty, and his manacles for golden bracelets studded with jewels, has not erred so widely as the man who has mistaken carnal license for Christian liberty.[6]

From the apostle's urging the Galatians to mutual love, and cautioning them against biting and devouring one another, it seems probable that the particular abuse of Christian liberty which he had in view was the ostentatious and untimely display of their freedom from the Mosaic law, in a way calculated to offend those of their brethren who, though they did not depend on the law for justification, yet conscientiously, though mistakenly, yielded obedience to its injunctions as an unrepealed divine institution. The apostle's advice seems equivalent to, 'Let not pride and vanity, or any other fleshly principle, induce you to make uncalled for displays of your Christian liberty, which may hurt the feelings and disturb the peace of some of your Christian brethren.'

It is a very important observation of a judicious commentator,[7] that "there is a great difference between Christian liberty, and the use of Christian liberty." Christian liberty is an internal thing; it belongs to the mind and conscience, and has a direct reference to God. The use of Christian liberty is an external thing; it belongs to conduct, and has reference to man. No consideration should prevail on us for a moment to give up our liberty; but many a consideration should induce us to forego the practical assertion or display of our liberty.

SECT. II. – AN EXHORTATION TO "SERVE ONE ANOTHER IN LOVE" SUPPORTED BY MOTIVES.

Instead of making such an ostentatious display of their liberty, the apostle exhorts the Galatians, – i.e. obviously that part of them who thought along with him – "the spiritual," as he terms them in the beginning of the next chapter – the same class whom he terms "the strong," in the Epistle to the Romans, – "by love to serve one another." Though free from the tyranny of human authority, they were readily, "in love," to act the part of servants to one another. "By love" signifies 'influenced by love;' and "serve one another" means, 'act the part of mutual servants; endeavor to promote one another's best interests; do not stand sturdily on your rights; do not obstinately assert, in every case, your undoubted prerogative as Christ's freemen; do not practically, and especially do not ostentatiously and invidiously, use that Christian liberty, which you cannot too sacredly preserve from violation; but, on the contrary, led by love, readily submit even to servile offices,[8] to promote one another's best interests.'

The apostle enforces his exhortation by two powerful motives: the one arising from love being the fulfilling of the law; and the other from the disastrous consequences of their allowing the flesh so to take occasion of their liberty, as to produce strifes and debate. "For all the law is fulfilled in one word, even in this, Thou shalt love thy neighbor as thyself. But if ye bite and devour one another, take heed that ye be not consumed one of another" (Gal. 5:14,15.).

1. LOVE IS THE FULFILMENT OF THE LAW.

"The law" here plainly does not signify the Mosaic law, but the law by which Christians are bound to regulate themselves; for, as the apostle elsewhere says, though completely free from the obligation of the Mosaic law, they are "not without law to God, but under the law to Christ." It is what the apostle calls "the commandment," when he says, "The end of the commandment is charity out of a pure heart, and of a good conscience, and of faith unfeigned" (1 Tim. 1:5.); and what the Apostle James terms "the perfect law of liberty," and "the royal law" (James 1:25; 2:8.), in opposition to the law of bondage.

Now, says the apostle, "By love serve one another," 'for love is the sum and substance of the law to which ye are subject.' "All the law is fulfilled in one word, even this, Thou shalt love thy neighbor as thyself." The precept here is quoted from Leviticus 19:18; but the words are plainly employed by the apostle in a somewhat different sense from that in which they are used by the Israelitish legislator. "Neighbor," with Moses, is equivalent to "one of the children of thy people;" "neighbor," with the apostle, is equivalent to 'every man.' The apostle had learned this mode of extending the meaning of the word "neighbor" from his Master. When, on our Lord's stating that the sum of the duty of man consists in the love of God, and the love of his neighbor, he was asked by a lawyer, "Who is my neighbor?" The parable of the good Samaritan was the answer (Luke 10:30-37.).

The command referred to has been by some considered as meaning merely, 'Thou shalt love thy neighbor as well as thyself;. that is, thou shalt not love thyself only, but thy neighbor also. This is certainly greatly below the true meaning. Others have interpreted it as equivalent to, 'Thou shalt love thy neighbor in the same degree as thyself.' This, as, from the constitution of human nature, it is impossible, is as obviously above the true meaning. The true interpretation is, 'Thou shalt love thy neighbor in a way similar to that in which thou lovest thyself − with the same sincerity, with the same constancy. Our Lord's words are the best commentary on it. "Whatsoever ye would that men should do to you, do ye even so to them."

Interpreters have wasted their ingenuity in endeavoring to show how the whole law can be said to be fulfilled by the love of our neighbor, when that law requires love to God, as well as love to man. The truth obviously is, that "the whole law" here is to be understood in reference to the subject of which the apostle is speaking. The whole of the law respecting out neighbor is fulfilled[9] by love. This precept is very fully illustrated by the apostle in his Epistle to the Romans: − "Owe no man anything, but to love one another: for he that loveth another hath fulfilled the law. For this, Thou shalt not commit adultrery, Thou shalt not kill, Thou shalt not steal, Thou shalt not bear false witness, Thou shalt not covet; and if there by any other commandment, it is briefly comprehended in this saying, namely, Thou shalt love thy neighbor as thyself. Love worketh no ill to his neighbor: therefore love is the fulfiling of the law" (Rom. 13:8-10.). When, then, Christians do not "serve one another by love," the law of Christ is not fulfilled but violated.

2. EVIL CONSEQUENCES OF AN OPPOSITE TEMPER AND CONDUCT.

Another motive which the apostle employs to induce the Galatian Christians to serve each other in love, is derived from the disastrous consequences of allowing the flesh so to take occasion of their liberty, as to produce strife and debate. 'But if ye bite and devour one another, take heed that ye be not consumed one of another" (Gal. 5:15.). The language is here highly figurative, but by no means obscure. By "biting and devouring one another" we are to understand violent strifes and debates in consequence of the new views which the Judaising teachers had introduced, − "vain contentions about the law," "perverse disputings," "foolish and unlearned questions gendering strife."

The natural consequence of thus "biting and devouring one another" was their being "consumed one of another." This may be understood of the mischievous effects of such contention either on the Galatians, viewed individually, or as a church. Such a state of contention would go far to destroy the life of Christian godliness in the hearts of the disputants. It would also materially affect the interests of the church. It would prevent accessions; for who would willingly join a society divided against itself? and it might very probably end in the dissolution of the church altogether, and the extinction of Christianity in that region of the world.[10]

The remark of the apostle is of general application. It is melancholy to mark how strikingly it has been illustrated in the history of the church in every age. How have the strifes and debates which have agitated the Christian church prevented edification within, and conversion without! It is not the conscientious differences subsisting among true

128

Christians which cause these evils. It is not the honest avowal of these differences, but the unchristian temper in which such questions are often, nay, almost always, debated that produces the mischief. The flesh takes occasion from them to seek its own gratification. The strifes and debates of Christians are one grand obstacle to the universal triumph of Christianity – the religion of love; and we have no reason to hope for this till we see the followers of Christ more influenced by the spirit of their Master. Blessed be God, we do see this in some measure. The love for debate in the Christian church is not extinguished, but it is greatly moderated; and the acrimonious and contemptuous spirit, which used to blow up its flames, is, we trust, decidedly on the decrease.

We strongly deprecate that spirit of insensibility to the importance of religious truth, which, if it produce tranquillity in the religious world, does so by producing death. That is the worst of all states. But it is very desirable that Christians – I mean true Christians – should deliver themselves more up to the cementing influence of those grand principles of Christian truth, in the belief of which they are all united; and, when they cannot help differing in opinion, maintain their conscientious views in a meek and humble spirit. It is in this way that we are to expect unity to flourish in the church, and to extend throughout the world. Nothing can produce this desirable state of things but a more general and diligent study of the will of God, as made known in His word, and a more liberal effusion of His Holy Spirit, who is the spirit of peace and love, as well as of truth and purity. To engage in this study, to pray for this effusion, is the duty of every individual Christian; and when

"Ὅρκον θ', ὃς δὴ πλεῖστον ἐπιχθονίους ἀνθρώπους
Πημαίνει, ὅτε κέν τις ἑκὼν ἐπίορκον ὀμόσσῃ."
—HESIOD, *Theog.* 226-232.

individual Christians generally set about the performance of this duty in the spirit of faith, and humility, and perseverance, glorious results may be expected. "How delightful," to borrow the beautiful words of Robert Hall, "could we behold in the church a peaceful haven inviting us to retire from the tossings and perils of this unquiet ocean to a sacred enclosure, a sequestered spot, which the storms and tempests of the world were not permitted to invade.

Intus aquae dulces vivoque sedilia saxo,
Nympharum domus. Hic fessas non vincula naves
Ulla tenent, unco non alligat ancora morsu."

Or in the more beautiful imagery and language of the inspired poet, – "Look upon Zion, the city of our solemnities: thine eyes shall see Jerusalem a quiet habitation, a tabernacle that shall not be taken down; not one of the stakes thereof shall ever be removed, neither shall any of the cords thereof be broken: but there the glorious Lord will be unto us a place of broad rivers and streams; wherein shall go no galley with oars, neither shall gallant ship pass thereby. For the Lord is our judge, the Lord is our lawgiver, the Lord is our king; He will save us" (Isa. 33:20-22.). "The Lord hasten it in His time."

SECT. III. – A GENERAL EXHORTATION TO "WALK IN THE SPIRIT" AS THE BEST MEANS OF OBTAINING DOMINION OVER THE LUSTS OF THE FLESH.

The best security against abusing the doctrines of grace is really to understand and believe them. It is on this principle that the apostle prescribes to a Christian evangelist a clear, full, and constant exhibition of the peculiarities of Christ's doctrine as the best method for securing that they who believe in Christ should maintain good works. "Not by works of righteousness which we have done, but according to His mercy He saved us, by the washing of regeneration, and renewing of the Holy Ghost; which He shed on us abundantly through Jesus Christ our Savior; that being justified by His grace, we should be made heirs according to the hope of eternal life. This is a faithful saying, and these things I will that thou affirm constantly, that[12] they which have believed in God might be careful to maintain good words. These things are good and profitable unto men."

It is on this principle, also, that, in thy passage which follows, he recommends the yielding of the mind up to the practical influence of the grand peculiarities of Christian truth as the best preservative from those immoral dispositions and practices in which, from the remaining depravity of their natures, even true Christians are in constant danger of indulging. "This I say then, Walk in the Spirit, and ye shall not fulfil[13] the lust of the flesh" (Gal. 5:16.). The word "Spirit" here does not seem to denote the Holy Spirit, that Divine person who, along with the Father and the Son, exists in the unity of the Godhead, and to whose operation all that is right in thought and feeling in created beings is traced in the Holy Scriptures; but that frame of thought and affection which is produced by His agency through the belief of "the truth as it is in Jesus."[14] It is contrasted with "the flesh," which is a general term for that frame of thought and affection which is habitual to man unchanged by Divine influence.

The introductory formula, "This I say,"[15] is obviously intended to mark the apostle's sense of the importance of the sentiment he was about to utter. "To walk"[16] is a common figurative expression for conduct. To "walk in the law of the Lord" is to regulate our conduct according to its precepts. To "walk in the Spirit," is to act like spiritual persons — to follow out to their fair practical consequences those views and affections to which, through the faith of the gospel, by the agency of the Holy Spirit, they were formed — to live habitually under the influence of the faith of Christ, and those dispositions which it naturally inspires. 'Deliver yourselves up to the native force of those new views and affections, and ye will not fulfil the lusts of the flesh.'

"The flesh," as we have just remarked, is the mode of thinking and feeling which is natural to man in the present state of human nature; and "the lusts of the flesh" are the desires which naturally rise out of this mode of thinking and feeling. From experience and observation, as well as from Scriptrue, we know that this mode of thinking and feeling is depraved — wholly depraved. Every man may truly adopt the apostle's language, "In me, that is. in my flesh, dwells no good thing" (Rom. 7:18.). The desires of the flesh then are foolish and criminal desires; and to "fulfil"[17] these desires is to endeavor to gratify them, to adopt the course of conduct to which they naturally lead.

The apostle's statement, then, is this, 'The best way of opposing the criminal biases of our depraved nature, is to yield ourselves up to the practical influence of that new and better mode of thinking and feeling into which we are brought by the faith of the gospel. This will put a more effectual check on the desires of the flesh than the most rigid observance of Mosaic ceremonies. Nothing mortifies pride, malignity, and impure desire, these lusts of the flesh, like walking in the Spirit.' Clear views of Christian truth, accompanied by corresponding affections, followed out to their obvious practical results, will do more to deliver a man from the power of vicious habits than the most minute, laborious series of external services or ritual observances.

It is probable that the Judaising teachers endeavored to recommend submission to the Mosaic law as a piece of moral discipline — an excellent method of "mortifying the flesh with its affections and lusts;" but Paul shows them "a more excellent way." If their "conversation was only such as became the gospel of Christ Jesus," They would find no want of the law as a means of nullifying sin. If they would but commit themselves to the influence of Christian faith and affection, they would experience that the school-mastership of the law was become unnecessary. Walking in the Spirit, they would walk in wisdom and in harmlessness, in purity and in love. "If ye walk in the Spirit, ye shall not fulfil the lusts of the flesh."

And it is plain, not only that it is so, but that it must be so. For the Spirit — the new way of thinking and feeling to which the faith of Christ forms a man — is directly opposite to the mode of thinking and feeling which is natural to man, and when the one prevails, the other must decay. This is the sentiment conveyed in the next verse. "For the flesh lusteth against the Spirit, and the Spirit against the flesh: and these are contrary the one to the other; so that ye cannot do the things that ye would" (Gal. 5:17.).

"The flesh" here, as above, is just a general term for that mode of thinking and feeling which is natural to man in his present depraved state, and which, although modified by an infinite variety of circumstances in individuals, is in its grand substantial character the same, common to the species; and "the Spirit," as opposed to it, is just a general name for that mode of thinking and feeling which is produced in the mind by the agency of the Holy Spirit through the instrumentality of Christian truth, which, though differing in degree, is substantially the same in all true Christians. "The flesh" is a phrase of equivalent meaning with "the old man," and "the Spirit" with "the new man." These two modes of thinking and feeling are here, as in many other parts of the apostle's writings, personified and spoken of as if they were living beings.

The flesh is represented as "lusting against the Spirit," and the Spirit against the flesh. These opposite modes of thinking and feeling may be viewed, either as existing in different minds, or in the same mind. In all men merely born of the flesh, the first of these modes of thinking and feeling reigns supreme. In all born of the Spirit, the second of these modes of thinking and feeling predominates; and it is to this that we are to trace that difference, that opposition, of desires and pursuits by which worldly men and true Christians are distinguished.

But it is not to this external struggle between these two modes of thinking and feeling that the apostle here refers, but to the opposition between them that is exhibited when they exist in the same mind. Every Christian is by nature a carnal man. He thinks and feels "according to the course of this world" (Eph. 2:2.). When he becomes a Christian by the belief of the truth under the operation of the Holy Ghost, he gets a new mode of thinking and feeling – he becomes a spiritual man – he is "delivered from the present evil world," and brought under "the power of the world which is to come." But he is not completely delivered in the present state. He is not thoroughly spiritualised. He still remains to a considerable degree under the power of his former mode of thinking and feeling, though his new mode of thinking and feeling gives a decided character to his habitual desires and pursuits.

Now, in such a person "the flesh lusteth against the Spirit, and the Spirit against the flesh." This is one of the subjects which are best illustrated by examples. Under the influence of that mode of thinking and feeling which the faith of the gospel and the operation of the Holy Ghost produce, the Christian earnestly wishes to acquiesce in the most severely afflictive dispensations of Divine Providence – to have no will but the will of God; but under the influence of that impatience of suffering, and that opposition to the Divine will, which are natural to man, he finds such acquiescence no easy attainment, and feels in extreme hazard of becoming fretful or sullen. This is "the flesh lusting against the Spirit."

On the other hand, when a Christian meets with unmerited ill-treatment from his fellow-men, he is very apt, under the influence of his natural mode of thinking and feeling, to cherish resentment and to seek revenge; but his new mode of thinking and feeling opposes this, and, remembering how God for Christ's sake forgave him all his trespasses, he is made, in opposition to the lustings of nature, to forgive his brother his trespasses. This is "the spirit lusting against the flesh."

In all this there is nothing but what is perfectly consistent with the constitution of human nature; though it must be confessed that, by forgetting that the representations in our text, and in the seventh chapter of Romans, are figurative; and that "the old man" and "the new man," "the flesh" and "the Spirit," "the law of the members" and "the law of the mind," are not separate living agents, but merely personifications of opposite modes of thinking and feeling, many Christian divines have involved this interesting department of Christian experience in a "darkness which may be felt – have perplexed and harassed the minds of the pious, and furnished to the falsehearted pretender to vital godliness an opportunity, of which he has not been slack to avail himself, of transferring the blame of his bad dispositions and criminal conduct from himself to some mysterious spiritual agent whom he terms "the old man," and for whose operations he does not feel himself answerable.[18]

These two modes of thinking and feeling are directly opposed to one another; "they are contrary one to the other." The one is occupied with "things seen and temporal," the other with "things unseen and eternal:" the desires and the pursuits to which they give origin must, of course, be opposite too.

The consequence of such a state of things in a mind in which both modes of thinking and feeling exist, where there is both flesh and spirit, is described in the close of the verse: "So that[19] ye cannot do the things that ye would." These words admit, and of course they have received, a considerable variety of interpretation. Some connect them with the first clause, – "The flesh lusteth against the Spirit; so that ye cannot do the things which ye would." They consider it as an expression of the same sentiment as the following passage in the Epistle to the Romans: "To will is present with me; but how to perform that which is good I find not" ' (Rom. 7:18.). 'Owing to remaining depravity, our holy resolutions are very imperfectly executed.' Others connect them with the second clause: "The spirit lusteth against the flesh; so that ye cannot do the things which ye would." 'In consequence of the tendencies of your renewed nature, you cannot – you dare not – yield obedience to the impulses of your depraved nature.' While a third class connect them with the third clause: "These two are contrary the one to the other; so that ye cannot do the things that ye would." 'You can neither follow your depraved nor your holy inclination without feeling resistance and opposition. You cannot follow your holy inclinations with that unmixed determination which distinguishes perfectly holy beings, nor can you follow your criminal inclinations with that unmixed determination that distinguishes completely depraved beings: the lustings of the flesh prevent the one; the lustings of the spirit prevent the other.' Did the passage stand alone, I would prefer this last mode of interpretation; but when I look at it in its connection, I can scarcely doubt that the second is the true mode of explanation. The verse before us is an illustration of the statement contained in the previous verse, that if they "walked in the Spirit, they would not fulfil the lusts of the flesh;" – that yielding themselves up to the practical influence of the new and better mode of thinking and feeling produced by the gospel, under the operation of the Holy Spirit, was the surest preventive of immoral conduct. 'Now,' says the apostle, 'I know indeed that the flesh will lust against the spirit, but the spirit will lust against the flesh (for these things are directly opposed); so that ye cannot do what, but for this opposite influence, you would be wholly inclined to do.' Just in the degree in which the Christian is influenced by the Spirit, the new and better mode of thinking and feeling, though he experience the natural desires of the flesh and the mind, he cannot fulfil them, he feels – not a natural, but – a moral impossibility of fulfilling them; and sets himself to mortify, crucify, destroy them.[20]

The observation which follows is obviously one made by the way, but, like all the apostle's occasional remarks, having an important bearing on his general object. "But if ye be led by the Spirit, ye are not under the law" (Gal. 5:18.).

"To be led by the Spirit" is another figurative expression, signifying to be influenced by the new mode of thinking and feeling to which the Spirit by the faith of the gospel forms men. To "walk in the Spirit" and to be "led by the Spirit," are nearly synonymous. The active influential nature of the Spirit is perhaps somewhat more clearly brought out in the last of these modes of expression. They who are thus influenced are not under the law. It has been ordinary to consider this verse as stating, that all who are the subjects of the leading influences of the Holy Ghost are delivered from the law, in its covenant form, from its condemning, and irritating, and commanding power. This proposition, if rightly explained, contains much important truth, but it does not, I apprehend, at all express the apostle's meaning. "The law" is here, as generally throughout the epistle, the Mosaic law, to which the Judaising teachers were endeavoring to subject the Galatians. And what the apostle says is this, – 'If you are influenced as you ought to be by these views and affections which grow out of the faith of the gospel, you will not be among those who seek to subject themselves to the Mosaic law, you will distinctly see that you stand in no need of it, that its genius does not correspond to the character of the new and better order of things which the Messiah has introduced, and refusing to submit to what are now nothing better than "commandments of men," you will "walk at liberty, keeping God's commandments." They who are led by the Spirit spontaneously[21] by "a law written on their hearts," follow that course which God approves, and have no need of the paedagogy of the law from which the church has been delivered.[22]

The great practical lesson taught us by this passage is, that, the true way of mortifying sin and making progress in holiness, is to yield our minds and hearts more and more up to the transforming influence of divine truth. Divine truth is efficacious only when attended by the operation of the Divine Spirit. The humble diligent study of the Bible, especially the New Testament scriptures, and fervent believing prayers for the assistance of the Holy Spirit, are the principal means of Christian sanctification.

That "the flesh" and "the Spirit" are direct opposites, and that of course the true way of escaping from the dominion of the former is to subject ourselves to the power of the latter, is strikingly and beautifully illustrated in the passage which immediately follows, containing as it does a view of the practical consequences of these two modes of thinking and feeling — the carnal and the spiritual mind. "Now the words[23] of the flesh are manifest, which are these: Adultery, fornication, uncleanness, lasciviousness, idolatry, witchcraft, hatred, variance, emulations, wrath, strife, seditions, heresies, envyings, murders, drunkenness, revellings, and such like: of the which I tell you before, as I have also told you in time past, that they which do such things shall not inherit the kingdom of God" (Gal. 5:19-21.).

As "the flesh" is, as we have repeatedly remarked, the mode of thinking and feeling natural to man in an unregenerate state, so "the works of the flesh"[24] are the practical results of this mode of thinking and feeling — the mode of conduct to which it naturally leads — just as we say, "the work of righteousness is peace," peace is the natural result of righteousness. "Now," says the apostle, "the works of the flesh are manifest."[25] There is no reason to doubt about them. It is quite plain what they are. There is no need of laborious inquiries to ascertain them. And then he proceeds to particularise a number of them. When the apostle represents all the different varieties of injustice, malignity, and impurity as the works of the flesh, he states the same truth as our Lord does when He says that, "out of the" unchanged "heart" of man "proceed evil thoughts, murders, adulteries, false witness, blasphemies." Every species of immorality of conduct is the result of depraved thought and feeling. What appears without is the index of what is going on within.

To enter into a minute description of the different crimes which are here mentioned, could serve no good purpose, and might serve some bad ones. There are immoral practices which are not even to be named among Christians, and there are others which, though they must be named, should scarcely be more than named. There are certain vices, and a number of them are mentioned in this catalogue, which can scarcely be made the objects of steady intellectual contemplation without tainting in some degree the purity of the mind. The greater part of the terms employed by the apostle are sufficiently plain. A few of them, however, to an English reader require a word or two in explanation.[26]

The word rendered "witchcraft"[27] is of ambiguous meaning. It is used to signify the preparation and administration of poison, and also the magical use of herbs and other substances for producing love, or hatred, or indifference. It is probable that it is in the last sense that it is employed here. The employment of such terms is no proof of the reality of magical influence. It merely establishes the fact, that magical arts were then practised, and that the practice of such arts was a work of the flesh.

"Sedition,"[28] in the modern usage of the English language, denotes a political crime, the endeavoring to excite disturbances and change in a government. There can be no reason to doubt that in very many cases this is criminal — a work of the flesh; but the meaning of the word used by the apostle is much more extensive, and describes all divisions which originate in other principles than a regard to truth and justice, whether in families, or states, or churches (Rom. 16:17; 1 Cor. 3:3.).

"Heresies,"[29] though the English word is little more than the Greek word in English characters, does not convey to an English mind anything like an exact idea of the apostle's meaning. Heresy in English means an error with regard to some fundamental principle of religion. We call Socinians and Pelagians heretics. In the apostle's usage of the term heresy it is nearly equivalent to sect, and, as used here, is very nearly synonymous with seditions, unreasonable and unnecessary divisions. This seems the ordinary sense in which the word is used in the New Testament, and it enables us to explain a passage which in the English sense of the term "heresy" is not easily explained. The apostle says that "a heretic is condemned of himself" (Tit. 3:11.). Now, certainly, every man who errs even on a fundamental doctrine of Christianity is not "self-condemned" in the ordinary meaning of these words. I have no doubt that many men have been perfectly sincere in maintaining what are commonly called heresies. The apostle's meaning is, – 'The man who unreasonably leaves the communion of the church condemns and punishes himself. By leaving the church he executes upon himself the severest sentence she can denounce against him, that of excommunication.

These particular immoral practices are mentioned by the apostle probably because they were very prevalent in the age and among the people to whom he was writing. He closes his catalogue, however, by the very general expression, "and such like."[30] The substance of his statement is obviously this, – 'The flesh, that mode of thinking and feeling which is common to all men in their unregenerate state, naturally produces every form of impiety and malignity, impurity and intemperance.'

What a humbling view of human nature! But is it more humiliating than it is just? In every age has not "the wickedness of man been great on the earth"? and is there any man who knows himself that is not ready to say with the apostle, "in me, that is in my flesh, dwells no good thing"? There is plainly something radically wrong with human nature. It stands in need not merely of improvement but renovation. We "must be born again." "Old things must pass away, and all things must become new."

To his enumeration of the works of the flesh, the apostle appends a very solemn declaration in reference to them, – "Of the which I tell you before, as I have also told you in time past, that they which do such things shall not inherit the kingdom of God." The importance of the statement appears from the solemn manner in which it is introduced: "in reference to these things I tell you before;" that is, 'I forewarn you,' – his declaration referring to something that is future, – "as I also in time past," when among you, warned you. When we look at such declarations as that before us, we are apt to suppose that, if once made, they would never need to be repeated – it seems that they would strike so deep into the heart, as to influence every future thought and feeling – and that, if once known, they could never be forgotten. But how different is the truth! The plainest and most interesting truths of religion need to be very often repeated. "Precept must be on precept, and line upon line;" and the minister who is more anxious to save his people's souls than to tickle their imaginations and gratify their curiosity, will, like the apostle, find it requisite to tell them again what he has often told them before. For him to say the same things ought not to be grievous to him, for it is not only safe but useful – aye, necessary for them.

The declaration is one that justifies the solemnity with which it is introduced, – "They which do such things shall not inherit the kingdom of God." "The kingdom of God," or "of heaven," is a phrase of frequent occurrence in the New Testament. It is plainly used in two ways, in the one of which Christians are viewed as the subjects, in the other as the possessors, of the kingdom. The first way of using the phrase naturally rose out of the mode of thinking common among the Jews, and produced by the phraseology of the prophets. The Messiah, or promised deliverer, is very often spoken of by them as a Prince; and the order of things to be introduced by him is naturally spoken of as his kingdom. In this view of the figure, the Messiah is the king, and all true Christians are his subjects. This is perhaps the most ordinary way in which the phrase is employed; and it is sometimes used with a reference to the laws, and sometimes to the privileges, of this spiritual kingdom, − sometimes in reference to its imperfect state on earth, and sometimes to its perfect state in heaven. In the second way of employing the phrase, it is used on the general principle of figurative language. To denote the dignity and happiness which await true Christians in their ultimate state, it is termed "the kingdom prepared for them." The figure is used in this way when the Apostle James speaks of poor Christians being "heirs of the kingdom which God has promised to them who love Him." When Christians are represented as "made kings," and when it is promised to such as overcome that they shall "sit down with Christ on His throne, even as He also overcame, and is set down with His Father on His throne," − wherever, indeed, the phrase before us occurs, "inherit the kingdom of God," − the phrase is obviously used in this last way; and to "inherit the kingdom of God" is just equivalent to 'obtain possession of that state of dignity and happiness, which is figuratively represented as a kingdom − a divine kingdom.'

The apostle's assertion, then, is that no man who does the works of the flesh shall be a partaker of the celestial blessedness. The assertion is a most solemn and important one. The man who is habitually characterised by any one of the habits above mentioned, or by any similar habit, cannot, if he die in this state, be saved. Let us all look inward, lest we come short of the heavenly kingdom. Eternal happiness is at stake. If we habitually indulge in any immoral habit, it matters not what it is; if we are habitually ungodly, or impure, or unjust, or intemperate, we cannot be saved. And let us remember that exclusion from that state of celestial royalty is but part of the evil. There are but two states in the eternal world, and they who do not "inherit the kingdom" must be "cast into outer darkness, where there is weeping, and wailing, and gnashing of teeth." There is no intermediate sentence between, − "Come, ye blessed, inherit the kingdom," and, "Depart, ye cursed, into everlasting fire."

It would be well if all who are living to the flesh would seriously consider these truths, − "If ye live after the flesh, ye must die." "If ye sow in the flesh, of the flesh ye must reap corruption." While men are "after the flesh," they will "mind the things of the flesh." The only way of securing abstinence from the works of the flesh, which end in perdition, is to be "born of the Spirit;" for "except a man be born again," he will not abstain from the works of the flesh, which must ruin him. The tree must be made good that the fruit may be good. "Ye must be born again," "not of corruptible seed, but of incorruptible, even of the word of God, which liveth and abideth for ever."

The apostle having thus stated the practical results of that mode of thinking and feeling which is common to all men in their unregenerate state, and which he terms "the flesh," goes on to give a contrasted view of the practical results of that new and better mode of thinking and feeling, to which men are formed by the Holy Spirit, through the faith of the gospel, and which he terms "the Spirit." "But the fruit of the Spirit is love, joy, peace, long-suffering, gentleness, goodness, faith, meekness, temperance: against such there is no law" (Gal. 5:22,23.).

"The Spirit" here, as throughout the whole context, is the new way of thinking and feeling to which a man is formed by the faith of the truth. Now "the fruit"[31] of this is just the disposition and habits that grow out of it. "Love"[32] is enlightened benignant affection toward God and man; "joy"[33] is holy cheerfulness; "peace"[34] is a peaceful disposition, rising out of "the peace of God keeping the mind and heart;" "long-suffering"[35] is patience under ill-treatment long continued (Rom. 2:4; Eph. 4:2; Col. 3:12.); "gentleness[36] is kindness − readiness to forgive and relieve (2 Cor. 6:6; Col. 3:12.); "goodness[37] is a disposisition to oblige (2 Thess. 1:4.); "faith"[38] is fidelity (Matth. 23:23; Rom. 3:3; Tit. 2:10.); "meekness"[39] is lenity, or a disposition to bear, forbear, and forgive (1 Cor. 4:21; Col. 3:12.); "temperance"[40] is continence − moderation, in our estimate, desire, and pursuit, of worldly good.

He who, through the belief of the truth, has the mind in him which was in Christ, is, in the degree in which he has this mind in him, good and happy − filled with benevolence −

happy in himself, and rejoicing in the happiness of all around him – at peace with God and himself, and disposed to be at peace with all men – not easily provoked, even by continued ill usage – mild in his temper and manners – distinguished by unbending integrity and inviolable fidelity – gentle to the infirmities of others – and, if severe in anything, severe to himself, in guarding against every approximation to sinful indulgence. Such is the kind of character which naturally grows out of that new and better mode of thinking, to which men are formed by the faith of the truth. It would not be difficult to show how every one of these holy amiable dispositions grows out of the new mind, – how the faith of the truth, or, in other words, the truth believed, naturally leads to these results. To do this with all of them would occupy too much room. I shall content myself with showing how one of these tempers is "the fruit of the Spirit" – gentleness of meekness, – and I shall borrow my illustration from the apostle's own writings. Christians are exhorted to be "gentle, showing all meekness unto all men; "for," adds the apostle, "we ourselves also were sometimes foolish, disobedient, deceived, serving divers lusts and pleasures, living in malice and envy, hateful, and hating one another. But after that the kindness and love of God our Savior toward man appeared, not by works of righteousness which we have done, but according to His mercy He saved us, by the washing of regeneration, and renewing of the Holy Ghost; which He shed on us abundantly through Jesus Christ our Savior; that, being justified by His grace, we should be made heirs according to the hope of eternal life" (Tit. 3:2-7.).

It will be a very edifying exercise, in our retirements, to go over the whole of the passage, and to consider how the faith of the grand peculiarities of Christian truth is calculated to produce all the various graces and virtues of the Christian character.

It is quite evident that the fruit of the Spirit and the works of the flesh – the practical results of the unregenerate and the regenerate frame of mind – are directly opposite, and that in the degree in which a man is under the influence of the latter will he be delivered from the influence of the former; and that of course "walking in the Spirit" is the best way of guarding against "fulfilling the lusts of the flesh." It is plainly morally impossible that the man full of "love, joy, peace, long suffering, gentleness, goodness, faith, meekness, and temperance," should indulge in the works of the flesh, as specified in the preceding verses; and that the shortest and only effectual method of becoming truly holy, and truly happy, is just to have the mind completely imbued with the grand distinguishing peculiarities of Christian truth.

Particular precepts, enjoining what is right and forbidding what is wrong, are very useful in their own place in promoting true holiness; but their place is, comparatively speaking, a subordinate one. What is chiefly wanted is a living spring of holy disposition – a habitual dislike of sin in all its forms – a habitual love of holiness; and this is nowhere to be obtained but in that "new mind," which is indeed "the mind of Christ," and which becomes ours when, and just in the proportion in which, under the influence of the Holy Spirit, we believe "the truth as it is in Jesus."

As it is "the Spirit," the new mind, alone which can produce these fruits; so, on the other hand, wherever there is the Spirit, the new mind, these effects will be produced. Whatever profession we may make, it is certain that we do not understand and believe the gospel, if we do not feel a happy, holy, transforming influence. "The Spirit" is an active principle. Wherever it exists it operates. If we are habitually strangers to the dispositions above enumerated, we have not "the Spirit of Christ;" and "if we have not the Spirit of Christ, we are none of His."

Alas! have not many who bear Christ's name reason to fear that they are altogether destitute of His Spirit; and even those who have something like satisfactory evidence that in them is the mind which was in Him, have they not much ground of regret and self-condemnation that they have it in so limited a measure. The only way of obtaining it by those who want it, is the belief of the truth under the influence of the Holy Ghost; and the only way of obtaining larger measures of the Spirit, is to grow in the knowledge and faith of this truth; and in order to the growth, and continued and increased operation, of this knowledge and faith, Divine influence is necessary; and this continued and increased operation is promised to sincere, believing, and persevering prayer.

The apostle adds, "Against such there is no law." This is one of those passages in which, though the words are perfectly plain, there is some difficulty in perceiving their reference, or the particular purpose for which the apostle employs them. "Against such,"[41] that is, not against such tempers and dispositions, but against persons characterised by such tempers and dispositions there is no law. Some have supposed that the apostle's meaning may be thus expressed, 'If all men were of this description, there would be no need of law.' These are not at all the class of people against whom "law" is directed. (1 Tim. 1:9-11.). We rather think that the following statement comes at least nearer his object in introducing this clause, 'The Judaising teachers, to gain their end, not only talked much of the advantages of submitting to the law of Moses, but also of the danger of not submitting to it. Now, says the apostle, 'these threatenings need not alarm you if ye thus walk in the Spirit. That law approves of such characters and corresponding conduct, that law has no curse for you.'[42]

The apostle then proceeds to state that all true Christians do, under the influence of the Spirit, endeavor to mortify the flesh – under the influence of their new mode of thinking and feeling endeavor completely to abandon their old mode of thinking and feeling; and calls on the Galatians who professed to be spiritually alive to prove this by a corresponding course of conduct in avoiding the works of the flesh, and displaying the fruits of the Spirit in their behavior to each other. "And they that are Christ's have crucified the flesh with the affections and lusts" (Gal. 5:24.).

"They who are Christ's" is a phrase just equivalent to the appellation Christians, when understood in its true extent of meaning. It is a word often employed in a very extenuated sense. Every man who makes a profession of Christianity – who pays some regard to its external offices – who has been baptized, and who has not formally renounced his baptism – every man, in a word, who is not a Pagan, or Mohammedan, or Jew, or infidel, is usually called a Christian. But there are many such Christians who are not Christ's. By their worldly, and often wicked, conduct, they dishonor His name and injure His interest; and on the great day of final reckoning He shall say to them, "Depart from Me, I never knew you, ye workers of iniquity." The general idea suggested by the expression is intimate connection – "They are Christ's," as "Christ is God's." They are His peculiar property, given to Him by His Father, redeemed by His blood, animated by His Spirit, subject to His authority, conformed to His image, devoted to His honor. They call no man master or proprietor – one is their master and proprietor, Christ. They are not their own, but His – His only – wholly – for ever. Now, all who are thus Christ's "have crucified[43] the flesh with the affections and lusts."

"The flesh" is, as I have so often had occasion to remark, a general name for that mode of thinking and feeling which is   natural to man so long as he continues a stranger to the regenerating power of Divine influence; and "the affections and lusts" are just those dispositions and desires which naturally grow out of this frame of thought and affection. The flesh and its attending lusts are here personified, spoken of as living beings; and true Christians are represented as putting them to death by crucifixion.

The figure is bold, and to our comparatively cold and tame occidental imaginations may appear harsh; but it is highly significant, and its meaning is obvious. Crucifixion was a punishment appropriated to the worst crimes of the basest sort of criminals, and produced death, not suddenly, but gradually. This seems to have been the idea present to the apostle's mind: True Christians regard with disapprobation and loathing that mode of thinking and feeling which is common to all till they are renewed; and they earnestly desire, and constantly seek, its complete extinction. They do not succeed in completely destroying it while here below; but they have fixed it to the Cross, and they are determined to keep it there till it expire. The phrase is similar in its meaning – but more emphatic – to the phrases, "mortifying our members which are on the earth" – "putting off the old man who is corrupt in his deeds."

Some have considered this passage as parallel with the following passage in the Epistle to the Romans, — "Our old man is crucified with Him, that the body of sin might be destroyed, that henceforth we should not serve sin."[44] But the two passages refer to two completely distinct, though very closely connected, subjects. The passage in the Epistle to the Romans refers to something done for the Christians — the passage before us to something which the Christian does for himself. The one describes the Christian privilege — the other delineates his character. The statement in the Epistle to the Romans is, 'The atonement secures the sanctification of all interested in it. What Christ suffered on the cross laid a secure foundation for the deliverance of His people from all immoral principles.' The statement before us is, 'Every true Christian regards with disapprobation and hatred that wrong way of thinking and feeling which is natural to him, and is engaged in endeavoring to root it out completely. He is treating it in a way analogous to that in which the basest criminal is treated.'

It deserves notice that the expression is unlimited — "the flesh, with the affection and lusts." It is not merely with some of the more unsightly products of the flesh that the Christian is displeased, it is with the flesh itself. It is not the pruning of the old stock which will serve his purpose, it must be dug up by the roots. It is not the improvement of "the old man," it is the putting him off. What the Christian is determinedly seeking after is complete deliverance from a mode of thinking and feeling at variance with the mind and will of God.

This crucifixion of "the flesh, with its affections and lusts" — the habitual desire and endeavor to master that wrong way of thinking and feeling, which is natural to us all, is peculiar to the true Christian, and it is characteristic of the true Christian. None but true Christians do so, — all true Christians do so. None but those who are Christ's "crucify the flesh, with its affections and lusts." Many who are not Christians dislike peculiar vices, and carefully avoid them. Many who are not true Christians set about a partial self-reformation, and for a time are very zealous in prosecuting it; but none but a true Christian makes war habitually with "the flesh," the worldly mode of thinking and feeling, in its root as well as in its fruit — in its most reputable as well as in its most disgraceful forms. Other men may chastise "the flesh," but it is only they that are Christians that crucify it.

And as it is peculiar to Christians, so it is common to them to "crucify the flesh, with its affections and lusts." Some of them are more successful than others in mortifying and crucifying their depraved modes of thinking and feeling; but they are all honestly thus engaged; and it is just in the degree in which they are successful that they give evidence to themselves and others that they are indeed belonging to Christ. The apostle's statement is not what many commentators have represented it. They who are Christians ought to "crucify the flesh, with its affections and lusts," though that is a truth too; but it is they who are Christians do crucify — a declaration which plainly implies, that if men do not "crucify the flesh, with its affections and lusts," they are not Christ's. The man who habitually indulges any of the affections or lusts of the flesh, makes it evident, whatever he calls himself, he is not in reality a Christian. He has not the Spirit of Christ, and therefore he is none of His. .

The apostle proceeds now to exhort the Galatians to prove the reality of their religion by producing its fruits. The exhortation, we should have naturally expected, would have been, — 'If, then, ye are Christ's, crucify the flesh, with its affections and lusts.' To be "in Christ," and to be "in the Spirit," are descriptive of the same persons. Not to "walk after the flesh," and to "walk after the Spirit," are but different views of the same kind of character and conduct; so that, to a person who is familiar with the apostle's mode of thought and expression, there is nothing unnatural in the phraseology of the exhortation that follows. "If we live in the Spirit, let us also walk in the Spirit" (Gal. 5:25).

To "live," in the phraseology of the apostle, is often equivalent to 'be happy.' "Now we live, if ye stand fast in the Lord" (1 Thess. 3:8.). "If ye through the Spirit do mortify the deeds of the body, ye shall live" (Rom. 8:13.). It is plain, however, that the word is not used in this sense in the passage before us. To "live in the Spirit" is just 'to be spiritually alive' — to be animated and actuated by the Spirit.

"The Spirit," as I have endeavored to show, is, in the whole of this context, that new mode of thinking and feeling to which a man is formed by the Holy Spirit, by the instrumentality of the faith of the truth as it is in Jesus; and to "live in the Spirit" is just to possess this mode of thinking and feeling.

To "walk," is, in Scripture language, descriptive of a course of conduct. To "walk in the Spirit"[45] is habitually to act spiritually — to behave like spiritual men — like men who think and feel in that new and better way to which the Holy Spirit forms all who are under His influence.

The force of the exhortation is obviously this, — 'If we are Christians, let us prove ourselves to be so, by acting like Christians. If we are spiritually alive, let us show that we are so by being spiritually active. If we really think and feel as all do who are believers of the truth, under the influence of the Spirit, let us make this evident by embodying our convictions and feelings in our behavior.'[46]

There are two important general principles obviously implied in this exhortation, — the one, that we must "live in the Spirit," in order to our "walking in the Spirit;" and the other, that "walking in the Spirit" is the natural result, and the only satisfactory evidence, of "living in the Spirit." "Living in the Spirit" is necessary in order to "walking in the Spirit." A man must be a Christian before he can act christianly. The tree must be good in order to the fruit being good; the fountain must be cleared that the streams may be pure. Christian conduct can spring only from Christian principle. Are we anxious to get to heaven, and, for this purpose, to obtain that "holiness, without which no man can see the Lord"? The only way of obtaining it, is to be thus "transformed by the renewing of our mind;" and this can only be brought about by the operation of the Holy Spirit, through the instrumentality of Christian truth understood and believed.

The other principle is equally important, — 'Walking in the Spirit is the natural result and only satisfactory evidence of living in the Spirit.' The state of the mind and heart is closely connected with that of the conduct. Whatever a man's profession be — however ingeniously he may speculate, and however plausibly and fluently he may talk about Christianity, — if, in his temper and conduct, he does not exhibit the native results of Christian principle and feeling, he makes it evident that he is not a Christian. "By their fruits," says our Lord, "ye shall know them." The Spirit is not there when his fruits are not there.

SECT. IV. — PARTICULAR EXHORTATIONS TO CERTAIN VARIETIES OF "WALKING IN THE SPIRIT."

The apostle follows up this general exhortation by a variety of particular ones, all of them included in it.

1. CAUTION AGAINST VAIN-GLORYING.

The first is contained in the 26th verse, — "Let us not be desirous of vain-glory, provoking one another, envying one another."[47] The English words, "Be not desirous of vain-glory," naturally signify, 'Do not eagerly desire, do not supremely seek after, a high reputation for qualities which are really not valuable in themselves, or are valuable in the estimation of those only whose good opinion is of little value.' True glory consists in being justly esteemed by good men for really good qualities. "Vain-glory" is to have the reputation of qualities which we do not possess, or to be praised for qualities which, though we do possess them, do not deserve praise; or to be highly esteemed by men whose esteem is of little value. To "be desirous of vain—glory," in any of these senses, is a very foolish and a very unchristian thing; but it does not seem to be the evil against which the apostle is here guarding the Galatians.

We apprehend the apostle's meaning is this, 'Let us not be vain-glorious.'[48] To be "vain-glorious" is to boast of what we do not possess, or of what, though we do possess it, is of no value, or is of far less value than we attach to it. For the meaning of the word, consult Phil. 2:3; 2 Cor. 10:17; 12:1-10; Phil. 3:3-10. The Galatian church was divided into two parties — the Judaising party, and their opponents. The first boasted of their circumcision, and their superior sanctity in keeping the Mosaic observances; and of their honors, as connected with Abraham, the father of the faithful. This was to glory in what was not really valuable. All these things, under the gospel, are utterly useless. The other party was in danger of glorying in their freedom from the restrictions of the Mosaic law, and to look down on their brethren as men of contracted minds. This liberty was in itself a good thing, but it was not a thing to glory in. It was not their chief blessing. The kingdom of God consists "not in meats and drinks," but in "justification" — in "peace" with God — in "joy in the Holy Ghost" (Rom. 14:17.). These were the blessings to glory in. This was true glory.

'Now,' says the apostle to both parties, 'be not vain-glorious.' Let not the Jew or the Judaiser boast of his subjection to the law; and let not the Gentile boast of his freedom from the law, as if either the one or the other was the great benefit by which, as Christians, they were distinguished.[49]

The natural consequence of indulging in this vain-gloriation was mutual quarrelling and mutual hatred, — "Provoking one another," — 'Calling out one another to the field of controversy.' When one said, 'I am better than you, because I submit to the Mosaic law,' and another, 'I am better than you, because I walk at liberty,' these statements naturally led to disputations and vain-janglings about the law, and these as naturally tended to strengthen mutual dislike into mutual hatred.

"Envying one another." The word "envy," in its most appropriate meaning, denotes a malignant uneasiness arising from perceiving the superiority of another. I do not see how, in this strict sense, it is very applicable to the case in the apostle's view. The word is sometimes employed to signify hatred, — as when it is said that Pilate knew that "through envy" — that is obviously malignity — "the Jews had delivered Jesus to him" (Matth. 27:18.). In this way we understand the word here. Controversies on such subjects generally end in setting the combatants farther than ever from each other, as to kindly affection. He, who in the commencement of such a controversy, only suspected the Christianity of his brother, generally ends with denying it. If he disliked him then, he hates him now. This is not to "walk in the Spirit," but in "the flesh."

It would be consolatory could we think that the exhortation in the text, though necessary in the apostle's time, had become unnecessary in ours. But alas! how different is the truth! How much vain-glorying is there among the professors of the name of Christ, even among those of whom charity obliges us to hope that their profession is genuine! How do they glory in their distinctions! One boasts of his connection with a rich and powerful, ancient and venerable establishment; another glories in his being a Dissenter. One boasts of the imposing splendor, and another glories in the primitive simplicity, of their respective modes of worship. Even far less discernible marks of distinction become grounds of glory: and this provokes to angry controversy; and this again produces strife, jealousy, enmity, malignity. Were we more spiritual it would be otherwise. We should glory chiefly in the grand principles of Christian truth, in which all really good men are agreed; and our attachment to these would produce attachment to all who really believe them. While every man sought after, and endeavored to communicate to his brother those views of truth and duty, which he conceived he had obtained from his Bible — "speaking the truth in love," — there would be no "provoking one another," except "to love and good works;" and instead of "envying and hating one another," there would be general edification of the body in love.

This state of things is to be brought about by the minds of men being brought more and more under the influence of Christian truth by the operation of the Holy Ghost. We may be able to do but little in the way of forwarding such a state of things, but we do something if we yield up ourselves to the enlightening, sanctifying, softening, influence of the truth as it is in Jesus.

2. DUTY OF "THE SPIRITUAL" TO THOSE "OVERTAKEN IN A FAULT."

The passage which follows is obviously so closely connected with what goes before, that it ought not to have been disjoined from it. It is the continued amplification of the general injunction to Christian duty contained in the 25th verse of the preceding chapter. "If we live in the Spirit let us also walk in the Spirit." Under the influence of the new and better spirit to which we are formed by the agency of the Holy Spirit through the instrumentality of the faith of the truth, let us not be vain-glorious, provoking one another to useless and mischievous contentions which have a direct tendency to produce mutual aversion and malignity. This was to walk after thy flesh and not after the spirit; this was to cherish instead of to crucify the flesh in its affections and lusts. Instead of seeking each his own glory, let us seek one another's true happiness; instead of triumphing over a fallen brother, and endeavoring to elevate ourselves by his depression, let us cherish a deep sense of deficiency and weakness; and in that meek disposition which such a feeling naturally produces, let us endeavor to reclaim the wandering, to strengthen the weak, and to raise the fallen. Such is the general import of the paragraph which follows, and to the more particular examination of which our attention must now be directed. "Brethren, if a man be overtaken in a fault, ye which are spiritual restore such an one in the spirit of meekness; considering thyself, lest thou also be tempted" (Gal. 6:1.).

It is plain that though the apostle's language be indefinite, "if a man be overtaken in a fault," the injunction does not refer to mankind generally, but to the members of a Christian church. It is just equivalent to, 'if any of you' − "any man that is called a brother" (1 Cor. 5:11.).

The phrase translated, "be overtaken in a fault,"[50] is somewhat ambiguous. For a man to be surprised or taken in a fault, or to be overtaken by a fault, is to fall into error or sin. The phrase seems to have been selected for the purpose of conveying the idea that the person referred to is not a habitual sinner − is not a person who lives in sin − who habitually does what is inconsistent with the will of Christ. He is not the person whom John describes as "a doer of sin."[51] A person of this description has no right to a place in Christ's church. If he has been admitted into communion with a scripturally organised church, it must have been by mistake; and when ever his real character manifests itself, it is their imperative duty to "put away from among them such a wicked person." The fault here referred to is obviously occasional; the man is "over taken" in or by it. From the force of temptation, the want of prayerful vigilance and humble dependence, every Christian, even the most eminent, may fall into error and commit sin.

Now, what is the duty of his fellow Christians to such a person? Is it immediately to expel him from their society? No; it is their duty to restore him, and to restore him in the spirit of meekness. The word rendered "restore"[52] properly signifies to put a dislocated member of the body into its proper place.[53] When a professed Christian falls into error or sin, he becomes, as it were, a dislocated member of the mystical body of Christ, incapable of properly performing its own functions, and occasioning pain and inconvenience to the other members of the body.

To "restore such an one," is to use the appropriate means of convincing him of his error and sin, and bringing him back to the path of truth and righteousness. He was not to be immediately excommunicated − that is thy last resort; but neither was he to be allowed to continue in a state dangerous both to himself and his fellow church members. When a member of the human body is dislocated, amputation is not immediately resorted to. But neither is it allowed to remain in a state of luxation. Means are immediately employed to have the dislocation reduced. Whenever a Christian man is "overtaken in a fault," means should without delay be used to "restore" him. And what are these means? By faithful, but at the same time friendly, statements of the truth, let him be led to see that he is in error and in fault. Show him the inconsistency of his opinion or his conduct with the doctrine and the law of Christ. Point out to him the bad consequences which are likely to result from it, both to himself and others. And when he is thus brought to a just sense of his fault, and in danger of being swallowed up of overmuch sorrow, turn his mind to the gracious promises made to the returning backslider, and receive him, as in that case there is reason to believe that Christ has received him.

All this must be done "in the spirit of meekness."[54] "The spirit of meekness"[55] is a Hebraism for 'a meek spirit.' The offending brother is not to be addressed in a tone of arrogant superiority, or angry rebuke. He is not to be "treated as an enemy, but admonished as a brother." Every thing that is done must be done in such a manner as to make it evident that there is no wish to give unnecessary pain, and that the ultimate objects in view are the honor of the Savior, the prosperity of His church, and the best interest of the individual himself. In performing this most important part of Christian duty, it is peculiarly necessary to be "gentle, apt to teach," "patient," "in meekness instructing those who oppose themselves."[56]

This injuction to restore an offending brother in "the spirit of meekness is addressed to "those who are spiritual." The appellation "spiritual"[57] is often used to denote converted men in contrast to unconverted men, who are denominated "carnal,"[58] "sensual."[59] But the word is also applied to Christians of a high order of attainment, to distinguish them from Christians of a low order of attainment. Enlightened, consistent Christians, as distinguished from their brethren of narrow prejudiced views and irregular and doubtful habits. This is plainly the meaning in which the apostle employs the term when he says to the Corinthians, whom he yet considered as Christian brethren, — "I could not speak unto you as unto spiritual, but as unto carnal, even as unto babes in Christ" (1 Cor. 3:1-4.). etc. "The spiritual" here are obviously the same class as the apostle in the Epistle to the Romans, chapter 15:1, calls "the strong."[60] "We then that are strong ought to bear the infirmities of the weak, and not to please ourselves." It is then thy peculiar duty of enlightened Christians who are enabled to act so as to "adorn the doctrine of God their Savior in all things," to restore such of their less enlightened and consistent brethren as have fallen into error or sin. And if, instead of this, they are disposed to treat their offending brother with arrogance and bitterness, it is proof that they are not so spiritual, nor so strong, as they ought to be, or, as they think they are. "For the fruit of the Spirit is love, peace, long-suffering, gentleness, goodness."

The apostle enforces the exhortation by a powerful motive — "considering thyself lest thou also be tempted."[61] But the apostle changes the manner of his address from the plural to the singular, to give it more force and point, — "each one" — "considering thyself lest thou also be tempted."[62] These words may either be considered as referring to the duty of restoring the offending brother, or the manner of performing the duty "with meekness." The spiritual were not to allow the offending brother to continue in error and sin, but were to take all proper means to restore him, to bring him back to truth and duty.

They were to do this from the consideration that error and sin, if allowed to pass unnoticed in a religious society, are likely to be hurtful not only to the individual but to the society, and not only to the reputation of the society, but to its real spiritual interests. "A little leaven leaveneth the whole lump." If first one brother and then another, when he falls into a fault, be allowed to continue in it, the danger of others falling before similar temptations is greatly increased; and the honest, yet meek and gentle, exercise of discipline in not overlooking faults, but restoring the faulty, by warning, and instruction, and rebuke, is one of the great menas of preserving others from falling into similar faults. But I apprehend that the apostle meant the motive contained in the concluding clause of the verse, to refer not so much to the restoring the fallen brother as opposed to the neglect of discipline, the letting him alone, as to the restoring him as opposed to the abandoning him, and the restoring of him with meekness instead of using the appointed means of restoration in a haughty overbearing spirit. 'Do not treat a brother, a fellow Christian, as if he were a determined apostate from Christ and Christianity; and in employing means to bring him back to the way of truth and righteousness, while you deal faithfully with him, deal kindly and gently with him. Make it apparent that it is because you love him that you cannot "suffer sin upon him;" and do this, remembering that you are also a man laboring under the remains of the same depraved nature, exposed to temptation, liable to sin, "lest thou also be tempted."[63] If placed in his circumstances you might probably not have acted a wiser or a better part. Most assuredly you would not if the grace of Christ had not enabled you. Let a sense of your own weakness induce you not indeed to spare the fault, but to pity the offender. And let the force of the general law of our Lord, "as ye would that others should do unto you, do ye even so to them," be strengthened by the consideration, that it is quite a possible thing that you, through the prevalence of temptation, may be placed in circumstances similar to those of the brother whom you are now called on to restore.[64]

This is a passage which is replete with important instruction to the members of Christian churches in all ages. Our Lord has informed us that offences must come; and the history of his church has in every age confirmed the declaration. In every Christian church, however careful they may be in their admission of members, − and the great body of Christian churches would require to be, in this respect, much more careful than they are, − individuals will be overtaken in faults. Now, what is to be done in such circumstances? Many Christians seem to think that the less that is said or done in such a case, so much the better; and that, at any rate, private church members have nothing to do in such matters.

But this is an important mistake. Regard − to the honor of Christ, who means His church to be an animated representation of His religion, − to the interest of the society, "for a little leaven leaveneth the whole lump," and "evil communications corrupt good manners," − and to the welfare of the offender himself, imperatively requires that violations of the law of Christ should not be allowed to pass unnoticed. The duty of church members is, to watch over each other, to be one another's keepers − to "look diligently lest any man fail of the grace of God, lest any root of bitterness springing up trouble them" (Heb. 12:15.). The course to be followed in such cases is distinctly marked out by our Lord and Savior, − Matt. 18:15-17. Members of Christ's church ought not to be "busy bodies in other men's matters," or lend an easy ear to every idle and slanderous tale; but when it is known that a Christian brother or sister, − a person in church fellowship, − has acted a part inconsistent with the Christian profession, they are bound to endeavor to restore such a person. He who is aware of the fact ought to go privately to the offender, and "tell him his fault" faithfully, yet tenderly; and in most cases this will serve the purpose. But if it does not do so, then he must take the second step with him − go with a Christian friend or two to the offender, and remonstrate with him; and if that also should be ineffectual, then the matter must be brought before "the church" − the assembly − that is, as I understand it, the assembly of elders; and if all these attempts to "restore such an one in the spirit of meekness" fail, then there remains nothing but that he be excluded as a person who will not submit to the law of Christ, and be to us "as an heathen man and a publican," till he come to a better mind.

If it is the duty of every chuch member to do all in his power to restore the brother that has been overtaken in a fault, it is peculiarly the duty of those who are appointed the overseers of their brethren. The elders should watch over the flock of Christ committed to their oversight, as they must answer at last to the great Shepherd of the sheep. They ought to wink at no violation of the law of Christ, to allow none to wander from the fold without warning them of their danger, and by every proper means endeavoring to bring them back.

It is of importance to recall to the mind that the paragraph we are illustrating commences with the 25th verse of the preceding chapter. "If, " says he, "we live in the Spirit, let us also walk in the Spirit," that is, "If we, through the knowledge and belief of Christian truth, are "renewed in the Spirit of our minds," let us prove this by a corresponding mode of conduct. If we are spiritual men, let us act like spiritual men. This general exhortation is followed by a more particular one, which is indeed just the application of the more general one to the peculiar circumstances of the Galatians. 'Let us act like spiritual men in guarding against that vain glorious spirit which finds its gratification in comparing our real, or supposed, excellence with the real, or supposed, deficiencies and faults of others, and which naturally leads to mutual provocation and mutual hatred. Instead of finding in the mistakes and faults of our brethren materials of self-glorification, let us do everything in our power to correct these in the spirit of true Christian affection, recollecting our own weakness and liability to sin, which may soon call for a similar exercise of Christian affection on the part of our brethren towards us. Thus, instead of being the means of cherishing a vain glorious disposition, which is a carnal temper, the mistakes and faults of our brethren will be the means of calling forth and strengthening true Christian charity, which is the most precious fruit of the Spirit, and the leading duty enjoined by the law of Christ.' We thus see how naturally the injunction comes in which follows in the 2d verse.

3. EXHORTATION TO BEAR ONE ANOTHER'S BURDENS.

"Bear ye one another's burdens, and so fulfil the law of Christ."[65]
The word "burden"[66] is obviously used here in a figurative sense. When thus employed it is significant of anything which produces painful exertion or depression, or which impedes easy unrestrained action. It is applicable to laborious duties – to painful restraints – to afflictions, whether external or internal, bodily or mental – to intellectual deficiencies, and to moral infirmities. All the ideas of which the term, in its figurative sense, is expressive, may perhaps be reduced to three – labor, suffering, infirmity.

The phrase "to bear a person's burden" must vary in its signification according to the particular sense we affix to the term burden. To bear the burden of a person who has a heavy load of laborious duty, is either to assist him directly in the performance of it, or to act towards him in such a manner as shall make the performance of it more easy; to bear the burden of a person who is oppressed with affliction, is to commiserate him, and do what we can to relieve and comfort him; to bear the burden of one who is encumbered with mistaken views, mental weakness, strong prejudices, and bad temper, is patiently to bear the annoyance which these unavoidably occasion; at the same time, employing all proper means for correcting these intellectual and moral obliquities, weaknesses, and faults.

It is without doubt the duty of Christians to bear one another's burdens, in all these senses of the term; and it is difficult to say how much it is in the power of Christians thus mutually to minister to each other's improvement and happiness. With regard to the burden of laborious duty, it may be often greatly alleviated by direct assistance, and when that is impracticable, or improper, by wise and friendly advice. When Christians are the objects of the laborious duties of their fellow Christians, the temper in which they meet dutiful exertions will either greatly increase or greatly diminish the burden. When a Christian people, for example, discover a readiness to adopt every measure proposed by their minister for their spiritual improvement – when his honest endeavors are affectionately seconded – the most burdensome occupations of the pastoral office become a pleasure. The people in this way bear their minister's burden. On the other hand, when all his exertions are met by a cold and heartless acquiescence, or, it may be, by direct opposition, then the weight of the pastoral duty is found a burden indeed. How much is it in the power of Christian parents to make the duties of their children easy, and in the power of Christian children to make the duties of their parents easy. Oh! how much might be done in, and by, the Christian church, if all its members could be induced, to use a homely but expressive phrase, to work to one another's hands!

Then, with regard to the burden of affliction, it is often practicable to remove at least a portion of it. I can bear a part of the burden of my poor brother by imparting to him of my substance. I can bear a part of the burden of my brother reproached for righteousness' sake by taking him by the hand, avowing my conviction that he has been falsely accused, and thus either removing the reproach, or bearing it along with him; and even in cases where there can be no direct participation, yet commiseration and consolation may be yielded, and these may go far in many cases to make a burden tolerable which otherwise would have altogether crushed the heart.

We apprehend, however, that it is to the last kind of burdens – those of intellectual deficiencies or moral infirmities – that the apostle here refers. Instead of despising and hating one another on account of their respective prejudices, mistakes, and faults, and finding in these food for self-conceit and vain glorying, they are to assist one another, and to promote one another's happiness and improvement. The exhortation seems nearly equivalent to that given by the apostle to the Roman church, – "We then that are strong ought to bear the infirmities of the weak, and not to please ourselves" (Rom. 15:1.).

To bear the mistakes and faults of our fellow Christians does not by any means imply that we flatter them in their erroneous opinions or improper habits; but it does imply that we, cherishing a deep felt sense of our own intellectual and moral deficiencies and improprieties, bear patiently the inconveniences which their mistakes and faults occasion to us, and in a truly friendly disposition do everything in our power to remove these mistakes and faults. A true Christian, to illustrate what I mean by an example, has a violent temper, which makes himself and all about him very uneasy. His fellow Christian must not, on this account, give up all intercourse with him; he must not take occasion from the infirmity of his brother to flatter his own self-complacency, but he must patiently bear the uneasiness which this infirmity produces, and use, in the spirit of Christian love, the appropriate means for curing it.[67] When a Christian brother under his burden stumbles and falls, we are not to let him lie on the ground and recover his feet in the best way he may; far less are we to insult him as he lies prostrate, and point him out to the scorn and derision of the world. We are to take him by the hand and raise him up; and as we have all our burdens, we are to journey on, hand in hand, endeavoring to keep one another from falling, and to press in a body forward along the prescribed course, that we may all obtain the prize of our high calling, in that "better country," where we shall be relieved from all our burdens at once, and for ever.

The apostle enforces his injunction to bear one another's burdens by a powerful motive: by doing so, Christians "fulfil the law of Christ." "The law of Christ" seems here plainly to be the law of mutual love, so often and so explicitly enjoined, and so powerfully and affectionately enforced, – John 13:34,35; 15:12. There does not seem to be anything emphatic in the word "fulfil."[68] It just signifies to obey. When Christians bear one another's burdens, they obey the law of Christ; and when they do not, they violate that law. When they act in the manner in which we have described, they show that they really love one another; and when they act in an opposite way, they show that they do not love one another. It is a very powerful motive with a Christian mind to reflect, 'If I do this, I do what is well pleasing to my Savior – what He has required of me as a proof of my love and obedience – and if I do not this, I displease Him, I trample on His authority, I dishonor His name.'

There seems to be a tacit contrast between the law of Moses, and the law of Christ. It is as if the apostle had said, 'This bearing one another's burdens is a far better thing than those external observances which your new teachers are so anxious to impose on you. To be sure, it is not like them, a keeping of the law of Moses, but infinitely better, it is a fulfilling of the law of Christ – the law of love.'

SECT. V. – CAUTION AGAINST OVER SELF-ESTIMATION.

The succeeding verses contain in them a powerful motive against the indulgence of a vain-glorious disposition. "For if a man think himself to be something, when he is nothing, he deceiveth himself. But let every man prove his own work, and then shall he have rejoicing in himself alone, and not in another. For every man shall bear his own burden" (Gal. 6:3-5.). For a man "to think himself something," or "somebody," is to entertain a high opinion of himself; as for a man to think himself "nothing,"[69] as the apostle has it, 2 Cor. 12:12, is to entertain a low opinion of himself. As the apostle is here speaking of professors of Christianity, we are to understand his words with that reference. The man who thinks himself something is the man who has a high opinion of his own Christian attainments, who thinks himself a very enlightened, accomplished Christian. The apostle obviously refers to the man who is vain-glorious – who, instead of restoring a fallen brother, glories over him, and who does not consider himself that he also may be tempted – who does not lighten his neighbor's burden by assistance or sympathy, but lets him bear it alone the best way he can, nay, perhaps adds to it.

Now, of such a man, the apostle says, "If a man think himself to be something, when he is nothing, he deceiveth himself." These words admit of two different interpretations, according as you connect the middle with the first or with the last clause. If we connect the middle clause with the first one, as our translators have done, the meaning is, 'If a man think himself to be a Christian of a high order, while he either is not a Christian at all, or at any rate a Christian of a very inferior order, he commits an important mistake – he falls into a hazardous error.[70] The man who supposes himself arrived at "the measure of the stature of the fulness of Christ," when in reality only "a babe in Christ," "deceives himself," and throws important obstacles in the way of his own improvement. Such a person is likely always to continue a babe.

This is a very common mistake among persons of the genuineness of whose Christianity charity obliges us to hope well; and it is one of the principal reasons why there is so much cause for complaining of many professors, that, "when for the time they might have been teachers of others they need yet some one to teach them what be the first principles of the oracles of God." In their own estimation they have little to learn, while the truth is, they have learned but little.

But the mistake is much more deplorable when a man flatters himself into the belief that he is a Christian, perhaps a Christian of the first order, while in reality he is not a Christian at all. The thing is quite possible – I fear not uncommon. We pity the poor maniac mendicant who thinks himself a king – we pity the man who has persuaded himself he is a man of wealth, while in reality he is in immediate hazard of bankruptcy – we pity the man who is assuring himself of long life, when he is tottering on the brink of the grave; but how much more to be pitied is the man who thinks himself secure of the favor of God, and of eternal happiness, while in reality "the wrath of God is abiding on him," and a miserable eternity lies before him! No kinder office can be done to such a person than to arouse him from his state of carnal security – to undeceive him – to convince him of his wants while they may be supplied, of his danger while it may be averted. A wo is denounced against such as are thus at ease in Zion. Such sinners have cause to be afraid. Fearfulness may well surprise these hypocrites. It will be well if they abandon their refuges of lies ere the overflowing flood of vengeance overtakes them.

But the words admit of another interpretation, which we are rather disposed to think the just one, 'If any man think himself to be something, seeing he is nothing, he deceiveth himself,' or 'If any man think he is something, he deceiveth himself, for he is nothing.' The apostle is cautioning the Galatians against a vain-glorious disposition; and in this verse I apprehend he means that the habitual indulgence of vain-glory is utterly inconsistent with the possession of genuine Christianity. Humility is a leading trait in the character of every genuine Christian. He knows and believes that he is guilty before the God of heaven exceedingly, and he feels that he is an ignorant, foolish, depraved creature – that of himself he is nothing, less than nothing, and vanity. Feeling thus his insignificance as a creature, and his demerit and depravity as a sinner, he is not – he cannot be – vain-glorious. Whatever he is that is good he knows God has made him to be. Whatever he has that is good he knows God has given him. The falls of others excite in him not self-glorification, but gratitude. "Who maketh me to differ?" "What have I that I have not received?" "By the grace of God I am what I am." The greater advance a man makes in true Christianity, the more humble he becomes. He gets better acquainted with himself, more emancipated from the dominion of self-love, and obtains higher and juster ideas of that holiness, which is the object of his ambition.

How humbly does the Apostle Paul speak of himself! How far was he from thinking highly of himself! "In me, that is my flesh, dwelleth no good thing." "When I would do good, evil is present with me." "Less that the least of all saints" – "the chief of sinners" (Rom. 7:18,21; Eph. 3:8; 1 Tim. 1:15.). A man, who had spent a considerably long life in very active labors for the honor of God and the salvation of mankind, and who, in the estimation of those who knew him best, had reached an uncommon height of Christian excellence, uses the following language in a paper obviously never intended for the public eye, "Lord, I am now entering of the thirty-fourth year of my ministry, an amazing instance of sovereign mercy and patience to a cumberer of the ground. How strange that thou shouldest have, for more than sixty years, continued to exercise mercy and loving kindness upon a wretch that has all along spoken and done all the evil that I could, nor even would yield but when the Almighty influence of free grace put it out of my power to oppose it. Lord, how often have I vowed, but never grown better – confessed, but never amended. Often thou hast challenged and corrected me, and yet I have gone on frowardly in the way of my heart. As an evil man and a seducer, I have grown worse and worse. But where should a sinner flee but to the Savior. Lord, all refuge faileth me: no man can help my soul. Nothing will do for me but an uncommon stretch of thy Almighty grace. To thee, O Jesus, I give up myself as a foolish, guilty, polluted, and enslaved sinner; and I hereby solemnly take thee as mine, as made of God to me, wisdom, righteousness, sanctification, and redemption. I give up myself as a poor, ignorant, careless, and wicked creature, who has ever been learning, and yet never able to come to the knowledge of the truth; to thee, O Lord, that thou mayest bestow gifts on the rebellious, and exalt thy grace in showing kindness to the unworthy. O Savior, come down and do something for me before I die."[71]

This is the spirit of genuine Christianity; and the man who thinks highly of himself, in thinking highly of himself shows that he is not what he supposes himself to be. He wants humility, which is essential to genuine Christianity; and if he feeds his self-conceit by glorying over the supposed or real inferiority of others, he proves himself destitute of that charity of which the apostle says, "Though I speak with the tongues of men and of angels, and have not charity, I am nothing" (1 Cor. 13:12.). "Not as though I had already attained" (Phil. 3:12.), is the true Christian motto. "If any man think that he knoweth any thing, he knoweth nothing yet as he ought to know (1 Cor. 8:2.).

As a cure for vain glory, the apostle prescribes an impartial and thorough examination of the individual's own conduct. "But let every man prove his own work, and then shall he have rejoicing in himself alone, and not in another. For every man shall bear his own burden" (Gal. 6:4,5.). The word "work" is just equivalent to conduct and character, as 1 Peter 1:17; Rev. 22:12. The word "prove"[72] signifies to try as metals are tried, and sometimes to approve in consequence of trial, – Luke 14:19; 1 Cor. 3:13; 16:3; 1 Peter 1:7; 1 Thess. 2:4; Rom. 14:22. "Let every man prove his own work." 'Let every man thoroughly investigate his own character and conduct. Instead of looking at the defects of his neighbor's character, and making use of them as a foil for setting off his own excellencies, let him examine his own character by the unerring test – the Divine law.' The consequence of such an investigation is stated in the conclusion of the verse, "and then shall he have rejoicing in himself, and not in another. For every one shall bear his own burden."

The ordinary way of interpreting these words is this.[73] 'If on fairly examining your own conduct and character by the test of the Divine word, it bears the trial, then you will not need to compare yourselves with others in order to secure a feeling of self-approbation. In that case you will have the satisfaction of knowing, not merely that your conduct is better than that of some other people, but that it is really such as to be well-pleasing to God. You will not need then to look around you to gather satisfaction from seeing that you are not worse, or even better, than others; you need only look inward to have the testimony of "the man within the breast." In this view of the passage what a fine illustration have we of it in the contrasted gloriations of the apostle and of the Pharisee,

– "Our rejoicing," says the apostle, "is this, the testimony of our conscience, that in simplicity and godly sincerity, not with fleshly wisdom, but by the grace of God, we have had our conversation in the world, and more abundantly to you-ward" (2 Cor. 1:12.). – "The Pharisee stood and prayed thus with himself, God, I thank thee, that I am not as other men are, extortioners, unjust, adulterers, or even as this publican" (Luke 18:11.). In this case, the 5th verse must be considered as a motive to, or a reason for, the duty enjoined in the beginning of the 4th, – "Let every man prove his own work; for every man must bear his own burden." The word here translated "burden"[74] is not the same as that so rendered in the 2d verse; but it is of nearly equivalent import. 'Let every man investigate his own conduct; for it is our own conduct for which each of us must ultimately be responsible. In this view of the words, they are nearly parallel to the passage, – "But why dost thou judge thy brother? or why dost thou set at nought thy brother? for we shall all stand before the judgment seat of Christ. For it is written, As I live, saith the Lord, every knee shall bow to Me, and every tongue shall confess to God. So then every one of us shall give account of himself to God" (Rom. 14:10-12.).

It is proper to state, however, that the 5th and the concluding part of the 4th verse have received another interpretation, which, to say the least, is not destitute of plausibility, – 'Let every man try his own work, impartially examine his own character and conduct, and the consequence will be, he will keep his glorying to himself[75] – he will not boast to another what he is – he will find so much wanting, and so much wrong, that he will find there is no room for glorying. He will no longer think himself something; for he will find himself to be nothing. It is self-ignorance which generally lies at the foundation of self-esteem. In this case the apostle recommends what he himself practised, – "For we dare not make ourselves of the number, or compare ourselves with some that commend themselves: but they, measuring themselves by themselves, and comparing themselves among themselves, are not wise" (1 Cor. 10:12.).

In this case the meaning of the 5th verse, 'for every one shall, or must, bear his own burden,' is – every one has his own faults and infirmities. None is without his burden, and therefore none is entitled to glory over others because they have burdens; and the dutiful and reasonable course is to bear one another's burdens, to exercise the forbearance we need, to yield the assistance we require, and thus fulfil the law of Christ.

SECT. VI. – THE DUTY OF THE GALATIANS TO SUPPORT THEIR TEACHERS.

Among the important purposes served by the apostolical epistles must be numbered the communicating of accurate information respecting the constitutional principles and particular laws of that spiritual society established by Jesus Christ, usually termed the Christian church.

Nothing is more obvious than that the Author of Christianity intended His followers to associate themselves together for the purpose of promoting their religious and moral improvement by a joint observance of certain institutions, and by mutual superintendence and incitement, warning and encouragement. It was not His purpose merely to make those who believe in Him wise, good, and happy as individuals, but to bind them together in a holy fellowship – the connecting bonds of which should be common faith and mutual love; and the objects of which should be the united worship of their common God and Father, the united promotion of the glory and interest of their common Lord and Savior, and their mutual advancement in the knowledge of Christian truth, the cultivation of Christian affection, the practice of Christian duty, and the enjoyment of Christian comfort. This society established by His appointment, subject to His authority, devoted to His honor, and blessed by His peculiar presence, is the Christian church.

To every man of enlightened curiosity it must be a desirable thing to understand the constitution and laws of so singular an association; and to every Christian such a knowledge must be peculiarly valuable, for how otherwise can he know how to "behave himself in this house of God?"

It is obvious that this society is entirely voluntary — that no man can become a member of it but by his own free choice; but it is equally obvious that the very act of connection with such a society is an act of obedience to the authority of Jesus Christ; and that the society, though voluntary, in submitting to His authority, are not at liberty to regulate themselves according to the dictates of their own humor or even reason, but are bound to conform themselves to His laws. The offices, the office-bearers, the qualifications and duties of office-bearers and members, all these have been the subjects of legislation by Him whom alone we are warranted to call Master, and to whose arrangements we are bound implicitly to submit. The Christian church is not to be considered, as many good men seem to consider it, in the same point of light as a bible or missionary society — a humanly devised method of gaining a divinely enjoined end. It is a divinely appointed means to gain a divinely appointed end. Its principles and laws, which are to be sought in the New Testament, are obligatory on the conscience, and we act a most unauthorised part when we attempt to substitute in their place principles and laws which may seem to us in particular circumstances better, fitted to promote the great object in view.

The church of Christ is a collection of men who, professing to believe the principles of Christianity, unite in voluntarily observing, and supporting, and extending those institutions, the object of which is the conversion of unbelievers and the edification of believers — the making bad men good and good men better. In conformity to the genuis of Christianity, which is much more a religion of principle than of statute, in which it is strikingly and most favorably contrasted with Judaism, whose place it occupied, the minor arrangements of time, place, and circumstance, are in a great measure left to be regulated by the judgment of particular societies; but everything that can be considered as essential to the being and well-being of the society in all circumstances, is fixed by the express appointment of its great Founder.

Among these vital points must be numbered the principle on which the society is to be sustained. The maintenance and the extension of the institutions of Christianity involve not only labor, but expense. How is this to be defrayed? How are the funds necessary for this purpose to be raised? The answer to this question is contained in the words to which the course of our exposition now brings us; and we are conscientiously persuaded that it had been well for the church and for the world had this sacred canon been strictly observed, and had Christianity been sustained and extended solely by the voluntary exertions and the voluntary contributions of those who themselves had experienced its invaluable blessings, and who felt the obligation under which both duty and gratitude laid them to supply the temporal wants of those who ministered to their spiritual necessities, and to communicate to their perishing brethren of mankind those benefits which sovereign unmerited kindness had bestowed on themselves. Here, as in every other case, the foolishness of God is wiser than the wisdom of man.

"Let him that is taught,[76] communicate unto him that teacheth in all good things" (Gal. 6:6.).

These words, though they seem so plain as scarcely to need interpretation, have yet divided not a little the opinions of commentators.

The concluding phrase, "in all good things," admits of being connected either with the word "teacheth," or with the word "communicate." In the former case the meaning is, 'Let him who is taught, impart of his substance to him who gives him instruction about "all good things." ' The objections to this interpretation seem to me insurmountable.[77]

The interpreters who connect "all good things" with "communicate," are not of one mind as to the meaning of the phrase. Some consider "all good things" as referring to the Christian teacher's knowledge of the doctrine and the law of Christ, and his living under the influence of the former and the practice of the latter, and view the verse as enjoining on the taught to have fellowship with him in all these good things, in other words calling on the disciples to be like their teacher.[78]

The other class[79] with whom we agree refer the words "all good things," to all things good for a comfortable subsistence. This sense the term undoubtedly has (Luke 1:53;

12:18,19.), and the general principle conveyed in the passage is, we think, this, − 'that Christian teachers should be supported by the voluntary contributions of those whom they instruct.'[80]

SECT. VII. − CAUTION AGAINST MISTAKE IN REFERENCE TO THE CONNECTION BETWEEN PRESENT CHARACTER AND CONDUCT, AND FUTURE PUNISHMENT OR REWARD.

To this exhortation to a liberal support of the institution of the Christian ministry, the apostle subjoins a most impressive warning against self-deception. "Be not deceived; God is not mocked: for whatsoever a man soweth, that shall he also reap. For he that soweth to his flesh, shall of the flesh reap corruption; but he that soweth to the Spirit, shall of the Spirit reap life everlasting" (Gal. 6:7,8.).

The injunction, "Be not deceived," when viewed by itself, is a very general one. It is a warning against all errors of all kinds, − a caution equally against allowing others to deceive us, and against deceiving ourselves. All religious error is dangerous, and ought to be carefully guarded against. "There is a natural connection between truth and holiness, and between error and sin." While the devil 'abode in the truth' he was holy; and no sooner was man deceived than he became a sinner. Every duty is acting out a truth, and every sin is the embodiment of a falsehood. Is it reasonable to expect that a man will walk in the right way if he does not know it? and if he is deceived as to this point, what can be anticipated but that he will stray into forbidden paths? Error is not, cannot be, either innocent or safe. It cannot be cherished without both sin and danger.

In the passage before us, the caution is to be viewed as referring to that species of error into which the Galatians were in danger of falling; and what that was, it is not difficult to discover from the preceding and following context. From the extreme importance attached to certain external rites and observances by the Judaising teachers, they were in danger of supposing that the essence of religion consisted in these, and to flatter themselves that they were truly righteous, merely because they attended to these rules and observances, though, at the same time, they were strangers to that spiritual mind, which is the essence of true Christianity, and were living in the neglect of duties plainly enjoined by the law of Christ, and to the performance of which the spiritual mind naturally leads. The error against which they are here so impressively warned is, that a man may live a carnal life, and yet be ultimately happy, − may "sow to the flesh" without reaping corruption, − or that a man may attain ultimate happiness without living a spiritual life, − may "reap life everlasting" without "sowing to the Spirit." To those who were in danger of being thus deceived by the Judaising teachers, and who were in danger of thus deceiving themselves, by supposing they were something, when, in reality, they were nothing, − by supposing themselves objects of Divine approbation, when, indeed, they were objects of the Divine displeasure, the apostle says, "Be not deceived," − 'Let no man deceive you; and do not deceive yourselves.'

Many, perhaps most, interpreters have supposed that the apostle particularly refers to those of the Galatians who, seduced by these false teachers, had been led to neglect altogether, or to perform in a very imperfect manner, their duty in supporting those instructors whom the apostle had placed over them. That such would be the natural result of the success of the ministrations of the Judaising teachers, and that the apostle's caution is very applicable to such a case, there can be no doubt; but we see nothing, either in the words or in their connection, which should lead us to limit their reference to this particular form of self-deception, − a person supposing himself a Christian, and cherishing the hope of eternal happiness, while living in the neglect of so plainly commanded a duty. It is well remarked by Riccaltoun, that "the unhappy selfish spirit − an attachment to the present world − inclines men to excuse themselves in neglect of that duty, and perhaps the neglect of this ordinance of God for the support of a gospel ministry, and substituting another mode of provision in its room, has contributed more than any one thing to the corruptions which have in all ages disfigured and disgraced the

Christian religion."[81] The injunction, "Be not deceived," which is common in the apostolic writings (1 Cor. 6:9; 15:33; 1 John 3:7; James 1:16.), appears to be here just equivalent to, "Beware of supposing that, in consequence of any external rite or distinction, you are objects of Divine favor – the peculiar people of God. It is not circumcision nor uncircumcision, but a new creature, that constitutes real Christianity.' "God is not mocked." God is often mocked by men, both explicitly and implicitly. There are men so fearfully impious, as to ridicule the attributes, and works, and word of God; and there are many more whose conduct can be accounted for on no other principle than that they have the most unworthy and contemptuous conceptions of God. The apostle does not mean to deny this: so far from denying it, he plainly intimates that those who deceive themselves, by cherishing the hope of eternal happiness while they live "after the flesh," do in effect attempt to impose on God, and thus mock Him. But He is not imposed on.[82] His unchangeable principle of moral government shall be applied in reference to such individuals, and they shall be treated, not as what they professed to be – not as what they perhaps had succeeded in convincing others, and to a certain extent themselves, that they were, – but as what they really are.

This leading principle of the Divine government is couched in plain and figurative language. "Whatsoever a man soweth, that shall he also reap."[83] The expression seems proverbial, and intimates that there shall be a strict conformity between a man's present character and conduct, and his future condition – a correspondence similar to that which exists between sowing and reaping. The proverb holds both as to the kind and as to the quantity of the seed sown. He who sows tares shall reap tares; and he who sows wheat shall reap wheat. Sin will produce punishment, and duty will lead to reward. "He who sows sparingly shall reap sparingly; and he who sows bountifully shall reap bountifully." The degree of punishment will be proportioned to that of crime, and the degree of reward to the degree of holiness.

The language seems also to intimate, that the connection between character and conduct in this world, and condition in a future world, is not accidental or arbitrary, but is just as much in the natural order of things in the moral government of God, as the connection between the quantity and the quality of what is sown and what is reaped, is in the physical government of God. To suppose that sin will not lead to punishment, is as absurd as to suppose that tares will not produce tares. To suppose that sin can end in happiness, is as absurd as to suppose that tares will produce wheat. To suppose that happiness can be obtained without holiness, is just as absurd as to expect an abundant harvest of precious grain when nothing has been sowed at all, or nothing but useless and noxious weeds.

The apostle amplifies the figure in the 8th verse, – "For he that soweth to his flesh,[84] shall of the flesh reap corruption; but he that soweth to the Spirit,[85] shall of the Spirit reap life everlasting."

In explaining figurative language, the first thing to be done is to endeavor to form a distinct idea of the figure which the author employs. We must understand what is the illustration before we can apprehend its force as an illustration. In the passage before us, "the flesh" and "the Spirit" seem to be represented as two fields, producing very different crops when cultivated.[86] He who cultivates the field of "the flesh" has a harvest of "corruption;" he who cultivates the field of "the Spirit" has a harvest of "life everlasting."

For a man to "sow to his flesh," and to cultivate the field of "the flesh," is the same thing as "to live after the flesh" – "to walk after the flesh" – to "do the works of the flesh" – to "fulfil the desires of the flesh." "The flesh" is just human nature unchanged by Divine influence – the mode of thinking and feeling which is natural to man. The man who is characterised by any of the enormities mentioned in the close of the fifth chapter of this epistle, is one who "sows to the flesh;" but he is not the only cultivator of the field "which bringeth forth nothing but briars and thorns, and the end of which is that it shall be burned." The man who is entirely occupied with sensible and present things, though he should not be what is ordinarily termed immoral – nay, the man who is strictly honest, and honorable, and punctiliously religious, so far as external morality and religion go, – who yet does not look at "things unseen and eternal," that man, too, sows in the flesh.

And both of these classes of cultivators of this field which the Lord has cursed, shall reap the same kind of harvest. Both shall "reap corruption." "To reap corruption" is a phrase which, had we met with it by itself, we should have said naturally signifies to obtain, as the result of our exertions, that which is corruptible and perishable. In this light it is strikingly true of the man who sows in the flesh. Let him be as successful as his heart can desire in the attainment of the pleasures, honors, and wealth of the world, what has he got? nothing but corruption. Short-lived, transitory, perishing are the leading characters of all things natural and earthly. But when we notice that "corruption" is contrasted with "life everlasting," and we compare the passage before us with the passage in the Epistle to the Romans, Chap. 8:13, with which it is obviously parallel. "If ye live after the flesh, ye shall die: but if ye through the Spirit do mortify the deeds of the body, ye shall live," we cannot doubt that "corruption" is here equivalent to death or misery – the second death, everlasting misery. 'The man who cultivates the field of the flesh shall find his labors end in his own ruin; a carnal life, whether spent in the grossest pollutions of open and unreatrained profanity, or in the strictest observances of a merely worldly religion and morality, must end in the destruction of the soul.'

As he who cultivates the field of the flesh shall have a harvest of everlasting ruin, so he who cultivates the field of the Spirit, who "sows in the Spirit," shall have a harvest of everlasting happiness. "The Spirit," as opposed to the flesh, is the new mode of thinking and feeling produced by the Holy Spirit, through the instrumentality of the gospel, understood and believed. To sow in the Spirit – to cultivate this field – is just to use the appointed means of improving and perfecting this new mode of thinking and feeling, the yielding ourselves up to its influence, the following it out to its fair results on our behavior. He sows in the Spirit who "lives by the faith of the Son of God," and abounds in all those holy dispositions and habits, which are enumerated in the end of the preceding chapter, as "the fruits of the Spirit." Such a person shall have a harvest of everlasting bliss and happiness, that is, he shall be everlastingly happy, and his happiness will be the result of his having sown to the Spirit.

The language of the apostle in both clauses deserves attention, and is very instructive. He who sows in the field of the flesh shall of the flesh reap corruption. He who sows in the field of the Spirit shall of the Spirit reap life everlasting. That very corrupted nature which the one has indulged shall be the source of his misery – the various carnal dispositions which he has cherished shall be, as it were, the fiends which shall torment him for ever. Lust, avarice, ambition, reigning with unabated, perhaps increased, force in the soul, while no means of gratifying them in any degree are afforded, must make the irreclaimably wicked inconceivably miserable in their final state. I do not deny, I do not even doubt, that in the regions of final punishment there are direct inflictions of wrath from the hand of a righteously offended divinity; but it surely deserves notice that, in very many passages of Scripture, the misery of the irreclaimably impenitent is represented as the native, necessary, result of their own conduct. The whole economy of God's moral government would need to be altered, the constituent principles of man's nature would need to be changed, before those who live and die "carnal" can be really happy in another world.

On the other hand, He who cultivates the field of the Spirit, shall of that Spirit reap life everlasting. That new and better mode of thinking and feeling which he has carefully cherished shall be to him the source of everlasting happiness. It shall be to him "a well of living water springing up to everlasting life." We are too apt to think of final happiness as something quite distinct from that holy frame of feeling and thought to which the gospel, as "the ministration of the Spirit," forms the human soul, while in reality it is just the perfection of it. Holiness is heaven. The spiritual mind – the mind of the Spirit[87] – the mode of thinking and feeling produced by the Holy Spirit through the belief of the truth

– not only leads to, but is "life and peace." We should not look on the cultivation of the Christian, the spiritual, character as in itself a hard, disagreeable task, by which – for which – we are at last to be compensated with an exceedingly great reward in heaven; but we ought to consider every attainment as bringing its own reward with it, every spiritual view, every spiritual feeling, as a part of the heavenly felicity. The Spirit is the "earnest" of the inheritance. It is a part of a whole – the beginning of what is to be perfected in eternity. The Christian is not like a laborer in the mines, who must look to the upper regions for nourishment and support, and who cannot turn to immediate use the results of his toilsome operation; but, like the agriculturist, all whose labor goes directly to the production of what is nourishing, and who is supported by the very same kind of material as that in the cultivation of which he is engaged. Every just view of Christian truth – every holy disposition – is a source of enjoyment opened to the Christian in this waste and howling wilderness; and it is perfect knowledge and perfect holiness which form "the river of life, clear as crystal, issuing forth from beneath the throne of God and of the Lamb," along whose banks all the nations of the saved repose, "and drink their fill of its pure immortal streams."

The passage which we have attempted to illustrate is considered by many interpreters as having a particular reference to the disposal of pecuniary substance. They understand the apostle as saying, he who expends his money in gratifying the flesh shall have a poor return – he shall purchase to himself nothing but ruin; but he who lays it out in accordance with the views and desires of a spiritual mind, that man shall be richly compensated in the treasures of eternity. This is no doubt a truth; but we do not apprehend that the words of the apostle so much embody that truth as the more general one which we have illustrated, and which implies this particular truth as well as a thousand others of the same kind.

SECT. VIII. – EXHORTATION TO WELL-DOING, AND CAUTION AGAINST BECOMING WEARY IN IT.

In the verses that follow the apostle warns against becoming weary in Christian well-doing, and enforces his warning by a very powerful motive. "And let us not be weary in well-doing: for in due season we shall reap, if we faint not. As we have therefore opportunity, let us do good unto all men, especially unto them who are of the household of faith" (Gal. 6:9,10.).

"Well-doing"[88] is a phrase which may be understood, either in a more restricted, or in a more extended, sense. In the first case, it is equivalent to beneficence; in the second, to dutiful conduct generally. It is a good general rule of interpretation, that when a word or a phrase occurs which admits of a more restricted and more extensive sense, the more extensive sense is to be preferred, if there is nothing in the passage or its context to fix it to the more restricted meaning. Applying this principle to the passage before us, we consider "well-doing" as a word of equal extent with "sowing to the Spirit" – as a phrase descriptive of the whole duty of a Christian. The Christian's business is, to "do good" – to perform all the duties that rise out of the various relations in which he stands to God and his fellow men. These duties are numerous; they are, many of them, arduous; they are constantly recurring; and their performance must be coeval with the Christian's life.

Owing to the number, the difficulty, and the never-terminating, never-remitting obligations of these duties, even genuine Christians are in danger of "becoming weary of well-doing." They become backward to undertake them, and languid in performing them. They multiply and magnify obstacles. They are ingenious in devising excuses. They leave them half done, and are strongly tempted to abandon them altogether. It ought not to be so. It would not be were Christians what they should be – what they might be. The great cause of weariness in well-doing is a deficiency in faith, and a corresponding undue influence of present and sensible things. To the man who has, through the faith of Christ, overcome the world, none of the commandments of God are grievous. On the contrary,

"In keeping them he finds a great reward." But whenever the Christian walks by sight, and not by faith, he becomes weak as another man, every duty is a burden. It is when in the exercise of faith he realises to himself the unseen realitites of religion and eternity, that he "renews his strength, mounts up on wings as an eagle, runs and does not weary, walks and does not faint."

Against this spiritual languor, which makes the discharge of duty tiresome, and strongly tempts to its utter abandonment, the apostle here warns the Galatian Christians, "Be not weary[89] in well-doing."

We have here a beautiful exemplification of the extent and spirituality of the law of Christ. It prohibits the neglect of well-doing, as well as positive evil-doing, and it reaches to the very spring of actions. It not only prohibits the neglect of well-doing, but that weariness in well-doing which is likely to lead to this neglect. It is not satisfied with the thing enjoined being done; it must be done in a right temper. The Lord loves a cheerful doer as well as a cheerful giver.

The motive which the apostle employs, for the purpose of guarding the Galatian Christians against weariness in well-doing, is at once appropriate and powerful. Nothing is so much calculated to produce languor as a suspicion that all our exertions are likely to be fruitless; and nothing is better fitted to dispel it than the assurance that they shall assuredly be crowned with success. "In due season," says he, "ye shall reap, if ye faint not."

"Ye shall reap." The language is figurative, but not obscure. Indeed it is far more expressive than any literal description could have been. It implies in it the idea of reward – of reward naturally rising out of, and proportioned to, the dutiful exertion. The Christian shall be rewarded for his well-doing. Every act of Christian duty, every sacrifice made, every privation submitted to, every suffering endured, from a regard to Christ's authority, with a view to Christ's honor, shall assuredly be recompensed. This reward is often – usually– granted in part, even in the present state, and shall be most certainly conferred in the future. This reward shall grow out of, and correspond to, the dutiful exertions of the Christian. It shall be his harvest. The happiness of a Christian, both in this world and the next, is, in a great measure, the natural result of his conformity to the will of God. Every holy temper is a capacity of enjoyment, and a source of enjoyment at the same time. The cultivation of holy dispositions, and the performance of commanded duty, are necessary to the true happiness of the Christian, not only from the Divine appointment, but from the very nature of the case.

The happy results of well-doing are not, however, in every case immediate – in no case are all the happy results of any act of well-doing at once and completely developed – and therefore the apostle adds, Ye shall reap "in due season."[90] Christians frequently act like children in reference to this harvest. They would sow and reap in the same day. When children sow the seeds of flowers in their little gardens, they are apt to become impatient for their appearing above ground; and then for their yielding blossoms; and by this impatience are often not merely disquieted, but induced to do what must retard, and may altogether prevent, the eagerly desired event. Like "the husbandman" who "waiteth for the precious fruit of the earth, and hath long patience for it, till he has received the former and latter rain," the Christian must also "be patient and stablish his heart." Our time is always ready; but it is not for us either to know or to regulate the times and the seasons. The Father has kept them in His own power. The harvest is certain. This we are assured of, and, moreover, that if our own fault prevent not, it will be abundant and joyful. Whether it is to be an early or a late one depends entirely on the arrangements of Him who is "wonderful in counsel, and excellent in working." And is it not right that it should be so? Is it not enough to be assured that in due season – at the period fixed by infinite wisdom and kindness – our objects shall be completely gained, our exertions abundantly rewarded?

The concluding clause deserves particular notice, "if we faint not," literally "not fainting."[91] This phrase, "not fainting," may, so far as construction is concerned, be connected with either clause of the verse. It may be considered as describing either the nature of the dutiful exertion, or of the gracious reward. They who take the last view consider the apostle as saying, Unwearying labor or Christian duty will terminate in unending reward. We shall never cease to reap if we but persevere in well-doing. There will be satisfaction without satiety, and that for ever. This is truth, important truth, but we rather think the more ordinary way of connecting the phrase brings out better the apostle's exact meaning.

The saint's reaping is suspended on his not fainting, that is, his reward is suspended on his "constant continuance in well-doing." The words obviously imply, 'If we faint we shall not reap.' No true saint will so faint as to abandon altogether the onward course of well-doing; but just in the proportion in which he does so shall he not reap; just in this proportion shall he come short of "obtaining a full reward;" and if a man who has exhibited all the appearances of saintship, who has been reckoned a saint by himself, and by those who were best acquainted with him, if that man should so faint as to habitually neglect the performance of Christian duty, no doubt he shall reap, but it will be "of the flesh, corruption," and not " of the Spirit, life everlasting." A great deal of the false and dangerous notions entertained in reference to a most important Christian doctrine, that of the perseverance of the saints, would be prevented were men but to remember that the perseverance of the saints is a perseverance in holiness, and that, though "eternal life is the gift of God through Jesus Christ our Lord," it is on those only who, "through a constant continuance in well-doing, seek for glory, honor, and immortality," that eternal life is conferred. It has been finely said, "He who becomes a Christian in the true sense of that word becomes such for eternity. He has enlisted for life – for immortal life – never to withdraw. He becomes pledged to do good, and to serve God always. No obstacles are to deter him, no embarrassments are to drive him off the field. With the vigor of his youth, and the influence and wisdom of his riper years, with his remaining powers when enfeebled by age, with the last pulsations of life here, and with the immortal energies of a higher life in a better world, he is to do good. For that he is to live. For that he is to die. And when he awakes in the resurrection with renovated powers, he is to awake to an everlasting service of doing good, as far as he may have opportunity, in the kingdom of God."[92]

No man who is habitually neglectful of, or allowedly languid and careless in, the discharge of Christian duty, can have satisfactory evidence of his being an object of Divine favor; and if, in these circumstances, he cherishes a confidence in the goodness of his state, and in the security of his salvation, his confidence is presumptuous.

From the consideration that every dutiful exertion of the Christian shall in due time receive its recompense, the apostle takes occasion to exhort the Galatians to act a consistent and dutiful part in reference to all men, and especially in reference to their Christian brethren. "As we have therefore opportunity, let us do good unto all men, especially unto them who are of the household of faith."[93]

The phrase, "doing good,"[94] like well-doing, may either be considered as expressive of benevolent exertion, or of dutiful conduct generally. In the passage before us it has almost universally been interpreted in its restricted sense. It is the Christian's duty to "do good;" to endeavor to lessen the amount both of moral and physical evil, of sin and of suffering; to add to the amount both of moral and physical good, of worth and happiness, in our world. To enlighten the ignorant and prejudiced; to rouse to consideration the inconsiderate; to lead the guilty to the blood of atonement, and the depraved to the laver of regeneration; to make the bad good, and the good better; to comfort the disconsolate; to relieve the poor and the miserable, – are so many varieites of the general duty of Christian beneficence. In the performance of this duty, the Christian knows no limits except those which are fixed by his power and opportunity of doing good. He is not to be confined by relationship, or neighborhood, or sect, or even religion. The possession of a common nature is claim enough on his good wishes and good offices. Every Christian is as really, though not quite in the same way as the apostle, a "debtor to the Greek and the

Barbarian, to the wise and the unwise." Whether a man be "a Jew or a Gentile, bond or free," learned or illiterate, good or bad, if he labors under evils from which we can relieve him, it is our duty as Christians to do so.

But while Christians are bound "to do good to all men," they are peculiarly bound to do good "to those who are of the household of faith." Jerome refers this appellation to Christian ministers, who are, in a peculiar sense, "the domestics" in the family of God; but it is better to refer it to Christians generally[95] – the believing family. The application is admirably expressive. All genuine Christians are bound together by a very powerful and a very tender tie. That tie is the faith of the same truth. It is this which unites them to God, "the Father of whom the whole family in heaven and earth are called;" to Jesus Christ, the elder brother; and to one another, as children of God and brethren of Christ, – "heirs of God, and joint-heirs with Jesus Christ." They love one another "in the truth, for the truth's sake, which is in them, and will abide with them for ever." Duty corresponds with relation. Christians, therefore, are particularly bound to do good to one another. Every poor and distressed man has a claim on me for pity, and, if I can afford it, for active exertion and pecuniary relief. But a poor Christian has a far stronger claim on my feelings, my labors, and my property. He is my brother, equally interested with myself in the blood and love of the Redeemer. I expect to spend an eternity with him in heaven. He is the representative of my unseen Savior, and HE considers everything done to his poor afflicted brother as done to himself. For a Christian to be unkind to a Christian, is not only wrong, it is monstrous.

The obligation to do good to our fellow-Christians extends both to their external and spiritual necessities. It is an important duty, "if we see a brother or sister naked, or destitute of daily food, to give them those things which are needful for the body." But it is not a less important duty, when we see a Christian brother or sister laboring under mistake, or in danger of falling into sin, to endeavor to undeceive them, and to warn them of their danger. Spiritual evils are the worst evils, and spiritual blessings are the best blessings; and we do good to our brethren in the most important way, when we deliver them from these evils, and put them in possession of these blessings. We are to love our brethren as Christ loved us, and do good to them as he does good to us.

Christians are to "do good to all men, and especially to those who are of the household of faith, as they have opportunity." The idea commonly attached to these words is, that Christians are bound to seize every opportunity of doing good, both to mankind generally, and to their fellow-Christians in particular. This is an important truth, but we doubt if it is exactly the truth which the apostle here expresses. The word "season"[96] in the 9th verse, and the word "opportunity" in the 10th, are the same in the original. That word is the link which connects the two verses. "In due season ye shall reap." While we have the "season" let us do good; as if he had said, 'The season of reaping will come in due time. Now is the season for sowing. While ye have the season, improve it. In a short time the objects of your beneficence will be beyond your reach, or you will be taken from them. The eternal harvest depends on the short seed-time. There is no time to be idle, for "whatsoever a man soweth, that shall he also reap."[97]

While I have explained the phrase "doing good," in the way in which it is ordinarily understood, as referring directly to benevolent exertion, I am strongly disposed to think that the word is employed by the apostle in its most general sense. "Work that which is good in reference to all men, but especially in reference to the household of faith.' It seems to us to refer to the duties of justice as well as mercy. "Render to all their due;" "wrong no man;" and, in reference to your brethren, let your conduct be scrupulously upright and dutiful. We find the apostle warning Christian servants against using improper freedoms with their Christian masters, as if their common privileges as Christians brought them nearer a level in civil society; and using the Christianity of their Masters as a powerful superadded reason why they should be obedient to them. "Let as many servants as are under the yoke count their own masters worthy of all honor; and they that have believing masters, let them not despise them, because they are brethren; but rather do

156

them service, because they are faithful and beloved, partakers of the benefit" (1 Tim. 6:1,2.). And we find him representing the Christian character of a person injured by another Christian as a great aggravation of the offence, – "Ye do wrong, and defraud, and that your brethren" (1 Cor. 6:8.). This gives unity to the whole paragraph, – "sowing to the Spirit," "well-doing," and "doing good," all of them being terms of nearly equivalent import.

The practical improvement to be made of this passage is not far to seek. Let us turn it to the use of serious self-inquiry. Let us ask, Have we never been, are we not now, "weary in well-doing"? Are we "doing good to all, as we have opportunity, especially to the household of faith"? If we press these questions honestly home, deep self-humiliation will be the result. But let us not, however, despair. The more languid we are, the greater is the necessity for earnest prayer and increased exertion. The less good we have done in the past, the more diligent should we be in doing good in the future. The season of doing good will soon close for ever. "What our hand findeth to do, let us do it with our might." The season of reward will soon come to those who, "by a patient continuance in well-doing, are seeking for glory, honor, and immortality." "Be steadfast, immoveable, always abounding in the work of the Lord, forasmuch as your labor is not in vain in the Lord."

And if the harvest seems long in coming – if the reward seems long delayed – still "faint not." "Cast not away your confidence, which has great recompense of reward. For ye have need of patience" – that is, you must persevere – "that after ye have done the will of God, ye may receive the promise" (Heb. 10:36.).

This seems to be the conclusion of the epistle, properly so called. What follows has all the ordinary marks of a Postscript.

PART VII.

POSTSCRIPT.

"See, in what large letters I have written you with my own hand. As many as desire to have a show in the flesh, these force you to be circumcised – only that they may not be persecuted for the cross of Christ. For they themselves who are being circumcised do not keep the Law, but they desire you to be circumcised so they might boast in your flesh. But may it never be for me to boast, except in the cross of our Lord Jesus Christ, through whom the world has been crucified to me, and I to the world. For in Christ Jesus neither circumcision is worth anything, or the lack of circumcision, but a new creation. And as many as shall walk by this rule, peace and mercy be on them and on the Israel of God. For the rest, let no one cause me troubles, for I bear in my body the brands of the Lord Jesus. The grace of our Lord Jesus Christ be with your spirit, brothers. Amen." – Galatians 6:11-18.

SECT. I. – INTRODUCTORY REMARKS.

In an age like the present, in which infidel principles are extensively entertained and zealously propagated, it is a matter of high importance, both to the satisfaction of his own mind, which may be disturbed by the hardy assertions or sly insinuations of unbelievers, and to the credit of his religion, which is apt to suffer when its supporters appear perplexed or silenced by the cavils of its opponents, that every professor of Christianity should be so well instructed in the grounds on which he has embraced that religion, as true and divine, as to enable him "to hold fast the profession of his faith without wavering," and "to give an answer to every one who asketh him a reason of the hope that is in him, with meekness and fear." The evidence of the genuineness, the authenticity, and the inspiration of the Holy Scripture, ought to be familiar to his mind.

To the questions, Why do I believe the books, received by me as sacred, as the compositions of the persons whose names they bear? Why do I give credit to their statements, and why do I consider these statements as not only characterised by strict truth, but possessed of Divine authority? he ought always to be ready to give an answer which is satisfactory to his own mind, and which is likely to be so to every candid inquirer.

A man may have a great deal of this kind of knowledge without being a Christian at all, in the true sense of that word. It is to be feared that some have most ingeniously and satisfactorily defended the truth and divinity of Christianity, who have lived and died strangers and enemies to all that is most distinctive and valuable in the doctrine of that religion, and utterly destitute of all those invaluable blessings which, when understood and believed, these doctrines uniformly convey to the soul; and, on the other hand, many genuine Christians are extremely deficient in this kind of knowledge, and still more deficient in the capacity of using with advantage that limited portion of it which they possess.

This is deeply to be regretted. "I take it," says the great and good Richard Baxter — "I take it to be the greatest cause of coldness in duty, weakness in grace, boldness in sinning, and unwillingness to die, that our faith in the divine authority of Scripture is either unsound or impure. Few Christians among us have anything better than an implicit faith in this point. They have received it by tradition. Godly ministers and Christians tell them so; it is impious to doubt it, and therefore they believe it; and this worm, lying at the root, causeth the languishing and decaying of the whole."

It is surely, then, the duty of the Christian teacher frequently to turn the attention of those whom he instructs in the numerous, varied, and powerful arguments which prove that, in receiving Christianity, "we have not followed a cunningly devised fable," but that we have embraced what is emphatically "the truth;" and to do this, not merely in presenting to them a complete systematized view of the evidence of revelation, but by seizing every opportunity of fixing their minds on those signatures of truth and divinity, which become apparent as we study the different doctrines, and duties, and institutions of Christianity, and the various parts of that inspired volume, in which these doctrines, and duties, and institutions are unfolded. With such an opportunity are we now presented, in reference to the genuineness of that portion of the inspired Scriptures — the Epistles of the Apostle Paul.

To the question, How do you know that these epistles are really the writings of the Apostle Paul, and not the forgeries of a late age? it is a most satisfactory answer, — 'I have the same kind of evidence, and a great deal more of it, as that on which the Commentaries of Julius Caesar, or the Epistles of Cicero or Pliny, are universally allowed to be the works of the great men whose names they bear. From the very period when the epistles are said to have been written, there is an unbroken succession of testimonies that, at that time and thenceforward, they were admitted by those who had the best means of ascertaining the truth, and the strongest inducements to employ these means, to be the undoubted productions of the age, and of the individual to whom they are ascribed.

But, apart from this evidence altogether, there is another species of proof of the genuineness of the epistles, which is calculated to convey most satisfactory conviction to every candid mind. I refer to the very numerous undesigned coincidences between the different epistles, and likewise between the epistles and that historical work, the Acts of the Apostles, in which many of the incidents of Paul's life are recorded. Dr. Paley, in the most original of all his very useful works, has fully expanded this argument, and has made it appear, to the satisfaction of every unprejudiced inquirer, that were a person to fall in with the Acts of the Apostles and epistles of Paul, without previously knowing anything about them — destitute of all external, direct, or collateral evidence, — he would find in these undesigned — obviously undesigned — correspondences good reason to believe the persons and transactions referred to, to be real, the letters genuine, and the narratives

To feel the full force of such an argument, the numerous minute and obviously undesigned coincidences must be brought forward; but a single example of the species of undesigned coincidence, on which the whole cogency of the argument depends, is enough to make a person understand its nature, and ought to induce him to study it in the admirable work already referred to — and what would be still better, to endeavor to develop it for himself, by a careful perusal of the inspired books in question.

SECT. II. — THE APOSTLE'S REMARK, THAT HIS LETTER WAS AUTOGRAPH.

The first verse of this postscript furnishes an example of that reference to circumstances in the apostle's history, not mentioned in the epistle, which furnishes so strong an evidence of the genuineness of his letters. "Ye see how large a letter I have written unto you with mine own hand" (Gal. 6:11.).

The circumstance to which we wish to draw your attention, as an exemplification of undesigned coincidence, of a kind altogether irreconcileable with the hypothesis of forgery, is Paul's directing the notice of the Galatians to his having written this epistle "with his own hand." To have noticed this was quite natural in Paul, who, as we learn from other epistles, was not accustomed to write to the churches entirely or chiefly with his own hand, but employed an amanuensis, and merely wrote his salutation in the close, as accrediting the letter. The Epistle to the Romans was written by Tertius (Rom. 16:22.). The First Epistle to the Corinthians, the Epistle to the Colossians, and the Second to the Thessalonians, have all, near their close, these words, "The salutation of me Paul with mine own hand;" and, in the last of the instances, it is added, "Which is the token in every epistle: so I write. The grace of our Lord Jesus Christ be with you all. Amen" (1 Cor. 16:21; Col. 4:18; 2 Thess. 3:17.).

To an impostor ignorant of Paul's custom alluded to — and you will observe it is no more than an allusion (for this passage does not state what we know from other sources to have been Paul's custom) — the reference could not have occurred; and an impostor, aware of Paul's custom, would have imitated it. It could not have occurred to a forger of the epistle to give plausibility to his claim by setting forth his epistle as written in a way different from that in which those of the apostle generally were.

If we admit the justness of the version of our translators as to the words rendered "how large[1] a letter," which, however, is doubtful, we shall find another obviously undesigned correspondence. The Epistle to the Romans and the two Epistles to the Corinthians are all of them larger than the Epistle to the Galatians. But none of these epistles existed at the time this epistle was written; and with the exception of these, and the Epistle to the Hebrews, of which it is by no means absolutely certain, though in a high degree probable, that Paul was the author, and which was also written subsequent to the date of this epistle, the Epistle to the Galatians is the largest of the apostle's letters.

The meaning of the apostle's phraseology in this verse is somewhat doubtful; and it deserves notice that this is a fair specimen of many of the difficult passages of Scripture. The way in which you understand them affects no principle, either of Christian faith or duty. The apostle's words might have been rendered in English, with a somewhat similar ambiguity of meaning as that which belongs to them in the original, 'Ye see what a letter I have written you with my own hand.' The reference may be either to the matter or manner, to the form, or the size, or the length of the letter. There is nothing in the words which absolutely fixes it to any one of them. It may be, you see how "weighty and powerful" a letter I have written you; or how faithful and affectionate a letter I have written; or how long[2] a letter I have written you.

Some of the earlier Greek interpreters suppose that there is a reference to the large and not very well formed Greek characters which the apostle, accustomed to writing in Hebrew, employed.[3]

There can be but little doubt as to the general idea which the apostle intended to convey by these words. He meant obviously to bring before the mind of the Galatians the fact of the deep interest he took in them, as expressed by his writing such a letter, and writing it too with his own hand.[4] It may be that, by drawing their attention to the circumstance that he had not, as usual, employed an amanuensis, he meant to show the delicacy of his affection. A friend will himself write to a friend with whose conduct he is dissatisfied in a manner very different from that in which he would do were he obliged to employ a third person to communicate his thoughts.[5]

SECT. III. – UNPRINCIPLED CONDUCT OF THE JUDAISING TEACHERS.

What follows consists chiefly of a caution to the Galatians against the acts of the Judaising teachers, drawn from the consideration of the mean and unworthy ends which they had in view in endeavoring to induce them to conform to the rites of Judaism. "As many as desire to make a fair show in the flesh, they constrain you to be circumcised; only lest they should suffer persecution for the Cross of Christ" (Gal. 6:12.).

The general meaning of thses words obviously is, 'These men who are so very zealous to make you submit to the initiatory rite of Judaism are not actuated by honest, though mistaken, conscientious views, as to the necessity of the observance of the Mosaic law to your salvation: their object is to secure the favor,or, at any rate, to avoid the persecution, of their unbelieving Jewish brethren. It is not an honest, though mistaken, wish to serve you, but the unworthy, selfish desire of serving themselves, that influences them. Let us look a little more closely at the phraseology in which this sentiment is expressed.

The apostle does not name the Judaising teachers, but he so describes them that they cannot be mistaken. They were such as desired "to make a fair show in the flesh."[6] "To make a fair show" is to assume a course of conduct which will be agreeable to those whom we wish to please. "To desire to make a fair show" is to be anxious to fashion our conduct so as to please. Now, these Judaising teachers were anxious to adopt a line of conduct which would please their unbelieving brethren. The phrase "in the flesh" modifies the expression "making a fair show." The best commentary on the expression, as used here, is to be found in the following passage in the Epistle to the Philippians, – "For we are the circumcision, which worship God in the Spirit, and rejoice in Christ Jesus, and have no confidence in the flesh. Though I might also have confidence in the flesh. If any other man thinketh that he hath whereof he might trust in the flesh, I more: Circumcised the eighth day, of the stock of Israel, of the tribe of Benjamin, an Hebrew of the Hebrews; as touching the law, a Pharisee; concerning zeal, persecuting the church; touching the righteousness which is in the law, blameless" (Phil. 3:3-6.).

In reference, then, to the Mosaic observances which were fleshly or carnal, that is, of an external ceremonial nature, these Judaising teachers wished to follow a course which would secure them from the persecutions of their unbelieving brethren. The same principle, in other forms, is still found operating among the professors of Christianity. How many are there who are constantly endeavoring to make a compromise between the demands of conscience and of interest, who are afraid to break with the world by giving up with its even to them very doubtful practices, and by a fearless avowal of Christian principle, and a determined obedience to the law of Christ. Such men play a losing game at best. They seldom gain even their immediate object. The world is a tyrant which requires unqualified submission; and if their conscience prevent them from giving this, all partial compliances will excite but the contempt of those whose favor they are courting. And even should the end be gained, if they should have their reward in keeping in the good graces of the worldly, it is a miserable one. They have gained, it may be, the good opinion of the world; but they have lost that of God, on whose decision their destiny through eternity depends. His words are by no means equivocal: "No man can serve two masters."

These time-serving, worldly professors of Christianity are among the most dangerous enemies of spiritual Christianity and spiritual Christians. They are continually endeavoring to bring these over to their side, and urging them to act as they do, under the pretence that Christianity may thus be rendered more palatable to worldly men, but in reality that they may be secured from what they account unnecessary reproach and suffering. Such was the part which the Judaising teachers acted. From a wish to ingratiate themselves with their unbelieving brethren, they "compelled"[7] the Gentile converts to be circumcised, that is, used every method in their power by persuasion, threats, and declining to associate with them unless they submitted to their favorite rite.

Had this originated in conscientious convictions, even then the apostle would have warned the Galatians against it. He would still have considered them as in a dangerous error; but their behavior would not, in his estimation, have been so contemptible as it was, originating, as he knew, and as indeed was made evident by their conduct, in low, selfish motives. In doing all that lay in their power to induce the Gentile converts to assume the external aspect of Jews, their object was to secure themselves from persecution. They did it "lest they should suffer persecution for the Cross of Christ." The early Roman emperors, according to Jerome, allowed the Jews throughout the empire to exercise their religion; and it has been supposed the circumcised Christians were considered as Jews, but if they were uncircumcised they were liable to persecution, as the professors of a "religio illicita." This supposed fact − for it is not authenticated[8] − has been considered as throwing light on this passage; but we cannot perceive this: for it was not by their own circumcision, but by the circumcision of others, these men sought security from persecution, so that the persecution here referred to was not from Pagans, but Jews, from whom, indeed, the principal persecutions of Christianity, directly and indirectly, in the earlier times proceeded (Acts 8:1; 13:50; 14:5,6; 2 Tim. 3:11.).

The Cross of Christ here, and in the 14th verse, is by many interpreters considered as equivalent to sufferings on account of Christ, as "the sufferings of Christ" is, in 2 Cor. 1:5, obviously expressive of sufferings in the cause of Christ, and accordingly they render the words,[9] 'lest they should be persecuted with the Cross of Christ, lest they should be called on to bear the Cross, which every true disciple, according to the declaration of our Lord, must bear.' Though, however, every true disciple must bear his own Cross, yet I do not know that the phrase, 'Cross of Christ,' is ever used in this sense in the New Testament. So far as I have been able to form an opinion, the expression, when used as in the case before us, always signifies the fact of the death of Jesus Christ on the Cross, as the expiation of human guilt − the only ground of human hope, superseding everything else as the foundation of acceptance with God (1 Cor. 1:17,18; Phil. 3:18.). It was this doctrine which was peculiarly unpalatable to the unbelieving Jews, − leading, as it plainly did, to a renunciation of all the expiatory rites of the Mosiac law as utterly useless, and indeed impious and criminal, if used as affording a method of obtaining the Divine favor. They could not bear that Gentiles should be recognised as of the household of God, merely because they believed in Christ, and trusted in His death on the Cross as the procuring cause of their salvation, and therefore nothing was so well fitted to moderate their antipathies as to throw this into the shade by continuing to observe the rites and ceremonies of the law. Now, these time-serving men thought the best way of rebutting the charge, that by becoming Christians they had become enemies to the law, was by yielding external conformity to its rites, and insisting that all Gentile converts to Christianity should also, by doing so, seem to have become proselytes to Judaism.

This tampering with truth and duty, even when it originates in a mistaken but sincere wish to serve the interests of Christianity, joined with dangerously lax notions as to expediency, is highly criminal; but when, as it often is, as it was in the case before us, a mere cloak for low selfishness, it is peculiarly detestable. That it was so in the case of these Judaising teachers is plain from what is stated by the apostle in the next verse.

"For neither they themselves who are circumcised keep the law; but desire to have you circumcised, that they may glory in your flesh" (Gal. 6:13.).

It is not easy to say whether these words in the first clause refer to the Judaising teachers or to those among the Galatian converts whom they had prevailed on to submit to the initiatory rite of Judaism. They state what was probably the truth with regard to both; all that they wished was to save appearances. The Judaisers insisted on the Gentile converts being circumcised: for to associate in a religious way, and in the ordinary offices of life, with persons known to have been heathens, and never to have submitted to the initiatory rite of Judaism, was something which could not be hid, and would have outraged the prejudices of the unbelieving Jews; but entire submission to the law in every case does not seem to have been required. The circumcised Gentile convert was not even by them, it would seem, required in everything to "live as a Jew." And even of themselves, it was probable that what Paul says of Peter was true, that though Jews, they lived in many things "as the Gentiles did." Their object was to make a fair show; and when legal observances were not necessary to serve their purposes, they could easily dispense with them.

Now, either of these courses of conduct on the part of the Judaising teachers was a proof that they had no really conscientious conviction of the obligation of the Mosaic law. If they had, they would have been consistent. Their object was to have, in the fact of having induced Gentiles to submit to the initiatory rite of Judaism, something that they might use as a defence against the persecutions of the unbelieving Jews. They could point to these circumcised Gentiles, and say, 'see the proof of our reverence for the law.'

Connected with this was the mean, unworthy motive of wishing to have substantial evidence of their power over the minds of the converts. There is no power which, by men of a certain cast of mind, is so much coveted as power over other men's minds – the being able to say, 'they embraced doctrines just because we taught them, and submitted to usages just because we prescribed them.' Nothing can be more absurd than this – as if their own responsibilities were not enough when called to "give account of themselves to God," they must ultroneously undertake other men's responsibilities, adding to their own burden, sufficiently heavy already, without at all lightening that of their dupes. For of every one of them it must still continue true: "Every one must give account of himself to God" (Rom. 14:12.). Such a principle is utterly unworthy of a Christian teacher; and whenever the slightest symptom of it appears, it is the duty and interest of the Christian people to watch it with the utmost care, and to resist it with the utmost pertinacity.

Let us bear on our souls the indelible mark of subjection of mind and heart to Christ; but let us bear neither on our bodies nor on our souls the brand of subjection to human authority. "One is our master, even Christ." "Be not the servants of men."

The fact that merely external conformity, and that to a certain length only, satisfied these false teachers – and, it would seem, served their purpose, also, in quashing the persecution of the unbelieving Jews, – is striking and important. Like cases are by no means rare. In almost every variety of corrupted Christianity we find materially the same thing. If a man will but profess his faith in the infallibility of the Roman Catholic church, and perform its rites regularly, he will be allowed almost any latitude he pleases, both as to opinion and conduct. Where there is nothing but an external religion, great uneasiness is often produced in families when some of the members, from conscientious principle, go not to the usual place of worship, or observe not the usual form of worship; – it does not matter whether the persons belong to the Established Church, or to a Dissenting body – to the Episcopalian or Presbyterian persuasion. The great matter is not the convicion of the mind, but the bringing them back to the orthodox place of worship. If they can be got back again to the church, or to the chapel, or to the meeting-house – if the external conformity be but yielded, all is gained. And, indeed, what else can be expected? Where a person's own religion is all of this external professional kind, how should he seek for anything more in another?

Let us learn from this passage to beware of bye-ends in religion. Let it be our constant object to maintain "a conscience void of offence to God and man," and to be able to say, "Our rejoicing is this, the testimony of our conscience, that in simplicity and godly sincerity, not with fleshly wisdom, but by the grace of God, we have had our conversation in the world" (2 Cor. 1:12.).

Let us also be warned against taking up with a mere outside religion – a thing of time, and place, and circumstance. Real Christianity is a religion as extensive as the nature of man as a being capable of thought, feeling, and action. Let our religion be the religion of the mind, the religion of the heart, the religion of the life, – not a theory of doctrine, however ingenious, or even correct, – not a feeling casually, though it may be strongly, excited, – not an external and ritual service, however simple or however imposing, – not an assumed garb, however splendid, and gracefully worn; but a constituent – the governing – element of our intellectual and moral nature: not speculation – not enthusaism – not superstition – not formalism – not hypocrisy: not exclusively doctrinal, or experimental, or liturgical, or professional, or practical; but all these in due proportion and degree, – the natural effect of the truth understood, and believed, and loved, – "faith purifying the heart, working by love, and overcoming the world." Let this be the religion which we cultivate in ourselves, and let this be the religion we endeavor to propagate among our brethren of mankind.

SECT. IV. – THE APOSTLE'S DETERMINATION TO GLORY ONLY IN THE CROSS OF CHRIST.

The sentiments of the apostle in reference to the cross, so directly opposed to those of the Judaising teachers, – the change produced on his views and feelings in reference to the world, and on the views and feeling of the world in reference to him, in consequence of his entertaining and avowing these sentiments, – and the influence of this faith and profession in producing these changes, – are very strikingly expressed in the following verse:[e] – "But God forbid[10] that I should glory, save in the cross of our Lord Jesus Christ, by whom the world is crucified unto me, and I unto the world" (Gal. 6:14.).

The connection of this passage with what goes before, indicated by the particle "but,"[11] may be variously stated. The particle "but" usually intimates contrast. The words before us may be considered as directly connected with the words immediately preceding. As if the apostle had said, 'Your false teachers glory or boast in their influence over you, proved by your submitting to the initiatory rite of Judaism in consequence of their urgency; but I have a more solid ground for my boasting. I glory not in the blind submission of men to my authority; I glory in the Cross of my Savior.' The contrast in this case is between the two different grounds of the glorying of the Judaising teachers and the apostle.

The words may, however, be viewed as connected, not with those which immediately precede them, but with the close of the 12th verse, while the 13th is viewed as a parenthesis. In this case, the contrast is between the light in which the Judaising teachers and that in which the apostle viewed the Cross of Christ. They greatly underrated its importance; they wished to conceal it; they were ashamed of it; and were afraid of suffering persecution on account of it. But, instead of this, the apostle gloried in it, and was determined to glory in nothing else. It does not matter which of these two views of the connection we adopt, though I am disposed to prefer the latter.

The meaning of the whole passage depends on the sense we affix to the phrase, "Cross of Christ." Some judicious interpreters understand "the Cross of Christ" here, of sufferings in the cause of Christ; and they consider the expression in the text as just synonymous with his declaration in 2 Cor. 12:5, "Of myself I will not glory, save in mine infirmities." "Most gladly therefore will I rather glory in my infirmities, that the power of Christ may rest upon me. Therefore I take pleasure in infirmities, in reproaches, in necessities, in persecutions, in distresses, for Christ's sake: for when I am weak, then am I strong." "We glory in tribulations also" (Rom. 5:3.). The same sentiment was strongly felt by the apostles, when they "departed from the presence of the" Jewish "council, rejoicing that they were counted worthy to suffer shame for His name" (Acts 5:41.). It is strikingly stated, when suffering for Christ is represented to the Philippians as a privilege, on the possession of which the apostle congratulates them, "Unto you it is given in the behalf of Christ to suffer for His sake" (Philip. 1:29.). If this be the apostle's meaning, he contrasts his own feelings with those of the Judaising teachers. 'These men are afraid and ashamed of bearing the Cross after Christ: I count this my highest honor; and through the means of these sufferings "the world is crucified to me" – the pleasures, and honors, and riches of the world have become, in my estimation, things contemptible and valueless; and, on the other hand, these sufferings have made me an object of contempt and dislike to the men of the world (1 Cor. 4:9.), so that I am under no temptation to court their favor, as these Judaising teachers are, by doctrines fashioned to their taste.'

There is no doubt that this is plausible. The sense thus given to the words is quite self-consistent. It agrees well enough with the context, and the obvious design of the writer, and it is perfectly agreeable to the analogy of faith; but it labors under one very important defect, — it gives the phrase, "Cross of Christ," a sense which, though not unnatural, nor inconsistent with the genius of the language or the analogy of Scripture expression, is yet altogether unsupported; for, as we have just observed, wherever the phrase, "cross of Christ," occurs in the New Testament, and does not express the instrument of our Lord's death, it signifies the fact that Jesus Christ expiated the sin of men by dying on a cross (1 Cor. 1:17,18; Phil. 3:18.).

This, then, is the sense in which we understand it here. In the fact that the incarnate Son of God had expired on a cross as the victim of human guilt — that He was "delivered for our offences" — that He was "made sin for us" — that He "gave Himself for us, the just One in the room of the unjust, that He might bring us to God," — the apostle gloried, and declares that, in comparison with this, He will glory in nothing else.

Now, what is meant by his thus glorying or boasting in the cross of Christ? This will be best understood by contrasting the apostle's sentiments on this subject with those of the Judaising teachers, who were ashamed of it. They did not place their dependence for salvation on the cross of Christ, or, at any rate, not wholly there. They concealed it: they thought that this concealment was necessary in order to the success of Christianity; and they shrunk from suffering on account of it. In all these ways they showed the low estimate they had formed of the cross of Christ; and just in an opposite way did the apostle show the high estimate he had formed of it.

It is difficult to say exactly what views these teachers had of the cross of Christ. It is plain, however, that they did not look to Christ's death as the price of their salvation — the ground of their hope. They did not submit to God's method of justification, but went about to establish a way of their own, "as it were, by the law." They depended, at least in part, for acceptance with God on circumcision, and the performance of ritual observances.

But, on the other hand, the finished work of Christ was the sole ground of the apostle's confidence: — "For we are the circumcision, which worship God in the Spirit, and rejoice in Christ Jesus, and have no confidence in the flesh. Though I might also have confidence in the flesh. If any other man thinketh that he hath whereof he might trust in the flesh, I more: circumcised the eighth day, of the stock of Israel, of the tribe of Benjamin, an Hebrew of the Hebrews; as touching the law, a Pharisee; concerning zeal, persecuting the church; touching the righteousness which is in the law, blameless. But what things were gain to me, those I counted loss for Christ. Yea doubtless, and I count all things but loss for the excellency of the knowledge of Christ Jesus my Lord: for whom I have suffered the loss of all things, and do count them but dung, that I may win Christ, and be found in Him, not having mine own righteousness, which is of the law, but that which is through the faith of Christ, the righteousness which is of God by faith."[12]

The Judaising teachers showed their low estimate of the doctrine of the cross by concealing it, or, at any rate, casting it into the shade. The apostle, on the contrary, showed his high estimate of it by giving it the greatest possible prominence in his exhibitions of Christian truth. Read his epistles, and you will find how closely he kept to his determination to "know nothing," among those to whom he made known the gospel, "but Jesus Christ and Him crucified;" that Jesus was "delivered for our offences;" that "He dies in our room;" that "we have redemption in Him, through His blood, who is set forth a propitiation;" that "we are bought with a price;" that "He was made sin for us, that we might be made the righteousness of God in Him;" that "we who are far off were brought nigh by the blood of Christ;" that "He gave Himself for us, a sacrifice and an offering, that He might bring us to God;" — these were the constant themes of the apostle's discourses (Rom. 4:25; 5:8; 3:24,25; Eph. 1:7; 1 Cor. 6:20; 2 Cor. 5:21; Eph.

2:13; 5:2.). "I declare unto you the gospel," says he, "which I preached unto you, which also ye have received, and wherein ye stand; by which also ye are saved, if ye keep in memory what I preached unto you, unless ye have believed in vain: for I delivered unto you first of all that which I also received, how that Christ died for our sins according to the Scriptures" (1 Cor. 15:1-3.). "The Jews," says he, "require a sign, and the Greeks seek after wisdom: but we preach Christ crucified, unto the Jews a stumbling-block, and unto the Greeks foolishness; but unto them which are called, both Jews and Greeks, Christ the power of God, and the wisdom of God" (1 Cor. 1:22-24.).

The Judaising teachers considered the doctrine of the Cross as a great obstacle in the way of the spread of Christianity. The apostle was of opinion that when the doctrine of the Cross was not received, Christianity was not received; and that that doctrine, opposed, as it is, to the pride and prejudices of men, is yet the divinely appointed and divinely adapted method for triumphing over that pride and these prejudices. It was the grand weapon of His warfare, and though not "carnal," he found it "mighty through God to the pulling down of strong-holds; casting down imaginations, and every high thing that exalteth itself against the knowledge of God, and bringing into captivity every thought to the obedience of Christ" (2 Cor. 10:4,5.).

The Judaising teachers shrunk from suffering on account of the Cross. The apostle, on the contrary, would not purchase life at the price of denying, or even of concealing, this doctrine. On the contrary, he thought shame honor, and suffering happiness, in such a cause. "Neither count I my life dear unto myself, so that I might finish my course with joy, and the ministry which I have received of the Lord Jesus, to testify the gospel of the grace of God" (Acts 20:24.).

But why did the apostle thus glory in the Cross of Christ? He saw, in the fact of the expiation of the sins of men by the death of the Son of God on the Cross, such a glorious display of the wisdom and power, the holiness and benignity, of the Divine character, as destroyed the native enmity of his own heart, quelled the jealousies of guilt, sweetly constrained him to love God, filled his mind with holy peace and joyful hope, delivered him from "the bondage of corruption," and brought him into "the glorious liberty of the children of God;" and he was persuaded that what the Cross of Christ was to him it was calculated to be to every one of the children of Adam, who, like him, understood and believed the truth respecting it. Therefore he gloried in the Cross — in Christ — in Christ crucified.[13]

"The doctrine of the Cross," as has been finely remarked by John Glas, in his "Testimony on the King of Martyrs," one of the most valuable theological treatises produced in this country during the eighteenth century — "The doctrine of the Cross is the distinguishing truth of Christianity, whereby it is differenced from mere natural religion, and from all the religions of the world, that any may compete with it. All the parts of the Scriptural revelation depend on it, and are connected with it, so that, take away this truth out of the gospel, it will become another gospel, and the whole of the prophets and apostles will be utterly made of none effect as to eternal life and salvation. This truth is the great means whereby the power of God is put forth to save sinners and to subject them to Him in His kingdom. It was by the revelation of Christ's righteousness in the gospel that Christ's kingdom was first set up and advanced in the world, and it was by the renewal of this great truth, after it had been bound under antichrist's reign, that the Lord began to "consume that wicked one." At the Reformation Luther said, "This article reigns in my heart, and with this the church stands or falls." Without this great truth all other means for promoting or defending the kingdom of Christ will be altogether ineffectual; yea, on the contrary, serve to advance the kingdom of Satan. The strength of Christ's kingdom, and its safety, lies all in this truth. So they who would advance this kingdom in the world must bear it about with them in their hearts, in all their preaching, and in all their conversation in the ministry; and truly this would be a spring of daily refreshment to themselves, and of great liberty and boldness in all the labors of the gospel ministry, and in all the sufferings that attend it.[14]

In this glorying in the Cross of Christ, the apostle sets an example which should be followed by every Christian, and especially by every Christian minister. Indeed, we are not Christians at all, in the true sense of that word, if we are not glorying in the Cross — in the Cross alone — as the ground of our hope. It is to be feared that multitudes are deceiving themselves on this all-important point. They say they are depending on Christ; but, in many cases, if they would but "examine themselves," they would find that they are depending on themselves. They expect pardon and salvation, not solely because Christ, the just One, died in the room of the unjust, but entirely, or in part, on the ground of their not being so bad as others, or of their repentance, their reformation, their good intentions, their alms deeds. If they think of the Cross as a ground of reliance at all, it is only as something to have recourse to in order to supply the deficiencies of other grounds of hope. This is not to glory in the Cross; it is to do it foul dishonor. "Other foundation can no man lay, save that which is laid." From the beginning to the end of Christ's religion, the weight of our eternal hopes must rest solely on the Cross.[15]

The example of the apostle deserves to be sedulously followed by the ministers of the gospel. Every Christian minister should himself be a Christian — should, for himself, as a poor, guilty hell-deserving sinner, glory in the Cross; and if he does so, the Cross is sure to occupy its proper place in his public ministrations. It is thus only that he can be faithful to his Master — it it thus only that he can gain the great object of his ministry in making men good and happy. Let a man preach with the greatest ability and zeal everything in the Bible but the Cross, he shall, as to the great end of preaching, preach in vain. While, on the other hand, the honest preaching of the Cross — though in great weakness, and even when accompanied with great deficiencies as to a full declaration of the counsel of God on some other subjects — has usually been accompanied with the divine blessing. The doctrine of the atonement ought not to be the sole theme of the Christian ministry, but every doctrine, and every precept, of Christianity should be exhibited in their connection with this great master principle; and the leading object of the preacher should be to kkep the mind and the heart of his hearers steadily fixed on Christ Jesus — Christ Jesus crucified.

SECT. V. — THE CRUCIFIXION OF THE WORLD TO THE APOSTLE, AND OF THE APOSTLE TO THE WORLD, BY THE CROSS OF CHRIST.

The influence which Paul's views of the Cross had on his views of the world, and the influence which his boastful manifestation of these views of the Cross had on the views of the men of the world respecting him, are powerfully expressed in the close of the sentence, — "By whom the world is crucified unto me, and I unto the world" (Gal. 6:14.).[f]

It was because Paul gloried in the Cross of Christ that the world was crucified to him, and he to the world; and it was because the Judaising teachers did not glory in the Cross of Christ that the world was not crucified to them, nor they to the world.

The relative which connects the two parts of the verse,[16] may either refer to Christ, or to Christ's Cross. From the way in which our translators have rendered it, it is plain they referred it to Christ — "by whom," that is, by Christ. With a large proportion of the best interpreters, I think it more natural to refer it to the Cross of Christ, and would render it "by which." The apostle's declaration then is, by the Cross of Christ[17] "the world is crucified unto me, and I unto the world." Such is the construction of the passage: let us inquire into its meaning.

"The world"[18] is a term that very often occurs in the New Testament in a somewhat peculiar sense. It designates present sensible things, viewed as exercising a malignant influence over the minds of men — directly opposed to the influence which future and spiritual things should exert over them.[19] It includes in it the external frame of nature — mankind — and their institutions, honors, pleasures, and wealth — disgrace, pain, and poverty — all that originates in this material system, and interests us, as belonging to it. It is plain that one man's world may be very different from another man's world. The world of the peasant and of the prince, of the theologian and of the statesman, of the Jew and of the Gentile, are very different worlds, but they are composed of the same sort of elements; and "the world" in each case means just the various earthly, external, influential objects, whether persons or things, objects or events, by which the individual is surrounded.

In the passage before us, and in many others, these sensible present things are personified, and termed "the world." Now, the apostle represents this figurative personage as crucified "to him;" that is, in his estimation. It deserves notice that the Apostle Paul is peculiarly attached to the word "crucify." He often uses it, when another word would nearly at least have expressed his idea, and when a person, whose mind and heart were less occupied with the cross, and Him who hung on it, would naturally have employed another term, – "Our old man is crucified;" "They that are Christ's have crucified the flesh;" and here, "The world is crucified to me, and I am crucified to the world."

But what is the apostle's meaning when he says "the world." – that is, present sensible things, as possessing and exercising influence – is as a crucified person, in his estimation? "The world," in the estimate formed of it by mankind in general, may be compared to a mighty prince, who has unlimited means of bestowing rewards and inflicting punishments, and whose favor, of course, it is of the highest importance to secure and retain. They conceive that happiness is to be found in present sensible things. To be rich and honorable, to have all the accommodation and pleasures of the present state, to enjoy the smiles of this potentate, is, in their estimation, to be happy. To be poor and despised, persecuted and afflicted, to be subjected to the frown of this potentate, is, in their estimation, to be miserable. This is the mode of thinking and feeling natural to man, and it was once the apostle's mode of thinking and feeling. He once counted worldly honor, and wealth, and pleasure, and power, gain; but now, instead of viewing the world as a mighty potentate, he regarded it as a condemned malefactor nailed to a cross. He no longer looked to it for happiness; he no longer regarded it either with admiration or fear; he no longer courted its smiles; he no longer dreaded its frowns. The wealth, and honors, and pleasures of the world could not seduce him, nor all its varied evils terrify him into an abandonment of the Savior or of His cause – make him renounce or even conceal one of His doctrines – neglect one of His ordinances, or violate one of His laws. In his estimate, to do anything inconsistent with duty to his Lord, in compliance with "the course of this world," in order to attain its richest reward, or avoid its severest punishment, would be as absurd as if to procure a favorable glance from the eye of a worthless expiring felon on a cross, a person were to sbuject himself to the displeasure of an accomplished and powerful sovereign, who had every claim on his affections and allegiance.[20]

The phrase probably intimates even something more than this. The apostle regarded "the world" viewed as man's idol; (for "covetousness" – just another word for the supreme love of the world – "is idolatry,") – that from which he seeks for happiness, – that which he substitutes in the room of God, and of his Son, with a species of horror similar to that with which a Jew regarded a crucified person – as one accursed of God; He shrunk back from the idea of making that which is the object of God's curse the object of His supreme affection.

This complete revolution in the apostle's mode of thinking in reference to the world, was brought about by the Cross. It was by the cross of Christ that the world was crucified to him; that is, 'It was the doctrine of the Cross, understood and believed by him, that led him into this way of thinking and feeling in reference to the world.'

How it did so it is not very difficult to explain. The death of the incarnate, only-begotten Son of God on a cross, in order to avert the miseries, and secure the happiness of eternity, is calculated so to impress the mind with the inconceivable importance of that eternity, as that the man brought under the "power of the world to come" is delivered from "the present evil world." Every earth-born thing, in such a case, "grows dim and disappears – shrinks to a thing of nought." Besides, the doctrine of the

Cross believed gives other and better sources of enjoyment, – it makes us acquainted with things far more to be desired than any worldly good, and things far more to be dreaded than any worldly evil; and it necessarily leads us to view "the world" in the aspect in which all men naturally consider it, as our most dangerous enemy, leading the mind away from God, and tending to form us to a character directly the reverse of that which Christ died on the cross for us to secure.[21]

But the apostle not only states that by the Cross "the world was crucified to him," but that by the Cross too "he was crucified to the world." Some interpreters consider these words as just a repetition of the same sentiment, under a different form of expression. 'I am crucified in reference to the world. I regard the world as a crucified person does; what are the riches, and honors, and pleasures of the world to one expiring on a cross? I see the world in the light in which he sees it.' In their way of understanding the phrase, it is equivalent to, "dead to the world."

But I am not disposed to think this the right mode of interpretation. There is plainly an antithesis; and the two parts of it must be explained on similar principles. If the first means, 'The world is as a crucified person in my estimation,' the second must mean, 'I am as a crucified person in the world's estimation.'[22] "The world," in the second clause, is not quite so extensive in its meaning as in the first. It plainly, from the nature of the case, refers to that part of "the world" which is intelligent – 'the men of the world.' To men of the world the apostle was a crucified person; he was an object of contempt, of hatred, and even of horror. There was a time when he was highly esteemed by his unbelieving countrymen – his living world – as a man of talent and worth. But it was now far otherwise. They reckoned him a wicked fool – a mischievous madman. His Jewish brethren regarded him with peculiar terror as an apostate, and hated him nearly as intensely as they did his Lord;[23] and the sentiments of the unbelieving Gentile world in reference to him were not materially different, – somewhat less of hatred – possibly somewhat more of comtempt. What the apostle says generally of his apostolic brethren, was peculiarly applicable to himself: – "For I think that God hath set forth us the apostles last, as it were appointed to death: for we are made a spectacle unto the world, and to angels, and to men. We are fools for Christ's sake, but ye are wise in Christ: we are weak, but ye are strong: ye are honorable, but we are despised. Even unto this present hour we both hunger, and thirst, and are naked, and are buffeted, and have no certain dwelling-place; and labor, working with our own hands: being reviled, we bless; being persecuted, we suffer it; being defamed, we entreat: we are made as the filth of the world, and are the off-scouring of all things unto this day" (1 Cor. 4:9-13.).

And as the world was "crucified to the apostle by the cross of Christ," so "it was by the cross of Christ that he was crucified to the world." It was the mode of thinking, and feeling, and acting, to which the faith of the doctrine of the Cross naturally led, that made him the object of the contempt and dislike of worldly men. It was this that led him to the bold avowal of the hated doctrine of the Cross, and of the doctrines connected with it, equally disliked by the worldly; and to that course of active endeavors to overthrow the power of the world over the mind and heart of men, which formed the business of his life.

The object of the apostle in making these statements is plain. It is as if he had said, 'Your Judaising teachers wish to keep well with the world; but all this is over, completely over, with me. Through the Cross, what is the object of their admiration and fear, as it was once of mine, is the object of my dislike and contempt; and indeed it were needless for me to attempt to court the world's favor, for I know that, through the Cross, I am become an object of its contempt and execration. But in the Cross I have infinitely more than the world ever gave me – ever could give me, – infinitely more even than I ever expected from it; and I have also what far more than compensates for its contempt and hatred. I glory in the Cross. God forbid that I should not glory in it, and God forbid that I should glory in anything else.'

What the apostle here expresses is not a sentiment and experience peculiar to him as an apostle, it is a conviction and feeling common to him with all in Christ. His declaration ought to be employed for the purposes of self-inquiry. Is the world crucified to us by the Cross of Christ, and are we by that Cross curcified to the world? We all naturally love and serve the world. In some of its forms it is the great subject of thought – the great object of affection. True faith in the Cross, and in Him who hung on it, crucifies the world to us, and makes us cease to love and serve it. "This is the victory that overcometh the world, even our faith." Men, to whom the world is not crucified, are certainly not believers; and men professing Christianity, who are not "crucified to the world" – men whom the world loves and honors, – have cause to stand in doubt of themselves. Where the Cross holds the place in the heart which it did in the apostle's, and exercises the influence over the character and conduct it did in him, it will be equally clear that the world is crucified to the individual, and he to the world.

Christians do not need to be greatly concerned though "they are crucified to the world," – though the world should strongly dislike them, and very clearly show its dislike. Its smiles are more formidable to their best interests than its frowns. It is not wise to provoke unnecessarily the ill-will even of the most decidedly worldly – this is fitted to do nothing but mischief; but Christians should do nothing inconsistent with their professed attachment to the Cross of Christ to secure the favor of the world. Either course of conduct throws obstacles in the way of their doing duty to the world, which is, to endeavor to save it from itself. They ought especially to be desirous to have the world every day more crucified to them – to be every day more and more delivered from its demoralising influence; and they must never forget that it is the Cross which is the grand means of emancipation from the world's power. The thought – Christ the Son of God – "the just One died in the room of the unjust," for our sins, to deliver us from "the present evil world" – clearly apprehended, firmly believed – ought ever to be present to the mind. "Forasmuch as Christ hath suffered for us in the flesh" – let us arm ourselves with this thought, – "He that hath suffered in the flesh is free from sin, that we no longer live the rest of our time in the flesh, to the lusts of men, but to the will of God." It is the grace of God, manifested in the Cross of Christ, that effectually teaches to "deny ungodliness and worldly lusts, and to live soberly, righteously, and godly; and to look for the blessed hope, the glorious appearing of our Lord Jesus Christ, who gave Himself for us, that He might redeem us from all iniquity, and purify to Himself a peculiar people, zealous of good works."

SECT. VI. – THE ESSENCE OF CHRISTIANITY AGAIN STATED.

The apostle now, in this Postscript, repeats substantially, as of supreme importance, a statement which he had already made more than once in a former part of the epistle (Gal. 3:28; 5:6.). This double repetition strongly marks at once his sense of the intrinsic value of the principle, and his conviction that the Galatians very much needed to have their attention directed to it. "For in Christ Jesus neither circumcision availeth anything, nor uncircumcision, but a new creature" (Gal. 6:15.).

The first thing requiring attention here, is the connection between this and the preceding statements, indicated by the particle "for."[24] I apprehend the following is the apostle's train of thought: – 'I do not glory in Jewish peculiarities, such as circumcision, for I know that in Christianity these are of no avail; but I do glory in the Cross of Christ, through which that radical spiritual change is effected, which is all in all in Christianity. These Judaising teachers, calling themselves Christians, are a most inconsistent set of men. They glory in what has nothing to do with Christianity, and are ashamed of what is its very essence. I act a more consistent part: I care nothing for what I know to be nothing in Christ's estimation; I care much for what I know to be everything in His estimation. "For in Christ Jesus neither circumcision availeth anything, nor uncircumcision, but a new creature." '

The phrase, "in Christ Jesus," may either be considered as signifying 'under Jesus Christ' – that is, under the New Testament economy; or it may be viewed as an elliptical expression, equivalent to "to the being in Jesus Christ," – that is, to the being a true Christian, so related to Christ, as to be treated as if we had done what He did, suffered what He suffered, and deserved what He deserved, – so as to obtain a participation in all the blessings of His salvation, – so as to be partakers with Him of the divine special favor; of the Spirit of truth, holiness, and consolation, which dwells in Him without measure; and of all the dignities, immunities, and delights of the children of the Lord God Almighty, whose only-begotten He is, yet "the first-born among many brethren." It does not matter much which of the two views you take; both express important truth, and both express truths quite appropriate to the apostle's object. We are rather inclined to consider the first as exhibiting the apostle's meaning; under Christ, as opposed to under Moses, "neither circumcision availeth anything, nor uncircumcision."

The term rendered "availeth"[25] seems a false reading. The idea plainly is, 'Neither circumcision nor uncircumcision is any recommendation to a man under the Christian dispensation. The proper signification of both phrases – "availeth," and "is" – is to have force, to be of importance, whether of a favorable or unfavorable kind. Under the law circumcision was something – it "availed," or was of force. It never secured salvation, but it opened the way to the possession of numerous important privileges; and, on the other hand, uncircumcision precluded the enjoyment of these privileges. A Gentile, on being circumcised, was admitted to the participation in all the external privileges of the chosen nation; and, on the other hand, a Jew, a descendant from Abraham, Isaac, and Jacob, if he did not submit to circumcision, was cast off from the people of the Lord, and had no more interest than an uncircumcised Gentile in the blessing of the natural covenant. But under Christ it is otherwise: circumcision is nothing; it has no force in introducing a man into the enjoyment of its privileges: uncircumcision has no force in excluding him from them. Submitting to the initiatory rite of Judaism has nothing to do with Christianity. He that has submitted to it is not on that account the nearer the enjoyment of the blessings Christianity promises: he that has not submitted to it is not on that account the farther from the enjoyment of these blessings. The circumcised and the uncircumcised stand, in reference to them, on the same level.

The words that follow – "but a new creature"[26] are equivalent to, 'But in Christ Jesus a new creature, or creation, is something – a new creature availeth.'

But what are we to understand by this "new creature," or new creation, which exists and avails in Christ Jesus? In the passage which is often quoted as parallel to that now before us, "If any man be in Christ, he is a new creature" (2 Cor. 5:17.). – or, there is a new creation, – it is probable that "new creation" describes the whole change which takes place when a man becomes a Christian, – the change of state, as well as the change of disposition, – the change of relation, as well as the change of character. It intimates not only that, when a man becomes a Christian, he becomes a new man, but that he comes into a new world. "Old things pass away, and all things become new." But, in the passage before us, it seems restricted to the change of character. The new creature, or creation, is but a figurative phrase for "faith that worketh by love" (Gal. 5:6.). It is that new mode of thinking and feeling which, growing out of the faith of the truth respecting the Cross of Christ – produced by the Holy Spirit, and manifesting itself in love and its fruits, – constitutes the essence of true Christianity, and, as the apostle says, crucifies the world to a man, and him to the world. The new creature is not a new soul, nor is it the addition of new faculties to the old soul – far less is it a portion of the Divine essence somehow or other amalgamated with the human spirit; but it is a new way of thinking, of feeling, and of acting – a new system of sentiments, affections, and habits, all of them the work of the Holy Spirit, growing out of the faith of the truth, which HE produces in the soul, – "faith working by love."

This is something – this, and nothing else, avails in Christ Jesus. A man, though circumcised, if he is not a "new creature," has neither lot nor part in the matter of true Christianity. A man, though uncircumcised, if he is a "new creature," is, in all the emphasis of the word, a Christian; he is one with the Seed, in reference to whom the promise was made, – identified with Christ, – "an heir of God – a joint-heir with Jesus Christ."

The great principle here taught by the apostle, though, according to the wisdom given to him, taught with a peculiar reference to those whom he was immediately addressing, is, that true Christianity does not consist in anything merely external, but in the state of the "hidden man" of the mind and heart. Nothing merely external can make a man a Christian. He may be baptised, but the washing of water is not "the washing of regeneration, and the renewing of the Holy Ghost."[27] He may observe the Lord's Supper, but eating bread and drinking wine, "not discerning the Lord's body," is not "the communion of the body and blood of Christ." He may attend the public ordinances of religion, but all this may only be bodily service. He may give much alms, and say many prayers, but all this may be to be seen of men. He may do many things commended by Christ, but his motives may be dangerously defective or fatally wrong. Nothing will suffice but the new creation – the mind and the heart transformed by divine truth regarding the Cross of Christ, made effectual by divine influence.

It is lamentable to think how often religion is placed in what has nothing to do with true Christianity, – in counting beads, and doing penance, and going on pilgrimages, – in wearing a particular dress, or speaking a peculiar dialect; and it is almost equally lamentable that, among those who are somewhat better informed, it is often placed in what, at best, is merely the expression of real religion, and which, of course, where the reality is wanting, is mere show and hypocrisy – nothing, or worse than nothing. It is not connection with religious parents – it is not membership in the purest church in the world – it is not the observance of external ordinances – it is not the most decorous course of general conduct, which makes the true Christian. It is the renewed mind and heart, and the transformation of character, which the renewed mind and heart produce.

"The word of the truth of the gospel" is the instrument by which alone, under the influence of the Spirit, the character connected with salvation – the character necessary to make a person capable of enjoying the blessings of the Christian salvation – is formed. It is this which gives such transcendent importance to the gospel, and to the faith of the gospel. Some seem to think that there is a way of faith leading to heaven distinct from that of holiness. But the way of faith and holiness is the same way. It is by believing that we become holy; and if we are not holy, it is the strongest of all evidences that we do not believe. It is a lamentable mistake to suppose that something called faith may be a substitute for spiritual practical religion – for a life of principled obedience and submission to the will of God. In believing we obtain a new mind; and if we have obtained this new mind, we must, according to its measure, be transformed: so closely connected are "the faith which worketh by love" of chap. 5:6, and "the new creature" of the verse before us.

SECT. VII. – THE APOSTLE'S PRAYER FOR ALL WHO POSSESS THE ESSENTIAL ELEMENT OF CHRISTIANITY, AND ACT ON IT.

On all who act on this principle, the apostle implores every heavenly and spiritual blessing, acknowledging them, and them only, as the true people of God. "And as many as walk[28] according to this rule, peace be on them, and mercy, and upon the Israel of God" (Gal. 5:16.).

These words contain the statement of a principle which the apostle obviously considered of cardinal importance, and the expression of a kind wish in reference to all who regulate themselves by this principle as their rule. Let us attend to these in their order; and first, of the apostle's principle.

It has been supposed by many good interpreters that there is only one class of persons spoken of by the apostle, that they who "walk by this rule," and "the Israel of God," are but different descriptions of the same class of individuals. They consider the particle, "and," as equivalent to, "even." There can be no doubt that the particle is used in this way, 1 Cor. 3:5, and elsewhere: at the same time, it is not a common use of it. We apprehend that the apostle refers to two classes of persons; that the first application refers to teachers of Christianity, and the second to private Christians.

The "rule"[29] is obviously the principle laid down in the preceding verse; and to "walk" by that rule, is to regulate their conduct according to this principle. The teachers of Christianity who walk by this rule are those who not only boldly avow it, but who, in receiving persons into the fellowship of the Christian church, will be satisfied with nothing short of, and require nothing more than, credible evidence of the new creation – a credible profession of the "faith that worketh by love." The Judaising teachers did not walk by this rule. A worldly, immoral man, if he would but submit to circumcision, they were ready to acknowledge as a disciple; and an enlightened, conscientious Christian, if he would not submit to circumcision, they were disposed to exclude from their fellowship. To such persons the apostle would not bid God speed, though he did pray "that God would give them repentance to the acknowledgment of the truth;" but on all who walked by the rule, "In Christ Jesus there is neither circumcision nor uncircumcision, but a new creature," he invoked "peace and mercy," that is, every blessing.

And he invoked these blessings, not only on them, but also on "the Israel of God,"[30] that is, the spiritual Israel in opposition to the carnal Israel.[31] "Ye," says the apostle, speaking to the believing Galatians, "Ye are the seed of Abraham, and heirs according to the promise." "We," says he to the Philippians – we, that is, believers, whether Jews or Gentiles – "We are the circumcision which worship God in the Spirit" (Phil. 3:3.). Paul had a strong affection for his unbelieving brethren, Israel after the flesh, and "his heart's desire and prayer to God for them was, that they might be saved" (Rom. 10:1.). But he regarded the Israel of God with an affection of a peculiar kind. They were his "brethren in the Lord;" it mattered not to him whether they were Jews or Gentiles. By faith they had become the Israel of God – God's spiritual people – and for them he supplicates all heavenly and spiritual blessings. Let us imitate the apostle. Let us show our disapprobation of all who either make terms of communion which Christ never made, or dispense with those terms which He has made. The two things commonly go together. Let us walk by this rule. Let us cordially love and earnestly pray for all who walk by it, whether they follow with us or not; and let our kind regards be as extended as those of our Lord and His apostles – let them reach to all the Israel of God.

SECT. VIII. – AN INJUNCTION TO CEASE TO HARASS THE APOSTLE, AS HE HAD BEEN HARASSED BY THE JUDAISERS AND THEIR FOLLOWERS.

The epistle now draws to a conclusion. The apostle makes a request, or rather issues forth a command, that he should no more be teased and harassed, as he had been, by these Judaising teachers in Galatia, and assigns a very good reason for this. "From henceforth[32] let no man trouble[33] me: for I bear[34] in my body the marks[35] of the Lord Jesus" (Gal. 6:17.).

The words have received two interpretations. They have been viewed as signifying, 'Let no man professing to be a Christian act the part of these Judaisers, in disturbing and harassing my mind: I am exposed, in the cause of Jesus Christ, to suffering enough already: let him look at the marks I bear in my body of suffering sustained in the common cause, and let him not heap up sorrow upon sorrow upon me.' Others consider them as meaning, 'Let nobody, after this clear statement of my views and determination, trouble me by seeking my sanction to Judaising principles or practices: I am a Christian – a thorough Christian: the marks which I bear in my body of the sufferings I have undergone in defence of the Cross, the grand peculiarity of Christianity as opposed to Judaism, are like the signs impressed on the bodies of priests to mark them as the property of their deities, or on slaves to mark them as the property of their master:[36] these are evidences that I have taken up my ground, and that my mottoes are, "Christ, and Him crucified." "None but Christ – none but Christ." "Christ is all, and in all." ' The latter appears to me the more probable meaning. A third mode of interpretation has suggested itself to me, as not without plausibility: 'Let those who harrass me take care what they are about. They need fear nothing from me; but I have a powerful Master: I am

His property, and bear His mark on me. He will take care of me, and He will not suffer those who abuse His property to pass unpunished.'

Every Christian, and especially every Christian minister, will find it highly advantageous to imitate the apostle in his decision on such points. There is nothing ultimately gained by seeming to "halt between two opinions" in such matters.[37] Decision commands respect, even when exciting hatred and fear. The apostle exemplified his own precept, "Let no man despise thee" (Tit. 2:4.).

SECT. IX. – CONCLUDING BENEDICTION.

The epistle closes, according to the apostle's custom, with a solemn benediction. "Brethren, the grace of our Lord Jesus Christ be with your spirit. Amen" (Gal. 6:18.). "The grace[38] of our Lord Jesus Christ" is just the favor or kindness of our Lord Jesus Christ. To possess this is an inconceivable blessing. To be the objects of the kind regards of one so excellent, so amiable, so kind, so wise, so faithful, who can estimate the value of this? It was the apostle's wish that the Galatian Christians might every day enjoy new proofs of this unaltered, unalterable love.

He does not pray simply that "the grace of our Lord Jesus Christ may be with them," but that it may be with their "spirit." The leading object of the whole epistle is to withdraw them more from external things, and fix them on things spiritual; and such a prayer is a most appropriate conclusion. May you have tokens of the Savior's kindness in His blessing you with "all heavenly and spiritual blessings" – in His making you more and more holy, and thus more and more happy – making you grow in knowledge, and faith, and comfort, and holiness. "Amen." So may it be; so shall it be. Thus does the apostle conclude this admirable epistle, and show us, by his example, what it is to "do all things in the name of the Lord Jesus, giving thanks to God the Father by him."

The illustration of this epistle is now concluded, and nothing remains but the improvement which ought to be made, and the account which must be given. God requires the things which are past, and so should we. Let me request my readers seriously to review the whole epistle – let them ask themselves, 'Do we understand it better, and do we feel more powerfully the sanctifying and consoling influence of the doctrines which it unfolds? Have we, in the course of studying this very precious portion of the volume of inspiration, become more decidedly, more thoroughly spiritual? Have we seen more distinctly that the finished work of the Savior is the only ground of our hope – that the faith of the truth is the only instrument of our justification, the principal means of our sanctification – that the Holy Spirit is the grand agent who works in us both to will and to do? And are we in consequence of thus depending more entirely and confidently on the Savior, believing more implicitly the truth as it is in him, and seeking with greater earnestness that Holy Spirit who is promised to all who ask him?' If it be so, even in one instance, the author's labor has not been lost; should it be so in many instances, he has received "a full reward," and the church of God may another day reap a rich benefit.[39]

In the "textus receptus" followed by our translators, the following note is added to the epistle, "Unto the Galatians, written from Rome."[40] Those hypographs subjoined to the epistles express merely the opinions entertained by the transcribers who added them, no man can tell when or where; and are of value just so far as they can be supported by evidence. We have seen[41] that it is not at all probable that the statement made here is correct; and that from whatever place the epistle was written, it is all but certain that it was not from Rome. "The copiers," says Dr. Wall, "could not have pitched on a more unlikely place; a place where St. Paul had never been: nor did he go thither for several years after this. There is, indeed, no certain character of time or place found in it. But as his last being in Galatia was but a little before this time, and he rebukes them for being so soon gone off from the principles he had taught them, and because Ephesus was the first place he settled at after he left them, Usher, Pearson, etc. conclude that it was written from thence not long after his settling there."[42]